Buddhist and Christian?

The last century witnessed a gradual but profound transformation of the West's religious landscape. In today's context of diversity, people are often influenced by, and sometimes even claim to belong to, more than one religious tradition. Buddhism and Christianity is a particularly prevalent and fascinating combination. This book is the first detailed exploration of Buddhist Christian dual belonging, engaging – from both Buddhist and Christian perspectives – the questions that arise, and drawing on extensive interviews with well-known individuals in the vanguard of this important and growing phenomenon.

The book looks at whether it is possible to be authentically Buddhist and authentically Christian given the differences in beliefs and practices. It asks whether Buddhist Christians are irrational, religiously schizophrenic or spiritually superficial; or whether the thought and practice of Buddhism and Christianity can be reconciled in a way that makes possible deep commitment to both. Finally, the book considers whether the influence of Buddhist Christians on each of these traditions is something to be regretted or celebrated.

Rose Drew is Research Scholar in World Christianity and Interreligious Studies at Uppsala University, Sweden, and Lecturer in World Religions and Inter-Faith Studies at the University of Glasgow, UK.

Routledge Critical Studies in Buddhism

Edited by Stephen C. Berkwitz, Missouri State University, USA
Founding Editors: Charles S. Prebish, Utah State University, USA, and
Damien Keown, Goldsmith's College, London University, UK

Routledge Critical Studies in Buddhism is a comprehensive study of the Buddhist tradition. The series explores this complex and extensive tradition from a variety of perspectives, using a range of different methodologies. The series is diverse in its focus, including historical, philological, cultural, and sociological investigations into the manifold features and expressions of Buddhism worldwide. It also presents works of constructive and reflective analysis, including the role of Buddhist thought and scholarship in a contemporary, critical context and in the light of current social issues. The series is expansive and imaginative in scope, spanning more than two and a half millennia of Buddhist history. It is receptive to all research works that are of significance and interest to the broader field of Buddhist Studies.

Buddhist and Christian?

An exploration of dual belonging

Rose Drew

Routledge
Taylor & Francis Group

LONDON AND NEW YORK

First published 2011
by Routledge
2 Park Square, Milton Park, Abingdon, Oxon OX14 4RN

Simultaneously published in the USA and Canada
by Routledge
711 Third Avenue, New York, NY 10017

Routledge is an imprint of the Taylor & Francis Group, an informa business

British Library Cataloguing in Publication Data
A catalogue record for this book is available from the British Library

Library of Congress Cataloging-in-Publication Data
Drew, Rose.
Buddhist and Christian? : an exploration of dual belonging / Rose Drew.
p. cm. -- (Routledge critical studies in Buddhism)
Includes bibliographical references and index.
1. Buddhism--Relations--Christianity. 2. Christianity and other
religions--Buddhism. 3. Identification (Religion) I. Title.
BR128.B8D68 2011
294.3′35--dc22
2011000313

ISBN: 978-0-415-61123-7 (hbk)
ISBN: 978-0-203-80911-2 (ebk)

Typeset in Times
by Taylor & Francis Books

MIX
Paper from
responsible sources
FSC
www.fsc.org FSC® C004839

Printed and bound in Great Britain by
CPI Antony Rowe, Chippenham, Wiltshire

For my mother and father,
with all my love

Contents

Acknowledgements

It is a pleasure to have the opportunity to thank all those who helped me in writing this book. Let me start with my interviewees: the late Roger Corless, Sr Ruth Furneaux, Ruben Habito, John Keenan, Sallie King, and Maria Reis Habito. I am enormously grateful to them for their willingness to take part in this research and to give so generously of their time and hospitality, opening their homes to me, ferrying me to and from airports, speaking freely with me about matters of deep concern to them, giving me many hours out of their busy schedules (in Roger's case, despite ill-health, and in Ruben and Maria's case, including hours spent repeating entire sections of interview when both recording devices malfunctioned simultaneously), and checking and editing transcripts (here, thanks too to Linda Klepinger Keenan). I am also grateful to Betty Obermann for driving a four-hour round trip in order to pick up an unknown student from Burlington airport and deliver her safely to the Keenans, and to all the friends and families of my interviewees who made me feel at home in Virginia, Vermont, California, and Texas.

This book began life as a doctoral thesis and a tremendous debt of gratitude is owed to my supervisor, Perry Schmidt-Leukel, whose thirst for truth, clarity of insight, vast reservoir of knowledge, and attention to detail have benefited this study enormously. I consider myself exceptionally fortunate to have had a supervisor whose unfailingly sound advice, generous support, and constant encouragement far exceeded the call of duty and continue to do so. I am deeply grateful.

I am grateful too to teachers, friends, and colleagues at the University of Glasgow for providing a lively and stimulating research environment, and to the Arts and Humanities Research Council for funding. Elizabeth Harris and Werner Jeanrond are due thanks for their challenging questions and helpful suggestions for improvement; and Heather Walton for her advice on qualitative research interviewing. For helpful comments on thoughts in progress, I thank David Cheetham and audiences at the universities of Glasgow, St Andrew's, and Winchester, the European Network of Buddhist–Christian Studies, and the World Council of Churches. My interest in Buddhist–Christian dialogue was first kindled while studying Buddhism with Rupert Gethin and the theology of religions with Gavin D'Costa at the University of Bristol.

I thank them for the seeds they sowed. A debt of gratitude is also owed to George Bain and Keith Moulsdale for their shrewd and generous advice and to Magdalen Lambkin for her assistance with the index. And for moral support and toleration of my frequently anti-social work schedule, I thank my family and friends, especially, Eleanor Drew and Lucy Pearson.

To my parents, Geoffrey and Allison Drew, boundless gratitude is due for their unfailing love, support, and encouragement (not to mention Dad's proof-reading skills). I thank them for all that they have done, and continue to do, for me. This book is dedicated to them.

Finally, I would like to thank my long-suffering fiancé, David Bain, for all the innumerable ways in which he has supported me over the years this book has been in gestation. For many helpful and challenging conversations, for all the time taken to read and comment on work in progress, for pushing me always to be clearer (especially about ultimate reality!), for being my on-call IT guy, for a beautiful study to work in, for putting up with countless evenings alone, and for so much more, I am profoundly grateful.

Glasgow, March 2011.

1 Introduction

Can a person be both Buddhist *and* Christian? Today it is no longer unheard of in the West for people to identify themselves as belonging to both traditions. But how is this possible when, for example, God is so central to Christianity yet absent from Buddhism; when Christians have faith in Jesus Christ while Buddhists take refuge in the Buddha; when Christians hope for heaven and Buddhists hope for *nirvāṇa*; and when Buddhists and Christians engage in different practices?

According to Keith Yandell and Harold Netland, 'if each religion is taken seriously on its own terms, as understood by traditional Buddhists and Christians, it is clear that the two religions offer very different perspectives on the religious ultimate, the human predicament, and ways to overcome this predicament'.[1] Surely, then, one cannot hold both perspectives. Yet increasingly we hear of individuals who claim precisely to hold both.[2] Perhaps the most prominent recent example is theologian, Paul Knitter. A practising Roman Catholic, Knitter declares that he is also 'a card-carrying Buddhist'.[3] Indeed, the title of his recent monograph goes so far as to proclaim that, without the Buddha, he could not be a Christian.[4]

So what's going on? Are those, like Knitter, who identify themselves as belonging to both traditions profoundly irrational, religiously schizophrenic or spiritually superficial? Or is it possible to somehow reconcile the thought and practice of Buddhism and Christianity in such a way that one can be deeply committed to both? And if it *is* possible, will the influence of Buddhist Christians on each of these traditions be something to be regretted or celebrated? John B. Cobb, Jr. asked more than 30 years ago, 'Can a Christian be a Buddhist, Too?' (1978) and 'Can a Buddhist be a Christian, Too?' (1980). But it is really only in the last decade or so that the question of dual belonging has begun to receive the academic attention it warrants and, until now, there has been no in-depth study. This book is such a study. It focuses on Buddhist Christian dual belonging, engaging the theological issues from Buddhist and Christian perspectives, and drawing on interviews with individuals in the vanguard of this important and growing phenomenon.[5]

A number of thinkers have rightly noted that, at this early stage in the academic attempt to understand the phenomenon, close attention must be paid to the experience of dual belongers themselves.[6] But, so far, there has been little thoroughgoing theological exploration which draws on their testimony. Hence, this book's empirical dimension is important. We will explore the questions to which this phenomenon gives rise within the concrete context provided by the reflections – in interviews and in print – of six individuals who have publicly identified themselves with both traditions. They are the late Roger Corless, Sr Ruth Furneaux, Ruben Habito, John Keenan, Sallie King and Maria Reis Habito.

Before we embark on our exploration in earnest, I shall in this first chapter say a little more to get the phenomenon of dual belonging into focus. I'll then identify what I take to be the central aspects of the challenge facing reflective dual belongers. And, finally, I shall note some crucial points about this study's methodology, before introducing my interviewees in more detail in Chapter 2.

Getting dual belonging into focus

The last century witnessed a gradual but profound transformation of the West's religious landscape. Fast global travel, mass communication, immigration and advances in technology mean that we're no longer confronted with just one religious option: Christianity.[7] Today we encounter an array of religious traditions, originating from all around the globe and taking numerous forms. In this newly heterogeneous landscape, it is not necessarily the lone voice of a single tradition which influences us. More than one voice may come to command our attention, perhaps because we have been raised by parents belonging to different traditions, or have studied another tradition in depth, or have spent time living in a community of practitioners of that other tradition. Hence, mixed religious identities are increasingly common, i.e. religious identities which are formed under the influence of more than one religious tradition.[8] This phenomenon has been described as 'multireligious identity' and, especially in its more radical forms, as 'multiple religious identity', 'multiple religious belonging', 'hyphenated religious identity' and 'bi-religious *appartenance*'.[9] It is a phenomenon currently receiving growing academic attention,[10] and deservedly so, since its implications for the way in which we think about religious belonging and identity, and about the future of the religious traditions and the relationships between them, are profound.

There have long been religiously plural societies in Asia. Unsurprisingly, then, the phenomenon of multireligious identity is not new. Indeed, Catherine Cornille suggests that, '[i]n the wider history of religion, multiple religious belonging may have been the rule rather than the exception, at least on a popular level' (2002b: 1–2). In India and Nepal, for example, people pray at shrines connected with various religious traditions, deities and saints. And, in Japan, many visit Shinto shrines on auspicious occasions, Christian churches for weddings and Buddhist temples for funerals. Still, it is potentially misleading to apply the term 'multiple belonging' both to Japanese religiosity and to the religiosity of those Westerners who are committed to more than one tradition. For, as Jan Van Bragt notes, in Japan the different religions are traditionally seen as fulfilling different functions, hence multiplicity in the Japanese context constitutes something of a unified system and is not considered anomalous. In the West, by contrast, 'multiple belonging is perceived as fundamentally at odds with the traditional understanding of religion. It appears as a deviating state of affairs', set against 'a presupposed normative pattern: exclusive belonging to a single religion, conceived as a particular system of beliefs in a bounded community' (Van Bragt 2002: 17).

In any case, even though there are countries in which multireligious identities have long been the norm, the question of how the phenomenon of multireligious identity is to be assessed from a theological perspective has only just begun to be discussed. The present study is an attempt to contribute to this theological assessment, focusing on the Western context and, in particular, on the combination of Buddhism and Christianity in the lives of individuals who were raised in a Christian context and came to Buddhism later.

There can, of course, be various degrees and kinds of Buddhist Christian identity. At one end of the scale there are the commoner, softer forms of the phenomenon. Here we find individuals who are influenced by both Buddhism and Christianity but nonetheless identify much more with, and have a stronger sense of belonging and commitment to, one rather than the other. For example, one might identify oneself as a Christian while at the same time practising a Buddhist form of meditation or being consciously influenced by some Buddhist ideas through reading popular Buddhist books by the Dalai Lama, say, or Thich Nhat Hanh. One might even incorporate into one's Christian doctrinal framework some Buddhist beliefs, such as belief in rebirth, for example, while at the same time remaining primarily Christian. At this softer end of the scale, there may also be people with no particular sense of rootedness in either tradition, but who select ideas and practices from both, perhaps along with elements of other traditions, as would be typical of some forms of New Age religiosity. And it is also at the softer end of the scale that we find those Thomas Tweed calls 'nightstand Buddhists'.[11] As Carl Bielefeldt explains, nightstand Buddhists are those who read about Buddhism, find what they read attractive and perhaps even describe themselves as Buddhist, but who don't belong to any Buddhist organisation (2008: 2). 'We might also call them "Buddhist sympathizers"', suggests Bielefeldt, 'and ... their nightstand reading as "public Buddhism" or "media Buddhism"'.[12]

It would be at best misleading to classify multireligious identities at this softer end of the scale as cases of dual belonging. Being immersed in one tradition and adopting the odd belief or practice from another does not imply *belonging* to that second tradition. In the case of New Age religiosity, moreover, it might be better not to think in terms of religious belonging at all.[13] Instead, then, I shall restrict the terms 'multiple belonging' and 'dual belonging' to multireligious identities at or near the harder end of the scale. At this end, people are firmly rooted in – and identify themselves as committed adherents of – more than one tradition. In the most unequivocal cases of Buddhist Christian dual belonging, people practise within both traditions, belong to a Buddhist and a Christian community, identify themselves as fully Buddhist and fully Christian and have made a formal commitment to both traditions (usually through baptism and the taking of the three refuges).[14]

How does this strong sense of identification with a second tradition come about? Often it is through participation in deep interreligious dialogue, involving serious and sustained engagement with another religious tradition and its teachings. In the most profound dialogue, a person attempts to experience another tradition as it is experienced by its adherents, 'from the inside' as it were. As Wilfred Cantwell Smith emphasises, understanding the faith of Buddhists requires more than looking from an outsider's perspective at something called 'Buddhism'; one must try to see the world through Buddhist eyes so as to learn *why* the Buddhist believes what he or she does.[15] To some extent, one's understanding will be limited by one's cultural and religious presuppositions, but through the process of dialogue one becomes increasingly aware of these presuppositions and hence freer to explore ways of experiencing and understanding reality which are not bound by them. In Buddhist–Christian dialogue, the Christian must get inside the Buddhist's experience of being Buddhist, and vice versa. This might be attempted purely at the cognitive level, by trying to understand another's teachings as they're understood by those who accept them and imagining what it would be like to see the world in terms of those teachings; or, in some cases, at the practical level too, by immersing oneself in a community of practitioners and joining them in their religious observances.

Aloysius Pieris advocates what he calls 'core-to-core dialogue'. The liberative experience at a religion's core, says Pieris, is 'ineffable and incommunicable but realizable'.[16] He recommends that Christians and Buddhists actively participate in each other's religious observances (1988a: 122). Both should temporarily leave behind their own religions, as far as is possible, practising the other religion as if it were their own, under the guidance of an authoritative practitioner of that faith. John Dunne describes the temporary adoption of a religious perspective other than one's own in terms of 'passing over' and 'coming back'. This idea is now well known to those involved in interreligious dialogue, and it is an experience with which many are familiar (though perhaps not to the dramatic degree experienced by Pieris himself).[17] 'The holy man of our time', writes Dunne, 'is a man who passes over by sympathetic understanding from his own religion to other religions and comes back again with new insights to his own. Passing over and coming back ... is the spiritual adventure of our time' (1972: ix).

For some Buddhist Christian dual belongers, their identity is the result of a process (or many processes) of passing over and coming back in which they have found it neither possible nor desirable to return to precisely the place which they left, for they find themselves and their understanding changed by this process to such a degree that the religion of the other is no longer perceived as 'other', and passing over to it comes to seem as much a return home as the return to the perspective and practices of the tradition in which they were raised. It is not difficult to imagine that if one has really succeeded in making another tradition one's own and believes one has experienced its truth and salvific/liberative power, one might not feel able to relinquish one's adherence to it. Then, if one is also utterly at home in the tradition in which one was brought up and takes oneself to have felt *its* salvific/liberative power too, one might end up considering both traditions one's own. In the process of striving to see the world from the perspective of the 'other' in dialogue, therefore, one may increasingly come to identify with that perspective oneself. If one comes to identify with it *more* than with one's original perspective, one may convert to the other tradition; but in other cases, one may identify roughly equally with both perspectives, as the dialogue between them becomes internal.[18]

Even if one's growing identification with a second tradition does not go as far as full-blown dual belonging, one's religious identity may nevertheless be profoundly changed by the process of 'passing over'. Indeed, King suggests that *all* those 'who take Buddhist–Christian dialogue seriously are ... some kind of a mix of the two traditions' (1990: 122). Elizabeth Harris, for example, does not self-identify as Buddhist and Christian, but as 'a Christian ... who draws deeply from the wisdom of another faith as well' (2010: 160–61). She describes going through the disorientating experience of letting go of Christian concepts in order to enable 'what was beautiful and distinct in Buddhism' to arise, 'as something perfect in its own right' (2004: 336). She explains: 'The "other" became part of me ... And there was a cost, the cost of not "coming back" to the place that I had started from' (2004: 345). Buddhism and Christianity, says Harris, now lie in 'creative tension' within her (2002b: 17; 2004: 332):

> I can say with utter sincerity that I revere the Buddha and take refuge in his teachings. I remain a Christian, one who seeks to follow the self-sacrificial path of Jesus of Nazareth, but I also feel at home in a Buddhist meditation centre.[19]

In other cases, the change goes even further and does result in full-blown dual belonging in the sense of identification of oneself as Buddhist and Christian. As Michael Amaladoss says, 'double belongingness enters into the picture when people really feel called to be loyal to two religious traditions' (2002: 307). Self-identified 'Christian Buddhist', John Malcomson, writes: 'Both of them are part of who I am. I cannot give up the way both of them speak to me. ... For me to practice only Buddhism or Christianity would be denying part of who I ... have become' (2007b: 3–4). And Fabrice Blée says, 'I didn't decide to simultaneously tread on the Christian and the Buddhist paths. I rather found myself in that situation after the event' (1999: 1). Blée sought refuge in the three jewels, was initiated in a Buddhist tradition, pledged allegiance to a Tibetan Buddhist Master and a Buddhist community, and took Buddhist vows. But he explains: 'This conversion to Buddhism ... did not translate itself in the rejection either of my Catholic faith or of my belonging to the Christian community'.[20]

It is likely that the majority of those involved in dialogue continue to identify first and foremost with one religious tradition and to judge what is learned of the other according to its criteria. In other words, it is likely that one tradition retains normative priority, establishing a standard of correctness in thought and deed against which the other is measured.[21] As Cornille notes, one might identify with both traditions but interpret Buddhism in Christian categories. Or normativity may shift. One might convert to Buddhism while continuing to identify with Christianity because one feels nostalgically attached to its symbols and rituals and remains convinced of the truth of some Christian teachings, even though these teachings are now interpreted in the light of one's new sense of religious belonging.[22] Such cases are not instances of *equal* belonging to each tradition. Yet there are also much rarer cases, as Cornille recognises, in which, during the process of dialogue, Buddhism may acquire a normative status without this resulting in Christianity losing its normativity, cases in which a clear sense of *primary* commitment is lost.[23]

At this point, Michael von Brück presents a challenge. He denies *a priori* that it is possible for a person's identity to be shaped *equally* by two traditions if that person has been raised in only one of them. He argues that one's early religious formation 'is similar to having acquired a mother tongue ... [O]ne may develop later in life multiple religious identities, but the emotional belonging is not the same and the relationship to the respective traditions is different in each case'.[24] Even if one converts to Buddhism, one is still shaped primarily by Christianity, he claims. And, as someone who was raised a Christian, he therefore does 'not claim to be a Christian *and* a Buddhist, but a Christian who is formed, changed, hopefully deepened etc. by Buddhist identity' (2007: 205).

However, while I think von Brück is right that we are formed by our childhood religion in ways which cannot be undone by any subsequent religious affiliation, it is not at all obvious that this entails that if one is raised a Christian one cannot avoid one's Christian identity forever being primary. (We would surely not expect a convert from Christianity to Buddhism to describe his primary religious identity as Christian, or to refrain from calling himself a Buddhist simply because he was not raised one.) Rather, von Brück's observation regarding one's emotional formation within one's 'mother religion' at most entails that one will belong *differently* to any subsequent religion, and not that any subsequent religion will necessarily constitute a *secondary* identity for one.

My focus in this book will be on hard forms of Buddhist Christian multireligious identity in which both traditions have come to occupy a strong normative status. We will be concerned with people who, through their interaction with these two traditions, have reached a point where they no longer identify themselves simply as Buddhist or simply as Christian, and have come to understand themselves as belonging roughly equally to both traditions.

Such cases pose the central questions of this study. As Jacques Dupuis says, the difficult challenge arises 'when two wholesale, self-contained, and self-consistent visions of reality claim the faith allegiance of a person, each with its intrinsic coherence and distinct outlook and perspective' (2002: 72). We will investigate what Dupuis aptly describes as the 'encounter, in one and the same person, of two ways of seeing and feeling, of thinking and being' (2002: 64). Can these two ways be reconciled? How do reflective dual belongers deal with the questions and potential difficulties posed by their dual affiliation? Are they able to do justice to both in their thought and practice? Is it possible for them to rationally affirm the truth of Buddhist teachings and Christian teachings? Does the Buddhist Christian have a Buddhist world-view and a Christian world-view, or an *integrated* world-view? If the latter, is this world-view fully and authentically Buddhist and Christian, or is it a syncretistic world-view which is neither Christian nor Buddhist but something else? How do dual belongers conceptualise their spiritual path or paths? Do they have one ultimate spiritual goal or two? How do dual belongers combine the practices of both traditions, and how is their understanding of their practice within one of these traditions affected by the presence of the other?

'I am intrigued by the condition of those of us who have more than one worldview in our hearts and minds', writes Sallie King:

> [E]ach worldview exists as an intact package. But it is not alone. There is another intact package functioning there. ... How, then, do we live? I don't know; I sincerely offer this question for discussion in the community of dialoguers. Are we building bridges as fast as we can between the worldviews? Does one worldview serve as a critique of the other, only to be critiqued, in its turn, by the other, which it has critiqued? ... Unfortunately, this condition and all its intriguing possibilities is very little explored.
>
> (1990: 125–26)

While Buddhist Christian dual belonging has received some attention since King wrote this in 1990, it remains too little explored. To begin *our* exploration, then, let us consider the challenge reflective dual belongers appear to face.

The Buddhist Christian's challenge

We've just seen what processes might lead to dual belonging. But dual belongers face a profound challenge, and whether or not their religiosity can be considered authentic from the perspectives of both traditions involved will depend on whether or not this challenge can be met.

Habito, one of my interviewees, reflects that the best thing about being Christian and Buddhist is 'being able to receive nourishment and enrichment from these two traditions', but that the most difficult thing is, on the one hand, 'trying to see how apparently contradictory or incompatible elements can be seen in a more coherent picture' and, on the other hand, trying to be faithful to each of these traditions and respect their integrity 'in a way that does not compromise either'. He describes grappling with this challenge as 'an ongoing task' (165).[25] Habito's reflection nicely encapsulates the challenge faced by *all* reflective dual belongers. It is two-fold. First, one must find satisfactory ways of *integrating* the Christian way of thinking and being and the Buddhist way of thinking and being, such that dual belonging does not involve turning a blind eye to apparently outright contradictions nor entail being pulled in opposite directions by one's religious commitments. Second, one must at the same time ensure that the unique character, insight and integrity of each tradition is preserved and that what is special and attractive about each is not lost. In order to do justice to these traditions and allow them to interact at the centre of their spiritual lives in a way that is sustainable, dual belongers must find a balance between the integration of Buddhist and Christian thought and practice, and the preservation of the distinctiveness of the thought and practice of each.

Taking each of these considerations in turn, let's take a closer look at what this challenge involves.

The need to integrate

There are perhaps three main – somewhat overlapping – reasons why it is necessary for dual belongers to pursue the integration of the two traditions.

(i) The compatibility of truths

Cornille, a sceptic about the possibility of authentic dual belonging, mentions the most obvious obstacle: 'the reality of conflicting claims to truth' (2008: 12). Buddhism and Christianity are not just different from one another but also appear to *contradict* each other. For example, central to the Christian faith is the emphasis on relationship with a personal creator God; Buddhism affirms no such God. According to Buddhist thought we are reborn again and again; according to Christian thought we are not. It is a basic law of logic that a proposition and its negation (P and not-P) cannot both be true. Their both being true is a logical impossibility. Keenan, one of my interviewees, has this point in clear focus. 'No absolute contradiction can be honestly maintained', says Keenan (1994: 171); and, as he elaborates in interview, this means one 'can't say that the same thing both is and is not, in the same sense at the same time' (265). So, to the extent that the Buddhist Christian wishes to affirm the truth of both Buddhism and Christianity, or wishes to rationalise his or her belief in the truth of two apparently contradictory ideas *within* Buddhist and Christian thought, it must be possible to identify some level at which the teachings of the two traditions do not contradict each other, a level at which the truth of each can be integrated with the truth of the other.

(ii) The threat of a split personality

The second consideration is psychological. It is one thing to answer the question of how it is that a plurality of religions can be equally true, but it is a further question as to whether it is possible for that plurality to be reflected in the thought and practice of an individual. It is not clear that understanding oneself as living two parallel but entirely separate religious lives, each with its own way of seeing, interpreting and being, is a self-conception that can be healthily sustained. At least some degree of integration would seem to be required in order to avoid the danger of something akin to a split personality disorder. As Furneaux says, without integration 'one leads a schizoid existence' (114).

Psychologists such as Erik Erikson argue that the development of a mature identity requires the integration of contrasting experiences.[26] Drawing on Erikson, James Fowler contends that our identities should be 'flexible and integrative enough to unify the selves we are in the various roles and relations we have'; a mature identity and faith 'must somehow bring ... diverse roles, contexts and meanings into an integrated, workable unity' (Fowler 1981: 19). If so, the Buddhist Christian must look for ways of integrating his or her Buddhist and Christian experiences so that they are capable of nourishing a single, central self-understanding. Without this integration, reflective dual belongers are susceptible to a range of potentially intolerable psychological difficulties. Abhishiktānanda (Henri Le Saux), for example, at times experienced his commitment to Christianity and Hinduism as a source of profound anxiety;[27] as we will see, Corless' experience of tension between his commitment to Buddhism and his commitment to Christianity was, at one time, so acute that he consulted a psychotherapist (1996a: 5); and Bernard Senécal speaks of moments in his life when his inability to reconcile Buddhist and Christian insights led to crisis point:

> This double-faced experience, going on for more than ten years, has met with some very heartrending moments of real identity crisis between faith in Christ and the way shown by the Buddha.[28]

If dual belongers are to attain a sustainable degree of psychological equilibrium, they surely require a way of bringing together the doctrines and practices in which they find truth and value, such that those doctrines and practices are capable of nourishing a single faith and contributing to a unified framework of meaning.

(iii) The need to follow one path

The third motivation for integration is the fact that skipping to-and-fro between two religious paths looks likely to hinder spiritual progress. If Buddhist Christian dual belonging cannot be shown to be in some sense the following of a *single* spiritual path, it is hard to see how dual belongers avoid being pulled in two different directions by their religious commitments, rendering them incapable of fully committing to either tradition and, therefore, of fully realising the insights of either. If the Buddhist and the Christian paths diverge, then Paul Griffiths may be right that 'it is performatively impossible to belong to both at once – in much the same way that it's performatively impossible simultaneously to be a sumo wrestler and a balance-beam gymnast';[29] or at least he would be right to say that one cannot at once be an 'accomplished' Buddhist and an 'accomplished' Christian. Most religious traditions, argues Cornille, regard 'full and exclusive membership' as the ideal, and generally conceive of religious belonging in terms of 'an unreserved and undivided commitment' (2008: 10–11). Certainly, *if* integration cannot be achieved, then Cornille is surely right that double belonging 'always implies a certain holding back' which hinders progress (2003: 49). In the final analysis, insists Cornille, '[t]he problem with multiple religious belonging is ... not merely one of conflicting truth claims or theological incompatibility, but rather one of arrested spiritual development and growth' (2008: 14).

Even staunch pluralist, John Hick, despite contending that 'facts of faith' such as the Buddha's Four Noble Truths and the recognition of Jesus as the Christ constitute different but equally valid 'ways in which the same ultimate Reality has impinged upon human life', claims that these primary affirmations conflict inasmuch as 'they are different and that one can only centre one's religious life wholeheartedly and unambiguously upon one of them – upon ... the Buddha's enlightenment, ... or upon the person of Christ, ... but not upon more than one at once' (1989a: 373). Apparently, then, Hick too takes spiritual progress to depend on wholehearted commitment to *one* religious tradition.[30] Perhaps he sees religious commitment as unlike other kinds of commitment: *religious* commitment is absolute; it is one's principal commitment, the commitment before which all one's other commitments bow, according to which everything else is (or should be) ordered. Given this, the thought goes, it must surely be *singular*. This consideration is apparently in Dupuis' mind too when he asks:

> To what extent is it possible to make each of the two objects of faith one's own and to combine both at once in one's own religious life? Even apart from any interior conflict that might arise in the individual, every religious faith constitutes an indivisible whole and calls for a total commitment of the person. It may easily seem a priori impossible that such an absolute engagement might be divided, as it were, between two objects.
>
> (2002: 64)

Dual belongers, then, would seem to require a way of understanding their principal commitment and absolute engagement as being in some sense singular, despite their adherence to two traditions.

There are of course clear Christological and Buddhological worries about the possibility of following a single spiritual path which is genuinely Buddhist and Christian. Many Christians, especially, argue that what it means to be committed to Christ and to find salvation in the person of Christ entails the incompatibility of this commitment with commitment to the Buddha and all that that means. Bonnie Thurston says, for example:

> I admit to being one of those persons who holds to the traditional Christian insistence on a clearly demarcated religious identity. ... Jesus Christ does make exclusive claims on my life, loyalties, and allegiances ... My understanding of my tradition does not allow me to be Christian *and* Buddhist.
>
> (1994: 177–80)

Clearly, dual belongers must reject this, and hold that there is a way of interpreting Jesus Christ and Gautama Buddha such that they can be seen as making *compatible* claims upon his or her loyalties and allegiances.

The need to preserve distinctions

It is also crucial for the dual belonger to ensure that the uniqueness of each of these traditions is appreciated and the distinctions between them not destroyed. There are two principal considerations which place restrictions on the degree and kind of integration that is possible and desirable.

(i) Buddhism and Christianity offer distinct insights

The most basic motivation to preserve the distinctions between Buddhism and Christianity is the simple fact that these traditions *are* distinct: they constitute two ways of thinking and being. Buddhists and Christians interpret reality in different ways, employ different concepts, engage in different kinds of formal practice, and so on. Even if there is much convergence, and even if some differences turn out to be differences in emphasis, the differences are nevertheless vital, since they give the traditions their distinctive characters and account for their particular strengths.

One cause of scepticism regarding the possibility of genuine dual belonging is a concern that it amounts to a syncretistic religiosity which does away with differences, effecting union by destroying one or both of the traditions, either by assimilating one into the other or by creating something quite different from either of them. Calling attention to the differences between Buddhism and Christianity, the Dalai Lama criticises attempts to 'put a yak's head on a sheep's body'.[31] And Pieris warns against an 'unguided zeal for personal integration', arguing that mixing religions is neither 'ecumenically helpful' nor 'spiritually fruitful' (1996: 184).

It is important, then, that one's integration of Buddhism and Christianity not be so thoroughgoing as to change the character of these traditions beyond what is sanctioned by demonstrable continuity with at least some significant strands of each. Relatedly, the Buddhism of dual belongers should be recognisable to at least *some* Buddhists, and their Christianity to at least *some* Christians. (One cannot expect that even a single belonger's way of being Buddhist or Christian will be recognisable to *all* members of their tradition, given every tradition's great internal diversity.) This requirement acknowledges that there is an objective dimension as well as a subjective dimension to religious identity and belonging. (The subjective dimension of belonging concerns one self-identification, one's own claim to belong; the objective dimension concerns that claim's recognition by others who belong.)[32] If dual belongers are to be recognised as authentic adherents of both Buddhism and Christianity, they must faithfully represent both these traditions in their distinctness; their Buddhism must be authentically Buddhist and their Christianity authentically Christian.

Most of my interviewees explicitly recognised this criterion in one form or another. Keenan says, for example, 'to keep the faith ... I think you would have to be in harmony with it and recognised by people within the tradition as being in harmony with it' (319). Corless says: 'I think that someone with dual practice should try to be authentically in each tradition ... Transformation should be authentically in line with the tradition ... There is a development which is authentic and a development which is inauthentic' (84). Reis Habito explains that it is important to her that her Buddhist Master accepts her as a Buddhist (454); and Habito reflects, '[t]he knotty theological problem that keeps emerging is precisely how to responsibly articulate my understanding of the way things are [in a way] that is faithful to the Christian tradition as well as to the Zen Buddhist tradition' (196).

Owing to the distinctiveness of each of these traditions, it may not in every respect be possible to relate oneself to, or to think about or experience, reality from a Christian *and* from a Buddhist perspective at one and the same time. It appears inevitable that, to some degree, reality will be thought about and experienced differently depending on whether one is thinking and practising *qua* Buddhist or *qua* Christian. Even if some synthesis between these two perspectives can be achieved compatibly with both traditions, it is hard to see how one could do justice to both without any perspective-switching whatsoever.

On the face of it, it is unlikely that people who are deeply immersed in, and committed to, both Buddhism and Christianity would be attracted to ways of thinking which eradicate the distinctions between them. For it is precisely *in virtue* of the distinctiveness of each that they belong to both. As King says, 'that's why there's a point in practising two: if it was the same darn thing why would you do it twice?' (406). Dual belonging is self-defeating if one's integration of the traditions removes the point of drawing on both in the first place.

(ii) Each tradition is efficacious in its own right

The final motivation for maintaining the distinctiveness of each tradition concerns the need to uphold the affirmation of both Buddhism and Christianity as effective vehicles for spiritual transformation. Being an authentic Buddhist and an authentic Christian rules out the idea that either tradition's efficacy is dependent on its being practised in conjunction with the other.

So, to take stock, an absolutely central task of this book is to investigate to what extent it is possible for Buddhist Christian dual belongers to meet both the demand for integration and the demand to preserve the distinctiveness of each tradition. Not all dual belongers will strike the same balance between integration and the preservation of distinctions. I will try to evaluate a variety of approaches, with respect to some of the key theological, philosophical, and practical questions which seem to face anyone who identifies himself or herself as Buddhist and Christian.

The plan of action is as follows. The next chapter introduces the thought and practice of my six interviewees. Then, in Part I, I shall address the putatively serious disagreement between Buddhism and Christianity concerning God (Chapter 3) and questions about how dual belongers might think about the nature and significance of Jesus Christ and Gautama Buddha (Chapter 4). In Part II, I shall examine (in Chapter 5) how Buddhist Christians conceive of the nature and goal of the spiritual life and whether Buddhism and Christianity are concerned with different salvations or liberations, or whether they can be legitimately interpreted as orientating the dual belonger towards a single salvation/liberation. Finally, in Chapter 6, I shall investigate how dual belongers combine the practice of Buddhism and Christianity, and whether it is possible to do justice to both traditions in this regard.

Before turning to my interviewees, however, it is worth reflecting on some crucial methodological features of this study.

Methodology

A theological focus

This book's focus is primarily theological (construing 'theology' so as to include Buddhist, as well as Christian, religious thinking)[33] and many – though not all – of the questions it addresses concern the extent to which Buddhist and Christian beliefs can be reconciled. One might object that this focus is unwarranted and perhaps even indicative of a typically Western approach to religion which prioritises belief at the expense of other dimensions of religious phenomena (cultural, political, economic, social, etc.) – dimensions which a more ethnographic study might reveal.[34] However, while there are certainly other approaches one could fruitfully take to this multi-faceted topic, a theological focus cannot be avoided if the phenomenon of dual belonging is to be made sense of and evaluated *from within the Buddhist and Christian traditions*. The question motivating this study is not simply 'What does it mean to be a dual belonger?' but, more specifically, 'Is it possible for individuals to combine Buddhism and Christianity in their thought and practice *in ways which do justice to both traditions?'*. The latter question is centrally a theological one.

A concrete context

As noted above, an important and distinctive dimension of this study is its empirical dimension. To some extent it is possible to identify and evaluate *in the abstract* various potential solutions to the conundrums faced by Buddhist Christian dual belongers, simply on the basis of a knowledge of both traditions, and with the logical, psychological and spiritual considerations in focus. Indeed, some of the discussions which follow draw heavily on work in the theology of religions, the implications of which for our topic may not have been considered by its authors or by my interviewees. However, since we wish to understand this phenomenon better, constantly referring back to the experience of people who for many years have been attempting to meet the challenge of being both Buddhist and Christian is likely to be far more illuminating than a purely abstract consideration of the theological, philosophical and practical questions such people face. As Dupuis says, in this area

> theology must start 'from below,' that is, from the lived experience of trustworthy witnesses, and must build inductively on such testimonies before it may claim to contribute, by way of deduction, 'from above' (from established principles), some apodictic and dogmatic answers that would run the risk of being unduly restrictive. ... In this matter, then, the 'first theological act' must consist of reflecting on the concrete experience of some of the pioneers who have relentlessly endeavored to combine in their own life their Christian commitment and another faith experience.
>
> (2002: 69)

Hence, the writings of, and long interviews with, my six 'pioneers' (Corless, Furneaux, Habito, Keenan, King and Reis Habito) provide a concrete context for our investigation. I offer brief preliminary introductions to their religious biographies, self-understandings and practice in Chapter 2. And their reflections inform the discussions throughout this study, offering an insight into what a number of highly reflective dual belongers actually do, think and feel. This empirical dimension allows certain possibilities to be explored as lived realities. When assessing how Buddhism and Christianity are combined in *practice*, this concrete context becomes indispensible, given the vast array of combinatorial possibilities. Here, the only sensible approach would seem to be to look at how the practices of these two traditions are combined in some actual cases. That said, theory and practice are of course interrelated and so, to some extent, I shall treat the cognitive and practical dimensions of various questions in conjunction with one another.

In short, the interview material and published reflections of my interviewees are essential to our enterprise. I draw on this material throughout and especially in Chapter 6, where we'll focus specifically on the question of how dual belongers combine Buddhist and Christian practice.

Qualitative research interviews

Given the importance of my interviews, it is worth clarifying in this and the next two sections the nature of these interviews, how my interviewees were selected, and what precise role in this study their reflections play.

In March 2006 I conducted a three-hour recorded interview with Furneaux at her hermitage near Chepstow, Wales. Between April and May, I travelled around the USA, spending a few days with each of my other interviewees, conducting approximately seven hours of recorded interviews with each. I transcribed the interviews myself,[35] and have arranged the transcripts in a single 501-page volume with continuous pagination. When referring to this material, I shall give page references in brackets. Whenever a page reference appears without a publication date, the reference is to my unpublished transcripts. I have given these references even though these transcripts are not publicly available primarily to make it easier to tell apart what my interviewees said in interview and what they said in print. (Where interview material and published work are discussed simultaneously, it would otherwise be difficult to distinguish.) Where quotes from different parts of an interview transcript appear side by side, the references also allow readers to see that the quoted remarks were not contiguous.

The empirical dimension of my research was not quantitative. Obviously a six-person sample would be far too small to generate meaningful statistics. Rather my empirical research was qualitative. In other words, my intention in conducting the interviews was to gain a detailed picture of the religious lives of my interviewees, how they understand their dual affiliation, the advantages and disadvantages they experience, the challenges they see themselves as facing, how they deal with these challenges, and so on.[36] The long interview is particularly well suited to this aim since it offers insight into the daily experience of an individual and a glimpse of how he or she sees the world.[37]

A questionnaire provided the framework for each interview, but within that framework there was much room for the exploratory, unstructured discussion essential to qualitative research interviews. My questions were developed on the basis of a number of sources: my interviewees' writings (especially, where available, those discussing their multireligious identities); literature covering the current debates and discussions regarding the phenomenon of multireligious identity; general literature on identity and conversion; major works on Buddhist–Christian dialogue; and seminal pluralist literature.[38] Engaging with this literature helped clarify what I take to be some of the most pressing and intriguing theological, philosophical, and practical questions faced by anyone attempting to live as both a faithful Buddhist and a faithful Christian. At an early stage it became clear, moreover, that the overarching challenge facing dual belongers is how to negotiate the demand both to integrate these traditions and yet also to preserve the distinctiveness of each. Hence a core aim of my interviews, reflected in my questionnaires, was to test this understanding and find ways in which my interviewees seemed to be succeeding or failing in maintaining a balance between these potentially competing considerations.

The questions covered a range of topics including the religious biographies of my interviewees; the nature of their religious practice; their degrees of identification with Buddhism and Christianity and the roles played by each tradition in their lives; their preferred ways of describing their religious identities, and their opinions of terms others have used; their understandings of, and ways of relating to, Jesus Christ and the Buddha; the respects in which Buddhism and Christianity can learn from each other; their beliefs about God, creation, rebirth, karma and salvation or liberation; the respects in which they feel Buddhism and Christianity are integrated in their lives and in which they remain separate; the aspects of dual belonging they appreciate most and the aspects they struggle with; their experiences of raising children in relation to both traditions; and their understandings of, and attitudes to, syncretism. Some questions I phrased deliberately bluntly in order to provide crucial opportunities for interviewees to explain the complexities of an issue in their own terms and more fully than they otherwise might. Other questions were of a highly detailed and theoretical nature. While such theoretical questions would not usually be appropriate in qualitative research interviewing, the academic backgrounds of my interviewees allowed for this level of intellectual engagement. Often these questions concerned their own work.

Choice of interviewees

Since I'm concerned with multireligious identity as a Western phenomenon, I chose interviewees who live in the West and who were raised in a Christian context, coming to Buddhism later.[39] I decided to interview academics in the field of religious studies (or people with some background in academia, as in the cases of Reis Habito and, to a lesser extent, Furneaux) partly because I wanted people who had identified themselves publicly as having a dual religious affiliation, and also because my investigation is, to a large extent, theological, hence it was illuminating to talk to people acquainted with many of the theological questions on which my research would focus. Moreover, I wanted people with a good knowledge of both traditions. It is one thing to think oneself a dual belonger if one has only a superficial understanding of the doctrines of each of these traditions, quite another if one's understanding is deep and detailed. One cannot, after all, have grappled with putative contradictions of which one is unaware. I was interested in individuals who to some extent would already have reflected on, or would at least be aware of, the kinds of questions I would be asking them and who might therefore provide insightful responses generated by their experience of living as well-informed and reflective adherents of both traditions. A further advantage of choosing mostly academics was the availability of their published material to supplement and help me interpret the interview material.

Among my interviewees, there are more and less thoroughgoing instances of dual belonging, and not all share the same characteristics. But the diversity among approaches was also of interest. It was this consideration which persuaded me to include Keenan despite the fact that, although describing himself as a 'Mahāyāna Christian', he neither practises within both traditions nor identifies himself as a Buddhist. As Cornille notes, Keenan's identification with the world-view and hermeneutical context of one religion and the symbolic framework of another is a special kind of case.[40] It is open to debate whether one can speak here of multiple belonging, and Keenan does not use such terms of himself. Although I do not see him as a dual belonger in the strict sense, I decided it would nevertheless be illuminating to interview him in the interests of providing examples of diverse approaches to the issues this study addresses. While I do not assess the consistency and Christian authenticity of his Mahāyāna theology as a whole (this would take another book), I draw on his reflections where relevant.

One bias in my group of interviewees which I did not choose as such is that all but one live in the USA. This was partly because a number of academics who have identified themselves strongly with both traditions happen to live in the USA, and partly due to the ease of interviewing in English, my native language. Hence it is in the American cultural and religious climate that they make sense of their multireligious identities. So, for example, the dominant strain of Christianity from which King is at pains to distinguish her own Quaker Christianity is a strongly evangelical strain, whereas this is not the Christianity which prevails in, say, the UK. Moreover, none of my interviewees raised any *legal* difficulties concerning their dual religious affiliations, whereas in Germany and Austria, for example, where one is legally obliged to identify oneself as a member of a particular religious tradition or none for tax purposes, identifying oneself as belonging to more than one religious tradition would create legal complications which might affect how Austrians and Germans would view the issue.[41] Still, this bias is mitigated by the fact that only King and Keenan were born and raised in the USA (and King anyway spent extended periods in Germany and the UK). The others were all born and raised elsewhere.[42]

The descriptive and the normative

This study is partly descriptive and partly normative. On the one hand, I aim to illuminate the religious lives of actual dual belongers by describing my interviewees' thought and practice, including how they engage with the difficulties dual belongers face. On the other hand, I will at times evaluate their approaches, and also address dual belonging and its challenges directly. This is the normative dimension of my project, which is guided by the demands for integration and the preservation of distinctions. The demand for integration requires us to ask which approaches are logically consistent and which are logically inconsistent; which are likely to be psychologically sustainable, yielding coherent world-views and self-understandings; and which allow for a singularity of spiritual purpose, as against the pursuit of two goals conceived of as mutually incompatible. And the demand for the preservation of distinctions requires us to ask how far each approach is both authentically Christian and authentically Buddhist, i.e. how continuous it is with both traditions.

Traditions are, of course, far from static, well-defined entities, being instead constantly emerging amalgams of diverse strands of thought and practice intertwined in complex and ever-changing ways. Certainly, then, we can expect some internal disagreement between different strands of Christianity and different strands of Buddhism over what constitutes continuity with the Christian or the Buddhist tradition. But to avoid unduly restricting the parameters of the following theological discussion, we will not be setting out with a set of specific criteria for Buddhist or Christian authenticity and then applying these to various approaches in order to assess them. Rather, in the context of each of the topics we will cover, the question of what constitutes fidelity to each tradition will be treated as a matter for investigation.[43]

To be clear, the normative dimension of this study, stemming from the two-fold demand for integration and for the preservation of distinctions, does *not* rest on an assumption that those with Buddhist Christian multireligious identities *should* remain utterly faithful to the Buddhist and Christian traditions. Rather, I simply wish to establish whether any approaches do remain faithful to both – and if any do, *which* they are, *how* they do so, and to what *extent* they do so; and which do *not* remain faithful, *why* they do not, and to what *extent* they do not.

Cautionary remarks

It is crucial that the interview material on which I shall draw not be considered a definitive statement of my interviewees' views. A number of them pointed out that were they to be asked the same questions a year later – or even the following day – they might well give different answers. As Habito put it, these interviews are snapshots of moving targets. Moreover, allowances should be made for the inevitable imperfections of conversational as opposed to written English.[44]

All my interviewees struck me as living conscientious, rich and worthwhile religious lives. And I am enormously grateful to them for agreeing to take part in this research and for their willingness to speak so openly and honestly about matters of the deepest concern to them (and to be named in connection with their reflections, thus allowing me to relate their interview material to what they have said in print). In what follows, I have done my best to present their self-understandings as accurately as possible on the basis of the material I have. But it is not without trepidation that I have undertaken the task of interpretation and analysis. If I have misinterpreted them in any way, I apologise. Where I am critical, it is for the reasons discussed above and certainly not because I think their spiritual paths are inauthentic or invalid in and of themselves. I hope they will view any critical evaluations as honest attempts to move the discussion forward.

Terminological notes

The question of how people with hard Buddhist Christian multireligious identities should be referred to is somewhat contentious. A number of my interviewees felt that terms such as 'Buddhist Christian' or 'dual belonger' are misleading in various ways and that it would be best if *all* labels could be avoided.[45] I shall in places discuss some of the ways in which certain labels might be misleading, but labels cannot be avoided altogether. The terms with which I most frequently describe those who are immersed in, and understand themselves as adherents of, both traditions are 'Buddhist Christian dual belonger', 'Buddhist Christian' or 'dual belonger'. These are terms I am using for the sake of convenience; I do not claim that all those to whom I apply them would use them of themselves.

I have not hyphenated 'Buddhist Christian' so as to avoid any suggestion at the outset of a new Buddhist–Christian religion. Moreover, I do not mean 'Buddhist' in 'Buddhist Christian' to act as a qualifier of 'Christian' – either to indicate the chronological order of the dual belonger's contact with these traditions[46] or to indicate that Christianity is primary in terms of normativity, i.e. that what is at issue is a Buddhist form of Christianity.[47] Rather, I take the term 'Buddhist Christian', as I am using it, to be interchangeable with 'Christian Buddhist'. Whether or not there are respects in which either a person's Buddhist commitment or Christian commitment can be seen to modify the other is a matter for the forthcoming investigation.

Note also that 'dual' in 'dual belonger' should not be thought either to suggest that dual belongers take there to be a sharp divide between their practice of each of these religions, or that they experience their commitment to these two traditions as two distinct spiritual undertakings. Again this is precisely a matter into which we will inquire. Nor should my use of the term 'dual belonger' be taken to imply an *a priori* assumption that belonging fully and authentically to both traditions is possible. Cornille, for example, questions the coherence of the category of 'multiple belonging', arguing that the supposition of its possibility is based on a subjective conception of religious belonging which clashes with the objective conception of belonging implicit in the self-understandings of the religions in question (2002b: 4; 2008: 16–18). I am not assuming that such worries are unfounded. Rather I am simply using this terminology to refer to people who practise within, and understand themselves as belonging to, both traditions, whether or not that understanding can in the end be vindicated. In other words, my terminology tracks, primarily, the subjective aspect of belonging.[48] The question of the extent to which their self-understandings are justified – in the sense that they reflect the self-understandings of these traditions more generally – is, again, a matter pending investigation. Where a dual belonger's thought and practice can be seen to be, in important respects, continuous with both traditions we might speak of 'full' or 'authentic' dual belonging.

Let us turn, then, to a preliminary introduction to the religious biographies, practices and self-understandings of my interviewees, before addressing head-on the challenges that dual belongers face.

2 Interviewee profiles

Roger J. Corless[1]

Professor Emeritus of Religion at Duke University, Roger Corless spent his academic career working in religious studies. From 1986, he identified himself publicly as someone who practised both Buddhism and Christianity.[2] Corless was a Roman Catholic and his Christian spirituality focused on the Mass and the divine office. He was also a Tibetan Buddhist in the Gelugpa tradition, his practice consisting largely of liturgy and visualisation (accompanied increasingly by Pure Land Buddhist practices). When I interviewed Corless in May 2006, he was living in Benicia in the San Francisco Bay area of California. He had been suffering ill-health and had recently undergone treatment for cancer. Just eight months later, on 12 January 2007, he died from complications associated with cancer. His memorial service included Buddhist and Christian elements.

Corless was born in Merseyside, UK, in 1938. His family were not particularly religious, but occasionally he attended either a Congregationalist, Methodist or Baptist church. Interested in religious questions from an early age, as a teenager Corless began to read as much as he could on the world religions. One of the books in response to which he experienced a deep sense of 're-cognition' was on Buddhism. 'I have become a Buddhist', announced 16-year-old Corless to his mother, though he admits that, at that time, he was not entirely sure what being a Buddhist meant (1996a: 4). Once at university, however, Christianity took on a new vitality for Corless and he dropped the course he had started in veterinary science and took up theology instead. While attending the Eucharist in the Anglican tradition, Corless began to sense a power that he felt 'called' to investigate and to commit himself to. 'So I said I suppose this is what Christians call God, so I suppose I'm Christian again now' (1996a: 4). Meanwhile, his interest in Buddhism had not abated and having completed his BA he moved to the USA to study for a PhD in Buddhist Studies, specialising in Pure Land Buddhism, at the University of Wisconsin-Madison. Once in the USA, in about 1964, Corless sought acceptance into the Roman Catholic Church, and was conditionally baptised and then confirmed.[3] At around the same time, he also became an Oblate of St Benedict at Mount Saviour Monastery in New York.[4]

Towards the end of his doctoral studies, Corless was offered a post at Duke University. In 1974 he undertook a post-doctoral study tour of India, and in 1975 and 1991 spent time studying in Japan. For a long time, it seemed to him that Buddhism was assisting him in becoming what he hoped was a better Christian. Gradually, however, he began to experience an increasingly acute degree of tension between his Buddhism and his Christianity, until he had to admit that he was equally convinced by Buddhist and Christian teachings and yet believed them to be incompatible. This 'dilemma' gave Corless 'a real existential problem'. 'I even tried psychotherapy to resolve it because it really tore me apart' says Corless, but 'the psychotherapist was not able to understand the problem ... [O]ne time I just got very depressed' (1996a: 5; 1989: 3).

Eventually, something of a solution presented itself to Corless. The question he had been asking himself, on which his existential dilemma centred, was 'Are you Christian or Buddhist?', when 'actually the problem is not which do I choose, but why do I concentrate on an "I" that must ... [do] the choosing?'. It occurred to Corless that when the 'I' that doesn't choose disappears, 'then the process simply goes on' (1996a: 5). This revelation brought about an end to his anxiety and allowed him to feel comfortable in both traditions. In trying to justify his insight intellectually, Corless hit upon the notion that Buddhism and Christianity relate to one another as two distinct 'absolutes' which 'co-inhere' in superconsciousness[5] – a notion we will investigate during the course of our inquiry. Corless now felt able to formally take refuge, and in 1980 did so as a Gelugpa Buddhist under Geshela Lhundup Sopa (having first obtained the permission of his Catholic spiritual director, and having explained his dual affiliation to Geshela). A fortnight later he took Bodhisattva vows and received a Tantric initiation (1986a: 133): 'Now there were (at least) two of me', writes Corless; 'Catholic Christian and Mahāyāna Buddhist' (2002: 21).

As well as his Tibetan practices and his Christian prayer and meditation, Corless devised a special 'Buddhist–Christian Coinherence Meditation' to acknowledge both traditions 'as two Absolute Systems coinhering on the same planet (in humanity as a whole) and in your own consciousness' (1994a: 139), which he practised in various forms over many years. Corless had also – in the last year of his life – taken up a morning practice of chanting the mantra of the Lotus Sūtra (the *Nam-Myōhō-Renge-Kyō*), and despite the interference of his ill-health with his daily practice, he was still managing to attend the weekly mass at his local Catholic church and the meetings of his local Buddhist group, the Benicia Sangha (26, 31).

Keen to become involved in interreligious dialogue in a more pastoral capacity after retiring, in 2005, Corless had been ordained as a minister in the Universal Church of the Master (UCM), a small church which originally developed out of the spiritualist movement in 1908 in Los Angeles; he hoped that this would be a way of him doing some pastoral counselling in an official capacity, perhaps as a hospital chaplain.[6] UCM does not have many churches with congregations, explained Corless, but aims to support the individual path of each of its members: it's 'a multi-faith Church in which we respect all traditions although we might have personal preference or commitment to one or other of them or to a few of them' (12).

Corless emphasised that he did not regard himself 'as a Buddhist hyphen Christian, or even as a Buddhist and a Christian' but as 'an entity that is able to function authentically in both Buddhism and Christianity' (1996a: 10). In one publication, he describes himself as a 'dialogian' since he sees himself as a person who, rather than simply being *engaged* in dialogue, *is* a dialogue (1993: 13). Corless regarded his dual belonging not so much as something he had chosen, but as a vocation (1994b: 182).

Sr Ruth Furneaux

Sr Ruth Furneaux (also known by her Buddhist name, Kashin sama)[7] is an eremitic Anglican Christian nun, and a Zen and *Satipaṭṭhāna* practitioner and teacher. She was born Avril Furneaux in 1947 into what she describes as 'a non-religious working class family with an unspoken but tangible denigration of anything "spiritual" or academic' (2006a: 1). She was raised in London. As a small child she persuaded her parents to let her go to church and subsequently attended a Methodist church until she was 10 years old, at which point she was baptised into the Anglican church,[8] receiving confirmation a few years later.

Between 1975 and 1978 Furneaux studied theology and philosophy at the University of Bristol. She recalls that it was around this time that contemporaries of hers were heading off to India 'and jumping on the Buddhist/Hindu bandwagon' whereas she was adamant that 'IT is all here, in your own heartmind' (2006a: 1). After leaving Bristol, Furneaux was involved in community work but in 1985, having begun to search for something 'deeper' and 'more spiritually based' (87), she discovered and felt drawn by 'the still small voice' to study and practice Zen Shiatsu. This included *Satipaṭṭhāna* (mindfulness) meditation, which Furneaux came to feel was what she had already been doing since her teenage years, 'prompted by the Holy Spirit'. Initially her teacher was a senior student of John Garrie Roshi,[9] followed by John Garrie Roshi himself (until his death in 1998); he confirmed that early experiences of hers had been authentic insights. Once the relationship was established, frequent contact with her teacher was maintained, with several meetings a day for the period during which she lived at the Sati Society centre in Wales. There, she was trained 'in all aspects of sati in everyday life – true spiritual training not just sitting meditation' (2006a: 1). In 1991 Furneaux was granted permission by John Garrie Roshi to teach in the Zen and *Satipaṭṭhāna* traditions.

Excluding a two-year period spent living with the Society of the Sacred Cross, Monmouth (an Anglican convent in the Cistercian tradition), Furneaux has, since 1993, lived as a hermit in various locations including the grounds of Christian and Buddhist communities. These communities have included the Society of the Sacred Cross, Elsie Briggs House of Prayer, Lam

Rim Buddhist Centre and Throssel Hole Zen Monastery. Between 1995 and 2000 she began work on a PhD thesis on practice in St John of the Cross with reference to *Satipaṭṭhāna* and Zen, entitled 'Way/No Way',[10] and subsequently attended a Pāli reading group for two years. There was a time when Furneaux wanted to become a Buddhist nun but, after much soul-searching, she came to believe that the 'inner teacher' was telling her that this was not her way. Instead, in 2000 she left the convent at Monmouth and took her first formal vows to solitude directly to the Archbishop of Wales (now Archbishop of Canterbury, Rowan Williams), and received the name Ruth. Up to the time of our interview in spring 2006, she had lived in three Buddhist communities and two Christian communities for between four months and two years at a time, and was also closely associated with the Christian and Buddhist monasteries where she had spent some time since taking her vows to solitude. At the time I interviewed Furneaux she was living alone in a small hermitage near Chepstow.

Furneaux's basic formal practice consists of sitting at least four times a day but there are times when she will do more. Asked about the nature of her sitting practice she explains that, at times, it is more formally *Satipaṭṭhāna*, but that, on the whole, it is *shikantaza* (or just sitting). Furneaux's regular practice also involves self-administering the Eucharist daily and saying the office four times daily and the Buddhist Sōtō Zen office twice daily. At certain points in the year, she refrains from saying the offices so as to concentrate on sitting, walking and moving meditation. She also does a significant amount of *chi* work and Zen brush work (having trained both in the UK and for a month in Japan, Furneaux now has permission to teach *Hitsuzendo* – The Way of the Zen Brush – in the Daito lineage). The formal elements of her practice tend to take up to about five hours a day, 'then the morning and afternoon are working meditation. So that means being here and now, absolutely present to what you're doing, and practising mindfulness in everything that you do' (101–2).

When Furneaux took her vows to solitude, Archbishop Williams assigned to her a ministry to those, as she describes it, 'on the Buddhist/Christian tight rope who seriously wish to solve this koan': 'The Way of the Cross and Lotus' (2006a: 1). In 2001, in recognition of this ministry and in response to requests, Furneaux met with a group of Christians she knew who were seriously engaged in Buddhist practice. This initial meeting was to be the catalyst for the birth of the Morning Star Sangha (MSS). MSS is a group of people from various Christian backgrounds all of whom have received training in Buddhist meditation and some of whom are formally Buddhists. This groups meets together 'for interpractice and to explore intercommunion, on a basis of "Beyond Identities" "Beyond the Opposites"'.[11] MSS, Furneaux explains, provides an environment for practitioners in which nothing about Christianity has to be put down or denied but is instead 'there to be explored and understood'.[12]

Furneaux explains that she feels 'at home within Buddhism and within Christianity', but prefers to avoid identity labels: 'What I say is my colours are nailed to the cross – you can see it in my habit' (Furneaux wears a brown Anglican nun's habit), 'but I also wear the cross and lotus: the cross is emerging from the lotus'.[13]

Ruben L. F. Habito[14]

Ruben Habito is Professor of World Religions and Spirituality at Perkins School of Theology, Southern Methodist University, Dallas, Texas. He is a practising Roman Catholic and a former Jesuit priest. He is also a Master in the Sanbô Kyôdan School of Zen, and founding director of, and teacher at, the Maria Kannon Zen Center in Dallas.

Habito was born in the Philippines in 1947 to devout Roman Catholic parents. As a child he prayed with the family every morning and evening, abstained from eating meat on Fridays, went to confession every Saturday and to Mass every Sunday. Habito felt a 'deep devotion to the Blessed Mother Mary' and kept a rosary in his pocket which he prayed daily for a number of years, into his early teens. He also loved going to mass – the Latin chants and 'the uplifting aroma of incense all around' (2007: 171). His childhood religiosity centred upon a belief in a 'God up there' – a benevolent and omnipotent judge who would reward good deeds and punish bad deeds (2003a: 130).

In his mid-teens, however, Habito began to question this religious worldview in the light of a couple of powerful experiences at around this time.[15] The first of these was an exhilarating yet disorientating realisation that 'there was no need to imagine another layer of reality over and above that which we called the universe. This was it!' (2003a: 131). In that moment, the 'white-bearded grandfather god' disappeared from Habito's horizon, never to return (2007: 172), leaving him questioning the nature and meaning of existence. The second experience was one of 'being enveloped in a mysterious yet intelligent, immediate, and most of all, loving kind of Presence' (2003a: 134), which left Habito with 'a new appreciation of the Mystery that is this universe, that underlies every heartbeat, every breath, every tree, rock, and star' (2003a: 134–35).

After school Habito started a degree in physics but, finding himself more interested in searching for answers to the questions with which the first of his profound adolescent experiences had left him grappling, he felt drawn to give his life 'to the pursuit of this Mystery', the presence of which he had been acutely aware of since the second of his pivotal experiences. In 1964 he joined the Jesuit noviate to train for ordination as a Catholic priest. However, Habito was still 'struggling with the basic issue of God's existence' (2007: 173), because of what seemed to him the incompatibility between the God of classical theism and the realities of suffering and evil. What kept him going was the 'inner nourishment' he received through the Spiritual Exercises of St Ignatius which intensified 'those glimpses of the inscrutable, unthinkable Wisdom' his adolescent experiences had afforded him (2007: 174–75).

Eventually Habito had an experience while pacing the Seminary corridors one day, worrying about his inability to affirm God's existence, which was to set his mind at ease. His eyes fell upon a wooden crucifix on the wall, and in the cross he felt he saw all the suffering beings of the Earth, 'many of them crying out, "My God, My God, why have you forsaken me?"' (2007: 175–76). As he looked, 'a voice came, gently yet clearly, from within, addressing the Figure on the Cross, saying: "*You are My Beloved, in whom I am well-pleased*"' (2007: 176). From that moment on, Habito felt an inner assurance, both that he could accept the fact of suffering, and that he could accept that 'there is "something" more convincing, more reassuring, more overpowering, than all this evil and suffering ... that made it all worthwhile undergoing this, and even dying as a consequence of it. That "something" remains for me a totally inscrutable Mystery', writes Habito, 'but I can only refer to it as the Source of that voice that I heard ... a voice of unconditional acceptance, of all that was, is, and ever will be, *no matter what*' (2007: 176).

In 1970 Habito was sent to Japan on mission and, in accordance with new Vatican II guidelines regarding the imperative of dialogue with other religious traditions, was assigned to study Japanese religions, predominantly Buddhism (2003a: 135–36). Not long after his arrival in Japan, Habito had his first taste of Zen when a Japanese friend of his invited him to join a Zen retreat (*sesshin*). This first retreat was 'a powerful and exhilarating experience' which whetted his appetite for more (2004: 1). Habito took up the practice of Zen under Yamada Koun Roshi, Zen Master of the Sanbô Kyôdan lineage in Kamakura.[16] In his first meeting with Yamada Roshi Habito was given the famous 'mu' *kōan* as the foundation for his practice.[17] '[W]ithin a few weeks', recalls Habito, 'came the Big Bang. ... in the flash of an instant, I *understood*, in a rather direct and intimate way, that is, *from within*, what was behind the intriguing half-smile of the Buddha figures we see in sculptures and paintings'.[18] Yamada Roshi confirmed that Habito had experienced *kenshō*,[19] and this marked his formal entry into the world of Zen (Habito 2004: 2). It also made him one of the first Roman Catholics to have *kenshō* confirmed by a Japanese Master.

In the following years, Habito undertook graduate study in the Department of Indology and Buddhist Studies at the University of Tokyo. Included in his programme of study were seminars reading Sanskrit, Pāli, Chinese and Japanese Buddhist texts. His PhD thesis concerned the understanding of the Absolute in Indian Buddha Nature thought. During this period, Habito also studied Christian scripture and theology at the Jesuit Theologate at Sophia University, Tokyo.

In 1976 Habito was ordained, and in 1978 he completed his doctoral study and subsequently took up a post teaching primarily Buddhism in the Philosophy Department of Sophia University, meanwhile taking opportunities to go back to the Philippines and to travel for brief periods in Thailand, Burma, Indonesia, India and Sri Lanka.

Habito studied *kōans* under the guidance of Yamada Roshi for the next 16 years. He explains that his ongoing practice of Zen meditation, combined with his study and teaching of Buddhism, led him to an increasingly profound 'understanding and appreciation of Buddhist perspectives on the world, on human existence, on spiritual practice' (2007: 168).

In 1987 Habito met Maria Reis and after two years of friendship with her, asked for dispensation from his Jesuit vows in the summer of 1989. In the same year, after 19 years in Japan, he moved to Dallas, Texas to take up a teaching post at Perkins School of Theology, Southern Methodist University. In 1990 he and Maria were married. Their two sons were born in 1991 and 1993, and between 1998 and 2000 they lived again in Japan on a University assignment.

Habito had received authorisation to teach Zen by Yamada Koun in 1988, and once in Dallas, he established the Maria Kannon Zen Center,[20] where he is still teacher and Director today. He is also a member of the American Zen Teachers' Association and the Buddhist Peace Fellowship.

At the time of our interview, Habito was attending the Zen centre every other Wednesday for a full period of three sittings and to receive interviews from Zen students at the centre, and once a month on a Saturday for an all-day sit. Habito also attends mass, prays regularly with his family and endeavours to maintain a sense of mindfulness and to find time for sitting practice before bed (148). Sometimes Habito also chants the *Nam-Myōhō-Renge-Kyō*: 'somehow there are just some moments when that seems to be the appropriate thing to utter and ... means simply: "praise to the *Sūtra* of the Lotus of the wondrous *Dharma*"' (160).

If asked whether he is a Buddhist, Habito says his response would be: '"By the merit of the countless Buddhas and Bodhisattvas throughout space and time, I aspire to continue in this path of Awakening". *I take refuge in the Buddha, the Dharma, and the Sangha*' (2007: 178). By this response, Habito intends to identify himself with those who take the Buddha's teachings as a guide, with the community of sentient beings, like himself, who seek to cultivate wisdom and embody compassion (2007: 178). If asked whether he is a Christian, Habito says his response would be: '"By the grace of God, with the guidance of the Holy Spirit, I aspire to live following the way of Jesus the Christ." *In the name of the Father, and of the Son, and of the Holy Spirit. Amen*' (2007: 178). By this, explains Habito,

> I express infinite gratitude and total surrender to that Unknowable Mystery, that whom Jesus called Abba, Father, in whose Motherly Love I find myself embraced every moment together with the whole of creation; to the Beloved who, begotten of the Divine, became emptied of this and took on the form of our humanity, revealing to us our own divine source; to the Consoler who manifests to all people throughout all ages and in all places, all that is good, true, holy, and beautiful.
>
> (2007: 178)

Habito intends to identify himself with all those who have followed, and currently try to follow, Jesus as their model in life, 'seeking to be on the side of the marginalized, the poor and oppressed of this earth in the way Jesus was, to witness to the *kindom* of God in our midst'.[21] Habito does not see himself as 'part Buddhist, part Christian' or 'sometimes Buddhist, sometimes Christian' (2007: 179). He intends to live as a Buddhist 'through and through' and also to 'live thoroughly in the Spirit of Christ Jesus' (2007: 179). He is not unaware that this leaves him with a theological task:

> I still have to do my homework, in a theological sense … The knotty theological problem that keeps emerging is precisely how to responsibly articulate my understanding of the way things are [in a way] that is faithful to the Christian tradition as well as to the Zen Buddhist tradition that I have been nourished by.
>
> (196)

John P. Keenan[22]

John Keenan is Professor Emeritus of Religion, Middlebury College, Vermont, and from September 2007 to May 2008 held the Roche Chair for Interreligious Research at the Nanzan Institute for Religion and Culture in Nagoya, Japan. Keenan is also an Episcopalian (formerly Roman Catholic) priest. He has spent most of his academic career translating Mahāyāna texts from Chinese into English and writing 'Mahāyāna theology' on the basis of those texts, 'borrowing Mahāyāna philosophical themes and grafting them onto the Christian mystic tradition' (1993b: 32). The main Buddhist influences on Keenan's thought are the philosophies of the Mādhyamika and Yogācāra schools of Buddhism, although he is also influenced to some extent by Zen Buddhism (218). He understands himself as doing Christian theology through the 'lens' of Buddhist philosophies, and describes himself as a 'Mahāyāna Christian' (Keenan LCC: 271).

Keenan was born in Philadelphia in 1940 into a Roman Catholic family of Irish descent. He was baptised as a baby and grew up in a Catholic culture. He learnt the catechism at his parochial school (where most of the teachers were nuns), went to Mass with his parents every Sunday and served at the altar, prayed regularly and attended Benediction. The faith of Keenan's childhood was a clear and simple one: 'God created the world and was the source of all things. Good was rewarded, if not here, then hereafter. Evil was punished in similar fashion. The choice was ours – either to follow the good or opt for the evil'. This was all taken for granted by Keenan, 'unchallenged … by outside forces and unquestioned within' (LCC: 8).

Keenan decided he wanted to become a priest and in 1956 at just 15 years old he left home to attend St Charles Borromeo Seminary, Philadelphia, where he was to live and train for the next ten years: 'In my Catholic culture', writes Keenan, looking back, 'there was no higher vocation. … It drew me into a space of an assured identity' (LCC: 45–46). Seminary life for Keenan was marked by a profound sense of belonging. His new world was full of 'the overarching presence of God in Christ' (LCC: 68), and he found healing after the death of his father in the 'comforts of devotion' (LCC: 69).

The fifth and sixth year of his seminary training focused on philosophy and, finally, years seven to ten were devoted to theology. Keenan's world was shaken by new theological insights as he acquainted himself with the writings of Teilhard de Chardin, Karl Rahner, and Bernard Lonergan, and had his first contact with Zen through Aelred Graham's *Zen Catholicism*.

As the ramifications of the Vatican II reforms began to reverberate throughout the Church, the lines between conservatives and liberals were drawn, and Keenan found himself firmly in the 'liberal camp'.

In 1966 Keenan was ordained and, during his second appointment, began to read a little about Asian religious traditions. The first books he read on Buddhism were those of Alan Watts and D. T. Suzuki, and though Keenan now sees these works as 'rather simplistic import Zen', they had an impact on him, reminding him of the early Christian spiritual traditions of 'quiet prayer and self-abnegation' that he had learned about in his first years in the seminary (LCC: 192). Yet Keenan was also attracted to Eastern religions because of their *differences* from his own tradition: 'I wanted new questions, so that new perspectives might emerge' writes Keenan (LCC: 193). Deciding he would focus on Buddhism, Taoism and Chinese language, he signed up for a graduate course in world religions at Temple University.

It was not long into Keenan's life as a Catholic priest before doubt and dissatisfaction regarding his membership of the clergy began to creep in, as he found himself impressed by the radical Monsignor Ivan Illich's argument 'that one could serve as a priest without being a clergyman, without the culture of clerical privilege and supernatural status that kept the laity in their pews and in their places'.[23] Moreover, Keenan had started to see the Church 'as exercising an all-mothering control', demanding celibacy not for its own value, 'but because its culture of institutional control could not co-exist with the demands of committed intimacy' (LCC: 186). In 1969 Keenan reluctantly left the clergy with the intention not of renouncing his priestly commitment, but of living it out by serving Christ in the world without elite clerical status (LCC: 206).

In 1970 he was granted admission to the East Asian graduate programme in the Department of Oriental Studies at the University of Pennsylvania, where he learned Chinese, read Taoist and Confucian texts, became familiar with the Kyoto school of Japanese philosophy, and developed an interest in Buddhist doctrine and history. Eager to study Chinese language and culture and to experience a new and different world (LCC: 229), Keenan spent about four months in Taiwan as part of his graduate school study.

He met Linda Klepinger in his Chinese class and in 1972 they were married. The following year, after spending four years studying Japanese language, literature and Chinese philosophy together in Tokyo and then Nagoya, they returned to Philadelphia to have their first child and later moved to Wisconsin where their second was born.

Having felt only marginally accepted in the Roman Catholic Church since his departure from the clergy, Keenan began to feel the need to belong to a church where he and his family would be completely accepted and able to participate fully. He found what he was looking for in the Episcopal church and was received in 1976.

From the mid-sixties, Keenan 'consumed books' on Mādhyamika and Yogācāra philosophy and, while studying for his MA in Chinese language and philosophy at the University of Pennsylvania, immersed himself in Chinese classics and works on Mādhyamika doctrine and history. He was profoundly impressed by the Mādhyamika teaching of emptiness – 'that the very being of beings is transient and ever-changing, that things stand in being not alone and all of their own accord, but interdependently, as three sticks form a tripod by leaning one on the other' (LCC: 270). He was struck deeply too by the teachings on the two truths, 'which offered a model of engaging in concrete historical and conventional discourse in constant and dynamic tension with the silence of ultimate meaning – while never pretending to have captured the ultimate in any verbal net' (LCC: 199). Between 1976 and 1980 Keenan undertook doctoral work at the University of Wisconsin-Madison under the supervision of Minoru Kiyota. His PhD thesis was entitled: *A Study of the Buddhabhūmyupadeśa: The Doctrinal Development of the Notion of Wisdom in Yogācāra Thought*. During his time as a student of Buddhist Studies he made friends with fellow students who were Buddhists, and came to realise: 'I'm sitting here … talking theology with Buddhists, the same way I've been doing it my whole life with Christians' (224–25).

Crucially, Buddhism provided Keenan with 'altogether new languages and perspectives in which to think theology' (LCC: 195). Just as Aquinas had drawn on Aristotle's thought to express Christian faith through newly discovered terms, wondered Keenan, might one not employ Mahāyāna philosophy in order to yield insights obscured by other approaches? He began to think that one could 'graft Mahāyāna philosophy onto the root of Christian faith' (LCC: 263), 'rethinking' and 'reliving' what was already within the Christian tradition by interpreting Christian doctrines using Buddhist categories (225–26). To insist that the Greek framework is normative or necessary to all theological thinking, is surely 'to muzzle the Spirit, who would speak in as many languages as there are human tongues' (LCC: 272), reasoned Keenan. 'I thought if we can think about it in terms that reject essences altogether, we'd be closer to where people are today in *this* culture, and perhaps better able to see different patterns' (226). So as Keenan studied Buddhism, he began to consciously engender and nurture a dynamic and 'creative tension' in his life and thought, 'between Asian forms of thought and the faith of his Christian commitment' (LCC: 261, 263–64), integrating the insights of Buddhism into Christianity from his Christian perspective.

Having received his PhD in 1980, Keenan and his family spent two years in Japan where he worked as a research fellow at the Nanzan Institute for Religion and Culture, Nagoya. On returning to the USA in 1986 he and his family settled in Vermont where Keenan took up a post teaching Asian religions to undergraduates at Middlebury College.

Keenan has been introduced to Buddhist meditation practices, although he has never felt a personal need to adopt such a practice: 'my own practices have remained Christian', writes Keenan – 'silent prayer, verbal prayer, Eucharist. That seems sufficient for me' (LCC: 196). In 1988, Keenan was 'regularised' as a priest in the Episcopal Church of the USA, i.e. his 1966 ordination was accepted as valid by the Episcopal Church. At the time of our interview, Keenan was serving as the priest of St Mark's Church in Newport, Vermont.[24] 'The Eucharist liturgy still reverberates through my bones and forms the core of my practice', writes Keenan, 'enriched by the many Buddhist texts I have read and invigorated by insights into God and emptiness that that liturgy engenders in me' (LCC: 282).

'Philosophically, I think I'm Mahāyāna', says Keenan. Moreover, if one takes the Buddhist Canon as a set of philosophic principles, 'then I'm Canonically a Buddhist, I suppose' (219). 'I am now persuaded of the elegance and truth of Mahāyāna Buddhist philosophy', he writes, 'and I read the gospel through its lens' (LCC: 195). Keenan explains that, by identifying himself as a Mahāyāna Christian, he means 'Buddhist philosophy, Christian practice and faith' (220). 'So I'm, by doctrine, very Christian – Incarnation and Trinity – by philosophy, I'm Buddhist: I use the Buddhism as the framework in which to understand Christian faith and doctrine' (284). However, Keenan does not describe himself as a Buddhist: 'it's not what I would call a faith commitment because it's not a participation in community or a commitment to a practice'. He can say he's committed to the *Dharma*, to *Dharma* study, 'and probably to the Buddha', but not that he's committed to the *Saṅgha* (222). Moreover, Keenan sets much store in the formal making of commitments, and emphasises that he has never actually taken refuge:

> I mean, you go and you *say those words* and you *mean those words*: 'I take refuge in the Buddha, the *Dharma*, and the *Saġgha*', and I've never said those words. ... I think it's really *important* when you say something ... in a liturgical context, and ... for whatever reason, by the simple fact that I have *not* taken refuge, I am *not* a Buddhist. Perhaps the real point is that my *Saġgha* is the Christian community.
>
> (230–31)

Sallie B. King[25]

Sallie King is Professor of Philosophy and Religion at James Madison University, Harrisonburg, Virginia. King is a Buddhist – formerly practising in the Zen tradition, now in the *Vipassanā* tradition – and a Quaker.[26] She publicly claims a 'double religious identity' and has had this dual commitment for more than 25 years (King 2005a: 88).

King was born in Washington DC in 1952 into a military family and raised as a 'generic Protestant' (2003c: 157). She was baptised as a baby and, in her childhood, her family attended combined Protestant services on the military bases where her father – an Officer in the US Air force – was stationed (all over the USA and in Germany and the UK). But her parents were not religious and their church attendance gradually became less frequent. King, on the other hand, became increasingly involved and, for a time, while she was still at high school, she taught the kindergarten class in a Protestant Sunday school. However, she eventually gave this up on the basis that she was unable to reconcile Jesus' teachings, which she took to be clearly pacifist, with teaching at a Sunday School located on a military base.

King describes her religious life in childhood and adolescence as one of 'intensive, private, individual seeking' and describes herself as an 'avid student of world culture and life-long ponderer of religious questions' (2003c: 157). While still in adolescence, she reached two conclusions: first, the idea of a benevolent, omnipotent God could not be reconciled with the terrible suffering present in the world and she must, therefore, give it up – 'The Problem of Evil ... discredited the idea of God as I had been taught it', writes King (2003c: 157); second, a loving God would not punish spiritual seekers within other cultures with eternal damnation just because they weren't Christian. From a Christianity which taught otherwise, King 'walked away ... disgusted' (2003c: 158).

At college, King discovered Buddhism and it 'made complete sense':

> The Four Noble Truths' direct naming and addressing of suffering as the central problem described life exactly as I saw it. Moreover, it did entirely without the God in whom I could not believe, was impressively irenic in its social relations, and did not go around denouncing and condemning people who thought otherwise ... best of all ... Buddhism assured me that I need not take what they taught on their authority, but should seek for answers myself, in my own experience. I could hardly believe such noble ideas and practices existed.
>
> (2003c: 158)

King learned how to meditate and went on a few Zen retreats. At around the same time she studied Christian mysticism and did not find there the difficulties she had identified in mainstream Christianity. Feeling an affinity with it, King started to practise what she came to call 'natural meditation' – long hours spent 'sitting with a silent mind, quietly watching the sunrise, the sunset, the night sky, the ocean, a candle flame'. King describes how these practices opened up for her 'an experiential world that crushed all ordinary things into complete insignificance' (2003c: 158).

It was not until 1977, when King met and married her husband Steve, who was a member of a Zen Buddhist group which she joined, that she became a member of a Buddhist organisation: Rochester Zen Center. They meditated with the group and attended occasional retreats. In 1981, Toni Packer, one of Philip Kapleau's students at Rochester Zen Center left to set up her own Zen centre in Springwater, upstate New York, believing that Zen in the West should be freed from inessential institutional, cultural and ritual trappings. King and her husband went with Packer, along with a number of other students from Rochester, and began sitting regularly with her. Packer acted as King's teacher at that time, though King is no longer in touch with her. King has attended many retreats over the years with different teachers, but does not currently have a single teacher.

From 1976 King undertook graduate work at Temple University, Philadelphia, on the concept of Buddha Nature in the Chinese Buddhist text, *Fo Hsing Lun* (Buddha Nature Treatise). For the last few years of her doctoral work she taught part-time in Buffalo, New York (where her husband was working on his Master's degree). After receiving her PhD, in 1981, King accepted her first full-time post at Colby College, Maine.

In 1983 King had her first child and in 1986 her second. Although, she continued to meditate with her husband, she struggled to keep up a practice while at the same time juggling the demands of motherhood and an academic career. Moreover, at that time there was no Buddhist centre where she and her family lived in Illinois. As her first child began to return from school with tales of 'an angry God that lived in the sky and punished children if they misbehaved', the need for a religious community which would offer her children an alternative began to seem pressing. King met this need by joining the Religious Society of Friends (Quakers), having first made sure, explicitly, that they had no difficulty with her also being a Buddhist.

> I soon decided that this was not just the 'next best thing' to Buddhism; for me it was a wonderful thing in its own right, different from Buddhism, but ... compatible with it. What particularly impressed me in Quakerism was its dual focus: inwardly, on direct, personal experience of spiritual truth, and outwardly, on nonviolent social action – with a serious, sustained effort to have the outward action express the spiritual lifeblood.
>
> (2003c: 158).

King attends Quaker Meetings every week. Her branch of Quakerism has no formal ministers, rather, everyone in the Meeting is considered a minister. Everything is done via committee work and Quakers see this work as practice (354). King sits on many committees and has held a number of leadership roles, including Clerk of the Meeting, and been involved in the religious education of young Quakers.

Asked whether she understands herself as a *Christian*, King explains that she does, but would wish to distinguish herself from the fundamentalist, conservative, exclusivist, evangelical Christianity which represents the mainstream where she lives, and which she feels 'very badly about'. She very much embraces contemplative Christianity and contemporary monastic practices and beliefs, and also connects deeply with Liberation Theology (344). She explains that there are important threads in the Christian tradition and in Christian scripture which are very important to Quakers and to her personally. For example, Quakers focus more on the third person of the Trinity, the Holy Spirit, than other branches of Christianity tend to, and also on the prophetic tradition, going back to the prophets of the Hebrew Bible. Also very important to King, as a Quaker, are Jesus' teachings – particularly the beatitudes and the parables – and Jesus' example.[27]

> [I]t's ... 100 per cent Christianity, but the things that are emphasised are things that other traditions overlook for whatever reasons. We overlook, granted, a lot of things that they tend to emphasise. But ... I feel legitimate about that because ... every tradition of Christianity picks some things and some threads and themes that they pull out and focus on, and leave some others
>
> (345)

The only explicitly Christian imagery in her home is a picture accompanied by the quotation: 'Blessed are the merciful' (360).

Feeling the absence of a Buddhist community in her area, in the early nineties King and her family spent a month living as part of Thich Nhat Hanh's Zen community at Plum Village in France. It was during this stay that she formally took the three refuges and the five precepts with Nhat Hanh, although she explains that since she already understood herself as a Buddhist, this was no 'big threshold' for her (342). When I interviewed King in May 2006 there was still no Buddhist group in her area, but she was meditating regularly at a Buddhist shrine in her home: 'I have a practice that's ... concentration on breathing and also a kind of *shikantaza* ... "just sitting"', explained King; '[a] certain amount of *mettā* practice as well (loving kindness) ... picked up from the Theravāda side of things' (355).

After our interview, however, King and her husband joined their nearest Buddhist group in Charlottesville (an hour's drive from them), which happened to be a *Vipassanā* (Insight) meditation group. For two years they meditated weekly with the group, attending frequent weekend retreats. Eventually, however, the long weekly trip became unsustainable and they established a *Vipassanā* group in their own neighbourhood, while maintaining a connection with the Charlottesville community. King and her husband co-lead this group, which meets regularly in the Friends Meeting House. King also co-teaches Buddhist-Quaker retreats with a *Vipassanā* teacher from California.

Although, initially, King switched from Zen to *Vipassanā* for accidental reasons, she explains that she has come to feel that American *Vipassanā* is more suitable than Zen for a lay, American practitioner like herself, both in terms of its teachings and in terms of the way practice opportunities are set up.[28] It is orientated towards a practice which does not depend on a monastic support system, explains King, but which recognises that practice must be made suitable for people with jobs and families who cannot responsibly focus solely and intensively on their own spiritual development. She points out, however, that American *Vipassanā* draws on *all* branches of Buddhism and that her own thinking is still very much influenced by Zen philosophy.[29]

King is happy to be described as a 'Buddhist–Christian' or a 'Buddhist-Quaker' (350) but emphasises that she understands herself as '100 per cent Buddhist and 100 per cent Quaker': she does not see it as a fifty–fifty commitment (348). The flexibility of Quakerism and Buddhism regarding doctrine as well as their shared emphasis on experience as the primary locus of religious truth, and on the provisional nature of verbal formulations, gave King reason to believe, for many years, that hers was the '"easy path' in Buddhist Christian dual religious membership' (2003c: 161). In 1994, for example, she speaks of 'personal wholeness', despite the fact that she is drawing on two traditions, and explains that she does not go about her life 'with some kind of internal warfare going on' (1994a). These days, however, she does not feel so entirely at ease with each tradition and finds that apparent inconsistencies between the Christian and the Buddhist world-views sometimes present her with 'a little bit of a challenge' (359). Nevertheless she sees the traditions as having different strengths (406), perceives 'profound truth in both', and feels that she *needs* both, despite the fact that she no longer sees them 'as so nearly reconcilable' (2003c: 170).

Maria Reis Habito[30]

Maria Reis Habito is the International Program Director for Taipei Museum of World Religions and for Global Family for Love and Peace, and Co-director of the Elijah Interfaith Institute. Between 1990 and 2002 she held academic posts at Southern Methodist University (teaching History of Modern East Asia, Chinese History and Culture, Women in China and Japan, Women in World Religions, Contemporary Spirituality and Japanese Language) and has published books and articles in the fields of Buddhist Studies and Inter-religious Dialogue. Reis Habito is a Roman Catholic and a Buddhist (her Buddhist Master has Chan, Theravāda, and Tibetan ordinations, and all these influences are present in her own Buddhist thought and practice. She is also influenced by the Sanbô Kyôdan school of Zen). She has identified herself publicly as a 'Buddhist Christian'.[31]

Reis Habito (née Reis) was born in 1959 in Cologne, Germany, into a Roman Catholic family, and grew up in Saarbrücken near the French border. Her mother was from a very traditional Catholic background (she 'took the Scriptures quite literally, and you have to go to Church, you cannot do this or that'), but her father was from southern Germany: 'they are the mystics' (2000: 28). She and her family attended mass every Sunday, although, as a child Reis didn't think much of going to church. She recalls, however, that from her father – who sung the psalms beautifully and movingly but slept soundly through the sermon – she learnt what she took to be a valuable lesson: 'God has not to do with the sermon, and maybe God does not have much to do with the priest. God has to do with the music and the love expressed in those Psalms' (2000: 28–29). Reis Habito emphasises that hers was a very happy Catholic upbringing (2000: 28). She remembers fondly 'all the beautiful celebrations' that were part of the Catholic calendar, and recalls how, since one's name day was comparable to one's birthday in significance, all through the month of May she kept fresh flowers in front of her picture of the virgin Mary (2000: 29).

Reis' first contact with Buddhism came in the summer of 1978, just after her graduation from high school. She and her mother spent a fortnight in Taiwan where they stayed with a Roman Catholic parish priest and auxiliary bishop of Taipei, Father Joseph Wang, and, during their visit, he took them to meet a devout Buddhist nun. Reis Habito recalls how this smiley 60-year-old nun asked them whether they were Catholic like Father Wang: 'When we nodded somewhat hesitantly, not knowing what to expect, her smile grew even bigger and she replied: "Buddhists or Christians – it does not make the slightest difference. We are all brothers and sisters"' (2003a: 203). This encounter was enough to leave Reis determined to learn more about Buddhism, and so the following year she returned to Taiwan to study Chinese language and culture at National Taiwan Normal University in Taipei.

In the spring of 1980 a philosophy student friend of hers invited Reis to accompany him on a visit to a spiritually accomplished Buddhist master. During their visit to his rural hermitage, Master Hsin Tao suddenly announced that there was a very deep *yuan* (karmic connection) between himself and Reis. He explained to her that he believed there to be a relationship between them from a previous life and that this was the reason for their meeting. Reis Habito recalls how Master Hsin Tao further confounded her by saying: 'You are a tree that can bring rich fruit. Therefore I want to plant your roots in fertile ground' (2003a: 204). Master Hsin Tao invited her to return as often as she could. She recalls how she was attracted to this Buddhist monk because she felt he spoke the truth, even if she didn't fully understand it, and she wanted to go back and learn more from him (2000: 19).

During one of her first visits to Master Hsin Tao, when she still knew little about Buddhism, she watched him place food in front of a statue of Guanyin (Kannon), light some incense and bow. Suspecting this to be an act of idolatry, she asked him who the statue was, to which Master Hsin Tao replied: 'Can't you see? This is you!' (2000: 30; 2003a: 202). Reflecting later on his response, Reis was hit by an explosion of questions: 'What am I? Who am I? ... What does he mean? ... What is my connection to this figure he calls Guanyin? What does he see that I don't?' (2003a: 202). One night she dreamt that God had dropped out of heaven and she woke up crying; 'I was desperate, but I still thought this must be a teaching. If I cannot find God where I thought He was all the time, I may be able to find him somewhere else' (2000: 30).

In 1981 Reis left Taiwan to study Chinese–Japanese studies and philosophy at Ludwig-Maximilians-Universität, Munich. Keeping in mind Master Hsin

Tao's words that '[i]t's wonderful you want to study Buddhism' but 'you will ... not be able to understand anything about Buddhism unless you sit down and practice' (2000: 30), she began to meditate every morning for 20–30 minutes.

In 1983 Reis returned to Taiwan to visit Master Hsin Tao and took the Three Refuges, formally becoming a lay disciple of his. This was for her a joyful experience in which all doubts about whether she was doing the right thing were dispelled.[32] 'And with that,' writes Reis Habito, 'I was a freshly hatched Buddhist Christian' (2003a: 208).

Also in 1983 Reis attended her first Zen retreat, run by Father Hugo Enomiya-Lassalle at a Franciscan Monastery in Germany. After that, he guided her practice until she met Yamada Koun Roshi in Japan in 1987 while at Kyoto University writing her PhD thesis on the Great Compassion Mantra of the Thousand Armed Guanyin. 'Both Father Lassalle and Yamada Roshi ... strengthened in me the confidence that it is also possible for Christians to practice the way of enlightenment', writes Reis Habito (2003a: 209). She recalls how her first Zen retreat took place at a time when she was seriously considering returning to Master Hsin Tao to be a Buddhist nun. At the same time she grappled with doubts and questions about her Christian identity: 'I felt attached to the Catholic culture I had been raised in', explains Reis Habito. 'But was that enough to be called Christian? Should there not be a direct, tangible experience of God? ... I was ... full of questions and doubts about everything ... God is love. What does that really mean?' (2003a: 210). She continued to struggle with these issues in subsequent Zen retreats. However, while on retreat with Fr Lassalle in Shinmeikutsu, Japan, in 1987, she had an experience which, she writes, 'completely resolved my mental and bodily tension and – like the encounter with Shih-fu – changed my life forever' (2003a: 210. 'Shih-fu' means 'Master'; it is the familiar way in which Master Hsin Tao's disciples and friends address him).

> I cannot describe it other than to say that I was touched by grace, enveloped in a love so gentle and so clear that tears of joy and repentance streamed down my cheeks. How could I have been so blind ... not realizing how loved I was and how everybody else was loved just as much?
>
> (2003a: 210)

Yamada Roshi later confirmed Reis' experience as a *kenshō* experience. This was followed by another profound experience six months or so later, which deepened the first (446).

In 1987 Reis met Ruben Habito, who was also studying under Yamada Roshi at that time, and in 1990 she finished her PhD thesis and joined Ruben in Dallas, where they were married. Within the following three years their two sons were born and life changed dramatically for Reis Habito: 'Gone were the quiet evenings at the Zen Center and the peaceful hours of early morning meditation that I had been used to for more than ten years' (2003a: 210).

Since the early 1990s Master Hsin Tao's project has been the building of a Museum for World Religions which he hopes will facilitate interreligious exchange, and he has travelled widely in order to promote this project. Reis Habito has accompanied him whenever possible, acting as his interpreter (2003a: 211). Since 2002 she has been the International Program Director for the Taipei Museum of World Religions.

Reis Habito explains that her encounter with Buddhism and her close connection to her Buddhist teachers, Master Hsin Tao and Yamada Roshi, have not uprooted her from Christian ground. 'On the contrary', she says, 'my Buddhist teachers, together with Father Enomiya-Lassalle, have done everything possible to fertilize these roots and to let them grow stronger and deeper' (2003a: 213).

Reis Habito goes to a Catholic church on Sundays and sings in the choir once a month and on Feast Days. She visits her Buddhist Master, Hsin Tao, in Taiwan fairly frequently and, while she is there, participates in the morning prayers; 'I can read all the Sūtras with them and I can recite the mantras with them and I feel fully one with them' (458–59). Once a week she practises Zen meditation at Maria Kannon Zen Center. And she explained, in interview, that her morning jog had become a period of practice: 'while I go jogging, very naturally, ... I start to recite the *Great Compassion Dhāraṇī* or a Hail Mary: 'one or the other comes out', she says; 'it's the same plea for compassion, no matter which language I use' (441). Having been studying *kōans* for many years, at the time of our interview, Reis Habito was nearing completion of *kōan* study under Habito's guidance. In 2007 she completed and, in 2008, was appointed Assistant Zen Teacher by Yamada Ryoun Roshi, giving her permission to teach in the Sanbô Kyôdan lineage. Since then, she has been conducting short Zen retreats in various locations (most recently, at the time of writing, in Florida and Ladakh).

Reis Habito explains that she did not set out to become Buddhist and Christian, rather, it gradually became impossible for her to be solely one or solely the other as, increasingly, she found herself nourished by and at home within both traditions (431, 460–61). She reflects that although she identifies equally with both traditions (430), this does not mean she identifies with or belongs to each of these traditions *in the same way* (429). She thinks her Christian upbringing makes her *emotionally* more Christian than Buddhist: 'there are things that connect me very deeply to my childhood, and in Buddhism, obviously, that's not the case because I encountered it later' (429), and since Christianity came first for her, she feels the description 'Buddhist Christian' is perhaps more apt than the description 'Christian Buddhist' (431). However, she nevertheless understands herself as *fully* Buddhist (428) and feels she owes much of her *insight* to Buddhism (429).

Part I
Facing the ultimate

3 God

Having introduced my interviewees, we can now turn to the task of addressing the crucial questions such individuals appear to face, beginning with the most obvious potential obstacle to authentic Buddhist Christian dual belonging: Christians believe in God; Buddhists don't. When it comes to apparent contradictions between these traditions, this one would seem to be by far the most significant and pervasive. We must, therefore, tackle it head-on and in some depth at the outset, otherwise our exploration of further questions will build on shaky foundations.

Let's start by getting the problem into clear focus. God is utterly central to Christianity and, from a Christian perspective, without God there is no salvation from sin and death. Indeed, without God, there would be no one to be saved since the very existence of the universe is thought by Christians to depend on God. Buddhism, on the other hand, while traditionally acknowledging the existence of gods with a lower case 'g', accords these gods a status in the hierarchy of beings lower than that of the Buddha *qua* Enlightened being who discovered for himself the way to liberation. Buddhism's gods are themselves trapped within the round of rebirth, hence liberation in no way depends upon them. They are, therefore, not relevantly akin to the God of Christianity upon whom Christians believe all salvation depends. It would seem that whereas God dominates the Christian world-view, in the Buddhist world-view God's existence is denied. How, then, is it possible to belong equally to both the Buddhist and the Christian tradition? As far as Cornille is concerned, it is not possible:

> [i]f one religion affirms the existence of a personal God and another religion denies it, one cannot logically claim to equally belong to the two religious traditions at the same time. Even though many of the beliefs and practices of the two religions may overlap, ascendancy to the truth of one would necessarily exclude simultaneous belonging to the other
>
> (2008: 12)

Paul Williams (a convert from Tibetan Buddhism to Roman Catholicism) goes further still, arguing that, so pervasive is the contrast between Christianity and Buddhism with respect to the question of God, that there is really *no* significant overlap between these two traditions:

> It is the presence of God in Christianity that makes Christianity so often the exact opposite of Buddhism. ... It is not that basically, fundamentally, Buddhism and Christianity are alike, with Christianity adding something called 'God' ... In the light of God, even those aspects of Christianity that seem similar to Buddhism are really quite different.
>
> (2002: 71)

These two traditions, insists Williams, confront us with a straightforward either-or choice between theism and atheism; we can 'take our choice' but 'we cannot have both Buddhism and Christianity' (2002: 56).

Are those who think of themselves as Buddhist and Christian then hopelessly deluded, or might there be some way to integrate the Christian affirmation of God and the Buddhist denial of God within a single logically, psychologically, and spiritually coherent world-view, while at the same time acknowledging and respecting this fundamental difference between the traditions (rather than glossing over it or interpreting it in a way which is inconsistent with one or both of them)? Habito acknowledges the *prima facie* problem presented by the question of God, and explains that there was a time when the recognition of this apparently serious contradiction troubled him:

> [H]ow do you reconcile the notion of a personal God with the kinds of things that Buddhism was presenting in terms of absolute reality as emptiness, and so forth? So, theological issues somehow jumped up and told me: ' ... I need to get this cleared up' ... I realised: ... I still have to articulate ... what all of this means in terms of the traditional formulations of doctrine and it's still an ongoing task.
>
> (137–38)

Is Habito's ongoing task doomed to failure or is there a level at which Buddhism and Christianity can agree on this issue? I suggest there are at least three ways of attempting to move beyond an either-or dichotomy with respect to the question of God. The first is to propose a non-realist interpretation of religious language. Let's consider that approach, before turning to two others.

Expressing values and aspirations?

Suppose that when the Christian says there is a God and the Buddhist denies this and affirms instead the possibility of realising *nirvāṇa*, we assume that each of them is trying to say something about objective reality, i.e. about the way reality is independently of themselves and their own particular mental states and feelings – in the Christian case that there is a God and in the Buddhist case that there is no God but rather the possibility of realising *nirvāṇa*.

In that case, they appear to be saying contradictory things about objective reality. One way of removing this apparent contradiction is to reject realism about religious language.

The realist takes religious language to in some way 'relate to' objective reality, either straightforwardly, by referring to and describing it, or more indirectly by – in senses which I shall try to flesh out later – gesturing at, pointing towards, or rightly orientating people with respect to it. Christians intend their God-talk to relate to God, and Buddhists intend their *nirvāṇa*-talk to relate to *nirvāṇa* (or the *dharmakāya* or the *Dharma* – there are a number of overlapping concepts in Buddhism which point to that which is considered ultimate). If this realist interpretation is rejected by dual belongers, then their Buddhist and Christian language does not describe the nature of objective reality in contradictory ways for the simple reason that it does not describe (or otherwise 'relate to') objective reality *at all*. Rather, such language simply reports or expresses their feelings, or prescribes or prompts certain kinds of behaviour. Don Cupitt, for example, argues that 'religious language is not descriptive or metaphysical but intensely practical. It is used in order to provoke and to prompt change within the self' (1980: 164–65).

As we shall see later in this chapter, it is possible to think that one's God-talk or *nirvāṇa*-talk fails to describe objective reality and hence to construe such talk as having a primarily *practical* function, and yet to nevertheless understand that talk as functioning basically *realistically*. For example, some think that religious language concerning the ultimate, for example, God-talk or *nirvāṇa*-talk, relates to a reality which is objective but indescribable. Such talk is not, therefore, thought by these users to *describe* the ultimate, but is, nevertheless, thought to bear some practical relation to that ultimate. We will look at this idea in more detail presently. For now, let us simply note that this is *not* Cupitt's understanding of how God-talk or *nirvāṇa*-talk functions: Cupitt does not think such language relates *in any way* to objective reality but *only* expresses feelings and prescribes types of behaviour.

Cupitt thinks that these days it is very difficult to accept the objective or metaphysical side of religion (1980: 1). In the Christian case, he says, 'we do not have sufficient evidence to justify objective theism' (1980: 7). This does not mean that we should abandon God-talk, argues Cupitt, but we should not interpret it as the realist does; rather we should recognise that its value lies in its being a symbolic way of representing what spirituality requires of us, of expressing our values and aspirations (1980: 9). On this non-realist view of Christian and Buddhist language the difference between God-talk and *nirvāṇa*-talk is simply a matter of different symbols being used to express speakers' values and aspirations; it is *not* a matter of different claims as to what objective reality includes, for example, God or *nirvāṇa*. According to Cupitt, the job which is done by 'God' for Christians is for Buddhists distributed between 'the *Dharma*' and '*nirvāṇa*'. Cupitt himself argues, on the basis of this interpretation, that '[t]he major religious traditions need not be considered as excluding each other. ... So far as world-view, spirituality and values are concerned everyone in our culture now puts together a personal package' (1980: 141). Cupitt's own preference is for 'Christian Buddhism': 'The content, the spirituality and the values, are Christian', says Cupitt, 'the form is Buddhist' (1980: xii).

Surely, however, if dual belongers are to reflect the self-understandings of both these traditions, then they must seriously reckon with the fact that the majority of Buddhists and Christians simply do not intend their language to be construed as Cupitt construes it.[1] Rather, they understand their language as functioning realistically. They use their language to at least gesture at, or point towards, the way reality objectively is, even when that language is deemed to be inherently inadequate with respect to the objective reality at which it is in some way thought to gesture. If one does not think there is any objective reality – or dimension of objective reality – towards which one intends to point, however inadequately, with one's God-talk, then one is surely an atheist. Cupitt denies that he and others who interpret God-talk in a non-realist way are atheists.[2] But surely, if the atheist label does not apply, it is only because Cupitt has defined theism out of all recognition. Similarly, if one does not believe in any objective reality at which one intends to point, however inadequately, with one's talk of the *dharmakāya* or *nirvāṇa*, then one affirms nothing beyond the finite, conditioned world (and as we will see later, this is not the position of traditional Buddhism). There are some contemporary non-realists who, like Cupitt, continue to identify themselves as Christian or as Buddhist,[3] but for dual belongers who share the realist assumptions of the majority of Buddhists and Christians, giving up on realism will be a high price to pay for coherence.

If religious language is construed as being devoid of any metaphysical clout, moreover, this severely undermines both traditions insofar as it makes it difficult to see how they can be the sources of fundamental optimism that they have been to those who have construed what they have to say realistically. Much religious language concerns a profoundly better quality of existence, not yet experienced; it looks beyond death to resurrection, beyond the sufferings of *saṃsāra* to the bliss of *nirvāṇa*.[4] Throughout history, the brevity and pressures of life, and the sheer struggle many undergo simply to survive, have meant that the vast majority of human beings make very little progress towards the fulfilment described in their religious traditions. As Hick (1989a: 207) points out, if they are ever to do so, then reality must be structured accordingly; and, to believe it is indeed structured accordingly, is to construe religious language in a basically realist way. If dual belongers wish to retain the cosmic optimism of both these traditions, they therefore have good reason to reject the non-realist solution to the question of God.

Let's explore, then, the two options which remain for the realist dual belonger: the first is to construe Christian God-talk as relating to one reality and Buddhist *nirvāṇa*-talk as relating to another; the second is to construe God-talk and *nirvāṇa*-talk as somehow relating to the same reality. In discussing these options, it will be helpful to draw on the work of pluralist theologians. Pluralism is one of three categories – alongside exclusivism and inclusivism – belonging to the taxonomy theologians often use to classify attitudes to other religions. Pluralists suppose that several (at least two) traditions may be equally true and salvifically/liberatively efficacious.[5] Their work is useful to us here because they tend to remove apparent contradictions between religious claims about what is ultimate in one of two ways. Either they interpret those claims as concerning *different* yet simultaneously existing realities or dimensions of reality (we'll call this a polycentric approach), or they interpret them as concerning alternative ways of responding to *one* ultimate reality, i.e. within different traditions one ultimate reality is experienced and spoken of in different but equally valid ways (we'll call this a monocentric approach).

So, let us consider these approaches as potential answers to the question of God, starting with the polycentric approach.

Relating to distinct realities?

If there is more than one ultimate, as polycentric pluralists assume,[6] then when thinking, speaking and practising within a Christian framework, the Buddhist Christian may be focusing on one reality or one dimension of reality – God – and when thinking, speaking and practising within the Buddhist framework, he or she may be focusing on a different reality or a different dimension of reality – *nirvāṇa*, *śūnyatā* or the *dharmakāya*.

Corless' polycentric approach

Of my interviewees, it was perhaps Corless who had experienced the greatest degree of tension between Buddhism and Christianity with respect to the question of God, as he gradually found himself 'equally convinced' by the Mahāyāna Buddhist teaching of interdependent arising, 'in which there is no room for God' and where 'the notion of a Creator-God is unintelligible', and by the Christian teaching 'on the necessity of God' (1996a: 5). Eventually, this led Corless to conclude that 'there are at least two realities, one that has God and one that doesn't'.[7] Corless came to believe that he had previously been working, mistakenly, with 'a logic or metaphysic which permitted only one reality and one absolute, such that either one religion was true and the other false, or both were relative truths within a yet undiscovered absolute' (1994b: 182); in fact there are several realities each with its own 'absolute' (an 'absolute' can, according to Corless, be either a transcendent ultimate reality or an ultimately correct teaching about reality).[8]

So Corless' is a radically polycentric response to the question of how one can affirm both God and no God. He thinks in terms of a 'polyverse' rather than in terms of a single universe, suggesting that when 'we approach reality as if there were something behind it, such as a God of the Abrahamic type, a universe appears which either contains that God or is empty of precisely that God'; whereas if, on the other hand, 'we approach reality as if it were sufficient unto itself, some sort of monistic universe, or the Buddhist universe of interdependent arising, appears' (2002: 18). Corless contends that we have long assumed that 'there must be, *by definition*, one Truth, one Reality, one Absolute' (2002: 3), but he argues that in the light of today's vastly increased knowledge of the variety of religious world-views this assumption is no longer sustainable:

> As we come to know them accurately, each Weltanschauung is found to be as profound, subtle, and potentially adequate, as any other. ... We are forced to consider that our understanding of Absolute as unique may be naïve. There may be many Absolutes existing simultaneously in many universes.
>
> (Corless 2002: 4)

Corless contends that Christianity takes its message to be superior to that of other traditions, as does Buddhism, and that these mutually exclusive positions must be taken seriously if one is authentically Christian or authentically Buddhist. He had come to feel that the hypothesis that 'there's more than one reality and more than one truth' (48) succeeds in both taking these positions seriously and affirming the truth of both. This understanding, combined with his sense of the mutual irrelevance of Christianity and Buddhism and of the contradictions between them (44), led Corless to conclude that it is not possible for 'a single entity' to be at the same time both Christian and Buddhist (14); for in which reality would a Buddhist Christian abide, and what truth would he or she affirm as ultimate? However, what *is* possible, thought Corless, is for a single entity to be a 'host' to a Christian and a Buddhist, and this is how he understood his own religious identity:

> I ... try to allow them to interact in dialogue to see what will happen. ... I say ... that Christianity is the absolute truth and other religions are ... at best only partially true, and ... do the same thing for Buddhism ... [W]hat I want to do is to take those two seriously ... and say: what would happen if we took those two exclusivist and absolutist positions and then let them interact?
>
> (15–16)

However, despite Corless' determination to affirm Buddhism and Christianity as he believed those traditions have understood themselves, the overall effect of affirming the absoluteness of ultimate truth as identified by Buddhists and the absoluteness of ultimate reality as identified by Christians, is to qualify both claims, making the Christian claim 'there is a God (in reality x)' and the Buddhist claim 'there is no God (in reality y)'.[9] This means that neither Buddhists nor Christians make claims that are truly universal in scope since both are restricted to making claims which hold true only regarding their own particular realities and not regarding reality as a whole: there is a God but only in the Christian reality, and there is dependent origination (and no God), but only in the Buddhist reality. I submit, therefore, that Corless' theory does justice neither to the Christian's nor to the Buddhist's conception of ultimate truth.

And there are further problems. Corless claims that the Buddhist absolute is greatest, and that the Christian absolute is greatest, and that these realities or truths are distinct. He explains that by 'absolute' he means 'something than which there is no greater; go as far as you can, as big as you can ... [S]omething that is at the back of all explanations'. There is, says Corless, 'more than one thing that is the greatest thing' (50). Now, superlatives are ambiguous between a strong and weak sense and it is certainly logically possible that two things could be greatest in the weak sense, i.e. in the sense that there is no reality or truth greater (there may be two tallest humans, neither of whom is shorter than anyone, yet neither of whom is taller than everyone). But what is not possible, surely, is for more than one reality to be greatest in the strong sense, i.e. in the sense that each is greater (in the same respects) than all others. Yet it is this strong sense of 'greatest' which Corless seems to have in mind. He acknowledges that his hypothesis 'is incomprehensible at present' (50), but nevertheless claims that the 'the data seems to demand that we assert it as the case and then search for a way to understand it. This is how a paradigm shift occurs' (2002: 4).

Recognition of a proposition's incomprehensibility would normally lead to its immediate dismissal yet Corless insists that the problem lies not with the assertion that there are many absolutes but with our faulty logic: 'from our present perspective' it is not logical, but this is 'merely a failure of our logic' (48). He suggests we think of Buddhism and Christianity relating to each other as two distinct absolutes according to the models of the co-inherence (*perochoresis*) of the divinity and humanity in Christ according to Nicæa, and the co-incidence of *saṃsāra* and *nirvāṇa* in the Buddhist teaching of the Mādhyamika school (1990b: 117). Corless supposes the existence of an extraordinary, non-binary level of consciousness capable of apprehending this mutual coinherence (1986a: 118). When we achieve this consciousness it will bring about a 'new way of understanding' analogous to entering a fourth dimension: 'when you're functioning in three dimensions the fourth dimension is mysterious' (48), but with the dawn of 'superconsciousness' – the consciousness in which the 'coinherence' of the different religions is manifest – all will become clear.[10] Corless felt that this understanding of the traditions enabled him to regard himself, *at the level of superconsciousness*, as both a Christian and a Buddhist (7, 45; 1986a: 121, 133). The trouble is, however, that unless we assume the fundamentals of logic – in this case the law of non-contradiction – we cannot even begin to debate the merits of Corless' hypothesis since rational enquiry depends upon the assumption that the rules of logic apply. It is also difficult, to say the least, to assess a claim which is supposed to be comprehensible only on the basis of a new kind of consciousness which we do not yet possess. I suspect that most dual belongers will prefer to look for ways of reconciling the apparent contradictions between Buddhism and Christianity *within* the framework of logic, than to accept a theory according to which our logic is wrong (in the hope that they will one day gain the necessary consciousness to understand how it could be).

A further problem with Corless' theory is that, if one assumes that individuals 'with multiple religious loyalties may be living, seriatim or concurrently, in more than one universe', each with its own absolute (2002: 4), then what is the common ground for the internal dialogue between one's Buddhism and one's Christianity about how reality is to be understood? Whose reality would be being discussed? And what if a new religious tradition were to emerge which described the way reality ultimately is differently from how other traditions have described it in the past: would a corresponding reality automatically emerge? This would seem to entail that the truth of a claim is determined by whether or not anyone (or perhaps whether or not a sufficient number of people) *believes* it to be true – an idea which is, at best, counterintuitive. Moreover, how should one account for different branches of a single tradition; is there one absolute for Anglicans, another for Catholics? Corless' response to the question of God arguably poses more problems than it solves.

Perhaps a less radical polycentric approach would not be so susceptible to the difficulties which beset Corless' theory. Let's consider one example.

A process theology polycentric approach

David Ray Griffin's model for the affirmation of several ultimate realities is based on the process philosophy of Alfred North Whitehead and the process theology of John Cobb.[11] Unlike Corless, process theologians take ultimate realities to be aspects or features of a single complex reality. According to Cobb's brand of Whiteheadian pluralism (which Griffin endorses), the Buddhist and the Christian are focusing on different 'features of the totality' (Cobb 1999: 184), features which are 'ultimate' in the sense that each constitutes a reality 'at which a line of questioning ends' (Cobb 1999: 184). Cobb affirms three such features. The first of these is the *formless* ultimate reality, corresponding to what Whitehead calls 'creativity'. Buddhists call this feature of reality 'Emptiness' (*Śūnyatā*) or 'Dharmakāya', Advaita Vedantists call it 'Nirguṇa Brahman', Meister Eckhart calls it 'the Godhead', and Tillich refers to it as 'Being Itself'. The second ultimate is 'the *Supreme* Being'. This ultimate corresponds to what Whitehead calls 'God', but it is also referred to as 'Christ', 'Allah', 'Saguṇa Brahman', 'Ishvara', 'Yahweh', and by Buddhists as 'Amida Buddha' and 'Sambhogakāya'. This ultimate is 'the source of forms (such as truth, beauty, and justice)' (Griffin 2005b: 47). The third ultimate is the cosmos or the universe – 'the totality of [finite] things' (Cobb 1999: 185). Griffin explains that these ultimates 'differ as the one Supreme Being, the many finite beings, and Being Itself, which is embodied by both God and finite beings' (2005b: 49–50). Although the three ultimates are distinct, they are in fact inseparable from each other (Cobb 1999: 185): 'without a cosmic reality there can be no acosmic one, and without God there can be neither. Similarly, without both the cosmic and acosmic features of reality there can be no God' (Cobb 1999: 121).

Griffin argues that this model enables us to affirm various kinds of religious experience as authentic:

> Although these three ultimates are inseparable, individuals and religious traditions can concentrate on one or two features alone. Insofar as there is concentration solely on God, on the universe in distinction from God, or on creativity, there would be the pure case of theistic, cosmic, or acosmic religious experience.[12]

Griffin suggests that Cobb's understanding of God and creativity as two ultimates plays a particularly helpful role with respect to 'how theistic Christianity and nontheistic Buddhism could both be oriented toward something ultimate in the nature of things' (2005b: 49).

When we consider Buddhist Christian dual belonging in terms of this model, we see that this polycentric approach – unlike Corless' – does not oblige the dual belonger to understand himself or herself as a host to two distinct selves who operate within distinct realities. Rather, whether praying or practising formless meditation, Buddhist Christians can be understood as relating to ever-present features of reality, and simply focusing predominantly for a given period on just one of those features – 'God' or 'creativity'. Both of these are features of the one reality we all share.

However, one of the disadvantages of this interpretation, for some dual belongers, will be that it requires breaking with certain strands of the Christian tradition which may be considered important. For while the God of process theology shares many characteristics with the Biblical God (Griffin 2005b: 61–62), process theology's God differs considerably from both the God of Aquinas and the Church Fathers, and from the God of classical theism.

The conception of God expounded by the Church Fathers (downplayed by various Christian thinkers in modern times) is not one of *a being* but of a perfect, necessarily existent, and radically transcendent reality. This is the conception of God which lies at the heart of traditional Catholic theology and was most comprehensively and influentially developed by Aquinas in the thirteenth century. Aquinas' God is wholly simple, immutable, and outside time and space. This God is not an individual someone or something, countable alongside other beings or things; God does not exist in the same way as *anything* else we know; as Aquinas says, God is *sui generis*,[13] not the greatest being among beings but *being* simpliciter – *esse* (being) rather than *ens* (something existent). Aquinas describes God as *ipsum esse* ('being itself') and *esse tantum* ('being as such', 'just being' or even 'suchness').[14] This does not mean that God is the sum of all being (*esse universalis*), explains Aquinas, since creatures, unlike God, receive their existence and essence from God; it means, rather, that God is *pure being*. The name 'God', says Aquinas, 'signifies ... something that is above all, is the principle of all, and distinct from all'.[15]

Aquinas was heavily influenced not only by Aristotle, but also by Plotinus, through the Neo-Platonism of Dionysius the pseudo-Areopagite.[16] Dionysius had a strongly mystical emphasis, believing that, in the final analysis, it is impossible for us to say anything about God because of God's transcendence. We can affirm God's nature positively with statements such as 'God is good', but we must also affirm that God is infinitely more good than we can conceive; and, insofar as we do the latter, we must acknowledge that the predicate 'is good' does not apply to God in any way that we can conceive of. As Aquinas says: 'God's essence is beyond what we can understand of God and beyond what we can signify through words'.[17] This means that God cannot be grasped by the concept of God, i.e. by applying theistic predicates. Even using articles such as 'a' and 'the' are misleading insofar as they suggest that one is talking about an individual when one is not. '[B]y its immensity,' says Aquinas, 'the divine substance surpasses every form that our intellect reaches. Thus we are unable to apprehend it by knowing *what it is*. Yet we are able to have some knowledge of it by knowing *what it is not*.'[18] The influence of Neo-Platonism on Christian theology has helped foster a long and tenacious strand of apophatic or negative theology (*Via Negativa*) within the Christian tradition, according to which one can only speak literally and univocally about what God is *not* and, ultimately, can only remain silent about what God *is*.

Although negative theology was endorsed by all the major Church Fathers and almost all the great scholastic theologians, modern theism ('modern' here referring to its development in the seventeenth and eighteenth centuries) tends to marginalise, deny or reject apophaticism, instead conceiving of God as *literally* describable in theistic terms, i.e. as *a being* literally in possession of all the classical attributes. In Antony Flew's *A Dictionary of Philosophy* (1979), for example, we find 'theism' described as the belief in God, in which

> God is understood to be the single omnipotent and omniscient creator of everything else that exists. He is regarded as a Being distinct from his creation though manifesting himself through it, and also essentially personal, caring for and communicating with mankind, and infinitely worthy of human worship.
>
> (1979: 351)

And the *Concise Routledge Encyclopedia of Philosophy* defines the God of 'monotheism' as 'a person or as very much like a person' (Craig 2000: 590). On this understanding, God is an individual spirit whose perfection is a matter of his perfect morality and whose being eternal is a matter of his being temporally everlasting. This God is transcendent in relation to his creation, i.e. is outside creation (though also immanent within it), but is not transcendent in the radical sense intended by the Church Fathers, since language can be used univocally of this God and humans (even though God, unlike humans, is thought to exhibit the qualities attributed to him to an infinite degree). This means that the descriptions of God in the Bible can be taken as a good representation of God's nature: this God can literally know things, love people, forgive people, think various things and get angry. This anthropomorphic conception of God as a kind of super-being – like us only without a body and very much more moral and powerful than we are – is popular, not only with theologically and philosophically uneducated Christians, but with various modern theologians and philosophers.[19] It is, however, a far cry from Aquinas' 'being as such'. Indeed, given the difference between Aquinas' understanding of God and the modern understanding, Rudi te Velde suggests that it may be misleading to characterise Aquinas' understanding as 'theistic'. 'There is something in Thomas' conception of God ... that does not fit very well into the picture of "classical theism"', says te Velde (2006: 85). Aquinas does not think 'that the theistic description of God corresponds to an independent reality, or that, in fact, a supreme being exists with the features attributed to God by the Christian religion'.[20]

The God of process theology ('the Supreme Being') differs – perhaps most significantly – from the transcendent, unchanging, perfect, incomprehensible, and ineffable God of Aquinas and the Church Fathers. According to process theology, the world is a dynamic process and God is a being involved in that process and, as such, God is subject to change and growth (though, unlike other entities, God is infinite and exerts an ordering influence within the process). Not only does this mean that God does not transcend the world, it also means that God is not perfect, since perfection entails no possibility of further progress and development. This puts Cobb's theism greatly at odds with the mystical theism of Aquinas and the Church Fathers, as does his contention that God lies within the comprehension of finite beings.[21] As far as process theologians are concerned, their move away from the conception of God expounded by the Church Fathers is not to be regretted, since it brings Christians more in line with the God of the Bible.[22] However, it does make Cobb's notion of God unlikely to be acceptable to any Christian for whom the affirmation of God's radical transcendence is fundamental (and, as we will see presently, my interviewees fall unambiguously into this category).

One could, of course, argue that, if one's understanding of God is more akin to the mystical theism of Aquinas than to the classical theist's conception of God as *a being* literally in possession of all the classical attributes, then one is not in fact relating to the 'Supreme Being' at all, but instead focusing on 'the formless ultimate reality' which Whitehead calls 'creativity' – Eckhart's 'Godhead' or Tillich's 'Being Itself'. But, if this is the case, then Cobb's theistic 'ultimate' becomes irrelevant to the problem with which we're grappling here and his theory ceases to present us with a potential polycentric solution. If mystical theists are relating to the formless reality, and if this reality is the same ultimate which Buddhists call 'Emptiness' (*Śūnyatā*) or 'Dharmakāya', then the discrepancy between how Christians and Buddhists experience and talk about what is ultimate remains unaccounted for. If Christians and Buddhists are relating to the same ultimate reality, why do they experience and speak about that reality so differently? It is this question on which *monocentric* pluralism has focused, hence we'll consider it in detail in the next section.

For the moment, then, let's stick with polycentric pluralism and assume that there are, at least in principle, dual belongers whose conceptions of God are more akin to Flew's than Aquinas'. The trouble now, however, is that, despite sharing certain features with the classical theist's God, Cobb's God differs even from the classical conception, since there are certain important features of that conception which are absent from Cobb's conception. According to the classical conception, God's power is both complete and necessary, unlike the power of finite beings which is only partial and contingent. Following Whitehead, Cobb rejects this distinction, deeming the embodiment of power in the finite actualities of the world to be as necessary as its embodiment in God. The God of process theology can influence and persuade beings to act in particular ways but is not able to *make* them act in any particular way. Thus, Cobb's God is not omnipotent in the classical sense. Cobb also rejects the traditional Christian doctrine of *creatio ex nihilo* (creation out of nothing) and hypothesises that the existence of finite actual entities *of some kind or another* is as necessary as God's existence. These moves away from the classical conception may be more than many modern theists are prepared to accept.[23]

But even if there are dual belongers who would find Cobb's notion of God sufficiently continuous with their own to be able to embrace it, the problem which *all* reflective dual belongers are likely to have is that it seems impossible to embrace Cobb's theory from *both* an authentically Christian perspective *and* an authentically Buddhist perspective. If God is understood as being within the world process and subject to change, then from a Buddhist perspective, this 'god' is likely to be seen as yet another being trapped in the wheel of existence. Such a being cannot be considered ultimate, for the Buddhist line of questioning looks for ultimate truth beyond the conditioned, ceaselessly changing realities of *saṃsāra*. The 'god' of process theology cannot be thought of as the ground of liberation, since it too requires liberation. Yet for *Christians* God *is* ultimate and *is* the ground of salvation. Hence, a process polycentric approach is, in the end, no solution for dual belongers who seek coherence between their Buddhist and Christian perspectives with respect to the question of God since, as Buddhists, they cannot accept the God of process theology as ultimate and, as Christians, they cannot accept that God is *not* ultimate.

This brings us to the more general concern to which *all* polycentric approaches (whether Corless' or Cobb's or anyone else's) would seem to give rise, however their various 'ultimates' are defined. When Buddhists or Christians speak of that which they consider 'ultimate', they speak of that reality or truth which they believe lies at the end of *all* questioning; they intend to speak about – or otherwise gesture at – the *greatest* reality or truth, the *supreme*, the *most fundamental*, the *most worthy of commitment*. If one deems more than one reality to be 'ultimate', then it is not clear that one has done justice to what Christians or Buddhists mean when they describe God or *nirvāṇa* as 'ultimate'. Christians consider God to be *uniquely* ultimate and Buddhists consider *nirvāṇa* to be *uniquely* ultimate. Indeed, as Reis Habito suggests, uniqueness is arguably implied by the very notion of *ultimate* reality: 'There can only be *one* ultimate ... I cannot imagine different ultimate realities', says Reis Habito (465). In the case of process theology this worry is exacerbated by the fact that no *non-ultimate* reality or realities seem to be affirmed. As Karl Baier points out, the meaning of 'Ultimate Reality' is 'always related to some notion of its counterpart – namely, the non-ultimate realities – and the links between the two' (2005: 87); on a theory which deems creativity, God, and the Cosmos 'ultimate', it is hard to guess at what the *non-ultimate* realities are to which these stand in relation; in Griffin's terms, there is no reality at which a line of questioning *doesn't* end. Given these difficulties, let's move on to consider whether a *monocentric* approach might fare better than these polycentric approaches, when it comes to meeting the dual belonger's needs with respect to the question of God.

Relating to one reality?

According to monocentric pluralism, God-talk and *nirvāṇa*-talk concern a single ultimate reality, i.e. a reality which is *uniquely* greatest, supreme, most fundamental and most worthy of commitment (greater than everything, rather than merely not lesser than anything). The differences between Buddhism and Christianity with respect to the question of God are accounted for, not by positing the existence of different 'ultimates', but rather by interpreting these differences as relating to differences between the Buddhist's and the Christian's respective *experiences* of *one* ultimate reality and how those experiences are *expressed*.[24] Different religions are seen as equally valid responses to this one ultimate reality.

Crucial to the monocentric hypothesis is the notion that ultimate reality transcends all human conceptualisation. Monocentric pluralism has been articulated most comprehensively by Hick, though not in relation to the question of dual belonging. Hick's model relies on a distinction, similar to Kant's distinction between the noumenal (reality as it is in itself: alien to, and not describable in terms of, our categories and concepts) and the phenomenal (reality as we represent it in experience and thought). Hick posits that within each religious tradition an analogous distinction can be drawn between the divine or transcendent reality – the 'Real' (a neutral term, allowing for personal and non-personal conceptions) – *as it is in itself* and the Real as humanly thought and experienced. The nature of the Real *an sich* is ineffable: we cannot properly attribute intrinsic qualities to the Real – 'its nature, infinitely rich in itself, cannot be expressed in our human concepts' (1995: 28).

Hick takes this claim to correspond to the affirmations of the ineffability of ultimate reality found within all the major religious traditions (1989a: 236–38). Though ineffable, ultimate reality is, nevertheless, 'capable of being authentically experienced in terms of different sets of human concepts' (1995: 25), for example as the Holy Trinity or as *nirvāṇa* or the *dharmakāya*:

> if in the activity of I-Thou prayer we approach the Real as personal then we shall experience the Real as a personal deity. ... Or if our religious culture leads us to open ourselves to the Real in various forms of meditation, as ... [for example] the eternal Dharmakaya ever expressing itself in the limitless compassion of the Buddhas, then this is likely to be the way in which we shall experience the Real.
>
> (Hick 1995: 26)

When Christians speak in personal terms about ultimate reality and Buddhists speak in non-personal terms, both are responding appropriately to ultimate reality as they experience it (Hick 1989a: 246).

When we apply this hypothesis to dual belonging, as someone immersed in the Buddhist *and* the Christian conceptual frameworks, the Buddhist Christian can be seen as having two different ways of experiencing and speaking of ultimate reality. With the exception of Corless, my interviewees seemed to incline towards this self-understanding: monocentric assumptions are implied by their consistent use of singular terms with respect to ultimate reality (and occasional use of the same term to refer to ultimate reality whether from a Buddhist or a Christian perspective) and some appeared to explicitly embrace the monocentric hypothesis. Reis Habito, for example, suggests that some people approach ultimate reality through the notion of God, while others do not, and that, in her own case, she uses both approaches (466). She says she thinks she understands herself as relating to one ultimate reality, whatever the context in which she is practising:

> Christians ... are based on the Jewish experience which is the prophetic experience, and ... Buddhists, ... on the personal experience of the founder, so, of course there are those different expressions ... So ... it comes from the same ... ultimate reality but the expressions are different.
>
> (466)

King says of ultimate reality that 'through meditation and all sorts of religious experience one is attempting to dive into it and discover it' (373); that Buddhism and Christianity are each in their different ways trying to 'mediate' or give people a 'route of access to' this reality; 'they're both getting at it and they both affirm that, ultimately, it's transcendent'; '[t]hese are just two efficacious routes of access that I have discovered', says King (373). Borrowing from Panikkar, Habito explains that he thinks of ultimate reality as 'Mystery with a capital "M"', as 'something that invites us deeper and deeper into an *unknown*' (168). He has faith in this Mystery, a faith which he explains as 'a giving of one's self to something much much bigger and something yet incomprehensible but still something that elicits that inner peace and that inner confidence that one is in good hands' (162). He says he has 'one faith but with two differing ways of being articulated, informed by these two traditions' (163).

Reflections such as these appear to express the assumption that there is one ultimate reality with which Buddhism and Christianity are concerned. However, despite this, and despite the fact that throughout the interviews their language suggested integration of their Buddhist and Christian perspectives via a monocentric interpretation of the relationship of these perspectives to each other, when questioned directly about whether they took themselves to be responding, or relating to, *one* ultimate reality, or *different* ultimate realities (or neither of these), some of my interviewees seemed somewhat ambivalent. Habito replies, for example, 'I can only say that there are grounds for saying both and I haven't fully resolved it yet, myself. ... I'll have to keep reflecting and listening' (168). Later in the interview, discussing the Zen metaphor of words as fingers pointing to the moon, Habito appears to demonstrate both his monocentric inclinations and his ambivalence:

> if the moon in this metaphor is that which refers to Mystery with a capital 'M', is that the same Mystery that the Buddhists refer to as the Christians? Well, they certainly have different conceptual frameworks in referring to it. So, if you look at their fingers, they may be pointing to different directions but, somehow, it's that which is beyond the finger, which the finger tries to point to, that is important. So, in that sense, is it the same [or] is it different? ... I am not able to answer with decisiveness here.
>
> (188)

When asked directly whether King thinks that Buddhism and Christianity are concerned with *one* ultimate reality, *different* ultimate realities, or neither, she replies: 'I don't see how anyone can answer that question' (371). In order to establish whether this reticence is well-placed, or whether dual belongers such as King and Habito can afford to be more confident with respect to their apparently monocentric inclinations, we must establish whether or not there are significant strands of thought within each tradition which justify monocentrism, and which strands of each tradition would need to be rejected in order to embrace it.

An ultimate transcendent reality?

First we must investigate whether Christians and Buddhists, respectively, take their God-talk and their *nirvāṇa*-talk to be concerned with a radically transcendent ultimate reality. For if they do not, the monocentric approach distorts their self-understandings.

The Christian affirmation

In the Christian tradition God is often talked about as if 'He' were an omnipotent and omniscient person who watches over us and listens to our prayers. Indeed, this is an image of God found in numerous passages in the Bible. As we have already seen, such a being cannot be considered ultimate from a Buddhist perspective; such a being, moreover, cannot be considered transcendent in the radical sense required by the monocentric pluralist hypothesis inasmuch as language can be used univocally of this being and us. However, as we have also seen, none of the major Church Fathers, nor any of the great scholastic theologians, construed God-talk univocally. The classical conception of God as 'a being' tends to be the conception over which Christian philosophers and atheist philosophers do battle. Consequently, many assume that those denying that God is an entity are non-realists about God-talk and are, therefore, atheists.[25] But to insist that it is not possible to be a realist about God-talk without holding a reified conception of God (a conception of God as an individuated being) and without thinking that the qualities attributed to God can be understood as literally applying to God is to fly in the face of traditional Christian theology.[26]

The conception of God passed down through the tradition from the Church Fathers is one of a radically transcendent ultimate reality: ultimate in the sense of being the greatest, supreme, and most fundamental reality, and transcendent, first, in the sense of being outside time and therefore beyond change and, second, in the sense of being beyond the concepts possessed by finite human beings. John Chrysostom refers, for example, to 'the inexpressible God, incomprehensible, invisible, and unknowable ... [who] surpasses all power of human speech ... [and] eludes the grasp of every mortal intelligence'.[27] Gregory of Nyssa, declares that God is characterised more by non-being than by being and is therefore known only by unknowing. And 'what God is', says Aquinas, 'transcends all that we understand of him'.[28] The Orthodox Christians who have espoused this conception do not *reject* Biblical images of God as *a* being, but take them to be rightly understood as symbols, metaphors or analogies, pointing beyond themselves to a greater reality.

Although negative theology has, in modern times, tended to be marginalised, denied or rejected, there have been a number of very influential modern theologians (Catholic and Protestant) who have strongly affirmed this dimension of the tradition. Karl Rahner, for example, describes the term 'God' as a symbol which reminds us of the existence of that ultimate unspeakable mystery (1978: 21), and Paul Tillich speaks of 'the God above the God of theism' (1952: 189). Theologians such as Rahner and Tillich, Christian mystics, and all Christians who take seriously the inconceivability of God show us a theism in which God is unlike everything we know and is ungraspable by the intellect. Their God is aptly characterised as a transcendent ultimate reality.

It was this notion of God with which my interviewees' reflections were in greatest accord and, as Keenan makes clear, it is a conception which contrasts much less starkly with Buddhism than does classical theism. He suggests that when Buddhists say there is no God they mean 'there is no Super Being in charge of things' (246). But as far as Keenan is concerned, the Christian does not – or at least should not – affirm the existence of such a being either: 'when a Christian says "there is a God", it means that you can entrust yourself to the source and end of everything. The Christian does not mean there is *a* Supreme being among beings, or shouldn't' (246). God is 'the very act of existing itself (*ipsum esse subsistens*), not an all-powerful being within the processes of being ... but rather an act; not a noun but a verb' (2006a: 265). Keenan's notion of God is very much in line with Aquinas'. 'I'm *not* a theist in the classical sense', says Keenan; 'I don't think God is an individual ... and I don't think there's any distinction between subjective and objective in God' (296). Keenan's God is simply an 'encompassing presence; the spirit that dwells within' (288). He recognises that Buddhism has strengthened his apophatic awareness and explains that Mahāyāna theology moves apophaticism into the centre of the Christian tradition (226); but as he points out, the notion of God he endorses is, nevertheless, the one he was taught in the Seminary (246).

Other interviewees offered similar reflections. Furneaux, for example, takes the notion that 'God is *a* being' to be a misunderstanding (109); Corless describes God as 'ultimately, incomprehensible' (53); and Habito says that God is that which is 'ultimately unknown and unknowable, unobjectifiable, *un-image-able*, and which no verbal description or intellectual formulation can ever approach' (2004: 108). He explains that he uses the term 'God' as a 'pointer' or 'place-holder' to refer to 'that experience of an opening in our lives towards the inscrutable – towards the unknown' (181). Defining the notion of God she finds acceptable, King explains that one of her 'basic affirmations is the epistemological transcendence of what we're talking about here' (385) and, while she says she believes in some kind of spiritual reality, she does not see this reality as '*a being with a will*' (386). Indeed, so determined is King to distance herself from classical theism that she now tends not to use 'God' language to talk about the spiritual reality she affirms, lest it be misunderstood. She understands the ultimate reality she affirms as akin to the God in whom we 'live and move and have our being' (Acts 17: 28) and sees this as compatible with certain Buddhist conceptions of ultimate reality.

The Buddhist affirmation

In Buddhism we also find a transcendent ultimate reality affirmed. As Karl Baier emphasises, Buddhists can be said to relate to an ultimate reality in so far as their most important concern relates to a reality that is more than just a part of the world in which we are living (even if it is the most important part); they affirm an ultimate reality in the sense of a 'numinous presence that transcends everything in the world and the finite world itself' (2005: 89).

Christopher Gowans emphasises that a characterisation of Buddhism as atheistic in the sense of materialism or naturalism is not supported by the Buddhist scriptures (2003: 53), and Nyanaponika suggests that the term 'atheism' could be misleading if applied to Buddhism due to its association 'with a materialistic doctrine that knows nothing higher than this world of the sense and the slight happiness it can bestow. Buddhism is nothing of that sort' (1981: 5). Bhikkhu Bodhi, although asserting from his Theravadin perspective that 'Buddhism is an atheistic system in the sense that it does not admit the existence of an all-powerful creator God', qualifies this by acknowledging that 'Nibbāna is a supramundane reality, a reality which is utterly transcendent to the world' and that, given this, 'Buddhists themselves prefer to describe their religion as "non-theistic" rather than "atheistic".'[29]

What makes Buddhism a non-theistic tradition, then, is not the denial of a transcendent reality but rather the fact that transcendent reality is not conceived of as a personal God. As Perry Schmidt-Leukel is at pains to emphasise, Buddhists do affirm a transcendent reality, and affirm it 'precisely as the precondition of salvation'.[30] Consider, for example, the well-known verse from the *Udāna* and *Itivuttaka*:

> There is, monks, a not-born (*ajātaṁ*), a not-brought-to-being (*abhūtaṁ*), a not-made (*akataṁ*), a not-conditioned (*asaṅkhataṁ*). If, monks, there were no not-born, not-brought-to-being, not-made, not-conditioned, no escape would be discerned from what is born, brought-to-being, made, conditioned. But since there is a not-born, a not-brought-to-being, a not-made, a not-conditioned, therefore an escape is discerned from what is born, brought-to-being, made, conditioned.[31]

As Schmidt-Leukel explains,

> [t]his passage does not only emphasise that 'there is' a transcendent reality. It also underlies its genuine transcendence in the most explicit way by distinguishing it ontologically from the major features of the saṃsāric world.
>
> (2007a: 72)

There are those, particularly among Western converts to Buddhism, who understand *nirvāṇa* simply as the state of mind of one who has achieved Enlightenment. But this interpretation does not do justice to Buddhist tradition. As important classical treatises – including the *Milindapañha* and Buddhagosa's *Visuddhimagga* – make clear, if *nirvāṇa* were just a state of mind, it would be a conditioned reality, having come into being as a result of a person completing the Noble Eightfold Path and would, therefore, be subject to death and decay.[32] *Nirvāṇa*, explains Schmidt-Leukel, 'is not conditioned by someone's attainment of Enlightenment. It is just the other way round. The unconditioned existence of *nirvāṇa* is the condition that makes Enlightenment possible'.[33] As Baier acknowledges, the term *nirvāṇa is* used to describe the peaceful state of the human mind which has attained ultimate release, but passages such as the *Udāna* and *Itivuttaka* 'relate this inner peace to a transcendent reality. ... [E]arly Buddhism is not interested in the simple extinction of an always painful and dissatisfying life but searches for eternity, immortality' (2005: 106).

Nirvāṇa is not only transcendent with respect to the samsaric realm, it is also transcendent with respect to all possible conceptualisation. As Nāgasena says in the *Milindapañha*, *nirvāṇa* 'has nothing similar to it. By no metaphor, or explanation, or reason, or argument can its form, or figure, or duration, or measure be made clear.'[34] Some of my interviewees were reluctant to say that Buddhism affirms a transcendent ultimate reality, due to reification worries. Keenan, for example, explains that, although he *does* think reality is transcended in Buddhism, he has difficulty with the 'a': 'it's not that there is *a* transcendent reality somewhere there, because that assumes that it's not *here*' (257), and Habito suggests that Buddhism can affirm ultimate reality in the sense of the unknown, but this 'unknown' should not be thought of as 'an object out there that we are calling "ultimate reality"' (169). But such reflections in fact serve to *highlight* the transcendence of the Buddhist ultimate by emphasising that language is radically inadequate with respect to it. As we found in the case of the God of the Church Fathers and Aquinas, even words such as 'a' and 'the', though often grammatically necessary, mislead with respect to that which is ultimate. Describing *nirvāṇa* as 'a transcendent reality' does not entail that it is understood as an individuated and conceptualised 'something'; rather, *nirvāṇa* is described in this way *because* it is beyond all individuation and conceptualisation.

Recognition of the inadequacy of language is one of the reasons the Buddha was reluctant to talk about *nirvāṇa*, and the Buddhist tradition still regards silence to be one of the best responses to questions about the ultimate. The scriptures tend to describe *nirvāṇa* using negative terms such as 'disappearance' and 'extinction' (indeed the word *nir-vāṇa* literally translates as 'blown out' and refers to the blowing out of the fires of greed, hatred and delusion that bind one to the wheel of *saṃsāra*). 'The often very tacit way in which many Buddhist scriptures and teachers refer to an Ultimate Reality', acknowledges Baier, makes it possible to misunderstand what is being said and conclude that no ultimate, transcendent reality is affirmed. But 'the silence of the Buddha and his followers has the advantage of avoiding the danger of reifying Ultimate Reality' (2005: 107).

It is certainly true that interpreting the Buddhist stance with respect to ultimate reality becomes trickier with the emergence of the Mahāyāna tradition. Here ultimate reality is spoken of more explicitly and new names emerge, such as *dharmadhātu* ('*dharma* realm'), *tathatā* ('suchness') or *bhūtakoṭi* ('peak of reality'). But, whereas in Theravāda Buddhism the divide between *saṃsāra* and *nirvāṇa* is a sharp one,[35] in Mahāyāna Buddhism, we find Nāgārjuna's well-known assertion that there is not the slightest difference between *saṃsāra* and *nirvāṇa*.[36] This assertion stems from his understanding of the doctrine of emptiness: *nothing* exists as a particular individuated object in reality; *all* our distinctions and discriminations are ultimately false mental constructs (including, even, the idea of mental constructs). The question of how Nāgārjuna's insight should be interpreted has been the cause of interminable debate amongst scholars and practitioners. For our purposes, it is only necessary to note that while there are those who believe that Nāgārjuna's claim reduces everything to the level of *saṃsāra*, there are also those who argue that the reverse is true, i.e. that his claim raises everything to the level of *nirvāṇa*. The latter is Schmidt-Leukel's interpretation. He argues that this interpretation follows from the fact that Nāgārjuna's equation of *nirvāṇa* and *saṃsāra* is mediated by his statement that *saṃsāra* is as ineffable as *nirvāṇa*. What is said of *nirvāṇa* can therefore be said of all that is; the whole of reality is as mysterious as *nirvāṇa*: there is nothing which can be said which is literally true of reality. Nāgārjuna is not denying that there is an ultimate reality which is transcendent, insists Schmidt-Leukel, but rather that it is possible to reach this reality by a dualistic approach whereby one sees *nirvāṇa* as separate from *saṃsāra*.[37]

Reis Habito points out, from a Mahāyāna perspective, that using the word 'transcendent' could mislead in so far as 'in Buddhism, the absolute is in the phenomenal and the phenomenal is in the absolute and, so, if you imagine one absolute that's completely transcendent from everything that happens down here, that's the wrong idea'.[38] But the worry that 'transcendence' could imply that ultimate reality is somehow *out there* as opposed to *right here* (or as opposed to anywhere else) is significantly lessened when we recognise that, when it comes to what is ultimate, both Buddhism and Christianity acknowledge transcendence as only one side of a dialectical tension, the other side of which is immanence. As Reis Habito says, 'the transcendent is totally immanent and vice versa' (469). Keenan acknowledges that, 'if there's nothing transcended … we're caught in … delusion' (257), but rightly points out that this does not mean it is not also 'right *here*'; in Buddhism we find a 'healthy dialectical tension between here and not here'.[39]

Traditional Christian and Buddhist recognitions of a transcendent ultimate reality lay the foundations for Christian recognition of the Buddhist ultimate and Buddhist recognition of the Christian ultimate. Maurice Walshe – a Buddhist and an expert in Christian mysticism – takes the verse from the *Udāna* and *Itivuttaka* to suggest 'fundamental agreement at a very deep level … that the terms "nirvana" and "God" both refer to the UNBORN, which being incomprehensible to the ordinary mind, is differently interpreted' (1982: 6). Schmidt-Leukel understands the verse similarly, asking 'whether this is not a clear Buddhist testimony to that reality which we [Christians] call – for various historical reasons – "God" '.[40]

However, the fact that there is Christian and Buddhist acknowledgement of a transcendent ultimate reality does not by itself justify an interpretation of the Buddhist and the Christian as relating to the same reality unless we can account for why Christians and Buddhists tend to think and talk quite differently about that reality. Let us turn, then, to this task.

Conceiving of the ultimate

Even among those Christians who affirm the radical transcendence of God and reject the notion of God as a 'super-being' to whom personal attributes literally and univocally apply, there are many who nevertheless speak about God as loving, wise, and purposeful; and who experience God as a 'Thou' with whom relationship is possible (even if it is impossible to define the precise nature of this relationship). In Buddhism, on the other hand, despite the awareness of the inadequacy of language being stronger than in Christianity, ultimate reality is nevertheless spoken about and non-personal language is predominantly chosen. Buddhists speak about *realisation* of *nirvāṇa* rather than worship of or devotion to it and, as Schmidt-Leukel notes, in the *Milindapañha*, for example, *nirvāṇa* is described using non-personal similes: it is 'pure like a lotus, cooling and thirst-quenching like water, healing like medicine, mighty and boundless like the great ocean, life-giving like food, immovable and incomprehensible like space, satisfying every desire like a wish-fulfilling gem'.[41]

First, then, we must enquire how each tradition justifies the use of *any* concepts with respect to a reality which is supposed to be conceptually transcendent. (As we noted in the first section of this chapter, there are Christians and Buddhists who do not understand their God-talk and *nirvāṇa*-talk as *describing* God or *nirvāṇa*, but who nevertheless construe their talk as functioning basically realistically insofar as they take it to *relate in some other way* to God or to *nirvāṇa*. As we investigate how each tradition justifies the use of concepts with respect to a transcendent reality, we will be fleshing out what that way might be.) Second, we must ask whether the justifications offered by each of these traditions are ones which could, in principle, be applied to language expressing alternative conceptions of ultimate reality; and, third, we must investigate why Christians tend to employ mostly *personal* concepts, while Buddhists tend to employ mostly *non-personal* concepts, and whether they have any grounds for recognition of one another's concepts.

The practical function of words

Let's start, then, with the question of how Christians and Buddhists are able to speak at all about that which is supposedly conceptually transcendent. In the Christian tradition, apophatic theology and cataphatic theology have traditionally gone hand-in-hand. Cataphatic theology makes positive affirmations about God's nature, while apophatic theology insists that these human attempts to conceptualise the Divine nature fall short of so doing, holding that in the final analysis one can only say what God is not. However, the precise relationship between these strands of theology has always been somewhat ambiguous.

Keenan explains that, for Dionysius, the apophatic and cataphatic fields of awareness are 'interwoven in the mind of the same theologian' (1989b: 378), cataphatic theology functioning as a kind of model which guides one to an understanding of that theology. Keenan takes this to mean that affirmative theology has no final linguistic validity: its function is 'to guide one toward what can be experienced only in unknowing' (1989b: 378). In other words, God-talk does not capture the nature of God but rather leads Christians to an experience of God. On this model the relationship between ultimate reality and the words chosen to describe ultimate reality would appear to be purely practical: words do not describe God but if they lead one to an experience of God, i.e. to an experience of the reality which transcends those words, then their use is legitimate.

This practical emphasis may leave one wondering what distinguishes *this* understanding from Cupitt's non-realist account of religious language (see pp. 42–45), according to which God-talk is not descriptive but 'intensely practical' insofar as it is used 'to provoke and to prompt change within the self'.[42] Note, however, that on the model we're now discussing, God-talk provokes and prompts change in the self *because* it causes one to experience that ultimate reality towards which it orientates one. Here, God-talk causes experiences of a reality which – though it cannot be described – is *objectively there* to be experienced. This contrasts with Cupitt's non-realist understanding of the function of religious language, in which an objectively existing ultimate reality plays no role whatsoever.

Dionysius' realist understanding of the practical function of words has something of a parallel in Mahāyāna Buddhism with Nāgārjuna's notion of two truths: a truth of worldly convention and an ultimate truth.[43] Worldly and conventional language and gestures are all that are available to us for the expression of ultimate truth. Conventional means are therefore skilfully employed in order to bring about the experience of ultimate reality. The use of conventional language is skilful if it is triggered by the direct awareness of ultimate truth and if it nudges one's interlocutor towards direct awareness. Concepts are always subservient to experience in Buddhism and are employed only in so far as they are useful in bringing about the experience of *nirvāṇa*; where they hold one back from experiencing that which is beyond them, they are to be rejected. This emphasis is particularly strong in Zen Buddhism where we find, for example, the ninth-century Master, Lin Chi's, famous exhortation: 'if you meet the Buddha on the road, kill him!' (the Buddha here is the conceptualised Buddha which inhibits if clung to). It is in Zen that the study of *kōans* takes place – riddles and paradoxes passed from Master to student which admit no conceptual solution but invite the student to a direct awareness of ultimate truth. *Kōans* employ concepts with the specific intention of challenging and undermining the student's attachment to concepts.

These Christian and Buddhist notions of concepts as useful in so far as they help bring about an experience of that ultimate reality which cannot be captured by them suggest that the success or failure of language might very well depend on a person's cultural and conceptual context, since this will determine whether a given concept has the appropriate associations for that person. If God-talk has the wrong associations for someone then, *for that person*, the experience of ultimate reality might not be best expressed as one 'of God'. This would, in turn, suggest that the Buddhist concept of 'skill in means' can be applied to a person's ability to identify and understand the particular cultural and conceptual context in which his or her interlocutor is located, in order to choose the appropriate concepts for leading that person to enlightenment. Moreover, since on this understanding a concept's validity is a matter of its nudging one towards an experience which is beyond it, it is an understanding which supports the contention, particularly strong in Zen Buddhism, that to be attached to one's particular concepts of ultimate reality is to prevent them from serving their purpose and, thus, to invalidate them.

Catholic nun and Zen Master, Elaine MacInnes, recognises that were she to use the word 'God' in front of 35 people, 35 'conceptualised gods' would appear, one in each person's mind (1996: 75). Certainly if a Christian is attached to his or her concept of God then Buddhists will reject that conceptualised god – 'if you meet God on the road, kill him!' But the Christian apophatic tradition also rejects such gods. As Augustine puts it, 'if you know it, it is not God';[44] or as Eckhart says, '[m]an's last and highest parting occurs when, for God's sake, he takes leave of God';[45] and, in the strongest terms, as Tillich declares, 'God does not exist'.[46] Could it be that the Buddhist's denial of God, like these Christian statements, is first and foremost a rejection of concepts of God which reify ultimate reality insofar as they are clung to in the false belief that they accurately represent ultimate reality (rather than functioning as symbols which direct people beyond them)? Conversely, when Christians do not cling to their concepts of God but recognise the inadequacy of those concepts (as the *Via Negativa* recommends),[47] could it be that Buddhists, on the basis of the resources within their own tradition, are capable of recognising God-talk as pointing beyond itself, as a skilful means appropriate to the Christian context which can successfully guide Christians to an experience of ultimate reality? It would seem to be this possibility that Nhat Hanh is recognising when he suggests that the Buddha was not against God, 'only against notions of God that are mere mental constructions that do not correspond to reality, notions that prevent us from developing our selves and touching ultimate reality' (1995: 151).

The experiences of Habito and Reis Habito suggest that Nhat Hanh is not alone in his preparedness to concede that God-talk could potentially serve as an alternative to *nirvāṇa*-talk when it comes to leading people to a direct awareness of ultimate reality. Habito completed sixteen years of *kōan* study under the late Yamada Roshi in the Sanbô Kyôdan school of Zen. He explains that while Yamada Roshi's predecessor, Yasutani Roshi, had believed that it was not possible to practise genuine Zen while retaining Christian presuppositions and beliefs, Yamada Roshi disagreed, believing that the practice of Zen does not necessarily require one to *completely* let go of one's idea of God provided that this idea leads to an experience of the reality which goes beyond it: it was 'not that Yamada Roshi was any less insistent on throwing out the *concept* of God', explains Habito, but he, nevertheless, accepted those Christians who came to him without prejudging them and, in so doing, came to realise that when Christians use the term 'God' 'it's not necessarily just a concept but ... a gateway to the experience of mystery' (135).

Reis Habito has also found Buddhist teachers prepared to acknowledge the idea of God as a potential skilful means: 'if "God" does something to you that opens up your wisdom then they let you use "God" ... But if "God" is a notion that prevents the opening up of wisdom then they say "let go of God ... you have to use something else"'.[48] Yamada Roshi's willingness to accept the notion of God as a potential gateway to an experience of ultimate reality is well demonstrated by his occasional adaptation of *kōans* for Christian students. Reis Habito studied with Yamada Roshi for a time and explains that he altered the second part of the well known 'mu' *kōan* – 'What is the origin of mu?' – making it 'What is the origin of God?'. She describes how she had felt that cracking the first part of this *kōan* had been a letting go of her concept of God, resulting in a profound experience 'of what might be called God's love' (446). In grappling with the second part of the *kōan*, she reflected on that experience, asking herself 'well, what's the origin of this?' until she realised that she was once again 'thinking about God in concepts' and that this wouldn't get her anywhere: 'using God like a philosophical problem ... takes away from the reality' (447). This realisation prompted another profound experience in which she felt that 'it was as if God was saying, "Why do you keep me so far away and you can think about my origins somewhere out there? Let me get closer"' (2000: 33). Yamada Roshi recognised these experiences as *kenshō* experiences (444–45). Reis Habito's Dharma Master in Taiwan (Master Hsin Tao), despite his initial scepticism, has also come to recognise that the notion of God need not be a stumbling block, and now employs it himself when speaking to Christians: 'he says: "I give you God in your heart". He doesn't say "I give you enlightenment" or something like that'. Reis Habito concludes that Buddhists 'are not scared of the term ... "God" as long as it can help to lead you to insight. They are scared of the term ... "God" as long as it is a concept and it keeps you from insight' (463).

Just as the traditional Buddhist notion of two truths enables Buddhists to accept God-talk as having the potential to function as an alternative to *nirvāṇa*-talk, might not the traditional Christian notion of God-talk as a cataphatic model which guides people to an experience of ultimate reality enable Christians to accept *nirvāṇa*-talk as an alternative cataphatic model with the same function?

Keenan provides further potential grounds for Buddhist Christian mutual recognition of one another's concepts by suggesting that all theologies are 'straw houses' from their inception (1993b: 20), and the value of any particular straw house is a matter of how conducive an environment it is for cultivating practice and for protecting and nurturing people (335). Insofar, then, as Buddhists and Christians are able to recognise each other's environments as conducive to practice and as protective and nurturing, on this basis too they might be able to recognise the validity of each other's concepts.

Hick offers yet further possible grounds for mutual recognition by interpreting language which appears to be about ultimate reality in itself as functioning mythologically: 'we speak mythologically about the noumenal Real', explains Hick, 'by speaking literally or analogically about its phenomenal manifestations'. The truth of a religious myth is a practical truthfulness, true religious myths being 'those that evoke in us attitudes and modes of behaviour which are appropriate to our situation *vis-à-vis* the Real' (1989a: 351). For an assertion about the nature of the Real to be mythologically true, suggests Hick, it must encourage a transformation from self-centredness to 'Reality-centredness' and this can be judged by observing the behaviour of the saints of the tradition in which such assertions are made. '[T]he salvific transformation', explains Hick, 'is most readily observed by its moral fruits, which can be identified by means of the ethical ideal, common to all the great traditions, of *agape/karuṇā* (love/compassion)' (1989a: 14). On the basis of this criterion Buddhists and Christians might be capable of recognising one another's conceptualisations of ultimate reality as 'mythologically true' to the extent that they are capable of recognising one another's traditions as fostering love and compassion in their adherents.[49]

Again, it is crucial to note the contrast between this model and Cupitt's: Cupitt's and Hick's models agree that God-talk and *nirvāṇa*-talk have value insofar as they produce loving, compassionate behaviour; but on Hick's model, unlike Cupitt's, this talk produces such behaviour *because* it *rightly orientates* people with respect to that ultimate reality at which it gestures. In other words, on Hick's model God-talk and *nirvāṇa*-talk bear a relation to objective reality; on Cupitt's model they do not.

Words as descriptive of human experiences of the ultimate

But do concepts have *only* these practical connections to ultimate reality,[50] or do they also tell us something about the nature of ultimate reality? According to Hick, in addition to the practical effect they have on people, the words people use to speak about ultimate reality do indeed tell us something about the nature of ultimate reality: they tell us what people's *experiences* of that reality are, i.e. they tell us about what ultimate reality is *for us*. In the case of God-talk Hick notes that 'Christian theology has always wanted both to acknowledge the ultimate ineffability of the divine nature, and yet at the same time, for devotional and liturgical purposes, to speak of God as a personal presence with distinctive human-like qualities' (1995: 59). He contends, however, that 'the relation between these seeming incompatibilities has never been made clear' and argues that it can be clarified if we posit a distinction 'between God in God's infinite self-existent being, beyond our conceptual grasp, and God as known to us in humanly conceivable and experienceable ways' (1995: 59). Christians say 'God is good' not only because of the effect this statement has on them, but because that is how they *experience* ultimate reality.

Likewise, *nirvāṇa*-talk tells us about how ultimate reality is experienced by Buddhists. Insofar as ultimate reality is conceptually transcendent, explains Hick, it 'cannot properly be said to be personal or impersonal, purposive or non-purposive, good or evil' (1995: 27); conceptual dualisms do not apply (because *concepts* don't apply). Ultimate reality – or, in Hick's terminology, the 'Real' – is not 'an entity of the kind that *could* be personal or impersonal' (1995: 61). In the context of an I–Thou relationship, however, the Real '*is* personal, not It but He or She' and, in the context in which the Real is experienced as non-personal, 'it *is* non-personal' (1989a: 245). Insofar as Christian and Buddhist conceptualisations of ultimate reality tell us about how that reality impinges upon human life, they can be said to gesture at (in the sense of pointing humans towards rather than describing) ultimate reality *an sich*.

Note that this does not necessarily mean there is a perfect fit between language and *experience*. The non-conceptual experiences of ultimate reality attested to by Buddhists and Christian mystics suggest that sometimes it may only be possible to interpret and describe an experience of ultimate reality indirectly – using metaphors and analogies or describing the effect an experience has on one and what it means to one, rather than describing the experience as such.[51] And in traditions which *emphasise* non-conceptual experiences the practical effect of language is likely to be emphasised over and above its descriptive function with respect to experience. However, even mystic texts which speak of the ineffability of the experience of ultimate reality, or attempt to describe how different a particular experience was from everything that had gone before it, have a descriptive function insofar as they still tell us something valuable about how ultimate reality impinges upon the conventional.

The recognition that talk relating to ultimate reality can have a descriptive – as well as practical – function enables Buddhists and Christians to suppose that they might be speaking differently about the same reality because they are emphasising different ways in which that reality impinges upon human existence and different aspects of how that reality is experienced. But what is still required is an account of *why* Buddhists and Christians tend to experience ultimate reality differently and, relatedly, an identification of Buddhist and Christian grounds for the recognition of one another's experiences as authentic.

Different formative experiences

God-talk tends to express the experience of ultimate reality as a personal reality with whom one can have a relationship analogous to a relationship with another human person – a reality worthy of worship, who loves us and whom we can love. Moreover, Christian prayer appears to be modelled on the relationship between a parent and a trusting child and the soteriological image of reconciliation reinforces the notion of relationship between God and humanity. Even Christians who would agree with Tillich that descriptions such as 'Father' and 'Lord' are *symbols* of greater realities (e.g. 1951: 240–41) may, nevertheless, experience God as a 'Thou' with whom they are in relationship or to whom they are devoted. Reis Habito says that although she does not think of God as a person and has no image of God whatsoever, she still addresses God as 'you' and has the experience of being seen and supported even though she does not think in terms of someone out there looking at her (442–43); 'I address a Thou to an unknown' (444), she says. Similarly, although affirming the incomprehensibility of the Divine (53), Corless says his prayer is addressed to a Thou (33). *Nirvāṇa*-talk, on the other hand, expresses in non-personal language the non-dual or non-conceptual experience of Enlightenment in which ultimate reality is experienced as neither self nor other. The Buddhist experience of ultimate reality is, as Steven Katz puts it, 'not a relational state, i.e., it is *not* the meeting of two distinct selves or realities who come together in loving embrace' (1978: 39–40).

Schmidt-Leukel attributes this difference in how Christians and Buddhists experience and conceive of ultimate reality to the differences between the *formative* experience of each tradition: for Buddhists this is 'the experience of death, or more broadly, the experience of perishableness or transitoriness', for Jews and Christians, it is 'the experience of interpersonal relationship' (2003: 272). Because of their respective formative experiences, when it comes to analysing the human predicament, Buddhists focus on existential suffering under the transitoriness of existence, whereas Christians focus on 'sin', which Schmidt-Leukel interprets in terms of 'broken relationship' – 'the turning away from God and one's neighbour' (2003: 273). He sees these categories, respectively, as formative in the Buddhist and Christian interpretations of transcendent reality:

> In Buddhism, a frequent equivalent for Nirvâna is *amata* or *amrita*, meaning the 'deathless'. … Everything *within Samsâra*, within the cycle of rebirth and re-death, is impermanent. But Nirvâna is totally other. Nirvâna is deathless. In Judaism and subsequently in Christianity, transcendent reality is understood as a personal God, that is, as a reality that can be approached like a person, or more precisely like a merciful father. It is the experience of the fatherly divine love that liberates sinners from their curvature in on themselves and opens them up. … In this liberating love, emerging from God and reflected in human hearts, not only sin but also transitoriness and death are overcome.
>
> (2003: 274)

In Christianity, the experience of ultimate reality provides the solution to the problem of the absence of love and in Buddhism the experience of ultimate reality provides the solution to the problem of the thirst for permanence. Hence Christians tend to conceive of ultimate reality as a personal reality with whom a reciprocal relationship of love is possible while Buddhists tend not to. But could there be grounds on which Buddhists and Christians might accept one another's experiences of ultimate reality as authentic and, hence, one another's conceptions as valid?

Despite the *dominance* of personal conceptions of ultimate reality in Christianity and the *dominance* of non-personal conceptions in Buddhism, both kinds of conception have long been present within each tradition and this provides a possible basis for mutual acceptance. As examples of variations in Buddhism which could be construed as 'theistic tendencies', Baier draws attention, for example, to the Lotus Sūtra's theology of an eternal Buddha (important in Japanese Nichiren Buddhism),[52] to faith in the boundless compassion of Amida Buddha, and to the concept of Ādi Buddha ('Original Buddha') as developed in some Tantras (2005: 102). Corless (36) and Reis Habito (433) point out that compassion and wisdom are personal traits; as Corless says, they are 'aspects of Buddha Mind ... [T]he Buddha has compassion for all living beings just as a mother has compassion for her only child' (36). Schmidt-Leukel takes the Buddha himself – 'the perfected person of the fully enlightened one' – to be the most powerful personal expression in Buddhism, most fully expressed within in the Trikāya doctrine (according to which the Buddha is a manifestation of the *dharmakāya*), but already present in the declaration, found in the *Anguttara Nikāya* (3:56), that *nirvāṇa* is 'visible' in and through the life of an enlightened one (2006b: 122). In Buddhism, the 'highest symbolic representation of ultimate, ineffable reality is the image of a person full of wisdom and compassion', says Schmidt-Leukel (2007a: 84).

Conversely, not all Christians think in terms of *relationship* with God and there is nothing in the idea of the wholly simple, transcendent God that entails that this is the only appropriate way of orientating oneself to God. Among my interviewees a number explained that they think more in terms of God as the loving presence in which we 'live and move and have our being' (Acts 17: 28) than in terms of *relationship* with God.[53] Talk of God as a loving 'Thou' is interpreted by some Christians as just one kind of valid cataphatic model. Influential alternatives include, for example, Aquinas' notion of *Being itself* (*ipsum esse*) and Tillich's notions of God as the 'ground of all being' and as our 'ultimate concern' (Tillich 1949: 63–64).

In Christian mysticism, especially, where the distinction between 'the knower' and 'the known' is less pronounced and God is sometimes experienced as a reality inseparable from oneself,[54] non-personal characterisations of the Divine are not uncommon. Dionysius, for example, recommends that Christians transcend the relationship of 'Me' and 'Thee' between themselves and 'the Uncreated Light' (Rolt 2004: 27). Williams (2002: 197) has little truck with Christian mysticism, believing, as he does, that the Christian orientation towards God is necessarily dualistic, that mystical experiences of non-duality have 'nothing to do with the goal of Christianity' (2002: 55), and that 'to implicate God in nonduality is to destroy God' (2002: 53). However, this dismissal of the testimony of orthodox Christian mystics who have not always experienced God as an 'other' with whom they're in relationship ignores the traditional affirmation of God as beyond all concepts and, therefore, as beyond the distinction between self and other. As Tillich puts it, 'God is neither object nor subject and is therefore above the scheme into which theism has forced him' (1952: 187); this makes a conception of God as neither experiencer nor experienced perfectly legitimate. Moreover, the traditional Christian belief that humans have the Holy Spirit within them provides clear support for the notion that God is not entirely separate from oneself.

Let's explore further the notion that ultimate reality might be authentically experienced either as a separate reality to whom one relates or as neither self nor other, and realisable in non-dual awareness.

Ultimate reality as separate and not separate

King offers an illuminating interpretation of the dichotomy between the experience of ultimate reality as separate from one (what she calls theistic experience) and of ultimate reality as not separate (what she calls monistic or unitive experience). She contends that all experience is primitively given as a unitary whole. Habitually we analyse our experience as an experience of a subject who perceives or conceives an object but in the moment of experience itself 'there is, experientially, no subject experiencing an object. There is just experiencing' (1988: 272). King takes all mystical experiences to be primitive experiences (experiences prior to the division into subject and object components) in which one encounters 'that which grounds one's existence, one's phenomenal selfhood, one's values' (1988: 275). The fact that mystical experiences are prior to the division between subject and object means that the experiencer has no basis on which to determine whether a monistic/unitive or theistic description is preferable, argues King (1988: 273).

She suggests, moreover, that mystical experience entails radical transformation of the 'experiential self-sense', as indicated by, for example, St Paul's 'Not I, but Christ in me', by talk of dying to the self, by Zen master Hakuin's 'Great Death', and by the notion of realising the true self (Buddha nature, original mind). The mystic path involves one's sense of who and what one is being 'overturned at its foundation'; the self is 'becoming other-than-what-it-was' (King 1988: 274). This too, thinks King, makes it impossible for the mystic to establish, on the basis of his or her experience, what is self and what is other. She insists that there are simply no grounds upon which one could set up a hierarchy between experiences in which a sense of separation is retained (and subsequently expressed in God-talk), and experiences in which there is no sense of separation (416). Since there is no subject–object distinction in experience as 'given', King feels happy to leave the question of God an open one: 'is there a God that's separate or not? I think it's very difficult to tell even if what you're basing that on is your own experience', and the fact that the self is 'becoming other', 'further muddies the water and leaves unknown whether God language is appropriate or whether more Buddhist kind of language is appropriate' (416).

The reflections of some of my other interviewees seem to resonate with King's analysis. For example, Furneaux says of her contemplative prayer: 'it's not the "me" – the "I" – that we normally think of as ourselves that's doing the praying' (103), and Reis Habito speaks of experiences in which it is no longer possible to distinguish between self and other:

> Is it the same as 'I' or is it different? ... it has to be much bigger, other-wise how could we let go of this limited 'I'? But is this thing that's much bigger ... a non-'I' or other? ... What, in the final result, are their distinctions? – we cannot say anymore.
>
> (480)

And Habito says that although he affirms God as a loving presence, God is not 'somebody out there ... dualistically opposed to myself' (184):

> that which constitutes myself is not just this little self but is something that is infinitely bigger than what I can ever imagine ... and, so, it's simply giving in to that. In one sense, it's not an other ... but, on the other hand, it's not *this* little self of mine so, in *that* sense, it *is* other. So it's self *qua* other – the Self with a big 'S' *qua* other than the small self but, at the same time, self *qua* true self.
>
> (193)

These experiences of self 'becoming other-than-what-it-was' (to use King's terminology) seem to suggest that the human experience of ultimate reality may contain an ambiguity which emerges out of the fact that we are *part of* that which we experience and attempt to understand; in Christian terms, it emerges out of the fact that ultimate reality is the One 'in whom I live and move and have my being' (Acts 17:28). Habito seems to be expressing this kind of idea when, in explaining what he understands by terms like 'ultimate reality', he says that even the 'grasping mind is already part of that which I'm trying to behold and listen to and understand, so I'm right there in the middle of that circle' (169), and also when he likens God to water and us to fish who swim in the water and are ourselves composed almost entirely of water (185).

King suggests a helpful way of conceptualising our participation in ultimate reality when she explains that she has come to think of the 'spiritual reality' she affirms as being on a *continuum* with herself and others:

> we are on a very ... small end of the continuum: not knowing much, not seeing much but we are continuous with a much greater reality and we are trying to dive deeper and deeper into that. ... [T]hat reality is *greater*

than us – but not entirely separate (386); we are part of that, ... we're on this lower, minute end of that continuum, ... trying to deepen that participation.

(389)

On this understanding, that humans can experience and speak of ultimate reality as a reality to be realised in non-dual awareness, or as a distinct reality to be loved and worshipped, is in part a reflection of the fact that we participate in a reality which is greater than our limited selves. King believes this account can be supported from a Christian perspective, particularly with respect to the notion of God *qua* the One 'in whom I live and move and have my being' and the emphasis – strong in Quakerism – on the Spirit within; and, from a Buddhist perspective, by texts which emphasise transcendent reality as continuous with Buddha Nature and those which see 'Mind with a capital "M"' as being somehow at the heart of reality (417–18).

While the notion of continuum can be understood as a purely phenomenological observation – as yet another way of conceptualising the human *experience* of ultimate reality – I suggest the claim that there is a limited sense in which we are part of ultimate reality can also be interpreted as a metaphysical claim, i.e. that we are literally – in some sense – part of ultimate reality. What the notion of continuum certainly seems to suggest is that, when it comes to ultimate reality, phenomenology and metaphysics may not be distinguishable from one another in any straightforward way.

Speaking from her own experience, King says: 'I feel *transcended*, but not totally separate. I retain an awareness that this is something I am a small part of' (389). She feels that

> devotion is the right language and the right religious expression and mood ... when ... we feel that separation ... Other times, we feel more the connectivity and then ... devotion isn't quite where you are; it's a different form of spirituality. ... '[D]ivinity' is appropriate language when one feels ... more the transcendent side of this.
>
> (387)

This could be taken to imply that the Buddhist conception, according to which there is no self relating to ultimate reality as an 'other', signifies greater spiritual progress than Christians demonstrate in their conception of relationship with, or devotion to, a personal reality. But King's insistence that there are no grounds for constructing a hierarchy when it comes to theistic and unitive experiences suggests that this may not be her intention. Crucially, there is no need to interpret the notion of continuum in this way since, whatever the degree to which we experience non-separation, there is always a sense in which ultimate reality is greater than – and therefore distinct from – us insofar as it is infinite and unconditioned while we are embodied beings (and, to that extent, finite and conditioned). If the continuum is pictured as a wedge stretching infinitely outwards, we are the thin end of the wedge, so to speak. As Reis Habito says, though we contain a timeless dimension, we are also historical and very limited kinds of beings (483), and as Habito puts it, the greater reality in which we participate is infinitely bigger than what we can ever imagine (193). And King explains that, although she does not take ultimate reality to be separate, her response to it includes 'awe and what Rudolf Otto calls "creaturely feeling"' (373). Similarly, although Furneaux speaks of 'non-separation' (104), she also speaks of 'the immensity of that which is greater, and the *gratitude* to that which is greater' (106).

If Christians and Buddhists can accept that we participate in ultimate reality but do so in a limited way then Buddhists have grounds to recognise expressions which entail a distinction between ourselves and ultimate reality (such as the notion of *relationship*, and expressions of worship, reverence, and devotion),[55] and Christians have grounds to recognise non-dualistic expressions (such as *realisation*). Both can accept that we can legitimately focus on the infinite majesty before us (acknowledging that we are the thin end of the wedge and hence revering or worshipping ultimate reality as greater than ourselves) or we can focus on our connection to, and participation in, that infinitely greater reality (acknowledging that there is one wedge and, hence, not thinking of ultimate reality as separate from ourselves but in terms of the need to realise, experientially, our participation in that reality). Excitingly, the notion that we participate in ultimate reality in a limited way suggests, moreover, that Buddhist and Christian conceptualisations of ultimate reality, far from contradicting each other, may even complement each other. Let's explore this idea briefly.

A necessary tension between spiritual poles

King suggests that, if we are to provide a comprehensive first-person phenomenological account of the human experience of ultimate reality (of our axiological and existential ground), then we must conclude that 'neither unitive nor theistic language seems fully satisfactory' (1988: 274). I would adjust this conclusion to make clear that neither type of language is fully satisfactory *on its own*. If we are on a continuum with ultimate reality, as King suggests, then *both* kinds of language are valid provided they are held in tension with each other, since together they provide the most accurate picture of our situation vis-à-vis ultimate reality. Similar conclusions are reached by a number of thinkers who in various ways affirm a polarity in the human experience of ultimate reality. John Robinson, for example, speaks of a tension between '[t]he primacy of the Thou and the primacy of the That'. This, says Robinson, is 'the polarity perennially experienced by those who would give an account of ... ultimate reality' (1979: 18). He notes that in many traditions the two have been held together in tension, with one playing the dominant, the other the subsidiary role (1979: 12). Lynn De Silva also affirms this polarity: 'Ultimacy and intimacy are both aspects of our experience of the

Transcendent', says De Silva (1982: 49); personal expressions evoke a sense of intimacy and impersonal expressions evoke a sense of ultimacy. 'Thus we could understand the THAT (Nirvana) and the THOU (God) as coincidence of opposites in a single Reality' (1982: 50). Affirming Robinson's observation, De Silva notes that although one type of expression is dominant in Christianity and the other in Buddhism, both are present in different ways within each tradition (1982: 51–53).

Pieris characterises the two poles in terms of the 'agapeic' instinct, which concerns redemptive love, and the 'gnostic' instinct, which concerns salvific knowledge. As Pieris explains, '[i]n the gnostic idiom, the Absolute is ... a "nonpersonal It" to be realized within oneself rather than a "Personal Thou" to be loved and revered' (1988a: 14). Yet these two instincts complement one another and should be held in tension, as they are in Christianity where, although the agapeic instinct is dominant, a clear manifestation of the gnostic current is the stream of Christian mysticism, and in Buddhism where, although the gnostic instinct is dominant, the agapeic instinct is nevertheless manifest in personal expressions of ultimate reality such as those discussed above (see p. 68).

These thinkers all agree that, although these two dimensions of the human experience of ultimate reality are, in a sense, opposites, both are essential. Robinson describes them as two poles which stand in need of each other since it is by maintaining the tension between them that one comes closer to truth, and both he and Pieris refer to these two modes of experience as the two eyes of the soul. The gnostic and agapeic instincts are mutually corrective, says Pieris: the Buddhist emphasis satisfies our 'innate thirst to *know* the liberating truth in its metapersonal ultimacy' and the Christian emphasis fulfils our 'need to *love* the redemptive source of all beings in interpersonal intimacy' (1996: 183). '[G]nosis and *agape* are two languages of liberation which the spirit speaks within each one of us', says Pieris, 'and therefore no religion can spur us to the fullness of the humanum without educating us to be fluent in both of them' (1996: 183).

These reflections would seem to suggest not only that talk of God (*qua* 'Thou' with whom relationship is possible) and talk of *nirvāṇa* (*qua* non-personal, non-dual reality which is to be realised) are not mutually exclusive, but that they are in fact mutually *fulfilling*, in the sense that the predominant Christian conception of ultimate reality and the predominant Buddhist conception, together provide a deeper and broader understanding of how ultimate reality impinges upon human existence. The recognition of this polarity *within* each tradition lays the foundations for Buddhist and Christian mutual recognition of this polarity *between* their traditions and helps justify the legitimacy of an interpretation of both traditions as concerned with a single ultimate reality.

Dual belongers, moreover, by thinking and practising within both traditions, may find it easier than single belongers to assume an 'elliptical model of reality' (Robinson 1979: 15), in which both dimensions of experience are maintained in an even balance. MacInnes articulates the contrast between these two poles of experience as one between transcendence and immanence and reflects that, although the Church has always taught that God is both transcendent and immanent, 'somehow the former seemed to dominate' (1996: 115). Through her Buddhist practice, MacInnes attests to feeling 'more spiritually balanced'.

> Because of our creaturehood, we relate to God as children and 'Father' ... We are therefore relational, so in a sense God has to be 'other' ... [T]he Oriental Way is all about the Immanent God, with whom all creation is ONE, and therefore not in a position of relationship ... For me it is no longer 'either-or' but 'both-and'.
>
> (1996: 116)

Affirming both emphases as they appear within the Buddhist and Christian frameworks is not necessarily easy for dual belongers, but King, for example, attests to finding the mutual challenge between the Christian and Buddhist conceptualisations of ultimate reality a valuable area of spiritual growth. In Christian thought, reflects King, 'there's a pretty strong thread that's suggesting there's something really *loving* coming our way from a ultimate reality direction. ... That comes out a *little bit* in Buddhism ... but it's not quite the same thing ... ' (376). Buddhist thought, on the other hand, strongly critiques any Christian notion of God as 'a being':

> I'm trying to hold it all – ultimately, realising that there is no finally adequate way to think of it or say it ... but [to] nonetheless hear the ways they do say it to the best of their ability. ... It's a very good challenge.
>
> (376)

To summarise, then, the models which Buddhists and Christians deploy to justify the use of language with respect to a supposedly conceptually transcendent reality could, in principle, be applied to alternative expressions. Moreover, though Christians tend to conceive of ultimate reality in *personal* terms and Buddhists in *non-personal* terms, both have grounds for mutual recognition of one another's conceptions. Indeed, both even have grounds to affirm a *complementarity* between their respective conceptions. So far so good for the potential coherence of the dual belonger's world-view with respect to the question of God. But there remains a final important aspect of the Christian understanding of the ultimate which we have not yet looked at.

Ultimate reality as creator?

In Christian thought, God is not only redeemer (salvation depends on God), but creator (the existence of the universe depends on God). In Buddhist thought, however, although *nirvāṇa* is the ground of liberation, the existence of the world and the beings in it is not generally thought to depend on *nirvāna*. So what is the dual belonger to say about this issue?

Although the question of personal versus impersonal characterisations of ultimate reality has received considerable attention in Buddhist–Christian dialogue to date, there has been much less focus on the question of the ultimate as creator.[56] Schmidt-Leukel suggests that a possible reason for this neglect may be fear on the part of those involved in dialogue that the question of creation may prove to be an unbridgeable gulf, and thus jeopardise bridges of understanding already built (2006c: 5), and he points out that the issue of creation features frequently in the history of Buddhist–Christian polemics.[57] The doctrine of creation is one of Christianity's most fundamental, yet from the Buddha (who rejected the idea that the Hindu God Brahma was creator) onwards, we find Buddhist arguments against the notion of a divine creator. These arguments, as Schmidt-Leukel points out, are of three types. First, there's the problem of evil. This takes, in part, the same form in Buddhist thought as it has done in the West. Second, and relatedly, there's the argument from human responsibility. The criticism here is that salvation requires human freedom and human freedom is incompatible with a creator God: either God creates in accordance with the law of karma, in which case God is either redundant or is just another name for that law, or God does not create in accordance with the law and thus jeopardises human freedom and responsibility as well as justice. Third, there's the argument from ontology according to which it is illogical to suppose that an immutable, eternal, omnipresent, simple and perfect God could have created an impermanent, temporal and diverse world.[58]

Yet, with the possible exception of Corless, my interviewees did not appear to be particularly troubled by the apparently fundamental disagreement between Buddhism and Christianity over the question of creation. Even where disagreement was acknowledged, none seemed thrown into the existential dilemma one might expect if this really is an issue so thorny as to lead the dialogue partners – who for the dual belonger are internal – 'to the edges of a chasm which cannot be bridged, leaving them speechless in view of an irreconcilable contrast' (Schmidt-Leukel 2006c: 5). One reason for this seems to be that the disagreement between Buddhism and Christianity on this issue is less stark, and Buddhist criticism of the notion of creation less tenacious, if one's conception of God is of a transcendent reality to whom no attributes – including that of creator – literally apply. Let's explore this point further.

Rejecting a literal, anthropomorphic interpretation

Keenan (2006a: 265; 2006b: 72–74), like Heinrich Dumoulin (1974: 176), argues that much Buddhist criticism of the notion of creation is aimed at the idea of a creator who is a perfect being, literally in possession of all the classical attributes including omnipotence, and is not aimed at the creator God of the Church Fathers and Aquinas (not *a being* but a perfect reality, transcendent of all of our thoughts and words).

The anthropomorphism which Buddhists find problematic is particularly evident in the mythical creation accounts found in Genesis. But, as Keenan points out, when we look at later creation theologies, we see that God is not understood as 'a great being' who at a particular point in time decides to create the universe. Creation neither alters God nor draws God into the created world (2006b: 73). Keenan explains that, in response to critics, Christians and Jews have argued that creation leaves God unchanged; that God does not become an agent; that God 'creates continually, holding beings in being at each and every moment'; and that God creates *ex nihilo*, without prior condition or cause (2006a: 265). Keenan stresses that there are many creation theologies and he acknowledges that some of these fall firmly within the scope of Buddhist criticism, 'for some do teach God as a supreme, omnipotent being among beings'. But, argues Keenan, these are not the only options and nor are they the most profound (2006a: 265).

If Keenan is right that much Buddhist criticism of the idea of a creator God is levied at the notion of a God who is *a being* who creates the world at a particular point in time in much the same way a human being with super powers might create something, then the Buddhist critique concerns an idea of God as creator of which many Christians would be equally critical. As acknowledged by Keenan, to the extent that the Buddhist criticism applies to anthropomorphic notions of God as creator, it hits its mark more squarely, and it is perhaps indicative of the Christian climate in which King lives in Virginia that it is this anthropomorphic notion of creation which she takes as 'standard'. Hence, she says, 'I don't believe God created the universe in the standard way in which that is meant, because that presupposes a theology of God as a being' (389). In a similar vein, Reis Habito says: 'the stories in ... Genesis ... I find them fascinating but I don't take them literally' (435).

But once it is agreed that God is not a being and literally has neither agency nor intention (nor, of course, non-agency nor non-intention), it is hard to know precisely how the doctrine of creation should be interpreted by Christians (whether or not those Christians are also Buddhists). Like many doctrines, once one has dismissed literal interpretations, the doctrine of creation starts to look somewhat mysterious. However, if Dumoulin's interpretation of the traditional understanding is correct, this sense of mystery is well placed. Dumoulin points out that the essential mystery of creation can be easily obscured, and that even when speaking of God as the first cause one must remember that the notion of cause, like that of being, is predicated analogically: 'That means that the manner in which God acts causally is radically different from any worldly causation. ... God is absolutely other and unique in his activity and in his being' (1974: 176). Certainly, as far as Dumoulin is concerned, the Buddhist repudiation of the anthropomorphism they see in the doctrine of creation is also present within Christianity itself (1974: 174).

A number of those I interviewed expressed their sense of mystery and lack of full comprehension in the face of the doctrine of creation. '[P]eople think it's so simple', says King.

[S]upposedly you go back all these links, and things have to come from somewhere, and you end up with God. What the heck's that? You haven't said anything yet. You end up with God because you have to end somewhere. What is that supposed to mean? What is God then? What are we talking about?

(391)

King explains that she is happy to endorse the notion of creation but only insofar as it is understood as pointing to what she considers 'hugely mysterious' (391). Reis Habito finds the notion of creation similarly mysterious: 'I don't really *know* what's ... implied by "creation by God"' (435); and Habito says 'yes ... I do believe that God created the world. But what do I mean by that?' (186); 'I really need to work on this a little more, and really reflect a little more' (183). Reis Habito points out that, from a Christian perspective, it is easy to say the words of the creed (in this case: 'I believe in God the Father Almighty, Creator of heaven and earth'), but how many people have really thought about what those words mean? She reflects that how she has come to think of dogmas owes much to the influence of Buddhism:

> [Buddhism] has changed my approach to what's put down in terms of credo ... [b]ut it has also changed my spiritual practice and, with that change or deepening of spiritual practice, of course, there is more experiential understanding of what's expressed in the dogmas – so a less literal taking of things and more understanding of the reality that's behind it.
>
> (490)

Reis Habito suggests that this approach often reveals compatibility with alternative expressions which on the surface may appear to be contradictory (462–63, 486–88).

Focusing on the here and now

No doubt due, in part, to the influence of the Zen tendency to look for the meaning of doctrines in terms of experience in the here and now and the general Buddhist tendency to think of time in terms of the present moment or in terms of cycles of birth and decay rather than in a linear way, a number of interviewees emphasised strongly the strand of Christian thinking which Keenan identified above as the notion that God 'creates continually, holding beings in being at each and every moment' (2006a: 265). These interviewees reflected that they tend to think of creation in terms of the here and now rather than as something that took place at some point in the past. Habito, for example, says that he does not think creation is something that happened once and for all: 'It's not just something that happened way, way back ... it's continuing to happen every moment'(186), and Reis Habito says 'I think that

the universe is in creation every moment that's sustained by God's love. ...
I don't have this linear understanding of creation ... ' (478); and again:
'I would say that God is creating the world every moment, or the Absolute is
bringing all these things about every moment' (435).

On this issue as on many others, Reis Habito thinks from the basis of a
mixture of Buddhist and Christian ideas and has no qualms about this
because she sees no serious conflict between them (435). 'I think I'm very
influenced by the Buddhist concept of interdependent origination', says
Reis Habito; 'that everything comes into existence as it is because it's
interconnected with everything else – and I think that's a perfect way of
looking at [the] Christian understanding of creation, in the same way'.[59] Reis
Habito explicitly interprets the doctrine of creation in terms of her Buddhist
world-view:

> we are creation by God in the Buddhist sense of interdependent arising
> comes together in every here and now [*sic*]. I think that every moment is
> created by a force – call it God, call it the Absolute – and everything
> happens in interconnection ... So, I don't see how things in the world –
> like this tree or the sea or this country – come into being so much as how
> does every moment come into existence. That's more ... my focus.
>
> (435)

Thinking along similar lines, Habito explains that he is trying to understand
the notion of creation in 'a way that perhaps can be enlightened by the Buddhist
notion of ... interdependent co-arising'; 'I'm still trying to work on that', he
explains.[60]

Corless perhaps came closest to being significantly troubled by the question
of creation since his sense of the incompatibility or mutual irrelevance of
these two traditions was closely connected to it and, specifically, to the contrast between the Christian proclamation of God as ontologically prior to
everything else and the Mahāyāna Buddhist teaching on the interdependent
arising of all phenomena. The latter appeared to him to leave no room for a
creator God (44). Given his theory of many universes and many absolutes,
moreover, it is perhaps unsurprising that the question of creation troubled
Corless, for it cannot be that this universe was both created by God
(in whatever sense this is understood) and – at the same time (and in the same
sense) – not created by God. We noted earlier Corless' suggestion that when
we approach reality as if God were behind it, a universe appears which contains God; whereas when we approach reality as if it were sufficient unto
itself, the Buddhist universe of interdependent arising appears.[61] But if, yesterday, I approached reality as if there were a God and today approach it
as if there is no God, does this mean that yesterday the universe was God's
creation but today it is not, or perhaps yesterday's God-created universe has
today ceased to be and I now find myself in a universe sufficient unto itself? It
is not clear that sense can be made of either idea.

Fortunately, Corless reflects further that 'something else may be going on and we may be being confused by the words "God" and "interdependent arising", I'm not sure,' he says, 'but it seems in other places they're not as incompatible as all that' (44). From his Christian perspective, he confirms that he does believe in creation but, like other interviewees, says he does not think of it as something that happened at a specific point in the past: 'I think that's a symbol. It's more that God is creating the universe every moment; that the moment is constantly fresh with a new creation' (70). He contends that this kind of understanding is more compatible with Buddhism, which doesn't see any beginning to the world (44). Furneaux perhaps also sees compatibility in this regard since, in response to the question of creation, she asks, rhetorically: 'What use is it to speak of beginnings and ends within that which is beginningless and endless?' (125).

Towards a teleological understanding

But even if one's understanding of creation is not an anthropomorphic and backward looking one, but one which applies to the present moment and is taken to be consistent with the Mahāyāna teaching on the interdependent origination of all things, does the notion of creation not entail the idea – absent in Buddhism – of God's *purpose* for creation? As Keenan points out, the Genesis creation myth tells us that Yahweh alone is the source of everything and, as such, forms part of the 'prequel' to Israel's salvation history (2006a: 263; 2006b: 70). Given this, the creation myth should not be understood solely as telling us about our origins but, just as importantly, it should be understood in teleological terms – as telling us about our *destiny* (see Keenan 2006a: 263–64). The doctrine of creation by God can be understood as telling us that the world is good and that there is meaning in the world, for its creation is the beginning of our road to salvation. Even when the creation story is not taken literally, this teleological emphasis and its implications concerning the nature of reality remain, and it is not clear that they are to be found in the Buddhist context where there is no such doctrine, where there is no benevolent force thought to explain our being here in the first place, and where worlds simply go in and out of existence in accordance with the impersonal law of karma unless and until beings eventually break free of this cycle.

Despite Corless' conclusion that his understanding of creation might be more compatible with Buddhism than it first seemed to him, he nevertheless continued to be concerned by the possibility that there is no *meaning* from a Buddhist perspective: 'for Christianity, things have meaning: the world has meaning; the world is, in a sense, a story, and for Buddhism it's just more of the same; it just keeps on going so it's kind of meaningless' (44). Having said this, however, Corless himself makes a remark which perhaps points to a way of moving beyond this apparent contradiction: 'But then, when we come to the transformation of consciousness in meditation, and the monastic tradition, and the practice of the moral life in the every day, they seem to be very consonant with each other' (44). Here Corless gestures at the teleological relevance our being has, even for Buddhists.

Keenan makes more of this idea, pointing out that for Buddhist thinkers such as Gadjin Nagao the world is not simply part of a cycle of meaningless suffering; rather it is

> the field of intelligent and compassionate bodhisattva activity. That indeed is the central import of Mahāyāna ... In its early and first sense, dependent arising is the arising of the *saṃsāric* delusion and suffering that lead to the world of meaninglessness. But in a second and deeper sense, the classical Mahāyāna thinkers taught that dependent arising is the course of this world in which an awakened person is meant to practice the deeds of intelligent compassion.
>
> (Keenan 2006a: 267)

Schmidt-Leukel takes the idea yet further. He suggests that we may have something approaching a Buddhist–Christian theology of creation if we understand the Buddhist notion of karma within the context of a soteriological teleology which construes it as functionally equivalent to the Christian belief that God is both redeemer *and* creator of the world (2006b). 'Whether in the ancient Hindu-Buddhist or in the modern Christian-Buddhist controversies, the great alternative seemed to be: *Is creation karmic or divine?* But in the future,' suggests Schmidt-Leukel, 'this alternative itself ... might be questioned' (2006c: 12). If certain lines of thought within each tradition are emphasised, argues Schmidt-Leukel,[62] it is possible to understand the doctrines of creation by God and creation by karma, respectively, as providing equivalent answers to what is essentially the same question:

> 'Why is there this universe?', but in both cases this 'Why?' and the respective answers do not refer to a chronologically first cause of the universe but rather to its teleological *raison d'être*. The 'Why' is a 'Why?' in the sense of 'What for?'. And in both cases, the answer is that the universe exists as the appropriate environment for the realization of salvation.
>
> (2006b: 177)

On this interpretation, there is just as much meaning and goodness in, and purpose to, the existence of the world and our existence in it in Buddhist thought as there is in Christian thought.

A number of my interviewees offered reflections consonant with this interpretation insofar as they tended to see an inherent goodness as somehow undergirding existence from both a Buddhist and a Christian perspective. Reis Habito, for example, recalls asking her Dharma Master what underlies all reality, and him replying: 'great compassion'. She reflects: 'whether it's great compassion or whether it's the love of God, to me, in the final result, it does not make a difference, ... I have faith that it is there' (432). And, although King finds the notion of creation mysterious and, hence, tends not to use 'creation' language, she reflects that what she is able to say is that what she calls 'Buddha Mind' is 'somehow at the *root* ... of existence'; 'I don't know about origins', says King, 'but somehow Buddha Mind is at the heart of life itself' (389–90). She takes this 'principle of wisdom and compassion' to be somehow at the very core of existence and explains that, although she is affirming this with Mahāyāna Buddhists, she also takes herself to be in line with Christian mysticism on this point (388–89).

When elaborating why she rejects what she takes to be the 'standard' understanding of creation, King explains that she sees it not only as pre-supposing a theology of God as a being, but also a separation between God and the universe which she does not accept (389). But when it comes to the duality between ultimate reality (creator) and us (created) implied by the notion of creation,[63] King's hypothesis of a continuum between us and ulti-mate reality again offers a useful interpretative tool. On the basis of the con-tinuum hypothesis it is possible to affirm a distinction between creator and created (God is infinitely greater than we finite creatures and therefore not the same as us), without supposing that there is a sharp separation between creator and created (our being participates in God's being in a limited way). We may also note Rahner's condemnation of the '*dualism* which places God and the non-divine simply as two things alongside of each other'. The differ-ence between God and the world, insists Rahner, is 'radically misunderstood if it is interpreted in a dualistic way' (1978: 62).

Avoiding double standards

Certainly there is further dialogical ground to be covered and theological work to be done on the question of creation before we can hope to precisely outline the extent of a Buddhist–Christian consensus. With the possible exception of Keenan,[64] arguably, none of those I interviewed had a fully worked out theology of creation. Habito, for example, acknowledges that his endorsement of the doctrine of creation presents him with a theological challenge which he still needs to work on (183, 186). One might be tempted to view the lack of a thoroughgoing response to the question of creation as casting doubt on dual belongers' claims to have embraced the teachings of both traditions, or even to see it as threatening *any* supposed coherence between their Buddhist and Christian perspectives. However, if we step back for a moment and look at this issue within the broader context of the dual belonger's overall attempt to do justice to both traditions, the fact that this particular dimension of the task is yet to be comprehensively tackled does not appear to invalidate that attempt.

Reis Habito describes working out how her Buddhism coheres with her Christianity as an 'ongoing process', explaining that 'from getting more familiar with the things you are able to integrate them more' (462). This suggests that unresolved questions present dual belongers with an ongoing impetus to deepen their understanding of Buddhist and Christian teachings. This makes the very process of grappling with these questions enriching, even – and perhaps *especially* – where fully fledged solutions remain elusive. In looking at this broader picture, we also become aware of the risk of demanding more of dual belongers than we do of other religious people. After a modicum of in-depth reflection, the majority of single belonging Christians (whatever their form of theism) would not find it utterly straightforward to explain – in a way which is logically consistent and contains no conceptual problems – what they mean by the sentence 'God created the universe'. And, while those I interviewed, by their own willing admission, do not have all the answers, they are at least giving serious thought to issues such as this and, by so doing, increasing their understanding of Buddhist and Christian doctrines and coming up with potentially helpful interpretations which benefit both traditions and offer pointers which move Buddhist–Christian dialogue forward. Reis Habito acknowledges that having a dual religious identity has made it trickier to articulate her beliefs, but she points out that even when she was only Christian, articulating her beliefs was a difficult task:

> I found it not so easy to clearly state what I believe as a Christian because if you just say the words of the credo that's all [very] well, but then there will be so many questions. So, I think it's always a challenge to say what you believe.
>
> (487)

It might even be that some dual belongers will never feel it necessary, or even helpful to arrive at a fully worked out theology of creation insofar as this might imply that creation can be fully understood when it cannot be. In the spirit of the Buddha's unanswered questions, when it comes to the question of origins (whether the world is eternal or not) perhaps dual belongers can afford to retain something of a sense of mystery.[65] Indeed, King attests to finding it useful to have a few possibilities in mind (402).

The necessity of a monocentric interpretation

In light of the above conclusions, I suggest that Buddhist Christians can be confident that a monocentric pluralist answer to the question of God does not distort either of these traditions but rather reflects important strands of each. In both traditions we find the affirmation that there is one ultimate reality upon which salvation or liberation depends and the affirmation that this reality transcends all that can be thought and said about It/Him/Her. We also find the idea that concepts are valid with respect to ultimate reality insofar as they guide people towards an experience of, and rightly orientate people with respect to, that reality; concepts can also be legitimately construed as describing how ultimate reality impinges upon human existence, and both traditions are capable of recognising the role of personal and non-personal concepts in these regards. Moreover, in both traditions we find the idea that the existence of this universe has to do with its being a suitable environment for the realisation of salvation or liberation. These strands of thought make it possible for Buddhists and Christians to interpret their respective ways of experiencing and conceiving of ultimate reality as different ways of experiencing and conceiving of one and the same reality. Dual belongers can, in turn, be understood as experiencing and conceiving of reality differently, depending on the conceptual and ritual framework in which they are operating.

As we saw, apart from Corless, my interviewees spoke in singular terms about ultimate reality but despite this, and despite the fact that some of their statements seemed clearly to embrace the monocentric hypothesis, when questioned explicitly on the subject, some seemed reluctant to unreservedly endorse this interpretation. Habito's ambivalence seemed to relate, at least in part, to a belief that it is not strictly possible to say of a conceptually transcendent reality that it is one rather than two, since 'one' and 'two' are concepts.[66] But as Hick points out, 'our language is such that we can only refer to the Real in either singular or plural terms' (1995: 71), and neither Christians nor Buddhists speak of the Real in plural terms (and nor does Habito, even when asking: 'Is *it* one? Is *it* two?'[67]). By saying that ultimate reality is one, the monocentric pluralist means only that ultimate reality is uniquely ultimate, i.e. that there is nothing as great, and not, as Hick explains, that ultimate reality 'is one in distinction from two or three or more. The Real remains beyond the range of our human conceptuality, including the concept of number' (1995: 71).

King's ambivalence seemed to relate to a belief that it is impossible for us to *know* whether Buddhism and Christianity are concerned with *one* ultimate reality or *different* ultimate realities (371), and she is right to the extent that it seems unlikely that one could ever *prove* the monocentric hypothesis. Hence, although there are good reasons from each perspective to embrace it, neither Buddhists nor Christians are logically obliged to accept it. I suggest, however, that individuals who belong to *both* these traditions *are* logically obliged to accept it. This obligation arises out of the fact that, if one endorses both perspectives, one is required to endorse both the Buddhist and the Christian claim that there is no more than one ultimate reality: one cannot say that there is more than one, and remain a faithful adherent of a religion which takes there to be only one. Nor can one endorse both the Buddhist and the Christian claim to be concerned with that which is uniquely ultimate unless one takes these religions to be concerned with the same ultimate. As our investigation into polycentric approaches suggested, if dual belongers wish to affirm God as uniquely ultimate and also to affirm *nirvāṇa* or the *dharmakāya* as uniquely ultimate, and if, at the same time, they want a logically coherent religious outlook, then, unlike single belongers, they have no choice *but* to endorse the monocentric interpretation since to do otherwise is to reduce either God, *nirvāṇa*, or both, to the status of non-ultimate realities. Far from implying a move away from the teachings of either of these traditions, then, a monocentric answer to the question of God is, in fact, *entailed* by the teachings of both traditions if one accepts *both* teachings as true. In short, dual belongers are obliged by their commitment to both traditions to accept the monocentric hypothesis.

Corless apparently held that one should not 'fool oneself' that one's Buddhist practice 'has anything … to do with God' nor that one's Christian practice has anything to do with the Triratna (Buddha, *Dharma*, and *Saṅgha*).[68] But how can one believe, from a committed Christian perspective, that the truth and goodness one has discovered in Buddhism has nothing to do with the ultimate reality one knows as God? Likewise, how can one believe, from a committed Buddhist perspective, that the truth and goodness one has discovered in Christianity has nothing to do with the ultimate reality one knows as *nirvāṇa* or the *dharmakāya*? The obligation to embrace a monocentric interpretation of one's dual belonging seems to be as much spiritual as logical. Amaladoss goes so far as to suggest that the possibility of dual belonging depends on 'a strong belief in, if not experience of, the oneness and transcendence of the Ultimate' (2002: 311), and perhaps there is some truth in this. Despite his theory of many absolutes, even Corless occasionally appears to speak in singular terms about that which is ultimate, as, for example, when he writes: 'when we feel a genuine vocation to a dual loyalty, something or someone leads us into a dark night, but … somehow, that something or someone is trustworthy' (1990b: 115). And there is perhaps some evidence in his reflections in interview that he might have been beginning to embrace a more monocentric interpretation of his dual belonging, in so far as he was starting to see some convergence between Buddhism and Christianity at the ultimate level:

> I've come to suspect that … I function as a Buddhist or as a Christian but then there's … some kind of level where they're happy with each other (11); I've come to believe … that the universe, whether seen from a Christian or Buddhist angle, appears to be wise and compassionate and energetic at its deepest level … it seems to me that, ultimately, … it is that way somehow and that somehow Christians and Buddhists … agree on some fundamental level that, to put it into Einstein's terms, the universe is friendly.
>
> (20)

Corless explained that this ultimate wisdom, compassion, energy, and friendliness was something he had come to believe in as a Buddhist and as a Christian.[69] This does not seem so far removed from Reis Habito's affirmation of a single ultimate reality or Absolute, which she describes as 'fully unimpeded wisdom and compassion … and love … – a compassionate loving energy' (468).

One factor which continued to fuel Corless' reluctance to embrace the idea that Buddhism and Christianity are concerned with a single ultimate reality seemed to be a concern that to do so would amount to claiming that Buddhism and Christianity are the same.[70] But to say that these traditions are concerned with the same ultimate reality is not to claim that *they* are the same, nor that they are saying the same thing. King, for example (despite expressing ambivalence about monocentrism elsewhere), describes Buddhism and Christianity as 'two efficacious routes of access' to 'ultimate reality' (373), but she nevertheless takes the value of belonging to both traditions to lie in the respects in which these traditions are unlike each other, i.e. where what is said by each of them differs.[71]

Another of Corless' objections was the way in which monocentric pluralism subordinates or relativises Buddhism and Christianity with respect to a greater Absolute or Truth.[72] But what I have tried to show is that, provided one acknowledges Christian apophaticism (as Corless appears to) and provided, from a Buddhist perspective, one sees doctrine as a finger pointing to the moon, then from a traditional Christian and a traditional Buddhist perspective, the subordination and relativisation of all linguistic expressions with respect to ultimate reality is entirely appropriate. As Abhishiktānanda says, each religion 'bears within itself an urgent call to men to pass beyond itself', for '[t]he mystery to which it points overflows its limits in every direction' (1975: 25–26); or, as Habito puts it, Buddhists are called by their Buddhism to go beyond concepts, and Christians are called by their Christianity to go beyond the concept of God (151). Smith warns that we fall into idolatry when we make the mistake of

> identifying with the divine, with the truth, with the final, with transcendence, the particular form in or through which we have been introduced to it, by way of which It or He or She has come into our particular lives – rather than relating that form to It/Him/Her, subordinating it, relativising it in relation to the Absolute that it serves.
>
> (Smith 1987: 59)

The monocentric hypothesis does not replace or diminish Christianity or Buddhism but rather highlights the contention of each that ultimate reality cannot be captured by concepts, and writes large this self-understanding in each case, in order to take account of the discovery of truth and goodness in the other. Far from glossing over the differences between how Buddhists and Christians think about, and relate to, ultimate reality, this interpretation allows those differences to become sources of profound complementarity and beneficial mutual challenge.

4   Jesus Christ and Gautama Buddha

So let us now turn to another area of potential conflict which Buddhist Christian dual belongers must negotiate. It concerns the presence of two key figures at the centre of their spiritual lives: Jesus Christ and Gautama Buddha. In this chapter we will look at how these figures might be understood by dual belongers: can their nature and significance be interpreted in ways which are continuous with both traditions and yet consistent with each other?

The problem is this. Understood as the historical mediator of God to humans, Jesus Christ came to be thought of as the Incarnation of the second person of the Trinitarian God – God the Son, the Logos incarnate. Jesus is God in the mode of God's self-revelation. In 325 the Council of Nicea pronounced that Jesus Christ was of one substance with the Father, and then in 451 the Council of Chalcedon added that he was also of one substance with humans.[1] This Christological understanding seems to imply that, from a Christian perspective, whoever the Buddha is or was, he is inferior to Jesus Christ. Moreover, if the salvation of all of humanity is thought to be constitutively dependent on Jesus Christ's death and resurrection, then the Buddha and his teachings seem redundant. From a Buddhist perspective, on the other hand, even if there is an interpretation of Jesus *qua* divine incarnation which might be acceptable, Jesus could never be accepted as the *only* such incarnation. Moreover, it is impossible for Buddhists to accept that salvation is constitutively dependent upon Jesus' death and resurrection, and many Buddhists would question whether Jesus was even a fully enlightened being. So, the question arises: is there any way for the dual belonger to see beyond this impression of incompatibility and competition?

One could interpret Jesus as an incarnation of God and the Buddha as a great teacher, but this seems to entail the Buddha's inferiority, and if one is authentically Christian and authentically Buddhist, one cannot embrace any notion which entails the inferiority of either the Buddha or Jesus Christ vis-à-vis the other. Moreover, on this option, the dual belonger would still face the question of how to interpret Jesus' divinity from his or her Buddhist perspective.

Perhaps dual belongers should give up on the doctrine of the Incarnation, and treat both Jesus and Gautama as simply great teachers and exemplars of right living? Some contemporary Christian thinkers, including Hick, argue not only that the doctrine of the Incarnation is a stumbling block for those who would acknowledge the validity of non-Christian traditions, but that it is anyway incoherent. Although the Council of Chalcedon stated that Jesus was of one substance with the Father and of one substance with human beings, the precise relationship between these two natures was not specified beyond their being pronounced to be united in one person and undivided yet not mixed. Jesus was to be thought of as at once fully human and fully God, yet how this is possible was considered a mystery. Unwilling to accept this mystery, Hick rejects the idea that there is any literal truth expressed by the doctrine of the Incarnation, arguing that the God-Man idea is as contentless and without meaning as the idea of a square circle,[2] and since no sense can be made of it as a statement of metaphysical fact, we should see it as a mythological idea (Hick 1977a: 178) or a metaphor (Hick 1993). Jesus Christ, he concludes, was not God but simply a human being 'in following whom we have found ourselves in God's presence and have found God's meaning for our lives' (1977a: 178).

Of my interviewees, King comes closest to advocating a rejection of the doctrine of the Incarnation – 'forget this "incarnation of God" thing ... and make ... [Jesus] a great teacher and Buddha's a great teacher' (381) – but as we will see, in further reflections King appears to modify this position, making it clear that it is in fact a particular *interpretation* of the incarnation that she rejects, and not necessarily the incarnation *per se*. Insofar as this doctrine is one of Christianity's most central, many Christians would consider a rejection of its literal truth to be too radical a break from the tradition and would argue that an interpretation of Jesus as merely a teacher does not do justice to their understanding of Jesus. Moreover, if Hick is wrong, and the affirmation of Jesus' two natures can be interpreted in a manner which is both intelligible and which allows for the possibility of other incarnations, then perhaps there is a way of interpreting the Buddha in a similar manner, thereby avoiding the implication of Jesus' superiority. Let's consider this possibility.

Grounds for Buddhist recognition of Jesus Christ as an incarnation

Given that Buddhism is non-theistic, if the notion of a divine incarnation is to be viewed from a Buddhist perspective as anything other than a deluded construal of Jesus as an incarnation of a God who does not exist[3] (or at best exists only as a being still trapped within the round of rebirth), it is vital to see this issue in the light of the monocentric pluralist interpretation advanced in the last chapter. Jesus' divinity can then be seen in terms of his being an incarnation or embodiment of the transcendent ultimate reality which he conceived of, and which Christians conceive of, as God. Hence, Buddhists might be able to recognise Jesus as an incarnation of the same ultimate reality, which they experience as *nirvāna* or the *dharmakāya*; and Christians might be able to recognise the Buddha as an incarnation of the same ultimate reality, which they experience as God.

Despite the tendency among Western interpreters of Buddhism to portray the Buddha as simply a human being of exceptional wisdom and insight, this is not the portrayal of the Buddha we find reflected in, for example, the religious imagery in Thai temples where, as Schmidt-Leukel points out, everything 'proclaims the supramundane, not to say "divine" nature of the Buddha' (2005c: 151). And Buddhist Taitetsu Unno (1999: 139) argues that right from the start Buddhism taught that the Buddha is more than simply human. Concurring with this, Schmidt-Leukel points out that, just as Jesus says, 'he who sees me, sees the Father' (John 14: 7–14), 'in the Pāli Canon the Buddha is repeatedly identified with the *Dharma*: "Seeing the *Dharma*", says the Buddha, "one sees me, seeing me one sees the *Dharma*"'.[4] And just as Jesus is described in Colossians as 'the image of the invisible God' (Colossians: 1.15), terms such as 'visible *Dharma*' and the 'visible *nirvāṇa*' are used to refer to the life of one who has reached the final goal and is free from the shackles of greed, hatred, and delusion.[5]

The notion of the Buddha as an embodiment of ultimate reality is further developed in Mahāyāna Buddhism where we find the Buddha portrayed in the *Lotus Sūtra* as a manifestation of the supra-mundane Buddha-reality referred to as the 'Father of the World', who manifests out of compassion for beings in order to show them the way to Enlightenment.[6] Tibetan Buddhist, John Makransky, describes Gautama Buddha as 'someone who became *perfectly transparent* to the unconditioned reality, *nirvāṇa*, so as to fully embody its qualities of unconditioned freedom, all-inclusive love and penetrating insight and to disclose the means for many others to realise them' (2005a: 177). Nowhere is the Buddhist notion of incarnation more developed than in the Mahāyāna Trikāya doctrine (three-bodies doctrine), according to which the historical Buddha is the Buddha's 'Transformation Body' (*nirmāṇakāya*) which is illusory in comparison with the Buddha's other two bodies. The *nirmāṇakāya* is a manifestation of the supramundane 'Enjoyment Body' (*saṃbhogakāya*), which is the transphysical and glorified body of the Buddha. Insofar as they are manifest and visible, both the *nirmāṇakāya* and the *saṃbhogakāya* are referred to as 'Form-bodies' (*rūpakāya*). These Form-bodies are manifestations of the 'Dharma Body' (*dharmakāya*) which is Formless (*arūpa*). The *dharmakāya* is the ineffable, transcendent, ultimate reality. Mariasusai Dhavamony explains that '[i]n the Mahāyāna ... [the Buddha] is interpreted as the projection or manifestation of the Absolute. He is in essence with ultimate being [*sic*]' (1978: 47). The notion of the three-bodies is developed further by Pure Land Buddhists. Shinran Shōnin,[7] for example, holds that the '*dharmakāya* as suchness' manifests as the '*dharmakāya* as skilful means' in the form of Amida Buddha who, out of boundless compassion, manifests as the human figure of Gautama Buddha, for the sake of the liberation of living beings. As Schmidt-Leukel explains, here we find the belief that 'the inconceivable transcendent reality is revealed to us as the mind of infinite loving-kindness finding its meta-historical expression in the figure of Amida and its historical expression in Gautama Buddha' (Schmidt-Leukel 2005c: 161).

So might Buddhists be able to similarly accept Jesus Christ as an incarnation of ultimate reality? Corless (1987) develops an interpretation of Jesus' two natures in accordance with the Trikāya doctrine. Although he is writing primarily from the perspective of a Christian theologian here (rather than a Buddhist or joint perspective), the interpretation of Jesus Christ he presents is one which could perhaps be accepted from a Buddhist perspective.[8] Makransky believes it is indeed possible for Buddhists to 'recognise Christ as a remarkable *rūpakāya* manifestation of Buddhahood itself, a powerful means through which followers of Christ have indeed communed with and learned to embody liberating qualities of *dharmakāya*' (2005a: 199). Even within Theravāda Buddhism there are rare individuals who are prepared to acknowledge Jesus Christ as another incarnation of the *Dharma*. Bhikkhu Buddhadāsa is one of them: 'If you agree that God is 'the Dhamma' (1967: 106), then 'Jesus Christ in his fourfold role as a son of David, a historical teacher of religion, a son of God and God,' asserts Buddhadāsa, 'may ... be understood in the same way as we Buddhists are familiar with our Lord Buddha' (1967: 107). The term 'son of God', suggests Buddhadāsa, should only be applied 'to those who can lead the world to perfect understanding of the dhamma' (1967: 106). Buddhadāsa was happy to apply this term to Jesus (1967: 29).

What cannot be accepted from a Buddhist perspective, however, is that Jesus is the *only* incarnation of ultimate reality. Buddhadāsa, for example, as Santikaro Bhikkhu (2001: 94) explains, is prepared to grant that Jesus was the Son of God, provided it is not claimed that he is the *only* Son of God; and Nhat Hanh (1995: 99–100), who has accepted Jesus Christ as one of his 'spiritual ancestors' and keeps an image of Jesus on the altar of his hermitage alongside statues of Buddhas and Bodhisattvas, says that 'God made Himself known to us through Jesus Christ', yet Nhat Hanh has difficulty with the fact that 'in Christianity, Jesus is usually seen as the only Son of God' (1995: 35–36). Jesus is 'the door for us to enter the Kingdom of God', says Nhat Hanh, but 'The Buddha is also described as a door, ... it is said that there are 84,000 *Dharma* doors, doors of teaching. If you are lucky enough to find a door, it would not be very Buddhist to say that yours is the only door'.[9]

The question, then, is whether the dual belonger can reject an interpretation of Jesus as unique as an incarnation of ultimate reality and remain authentically Christian? Certainly Jesus has traditionally been understood by the vast majority of Christians as unique as an incarnation of ultimate reality, but is it necessary for Christians to continue to construe Jesus' uniqueness in this way (especially in the light of increased awareness of other potential candidates within other traditions)? Does the Christian tradition have the resources within it to justify interpretations of Jesus *qua* incarnation which might allow for the recognition of other incarnations?

Grounds for Christian recognition of Gautama Buddha as an incarnation

From the beginnings of Christianity to the present day the nature and significance of Jesus Christ has been the source of ongoing debate among Christians. Increasing awareness of religious diversity in recent times has lead much of this debate to focus upon the question of Christ's uniqueness.[10] Paul Knitter (1985: 186) points out that much modern Christological reflection is moving towards a reinterpretation of Jesus' uniqueness, even if the conclusions of this reflection are not always fully drawn out. Rahner's influential 'transcendental Christology', for example, although continuing to construe Jesus as the only divine incarnation, arguably lays the foundations for a reinterpretation, since Rahner sees Jesus, *qua* incarnation, as representative of the fulfilment of what *all* human beings are, insofar as they reach beyond themselves and experience themselves as 'Spirit in the world'. In Jesus Christ, says Rahner, human nature 'reached the ... point towards which it is always moving by virtue of its essence' (1978: 217). Jesus gave his whole life in an act of trust to the mystery of God and, thus, divine communication reaches fulfilment in him, thinks Rahner; but the presence of God in Jesus is not different from the presence of God within all human beings.

Admittedly, Rahner still insists that Jesus is in a unique way the *assurance* of God's presence in all human beings since he is the '*highest* instance of the actualization of the essence of human reality'; 'the most radical culmination of man's essence' (1978: 218). But why must we conclude that the essence of human nature has been fully realised only once in history? Knitter is bemused by Rahner's insistence 'that this culmination/fulfillment has taken place and can take place *only once*' (1985: 188). He and Schmidt-Leukel see Rahner's arguments as leading instead in the direction of a pluralist Christology capable of recognizing other incarnations. The universal presence of the divine Spirit in the depth of everyone's existence, points out Schmidt-Leukel,

> allows for the possibility of something like a 'gradual incarnation', according to which everyone incarnates or embodies the presence of God, in so far and to the degree that he or she resonates in his or her life with the divine Spirit. But why should we then not seriously reckon with the possibility that there are several 'highest instances' of such an 'actualization of the essence of human reality', that is with the possibility of several incarnations so conceived?[11]

Perhaps the most impressive attempt to construct a pluralist Christology which recognises the presence of the Spirit within all humans and, relatedly, the possibility that others besides Jesus might manifest this Spirit to as great a degree as did he, is Roger Haight's Spirit Christology. Haight offers an interpretation of Jesus' two natures which is both intelligible and also conducive to the recognition of other incarnations by construing Jesus' identity in terms of 'the presence and operation in him of God as Spirit' (1992: 262). The (meta-phorical) symbol of God as Spirit concerns God's active presence at work in creation, outside of God's immanent selfhood. 'God as Spirit', Haight writes, 'inspires human beings and is thus responsible for the dramatic saving events that are accomplished by God's agents' (1992: 267). Haight describes ultimate reality as presenting itself to us as 'unfathomable and incomprehensible mystery': since 'ultimate reality is transcendent, human beings can only perceive and appreciate it through finite this-worldly symbols' (2005a: 152). The hermeneutical key Haight uses to interpret Jesus' two-natures is the definition of a symbol as that which 'mediates a perception and knowledge of something other than itself' – in so doing the symbol both participates in the reality symbolised and is distinct from it (1992: 263). In other words, a symbol necessarily has two natures. Jesus Christ, says Haight, is 'the historical medium that stands at the source of Christianity' and is its 'central symbol': 'as a human being, he is the historical symbol that focuses Christian faith in God. ... Jesus is ... the way of the Christian, to God ... All who became Christians experienced Jesus as the mediator of God's salvation' (1992: 263–64).

The symbol of God as Spirit, explains Haight, 'refers simply and directly to God' but also 'points to God as immanent in the world' and as personally present and active within the world and within people (1992: 268). Haight upholds Nicea and Chalcedon by asserting that God 'is really present to and at work in Jesus, ... Jesus is a manifestation and embodiment of the reality of God' (1992: 275). He insists, however, that the notion of incarnation must not undermine Jesus' humanity, as Logos Christology has often done, and argues that this entails dropping the idea of Jesus as pre-existent; 'what is preexistent to Jesus is God, the God who became incarnate in Jesus. ... Jesus is really a creature like us, and a creature cannot preexist creation' (1992: 276). Jesus embodies God as Spirit. In him we see God at work *within* human freedom, 'not from outside and dominating nor from inside and taking over, but actualizing human freedom to its full capacity' (1992: 276). So Haight moves away from the traditional understanding of Jesus as qualitatively different from other human beings, arguing that this understanding undermines the message of the New Testament and 'the very logic of Christian faith'. Rather, argues Haight, Jesus should be understood as distinct to the extent that he embodies God as Spirit in a most intense, complete, and fully effective way (1992: 279–80).

Haight acknowledges that Spirit Christology does not reflect the idea of the *immanent* Trinity (which concerns God's internal nature), but argues that it expresses clearly

> that which is the very point of the doctrine of the immanent Trinity, and that is to reinforce ontologically that no less than God really acted for our salvation in Jesus, and that what is experienced in the Christian community today as Spirit is no less than God.
>
> (1992: 285)

Thus Spirit Christology guarantees the *economic* Trinity (which concerns the way in which God is known through revelation in history) insofar as it reflects the New Testament language of the economy of God's saving action through Jesus. It is the economic Trinity which is essential to Christian existence and thought, argues Haight, and the doctrine of the *immanent* Trinity – i.e. 'that God is one in nature, but God is also Trinity, for there are three distinct persons in this one Godhead' – is not entailed by the economic Trinity, does not appear in the New Testament, and has no status independently of the experience of the *economic* Trinity (1992: 284–85).

Haight argues that a pluralist Christology such as his succeeds in recognising that 'other religions and other religious symbols mediate the "same" transcendent source and power of salvation', while at the same time remaining faithful to Christian orthodoxy in so far as it affirms 'the basic experience and conviction of Christians regarding the true divinity of Jesus' – it simply construes that divinity non-competitively (2005: 161). Christians should not be surprised to find salvation mediated within other religious traditions, contends Haight: 'Given the limitation of all historical mediation, and given the transcendent character of ultimate reality, no single salvific mediation can encompass God's reality or human understanding of it'.[12]

Cornille argues that Christian belief in 'Jesus Christ as the unique son of God whose death and resurrection have brought about the forgiveness of sins and eternal life' is 'radically incompatible' with Buddhism (2003: 49, fnt. 3). However, Spirit Christology not only provides Christian grounds on which the dual belonger may recognise the Buddha as another incarnation who also mediates salvation to his followers, but also construes Jesus Christ *qua* divine incarnation in a manner that is more in keeping with Buddhism insofar as it construes his divinity in terms of its being the fruition of the seeds of divinity which are within us all. This notion coincides with the Christian idea of 'Christ Within' and can be seen as reflecting St Paul's exclamation: 'I live now not with my own life but with the life of Christ who lives in me' (Galatians 2: 20). It is an understanding of human destiny in relation to Jesus Christ's achievement which functions similarly to the Buddhist understanding of the destiny of beings in relation to the Buddha's achievement, most developed in the Mahāyāna Buddhist doctrine of Buddha Nature or Buddha Germ (*tathāgatagarbha*), according to which, all beings contain within them the innate potential to become Buddhas; each of us has within us the seed of Buddhahood which is rooted in the *dharmakāya*. These notions within both traditions allow Jesus and Gautama to be seen, within their particular historical contexts, as fruitions of the spiritual potential we all possess. It is this fruition which makes both of them 'Mediators of the Transcendent' as Schmidt-Leukel (2005c: 151) puts it, or 'embodiments of the Mystery', as Habito puts it (174).

Given that Nhat Hanh sees the 'Holy Spirit' as equivalent to 'the energy of mindfulness (which is the energy of the Buddha)' (1999: 194) and says of Jesus that, '[a]s someone animated by the energy of the Holy Spirit, He is the

Son of God' (1995: 35–36), Haight's is a Christology which Nhat Hanh would likely find acceptable: 'The Holy Spirit is already there, within us. If we are able to touch it within ourselves and help it to manifest in us we can cultivate the Holy Spirit the way we cultivate mindfulness'.[13] Nhat Hanh distinguishes between the historical Buddha and the 'living Buddha' and sees a parallel distinction within the Christian tradition (1995: 34–35). He takes the living Christ to be manifest in those who faithfully follow the way shown by Jesus, and argues that we are all 'the sons and daughters of God and the children of our parents' (1995: 44), thus echoing St Paul's declaration: 'Everyone moved by the Spirit is a son of God' (Romans 8: 14). Buddhadāsa might also have found Haight's understanding acceptable for, as Santikaro explains, Buddhadāsa was of the opinion that when wisdom, compassion, and freedom ripen in individuals, 'their lives become a complete expression of God or Dhamma. In this sense, they can be spoken of as being Dhamma or God' (Santikaro 2001: 95).

Christological understandings akin to Haight's seemed to be implicit in the reflections of a number of my interviewees. Reis Habito, for example, expresses her belief that what Jesus achieved is a possibility for us all, saying: 'I think we can all be completely open and transparent to God as Jesus was' (483). King, rejecting what she sees as the usual interpretation of the Incarnation, offers what she takes to be the Quaker understanding: as 'a way of saying that the Holy Spirit was very alive in him ... and that's how I do see Jesus' (382). King appears to reject the immanent Trinity on the grounds that it implies Jesus' uniqueness: 'the uniqueness thing – that's a big problem', she says. 'Why should we accept a theology – namely the whole Trinity thing – ... that it's somehow absolutely required of us to believe just one way of thinking about it. I don't think it holds any particular compelling truth or compelling authority' (382). Nevertheless, like Haight, King arguably preserves the economic Trinity insofar as she accepts the doctrine of the Incarnation when it is interpreted in terms of the operation of the Holy Spirit within Jesus. She explains that, for Quakers, Jesus is 'a paradigm of the ideal form of the life one aspires to' (344). The Holy Spirit is within every person which means every person is 'perfectible' – 'it's kind of a principle of enlightenment, in a sense' (366). King distinguishes between the historical figures of Gautama and Jesus and Buddha Nature or Christ Within, and takes the latter notions to be overlapping concepts which refer to the spiritual potential we all have as 'part of being human'.[14]

Jesus Christ as saviour?

However, what dual belongers seem to further require if they are to understand both Jesus Christ and the Buddha as *equal* blossomings of the spiritual potential within us all, is a *non-constitutive* interpretation of Jesus Christ's role in salvation. From a Christian perspective, if one relates to Jesus Christ as 'saviour' and means by this that salvation is constituted by Jesus' death and resurrection, then even if the Buddha is seen as another embodiment of ultimate reality, one must still consider him vastly inferior to Jesus Christ and his teachings, as, at best, a preparation for the acceptance of Jesus Christ as saviour.[15] Moreover, constitutive Christologies are virtually impossible to understand from a Buddhist perspective: how can Jesus Christ have brought about my salvation 2,000 years ago without my doing a thing? José Cabezón says that Buddhists cannot accept that the death of one individual could act as 'the direct and substantive cause for the salvation of others', since every person is considered to be ultimately responsible for his or her own liberation (1999: 27). '[S]alvation is not dependent on any one historical event' or, specifically, upon the appearance of any particular person in history, argues Cabezón. Other individuals may help us or hinder us, but they cannot seal our fate: 'Salvation is not granted to us, or withheld from us, by some external force. It is self-earned'.[16]

First, it should be noted that the imperative to bring one's thoughts, words, and deeds in line with the nature of ultimate reality as revealed by Jesus has always been present in Christianity. This imperative seems to resonate with Cabezón's claim that '[w]hat brings about salvation is not mere belief or faith ... but the long and arduous process of radical mental transformation, which requires more than simply belief' (1999: 28). Reis Habito recalls, for example, Jesus' saying that it is 'not those who say to me, "Lord, Lord", who will enter the kingdom of heaven, but the person who does the will of my father in heaven'.[17]

Second, and crucially, much contemporary Christological reflection is moving away from a constitutive construal of Jesus' role in salvation and rejecting the notion that Jesus' death on the cross was necessary in order to atone for the sins of humanity. Schmidt-Leukel goes as far as to say that the 'theological construct that God would require the bloody sacrifice of Jesus so as to be able to forgive our sins is as bizarre as it is repulsive' (2005d: 201). He points out that many theologians these days reject the medieval notion that Jesus' death constitutes salvation, seeing salvation instead as *represented* through Jesus' life and death (2005d: 201). On this understanding, by his life, death, and resurrection Jesus *demonstrates* that which constitutes the salvation of all. As Haight puts it, historically speaking, 'salvation did not begin with Jesus. Rather Jesus saves by being the revealer of God and God's salvation ..., the revelation of what human life should be, and the empowering example of life for disciples' (1992: 278). Haight does not abandon a construal of Jesus Christ as 'saviour' but argues that Jesus saves by mediating God as Spirit and by being followed and imitated. 'Resurrection is the climax of a life that follows the pattern of Jesus' (Haight 1992: 278).

Regardless of the dual belonger's needs, this understanding has clear merits and it is arguably much closer to Jesus' own understanding. Indeed, if Jesus' message concerns the Father's unconditional love and forgiveness, this message is seriously undermined by a Christology which construes God's mercy as *conditional* upon the sacrifice of an innocent life.[18] For the dual belonger,

Haight's understanding has the additional advantage of presenting Jesus as saviour in a way that is much more acceptable from a Buddhist perspective: it is down to me to cultivate the divine spirit which resides in me by living in faithfulness to Christ and to the possibility for all people to which he bore witness. In other words, it is down to me to realise Christ Within, just as it is down to me to realise my Buddha Nature.

Grace Burford, contrasting her Buddhism with Christianity, asserts that

> the central religious task ... is inherently a task I must do and not have done for me. ... So give me a map, lend me your car (or raft?), show me a shortcut, even protect me along the way if you can – but do not make the trip for me!
>
> (1999: 137)

But this contrast appears too simplistic. The question of 'self-power' versus 'other-power' with respect to salvation or liberation is a complex and much debated one, not only between Buddhists and Christians but also *within* both traditions. There is not the space to properly address this issue here, though we will touch on it again in the next chapter. But suffice it to say that the contrast between Christians who see salvation as dependent upon Jesus Christ and Buddhists who see salvation as 'self-earned' (Cabezón 1999: 27) is too crude to do justice to the complexities of each of these traditions, not least because in neither case is it clear what is meant. *Both* Christianity *and* Buddhism affirm that, in the end, it is ultimate reality (God/*nirvāṇa*) which saves and ultimate reality is unconditioned and impervious to manipulation of any kind. As Buddhagosa says, one can cultivate the right conditions for the encounter with *nirvāṇa*, but one cannot produce this encounter (*Visuddhimagga*, XXII, 126); 'personal effort is only the "setting" for the realization of the highest religious truth', explains Mahinda Palihawadana, 'the highest realization can take place only when effort ceases to be' (1978: 193). Moreover, to the extent that so-called 'self-power' is relied upon by many Buddhists, '[t]he self here is not the unenlightened ego self', explains Unno, 'but the enlightened non-ego self imbued with *dhamma*' (1999: 142). If this is the 'self' Cabezón has in mind when he speaks of salvation being 'self-earned', then notions of God as Spirit within each of us, or of Christ Within, present us with equivalent Christian ideas: Christ, as an incarnation of God as Spirit, is not merely a saviour figure who is external to me but is also a seed within myself.

Moreover, although Cabezón may see the Buddha as primarily guide and teacher, there are plenty of Buddhists for whom the Buddha – or a Bodhisattva – functions as saviour,[19] particularly in Pure Land Buddhism, as taught by Shinran, where liberation is taken to result from placing one's trust in the all-encompassing compassion of Amida Buddha who transfers merit to those who call on his name in faith.[20] Habito and Corless were both significantly influenced by Pure Land Buddhism. Habito explains that Shinran's recognition of his inability to save himself resonates with the realization of one's own weakness; 'the only way is to really surrender to that other power ... which really is a power of compassion that permeates throughout the universe' (133). Similarly, from a Christian perspective, he says: 'Not by our own efforts are we saved, but precisely by the power of God's grace and ... that's the good news. You don't need to keep trying to save yourself because you can't anyway' (192). Corless explains his attraction to Pure Land Buddhism, saying:

> I'm not a very good meditator – I can't concentrate that well, I can't do visualisations all that well – and so the Pure Land approach where you say 'I can't do this myself' and you rely on the power of the Buddha has become more attractive over time.
>
> (9)

Conversely, there are Christians who do not think of Jesus Christ primarily as an external saviour figure, choosing instead to emphasise the historical Jesus as teacher or guide and paradigm of behaviour, and the trans-historical Christ as an internal reality to be realised. Among my interviewees, this orientation was perhaps most evident in King's reflections (344–46, 381). She contrasts the emphasis on Jesus as 'our salvation' with the Quaker emphasis on Jesus as the 'ultimate spiritual teacher' (2003a: 21), a reading she takes to be closer to the synoptic gospels which, as she puts it, do not present Jesus as saying 'I'm the saviour, I am God, you should worship me'.[21] It is one's Buddha Nature or Christ Within which saves one, thinks King; 'the indwelling Christ or the indwelling Buddha: that's the reality that's unfolding'.[22] She thinks of 'Christ Within' as a reality each of us is to realise within ourselves – 'a part of me and yet not me' (380). As far as Habito is concerned, Jesus Christ is not 'an external element out there that saves me' but, rather,

> that which ... enables me to die to my little self and to be born to the newness of life toward a life of unconditional love and compassion. ... that dynamic reality that empowers me to live in that way. That's what I would call 'Jesus Christ in me'.
>
> (194)

Here Jesus Christ *is* affirmed as saviour but affirmed as saviour *qua* my true self. 'The basis of the Christian life is this cross and resurrection', says Habito, but this is not just something which happened two thousand years ago, but an invitation to experience 'total self-emptying and total newness of life' as a present reality; ' ... no longer I that live, but Christ in me' (2004: 37).

Even if most Buddhists do relate to the Buddha as a teacher or guide rather than a saviour and most Christians relate to Jesus as saviour rather than merely teacher or guide, this can be seen, within the context we have been sketching, as an indication that there may be more than one way of realising the salvation demonstrated by each of these figures, i.e. salvation can come about primarily through commitment to following a set of teachings *or* primarily through ongoing love of, and entrustment to, a saviour figure who embodies ultimate reality – a love that responds to the saviour's love and compassion, and extends love and compassion to all people in accordance with the saviour's example. Peter Hodgson reasons that, 'if the teaching is completely realized in a teacher, as is believed to be the case with both the Buddha and Jesus, then the teacher and the teaching, while distinguishable, are inseparable' (2005: 150). Hence, to love and entrust oneself to the teacher as one's saviour is to love and entrust oneself to the teaching. Provided the salvific or liberative transformation occurs then does it matter precisely how one thinks about and orientates oneself towards each of these figures? As Pieris emphasises, in both Christology and Buddhology 'it is not the interpretation that saves! What saves is the *mediating reality* itself' (1988a: 133).

Not all of my interviewees thought of and orientated themselves towards Jesus Christ in the way that they thought of and orientated themselves towards the Buddha. Nor did all of them think of and orientate themselves towards Jesus Christ or the Buddha, respectively, in the same ways as one another. Reis Habito, for example, explains that although she sees both Jesus Christ and the Buddha as people who were 'completely selfless', there are also differences in how she thinks about and relates to each of them:

> the Buddha is the one who gives me the path to insight – a concrete method in looking at the self and helping me to overcome all the hindrances that the 'I' or the ego builds up, and Jesus Christ is, for me, personally, different from the Buddha because I have a more personal connection to Jesus Christ.
>
> (481)

She says she thinks of Jesus as seeking a very intimate connection with us and as asking for our love, whereas the Buddha is asking us to try out his teachings and find out for ourselves whether or not they are true (443). Hence, 'there's *bhakti* aspect in Jesus that's not there with the Buddha'.[23] She finds descriptions of Jesus as 'the lover of our souls' or as 'beloved' fitting. Reis Habito feels that these two figures function differently in her spiritual life: Jesus extends an invitation of love to which she feels called to respond and this causes her to ask herself why we respond to this invitation of love – 'is it because you are loved in the first place? Probably' (472). The Buddha, on the other hand, functions primarily as teacher of mindfulness: 'in my Buddhist practice the Buddha is very important as the one who taught all of these things' (473). Corless also felt he had a 'very warm, personal relationship' with Jesus (Corless: 63) but, unlike Reis Habito, did not feel that there was a significant difference here between how he related to Jesus and how he related to the Buddha – or, in his case, *Buddhas*, since his Buddhist practice focused on the personalities of the Buddhas (especially Amitābha Buddha and Medicine Buddha) and the Bodhisattvas (especially Tārā, Chenrezi, Avalokiteśvara and, to a lesser extent, Mañjuśrī) and not 'on some abstract awakening' (63–65).

My other interviewees tended not to place emphasis on personal *relationship* with either Jesus Christ or the Buddha, emphasising instead Christ Within or Buddha Nature (i.e. the reality represented by each of these figures which is to be realised within oneself).[24] Keenan, for example, explains that, for a long time, he had 'that kind of a *bhakti* relationship' with Jesus, and would talk to Jesus as a friend, but eventually began to feel that he was imagining Jesus' responses – that it was 'much too *imagined* a relationship' (280); 'whether it's the Buddha or Jesus … it's a question of who we are' (282): 'relationship spirituality' is 'too discriminatory and dichotomous' (251). Keenan does think of Jesus Christ as saviour (306) but tends to think of being *in Christ* or in terms of the indwelling Spirit: 'In living in Christ we mirror the Father' (306). For Keenan, the Buddha functions as 'teacher of wisdom and philosophy' (301, 307).

Appreciating differences

The interpretation of Jesus as not unique *qua* incarnation does not entail that he is not a unique incarnation in the sense of being unlike other incarnations, and the same is true of Gautama. These figures embody ultimate reality in unique ways appropriate to their particular cultural, religious, and political contexts and it is only by attending to the uniqueness of each of them that each can make a distinct contribution to one's understanding of how ultimate reality impinges on human existence. Many similarities can be identified between them, but the fact that each was situated within a particular concrete historical context means that each will bring out aspects of what it is to embody ultimate reality, and how that reality can be experienced, which might not come to the fore within the other's context. Therefore, as Harris (1999a: 94) notes, although there are many qualities shared between great religious leaders such as Jesus and the Buddha, it is the *differences* between them which present the greatest potential for growth and mutual enrichment.

Buddhadāsa sees Jesus as an excellent exemplar of mettā (loving kindness) and karuṇā (compassion) whom, if emulated, could eradicate selfishness. He was also convinced that Jesus taught a path of wisdom and karma (action) and that wisdom could be found in the teaching of Jesus Christ '*in full measure*'.[25] Santikaro Bhikkhu concludes from Buddhadāsa's reflections that Buddhadāsa saw Jesus' teaching as sufficient for realising the goal of Buddhism. 'In other words,' says Santikaro, he 'was willing to accept Jesus as an equal of the Buddha' (2001: 93). Nhat Hanh also appears, at times, to interpret Jesus Christ as being as spiritually accomplished as the Buddha: 'we can see that Jesus Christ was … enlightened. He was in touch with the reality of life, the source of mindfulness, wisdom, and understanding within Him' (1995: 37). Arguably, however, Buddhadāsa and Nhat Hanh downplay the differences

between Jesus and Gautama to such a degree that one wonders if the Jesus they affirm as equal to the Buddha would be recognisable to Christians.[26]
Both downplay the crucifixion, for example. Nhat Hanh, like many Buddhists, has difficulty with the image of Jesus on the cross:

> This is a very painful image … It does not convey joy or peace, and this does not do justice to Jesus. I hope that our Christian friends will also portray Jesus in other ways, like sitting in the lotus position or doing walking meditation.[27]

And Buddhadāsa suggests that 'whether Jesus Christ did or did not sacrifice His life is incidental to natural circumstances, and may have nothing to do with redemption whatsoever' (1967: 115). By interpreting images of Jesus suffering as not doing justice to Jesus, Nhat Hanh overlooks the possibility that the crucifixion may reveal something important about what it is to fully embody ultimate reality which may be less clearly expressed in the Buddha's historical circumstances. Relatedly, while it is true that Jesus' whole life was his teaching and not just his dying, to see Jesus' death as *incidental* is to miss a possible interpretation of his willingness to sacrifice his very life and to accept utter self-defeat on the cross without anger towards his persecutors, as Jesus' ultimate act of love, as the pinnacle of his uncompromising commitment to truth, and as crucial to his demonstration of the power of love over suffering and death.

Reis Habito sees Jesus' death on the cross as expressing something important about how ultimate reality impinges upon human existence: 'the extent of that kind of love which, to me, seems different from the love that the Buddha had in teaching for eighty years – just giving up your life like that – and so what does that mean for us?' (474). E. Dale Saunders points out, with reference to Suzuki's suggestion that the Christian focus on the cross is sadistic (Suzuki 1957: 136–37), that 'the cross to Christians, despite the fact it is an instrument of torture, symbolizes the idea of suffering for love' (Saunders 1957: 255). There is plenty of Buddhist literature associated with the Bodhisattva-ideal which extols the sacrifice of one's life for the sake of others, especially the *Jātakas* in which the Buddha, as a Bodhisattva, sacrifices his life on numerous occasions. Saunders points out that 'the Buddha who sacrifices his body for the nourishment of the tiger cubs, a scene which is often represented in Buddhist iconography with startling realism … cannot but be thought of as blood-chilling' (1957: 255). But perhaps Buddhists can appreciate a parallel here? By not dismissing too readily aspects of another figure's mediation of transcendent reality which may initially appear new or strange to one, dimensions of what is revealed by the mediator with whom one *is* familiar may come to be better understood and more deeply appreciated.

Christian pluralist, Diana Eck, cannot help feeling that images of Jesus in meditation somehow miss something important about Jesus: 'Jesus the carpenter's son did not sit peacefully on a lotus, but walked the roads of

Galilee and challenged the powers of Jerusalem with such boldness that he
ended up crucified with two thieves', writes Eck (1993: 85); 'Jesus did not
point the way out of suffering, as did the Buddha. ... Jesus took on suffering
himself ... Only in going through the valley of the shadow of suffering and
death did Jesus overcome the grip of suffering and death' (1993: 90–91).
Similarly, Corless says: '[S]uffering related to Christ is the transformation of
suffering ... one can offer one's suffering to Christ. It can be linked with his
own suffering and transformed into glory' (65). In the Buddhist tradition, on
the other hand, it's a question of seeking the cause of suffering (which is
grasping) and of letting go of suffering, says Corless (65). Reis Habito suggests that images of Jesus suffering are important to Christians because they
show us 'that God is with us in our deepest suffering and, if you ... only have a
peaceful, serene Jesus, ... people who are really in a situation of suffering – there
is nothing they can turn to' (477), and Habito sees the cross as 'an affirmation
of that unconditional love in and through our human suffering' (213).

There are Buddhists who have written appreciatively about the message of
the cross – Momozō Kurata writes, for example: 'I have come to realize the
foolishness of speaking about love without knowing that love necessarily
becomes a cross. The essence of love is sacrifice'[28] – and others have suggested
further aspects of how ultimate reality impinges upon our lives which may be
more clearly demonstrated by Jesus than the Buddha. Cabezón, for example,
believes that although there are parallels between the reformist tendencies of
Jesus and Gautama, 'as a program of social reform, Jesus' must be recognized
as the more radical and far-reaching ... We Buddhists have a great deal to
learn from this aspect of the life of Jesus'.[29] This feature of Jesus' life is
strongly emphasised in Pieris' liberation Christology, in which Jesus is construed as the symbol of a twofold ascesis, the first form of which focuses on
interior liberation, 'well symbolized by the Buddha seated under the *tree of
gnosis*' and the second of which involves

> a ruthless demand for a structural change in human relationships in view
> of the new order of love or the kingdom of God, a demand that led Jesus
> to a type of death reserved for terrorists (zealots) on what turned out to
> be the *tree of agape.*
>
> (Pieris 1988a: 134)

As Pieris sees it, a Christology based on the recognition of this double ascesis
'does not compete with Buddhology'. Rather, it 'complements it by acknowledging the *one path* of liberation on which Christians join Buddhists in their
gnostic detachment (or the practice of "voluntary poverty") and Buddhists
join the Christian *agapeic involvement* in the struggle against "forced poverty"' (1988a: 135). On this model, having both these figures at the centre of
one's spiritual life may assist the dual belonger in maintaining the fruitful
spiritual tension between the poles of agape and gnosis which represent
essential aspects of the way in which ultimate reality impinges upon human

existence (see p. 72–74). Certainly, Buddhist Christians would seem to have most to gain from their dual belonging if they focus on the uniqueness of each of these figures as well as on the similarities between them for, as Harris asserts, difference and uniqueness can be beneficial sources of mutual inspiration and mutual challenge (2003: 131).

Appreciating each figure in his uniqueness does not require dual belongers to look at Jesus only through Christian eyes or at Gautama only through Buddhist eyes. On the contrary, an advantage that Buddhist Christians have when it comes to appreciating these two mediators is that they have two lenses through which to look at each of these figures. This may help them appreciate aspects of each figure which may be less apparent to those operating with only one interpretative framework. Reis Habito, for example, explains that having a Buddhist Master and being aware of the importance of gurus in Buddhism has been helpful in leading her to explore the benefits of looking at Jesus as a spiritual Master, and this has opened up new dimensions of her relationship to Jesus. On the other side, she says she takes very seriously Christ's assertion that he is with each one of us every day, and explains that this has encouraged her to think about the Buddha, as *dharmakāya*, in a similar way: 'I know that I'm also in the Buddha's awareness ... There is ... a consciousness of the body – of the universe – that's aware of all the members' (474). Keenan has systematically attempted to interpret Jesus according to Mahāyāna Buddhist categories as opposed to the categories of Greek philosophy. This, explains Keenan, allows the dual nature of Christ to be seen to indicate 'not two essences somehow intercommunicating, but the identity of emptiness and dependent co-arising embodied in Jesus Christ' (1989b: 394), revealing facets of meaning in Christ not in focus in western thinking.[30]

Cornille is sceptical about whether what Keenan sees through his Mahāyāna lens is genuinely Christian. She suggests that if 'traditional belief in the uniqueness of Christ is constitutive of Christian faith', then it might be 'tempting to say that one who believes in Christ from within a Buddhist ... hermeneutical framework has in fact unwittingly come to belong to Buddhism, while remaining attached to a symbol which has quietly been drained of Christian meaning' (1999: 7). But, contra Cornille, I have argued that the dual belonger might legitimately reject both the notion that Jesus is unique in the sense of being the *only* incarnation of ultimate reality and the idea that belief in Christ's uniqueness is constitutive of Christian faith. However, if uniqueness is interpreted in terms of Jesus being different from all other incarnations of ultimate reality, her concern to preserve a recognition Christ's uniqueness is well-placed. Cobb, for example, suggests that Keenan's 'Christology is essentially a Buddhology. That is, Jesus is an enlightened one' (1993: 47). If this interpretation is justified, it should perhaps ring a warning bell. If through Keenan's Mahāyāna lens he sees a Jesus who reveals nothing more about what it is to be rightly orientated towards ultimate reality than that which is just as clearly revealed, if not more clearly revealed, by the Buddha, then Cornille's criticism seems justified. Keenan's reflections on the roles of Jesus and the Buddha with respect to salvation go some way to speaking to this worry: 'Jesus is the Incarnate Word of God and the Buddha is the Awakened One', says Keenan (274). However, to fully defend his Christology against the charge that it downplays Jesus' uniqueness, one would have to try to show that Keenan's understanding of what it means for Jesus to be the Incarnate Word of God is not so imbued with Mahāyāna Buddhism as to be indistinguishable from what it means for Gautama to be the Awakened One. It is by appreciating the differences between Jesus and Gautama, within the context of the acknowledgement that both are embodiments of ultimate reality, that the unique contribution of each emerges.

Unique but not superior

Buddhist–Christian dialogue is gradually producing Christians and Buddhists prepared to concede that Jesus Christ and the Buddha might be equally effective mediators of transcendent reality. For example, King points out that the Quaker institutions to which she belongs affirm the status of the Buddha as equal to Christ's (381), and the ever growing body of Christian pluralist literature indicates that the same is true of an increasing number of Christians. However, even among those who acknowledge the virtues of Jesus, *Buddhists* who are prepared to see these figures as equals are fewer and further between. If Nhat Hanh and Buddhadāsa are rightly interpreted as asserting the equality of Jesus Christ and the Buddha,[31] they appear to be unusual in so doing. Amoghavajra Karl Schmied suggests that, although most Buddhist teachers today would acknowledge 'the living Christ [as] a spiritually transforming inner reality', they would see the historical Jesus as a Bodhisattva (2001: 134), i.e. a spiritually accomplished and greatly compassionate being but one still on his way to Buddhahood.[32] It should be noted that identifying Jesus as a Bodhisattva should not *necessarily* be taken to imply a judgement of Jesus as inferior to the Buddha. The Dalai Lama, for instance, has sometimes identified Jesus as a Bodhisattva but has also made statements which seem to suggest he does see Jesus and the Buddha as equally spiritually advanced.[33] Michael von Brück suggests that the Dalai Lama sees Jesus as coinciding 'with what the Bodhisattva Avalokitesvara stands for' (2001: 167); and, as Schmidt-Leukel explains, the praise lavished upon supramundane Bodhisattvas such as Avalokiteśvara, 'is at times so extraordinary that the boundaries between them and the fully developed Buddhas blur' (2006e: 103). Nevertheless, many Buddhists who identify Jesus as a Bodhisattva *do* mean that he had not quite reached a level of attainment equal to the Buddha's.

What may be motivating Buddhist reluctance to accord Jesus the same status as the Buddha is a belief that to do so would be to interpret Jesus *as* a Buddha, and this might be felt by many Buddhists to conflict with the traditional assumption that there can only be one Buddha's teachings in the world at once. All Buddhist schools assume an infinity of worlds and hold that there have been, are, and will be many Buddhas. However, Theravadins, especially, tend to assume that there can only be one Buddha or one Buddha's teachings in a world at any one time and hence the most they tend to acknowledge is that Jesus Christ is a Bodhisattva on his way to full Enlightenment.[34] In Mahāyāna Buddhism it is not always clear whether more than one Buddha can operate within the same world at the same time. Hence, if one is a Mahāyāna Buddhist it may be easier to construe Jesus as a Buddha.

But does one have to see Jesus as a Buddha in order to see him as an embodiment of ultimate reality equal to the Buddha? Does seeing Jesus as a Bodhisattva, *from a Buddhist perspective*, necessarily prevent one from recognising that, when it comes to how Jesus functions within the Christian framework, he is indeed equal to the Buddha? In order not to betray either tradition, the dual belonger must assume that neither Jesus nor Gautama is inferior in his mediation of transcendent reality, but this does not mean he or she must place them on the same level *within* the Buddhist framework or *within* the Christian framework. Inside the Buddhist and the Christian frameworks, respectively, one of these figures inevitably occupies primary status because each of these frameworks prioritises one or other way of manifesting ultimate reality. We can describe Jesus Christ in neutral terms as an incarnation of ultimate reality, but he is also a *particular* incarnation who experienced ultimate reality as personal and encouraged his followers to think of that reality as a loving God who can be addressed as 'Abba' ('Father'). '[T]he Buddha never talked about the Father and he didn't empty himself in the same way', says Keenan; 'Christ was emptied on the cross'. To speak about the Buddha, 'you're going to have to switch contexts and languages' (279).

If we take the term 'Buddha' to apply to one who has experienced, embodied, conceptualised, and mediated ultimate reality as Siddhartha Gautama did, then to call Jesus a Buddha would indeed be misleading. Similarly, if we take the term 'Son of God' to apply to one who experienced, embodied, conceptualised, and mediated ultimate reality as Jesus of Nazareth did, then it is misleading to call the Buddha a Son of God. If these terms are applied in this way, then the acknowledgement of these figures as equal embodiments of ultimate reality does not require one to think of them both as Buddhas or both as Sons of God. Dual belongers do not have to say that the Buddha's experience and embodiment of ultimate reality was the same as Jesus Christ's, nor that the Buddha's teachings are as effective as Christian teachings in bringing about the kind of experience and embodiment Jesus exemplifies. Similarly, dual belongers do not have to say Jesus had the same experience of ultimate reality as Gautama or that his teachings are as effective in bringing about that experience. When operating within a Buddhist context, therefore, dual belongers may think of Jesus as a Bodhisattva who did not embody the same sort of enlightenment as the Buddha, provided they do not take the enlightened Buddha to be a superior mediation of ultimate reality *overall*.

Following two masters?

It could be argued that alternating between the prioritisation of Jesus Christ and the prioritisation of the Buddha shows a lack of full commitment to both. If Christian authenticity requires that one be solely dedicated to Jesus Christ and the way shown by him, and Buddhist authenticity requires that one be solely dedicated to the Buddha and the way shown by him, then the dual belonger's alternating prioritisation of each of these figures is inauthentic from both perspectives and constitutes an unacceptable division of his or her commitment and loyalty. As Dupuis says,

> [t]o be a Christian is not only to find in Jesus values to be promoted or even a meaning for one's life; it is to be given over to his person, to find in him one's way to God. Is it then possible to be, at one and the same time and on the same level, given over to Jesus and to another person, such as Gautama the Buddha, in order to trace our way to God?
>
> (2002: 64)

Schmidt-Leukel points out, moreover, that Eastern traditions, particularly, often hold that following a spiritual path implies surrendering oneself to the guidance of a specific guru or master, 'to the guidance of *one* master! It is frequently and rigorously asserted that one cannot belong at the same time to the schools of two different masters' (2009: 53). Schmidt-Leukel also suggests that ordinary experience reveals that 'it can be disastrous if in the education of children two parents don't pull together. Or even worse, if two sides constantly interfere in educational matters' (2009: 53). Cornille argues that it is only by withholding full commitment in each case that one is able to belong to two traditions at once (2008: 17). She likens multiple belonging to 'following many masters, selectively appropriating different aspects of their teachings and profiting from each of their particular charismatic gifts and/or miraculous powers' (2008: 16), despite the fact that, as far as the traditions themselves are concerned, religious belonging and spiritual growth ideally involve 'unreserved and undivided commitment' (2008: 11, 14).

However, if it is acknowledged that what gives both Jesus Christ and the Buddha their authority and makes each of them worthy of being followed is that each is an incarnation or embodiment of the one transcendent ultimate reality, then it is not obvious that entrusting oneself to the teachings of both these figures entails a fundamental division of commitment. Jesus Christ and the Buddha do not compete for the dual belonger's allegiance insofar as it is the singular pull of ultimate reality which draws him or her to both; and there is no disloyalty to Jesus Christ implied by prioritising the Buddha within a Buddhist framework, nor any disloyalty to the Buddha implied by prioritising Jesus Christ within a Christian framework, provided that at no stage one is thought to be a superior embodiment of ultimate reality *overall*. Arguably, the only one of my interviewees to fall foul of this criterion is Corless.

Corless explains that, if he thinks about Jesus while he is thinking and practising as a Buddhist, he tends to see Jesus as a Bodhisattva (66), but that when he is operating as a Christian he accords primary importance to Jesus:

> when I function as a Buddhist, the Buddha is the one who has the key to liberation and then, in the Christian tradition, Jesus is the one who has the key to salvation. So within each tradition they are of great importance and are, therefore, similar.
>
> (64)

This would be fine on the model sketched above, except that, when Corless prioritises the Buddha, he sees the Buddha as superior *overall*, and when he prioritises Jesus Christ, he sees Christ as superior *overall*: 'I don't see that a Christian could remain a Christian and put Buddha on the same level as Christ or the other way around', says Corless (67). In this respect, as in others, Corless' position seems to entail either a logical inconsistency and problematic lack of psychological integration, or frequent and ongoing changes of mind about which of these figures, and which tradition, is superior. This makes his position susceptible to the charge of disloyalty to each of these figures since each is thought to be inferior to the other roughly half of the time. Yet it is hard to see how Corless can move beyond this 'flip-flopping' with respect to his commitment to Jesus Christ and the Buddha insofar as he rejects the monocentric pluralist hypothesis; as far as Corless is concerned, when he is operating as a Buddhist, the Christian ultimate reality does not even exist.

Although she does not reject the monocentric pluralist hypothesis, Reis Habito appears somewhat reluctant to draw conclusions about the relationship in which Jesus Christ and the Buddha stand to one another. She says, for example,

> I would say Jesus had the greatest degree of transparency to God and, in the same way, I would say that the Buddha had the greatest degree of transparency to Ultimate Reality – without wanting to say whether this is the same or different; just using the language as it's used in the traditions.
>
> (483)

But if Reis Habito is not prepared to interpret each of these figures as transparent to one transcendent reality to which she is committed, then she leaves herself vulnerable to the accusation that her loyalty is divided and her commitment to both figures, less than wholehearted. Would it not be better, from this perspective, for her to explicitly integrate her commitment to each of these figures in terms of the monocentric hypothesis? This interpretation is supported by Reis Habito's own assertion that, despite the differences between how Jesus Christ and the Buddha function in her life, 'when it comes back to the one ultimate reality', she does not 'make the distinctions anymore' (474).

Of course there is still the possibility that Jesus Christ and the Buddha embody ultimate reality in mutually exclusive ways, such that it would be impossible for a single person to achieve both the liberation demonstrated by the Buddha and the salvation represented by Jesus Christ. Relatedly, even if these figures lead people to the same goal, they may lead them via mutually exclusive routes and, if this is the case, then attempting to follow both Jesus Christ's way and the Buddha's way may result in the stunted spiritual growth against which Cornille warns. It is, arguably, this kind of worry which lies behind the injunction, common in Eastern traditions, to submit to the guidance of just one guru. We will look at these issues in detail in the next chapter but, for now, let us simply note Habito's insistence that the way shown by Christ and the way shown by the Buddha are 'not two different ways' (175), and King's contention that, ultimately, these unique figures lead people along one path:

> They're unique, of course, and yet their values seem to be, ultimately, the same ... [B]oth of them point to a path ... almost no one's leading ... – have no material possessions whatsoever and don't worry about tomorrow whatsoever ... [T]hey offer very high ideals and they offer ... a profound enigma that draws us in and makes us want to try to find ... where's that coming from?
>
> (381)

No Christian will ever embody ultimate reality in precisely the way Jesus did, nor any Buddhist, in precisely the way Gautama did. Since every person's life is unique, we can assume that anyone who reaches the full blossoming of Christ Within or Buddha Nature will 'blossom' in his or her own unique way. Schmidt-Leukel asks whether it is not, in the end,

> the aim of every education, whether spiritual or ordinary, that the disciple shall eventually become a master and that the child shall not remain a child but reach its own maturity with the capacity of making its own decisions and choices and of listening, in the course of that process, quite deliberately and increasingly so to more than just one voice?
>
> (2009: 53)

In Reis Habito's case, pursuing her interest in the way of the Buddha was initially a case of learning from Master Hsin Tao. 'Am I betraying Jesus by listening more to a Buddhist master than by listening to a priest?' she wondered (2000: 19–20). Yet, praying over this question, she came to feel that Jesus was encouraging her to go, as if saying: 'You go there and listen. I will be with you' (200: 20). At the beginning, she reflects,

> you're a bit hesitant because you grew up and ... somewhere in the background you heard something about 'heathen' and 'idolatry' ... But

then you meet a Buddhist Master, where you think: this person is so much wiser than I will ever be, maybe. So how can you ever think that this is somebody you could not learn from?'

(448)

Habito describes how his encounter with Buddhism cast a new light on the quest to discover 'who I am and what I am called to be' (176). He believes that, 'in their own distinctive ways', Christ and the Buddha can be thought of as icons of the true self of every person. For him, these icons have come to be 'mutually reinforcing and mutually supportive', intensifying the force of one another in the transformation from 'little selfish being to something that is really more able to live in the light of that Mystery with a capital "M"', drawing forth 'that which is most intimately what I am, [and] calling forth its continuing cultivation and activation in my life' (176). Habito suggests that Jesus and the Buddha may also speak to other sentient beings in a similar way. If this is to happen, he says, Christians need to be open to learning from the Buddha's teachings, and Buddhists need to be open to learning from the teachings of Jesus Christ (176).

As far as Schmidt-Leukel is concerned, 'a Christian who encounters the Buddha in such a way that thereby a deep and existentially relevant truth is revealed to him or her, has simply not the option to reject the Buddha' and, if that Christian does not experience this revelation in terms of a break with his or her Christian faith (in which case he or she will convert to Buddhism), then what is required is integration (2009: 49–50). As Furneaux says, 'either one attempts to blank it out (perform a partial lobotomy)' or one engages fully with the practices and teachings in which one has found truth, such that one is 'irrevocably changed and enlarged' (2006b: 15–16). I suggest that, at the conceptual level, integration is best achieved by interpreting both figures as equally effective mediators of one transcendent ultimate reality. On this understanding, committing to a second mediator does not compromise one's commitment and loyalty to the first, since one's ultimate commitment is not to either of these figures *per se*, but to transcendent reality *through* one or both of them. Moreover, by focussing on the distinctiveness of Jesus Christ and the Buddha, as well as on the similarity between them, these figures can be experienced as complementary, each making a distinctive contribution to one's understanding of what it is to embody ultimate reality in one's own life.

Part II
Treading the path

5 Salvation or liberation

Building on the conclusions of Part I, in this chapter we will investigate how the Buddhist Christian might balance the need for integration against the need to preserve the distinctiveness of each tradition when it comes to questions about the goal of the spiritual life and, relatedly, whether practising both traditions can be legitimately understood as the following of a single spiritual path. If Buddhists and Christians have different spiritual goals – Buddhists aiming for liberation from *saṃsāra* and the eternal bliss of *nirvāṇa*, and Christians for salvation from sin and eternal communion with God and the saints in heaven – then what are Buddhist Christians aiming for? Is the dual belonger attempting, in vain, to follow two paths which lead in different directions, or is he or she somehow treading a single path to a single destination?

Two distinct aims?

The hypothesis that Buddhists and Christians, respectively, pursue different objectives – in this sense following different paths to different destinations – has been argued for by a number of contemporary thinkers, perhaps most notably S. Mark Heim. Heim offers a theory of multiple religious ends which depends on the notion that ultimate reality is complex and, therefore, capable of supporting this diversity of ends. He rejects the widespread assumption that salvation is 'an unequivocal, single reality' with which all the major religions are concerned (1995: 4). Rather than forcing the traditions into a single soteriological schema by ignoring or downplaying differences of opinion over what the nature of the goal is and how it is to be achieved, argues Heim, those differences should be understood as relating to real distinctions between achievable religious ends: Christians hope for communion with God and this end is attainable; Buddhists hope for *nirvāṇa* and this end is also attainable (1995: 151–52). As final states, however, these goals 'exclude each other', argues Heim (2001a: 288). One's religious thought and practice condition one for the achievement of a particular end and not another. In this sense, the logic of the faiths is radically disjunctive, insists Heim (1995: 169). If this theory is correct then trying to pursue the Buddhist and the Christian goal looks likely to reduce one's chances of achieving either.

However, many dual belongers will reject Heim's theory outright on the basis that, while he takes there to be various religious ends, he does not see them as equal: the Christian end is taken to be superior to all others; the Buddhist end, while achievable is a lesser aim which is not completely salvific (Heim 1995: 160; 2001b: 28, 44). The complexity of the Trinitarian God allows for a diversity of ways of approaching God, thinks Heim. It is possible to concentrate one's response to the divine 'in a particular dimension of the divine life' (2001b: 31) – often by elevating a single dimension of the relations between the three persons of the Trinity and a single dimension of their relations with the world, to the exclusion of other dimensions (2001b: 32–33) – and this is what the non-Christian traditions encourage, thinks Heim. If a channel of relation is maintained in isolation, the religious end which is realised may fall short of full salvation (2001b: 31). '[E]mptiness', says Heim, '*is* one of God's relations to creation', and 'a feature of the inner-trinitarian relations of the divine persons' (2001b: 36). Thus, Buddhists meet God 'in a particular phase of God's relation to us as creator' and this relation is real and valid (2001b: 39); but *a* relation with God 'is not the same thing as salvation' (2001b: 31). Those who achieve the Buddhist end 'are "let be" by the divine love' (1995: 166), but only the end of communion with the triune God encompasses dimensions of other fulfilments, thinks Heim; and it is the best fulfilment since it is more consistent with the true nature of the ultimate (1995: 165). Hence Heim takes non-Christian ends to be 'something to be avoided' (1995: 163), embodying, as they do, 'some measure of what the Christian regards as loss or damnation' (2001b: 31). This interpretation of the Buddhist end makes Heim's theory unacceptable from a Buddhist perspective, of course, and therefore unacceptable to the dual belonger.

Makransky's approach to religious diversity is inspired by Heim's, although he argues, from his Mahāyāna Buddhist perspective, that the Buddhist integration of aspects of engagement with ultimate reality is the 'fullest' integration (2005a: 191–92). Buddhist means for expressing the Absolute are, according to Makransky, 'uniquely liberating' insofar as

> they express a fuller knowledge of the ways that persons mistake their representations for absolute reality, not only in religious philosophy, but also in moment to moment experience and behavior ... so the Absolute, the unconditioned, radiant, empty nature of reality, may actually dawn, be realized, and embodied
>
> (2003: 358–59)

Whereas Christians believe that the Christian representation of the Absolute is closer to the Absolute than all other representations, argues Makransky (2003: 558), Buddhists understand that no word, image or expression *per se* is closer to the Absolute, and view each as 'salvifically effective, to the extent that it releases the person's most deep-seated self-grasping, harmonizes him with the ungraspable, the unconditioned reality of wisdom and compassion, and prepares him to be liberated unto it' (2003: 360). When Makransky is speaking about the results of practice in this life only, he expresses his judgement that Buddhist practice is soteriologically superior to Christian practice in terms of the notion that Buddhist and Christian practice lead to different ends (the Buddhist end being superior). When he is speaking about the results of practice across *all* one's lives (assuming, from his Buddhist perspective, that we are reborn again and again), he expresses it in terms of the notion that Buddhist and Christian practice lead people towards the same end (*nirvāṇa*), but Buddhism does so more fully than Christianity, leading people all the way there rather than just part of the way.

Of my interviewees, Corless comes closest to embracing the notion that Buddhism and Christianity orientate people towards distinct ends. 'I don't think that there's one path', he says. 'That is to say, it's not all going into the one place' (46); 'there seem to be different ends' (62). Jesus Christ and the Buddha offer remedies to problems which are, in a sense, irrelevant to one another, thinks Corless: salvation is 'overcoming the enmity or alienation between God and the soul … and liberation in the Buddhist sense is the disappearance of all conditions … one is suddenly without boundaries' (72).

Corless was, in a sense, attempting to embody in his own religious life a mutual inclusivism similar to that to which Heim's and Makransky's theories amount when held side-by-side. His Christian 'self' saw the Christian goal as superior overall and his Buddhist 'self' saw the Buddhist goal as superior overall. Indeed, at times he appears to embrace a mutual *exclusivism*, perceiving the success of the dialogue between Buddhism and Christianity within him to be dependent on each of his 'selves' being allowed to be as 'exclusivist and absolutist' as it liked (16). He explains that he wanted to see what would happen when these two apparently mutually exclusive positions interacted within him (15). However, unless one can make sense of the notion that Corless somehow really had two distinct selves, then this position must be deemed self-contradictory. Even if sense *can* be made of it – and the contradiction involved in taking each of these traditions to be superior to the other is, thereby, put to one side – it remains the case that understanding oneself as having a Christian 'self' and a Buddhist 'self' who disagree about what the ultimate spiritual fulfilment is and, hence, aim for two distinct religious ends, looks both psychologically and spiritually problematic. I suggest that many dual belongers will require a more coherent self-understanding.

Insofar as Makransky interprets Christianity as inferior to Buddhism, his theory is as unacceptable from a Christian perspective as Heim's is from a Buddhist perspective. Since neither of these inclusivist theories understands the other religion as its adherents understand it, each construing the other as pursuing an inferior goal, neither theory will satisfy those who take themselves to be authentically Christian *and* authentically Buddhist. (Remember that Corless did not see himself as Buddhist *and* Christian, but rather as a 'host' to a Buddhist and a Christian.) Both theories suppose that, eventually at least, Christian and Buddhist practice lead to distinct destinations and neither theory endorses both the Buddhist's and the Christian's claim to be orientated towards the uniquely ultimate goal.

If the goals of Buddhism and Christianity are distinct and mutually exclusive then George Bosworth Burch seems right that 'to follow more than one [religion] and so seek incompatible goals leads to religious frustration' (1972: 102) for 'a person can plant his two feet on two mountains only at the lowest point of the valley' (1972: 111). On the other hand, there's a worry for the dual belonger even if these goals are not mutually exclusive (at least insofar as one might be able to attain one and then the other), namely, that if these goals are *distinct*, then they cannot both be *uniquely* ultimate, hence either Buddhists or Christians are mistaken about the nature of their goal. Just as we concluded that in order to do justice to Buddhism and Christianity and to the demands of logic the dual belonger must say that there is only one ultimate reality, so too it would seem that, if the dual belonger is to be able to endorse both the Christian claim to be orientated towards the ultimate spiritual goal and the Buddhist claim to be orientated towards the ultimate spiritual goal, he or she must interpret Buddhism and Christianity as orientating people towards what is in some sense the same goal.

Let us consider then, whether this interpretation is justified.

A single aim?

From his monocentric pluralist perspective, Hick argues that there is indeed a sense in which Christians and Buddhists share the same aim. He contends that all the major world religions draw attention to the unsatisfactoriness of ordinary human life, attest to the possibility of a limitlessly better quality of existence, and show how that radically better possibility is to be realised (1989a: 36). Looking at Buddhism and Christianity, Hick sees variations within different conceptual schemes on a single fundamental theme:

> the sudden or gradual change of the individual from an absorbing self-concern to a new centring in the supposed unity-of-reality-and-value that is thought of as God, ... the Dharma, [or] *Śūnyatā* ... [T]he generic concept of salvation/liberation, which takes a different specific form in each of the great traditions, is that of the transformation of human existence from self-centredness to Reality-centredness.
>
> (1989a: 36)

In Christianity, says Hick, this transformation is conceived of, in St Augustine's language, as a transformation 'from a heart curved in upon itself to a heart open and responsive to the love of God' (1995: 107). In Theravāda Buddhism it is conceived of as 'the realization of the non-substantiality of the self, bringing a loss of the ego point of view and a nirvanic transformation of awareness' and in Mahāyāna Buddhism 'it's likewise a transcendence of the ego point of view, culminating in the discovery that the process of *samsara* (ordinary human life with all its pain and suffering), when experienced completely unselfcentredly, is identical with *nirvana*' (Hick 1995: 107–8).

Hick acknowledges that in the Christian case, the interpretation of salvation as essentially a transformation from self-centredness to Reality-centredness needs a little more by way of defence inasmuch as the doctrine of atonement presents this transformation as *a result of salvation* – which is constituted by Jesus Christ's death and resurrection – rather than as salvation itself (1989a: 44). As we saw in Chapter 4, the Christian tradition has within it the resources to justify a non-constitutive understanding of Jesus' role in salvation and it is a non-constitutive understanding for which Hick argues. He takes the notion that Jesus' death was necessary in order to atone for our sins to be unsupported by the portrayal of Jesus in the synoptic gospels: 'Virtually the whole weight of Jesus' message', says Hick, lies 'in the summons to his hearers to open their hearts now to God's kingdom, or rule, and to live consciously in God's presence as instruments of the divine purpose on earth'. There is, he insists, 'no suggestion in Jesus' recorded teaching that the heavenly Father's loving acceptance of those to whom he was speaking was conditional upon his own future death' (1989a: 44–45). Hick points out, moreover, that whereas the various forms of the atonement doctrine are theoretical constructs, 'the new reconciled relationship to God and the new quality of life arising within that relationship are facts of experience and observation' (1989a: 44). The reality of Christian salvation is 'no juridical abstraction but an actual and concrete change from sinful self-centredness to self-giving love in response to the divine grace' (1989a: 46).

Evidence of the idea that there is one transformation which both Christianity and Buddhism endeavour to bring about, but which they conceptualise differently, can be found in the thought of most, if not all, of my interviewees. All emphasised the fact that in both Christianity and Buddhism, the salvific or liberative transformation involves moving away from self-centredness and self-concern. Furneaux, for example, describes both traditions as fostering selflessness and an 'awareness of "not my will" ... not "I", "me" or "mine"' (126), and Reis Habito reflects that she probably thinks in terms of one transformation that is expressed differently in each tradition, a crucial aspect of which, in both expressions, is getting rid of selfishness (480). She describes salvation/liberation as 'letting go of all that hinders us to reaching this fullness of being' (479). Habito suggests that both traditions 'function in a way that liberates human beings from whatever leads to their dissatisfaction and selfishness, and that leads to the suffering of one's self and others, towards a life of liberation and of compassion' (193). Summarising his understanding of salvation/liberation, he says:

> whatever constitutes a fullness of life, ... involves a death to the ... egoic self that wants to grasp things and that wants to just hold on, and possess, and cling to things – a death to that, and a letting go of that self,

towards a way of life that is able to embrace all and be grateful for all. ...
[T]hose are aspects of what I would call salvation slash liberation.

(Habito: 191)

Habito sees this formulation as derived from both traditions and as a way of describing salvation/liberation on which both Buddhists and Christians would agree (191).

If, however, we are to be sure that understanding salvation/liberation as a single transformation from self-centredness to Reality-centredness preserves the distinctions between the traditions rather than ignoring them in order to achieve coherence, then we must address further questions about the particular ways in which Christians and Buddhists conceive of this transformation. Categorise any two things generally enough and one can say they are the same, but if the differences between what Buddhists and Christians think Reality-centredness consists in are significant, then the notion that Buddhists and Christians both seek to move away from self-centredness and towards Reality-centredness may not be enough to provide the coherence the authentic Buddhist Christian seems to need. It is the specific features of Buddhism and Christianity which constitute in each case the medium which facilitates the transformation from self-centredness to Reality-centredness and if those specific features clash with one another, then this may make a real difference to whether a dual belonger is justified in understanding himself or herself as pursuing a single aim through the practice of both these traditions.

Even if the construal of Buddhism and Christianity as concerned with a single salvation/liberation is *not* misleading, it might yet be the case that Buddhist and Christian ideas about how that transformation is to be brought about diverge significantly enough to make it difficult – or even impossible – for a single person to achieve it by practising both traditions. Griffiths argues that religions bear the relation of 'noncompossibility' one to another.

> This is because ... your religion ... by definition provides answers to (or at least a mode of addressing) those questions that seem to you of central importance to the ordering of your life. Such questions might include: Should I kill other humans? Is sensual pleasure the highest human good? Are there duties to God? – and so on. Simultaneous assent to or acceptance of different answers to these questions is both practically and logically impossible, from which it follows that simultaneous habitation of more than one religion is also impossible.
>
> (2001: 34–35)

As far as Griffiths is concerned, 'being religious ... is a monogamous affair'. Even if this is too strong, if Buddhists and Christians pursue the salvific/liberative transformation in mutually exclusive ways, then it looks as though simultaneous habitation might, in the end, hinder that transformation in one's own life. Cornille may be right when she suggests that spiritual growth depends upon complete surrender to the teachings of *just one* of these traditions (2008: 14). Indeed, despite taking the traditions to be concerned with a single salvation/liberation, even Hick suggests that one can only centre one's religious life wholeheartedly and unambiguously on *either* the Buddha's Enlightenment or on the person of Christ, not on both.[1] In other words, even if Buddhists and Christians reach the summit of a single mountain, they may arrive there by different routes and hence a choice between those routes may be necessary if an individual is to make significant progress.

Let us turn, then, to address six – somewhat overlapping – questions regarding the specific features of the Buddhist and Christian understandings of salvation/liberation in order to try to establish whether or not those understandings are compatible with one another, both in the sense of whether or not they contradict one another, and in the sense of whether or not it is possible for an individual to live according to both these understandings.

What are we being saved/liberated from?

While Buddhists and Christians both relate to one ultimate reality and both seek the freedom of salvation or liberation, contends Makransky, they seek it in different ways because they understand differently the predicament from which we require freedom. Mahāyāna Buddhists consider bondage to be the result of 'patterns of thought that construct, reify and cling to an autonomous sense of "self" and "other"'.[2] The problem is one of 'mis-knowing' (Sanskrit: *avidyā*, which Makransky defines as 'the deluded consciousness that reifies and grasps to a substantial sense of self and world, giving rise to grasping, fear and consequent suffering'[3]). Christians, on the other hand, seek salvation from sin, understood as broken relationship with God; bondage is understood to be the result of our having turned away from God. Makransky takes this difference to be one reason that Buddhist and Christian practices are differently targeted, hence one reason why these practices 'may function differently enough to make a real difference in salvific qualities realized and the type or degree of liberation attained' (2005b: 210).

Makransky is not alone in pointing out that Buddhists and Christians do not characterise our negative predicament in the same way. Hick notes that, for the Christian, our situation is one of 'fallen' existence, 'ruined by the primordial sin of our first ancestors. Inheriting their fault, or its consequences, we live in alienation from God, from ourselves and from one another'. Buddhists, by contrast, analyse our defective situation in terms of the first Noble Truth: all life involves *dukkha* ('unsatisfactoriness', including all kinds of suffering) (1989a: 32–33). Schmidt-Leukel describes the Buddhist understanding of the human predicament as 'an existential suffering under the transitoriness of existence' and the Christian understanding, as 'sin' which, like Makransky, Schmidt-Leukel understands as 'broken relationship' (2003: 273). Ninian Smart draws the contrast as one between *ignorance* and sin: the

Buddhist takes ignorance to lie 'at the root of our troubles', whereas, in Christian soteriology, 'sin is original, the primordial force which through a human *act* brings alienation from the Divine Being' (1993: 109). While these traditions agree that things are not right, contend Yandell and Netland, '[*t*]*he ways in which things are not right* is a matter of disagreement between Buddhism and Christianity. Correspondingly, there is deep disagreement about how things can be made right.' (2009: 181).

However, while Christians and Buddhists clearly do characterise the predicament from which we require freedom differently, both traditions, as Paula Cooey notes, 'clearly see egocentricity as the root of suffering and damage – an egocentricity that can be transformed' (1999: 130). Might it not be that, rather than fundamentally disagreeing, Buddhism and Christianity simply come at this problem of self-centredness from different angles?

Interpreting the Eden myth

As Harold Coward explains, after Jesus, it was Paul's understanding of the human predicament which had the most influence on the Christian tradition (2003: 31). Paul understood all humans to be in a state of sin as a result of Adam and Eve's disobedience to God; our moral corruption and physical death results from our having inherited their disobedience. Able to control neither body nor will, we find ourselves divided: the will, made to love God, has turned in upon itself in self-love. Thus, Coward explains, human nature as Paul sees it, is 'turned away from God and toward ignorance and death' (2003: 43). However, as Hick points out,

> most educated inhabitants of the modern world regard the biblical story of Adam and Eve, and their temptation by the devil, as myth rather than history; and ... far from having been created infinitely perfect and then falling, humanity evolved out of lower forms of life.
>
> (1990: 90)

This leaves Christians with a question: as Smart puts it, '[i]f the first Adam is imaginative myth, then what does Christ's salvation amount to? From what? In the light of evolutionary theory the whole story has ... to be retold' (1993: 110).

Hick suggests the human race be understood, along Irenaean lines, as evolving to perfection from a state of spiritual and moral immaturity (1990: 92). Also seeing humans as growing towards their destiny, Smart construes the fall from innocence in evolutionary terms, giving it a positive spin by interpreting it as the first stage in the rise to our becoming god-like. '[I]t is true', says Smart,

> that it was by action we were alienated from God, for we were designed as beings or processes who were physical and at the same time free to act.

This inevitably gives us a self-centredness which is the first stage to freedom.

(1993: 110)

Smart suggests that, thus interpreted, it is perfectly plausible that when it comes to giving an accurate account of our predicament, ignorance might be as important as faults in our *will*, i.e. sinfulness (1993: 110). Adrian Smith writes on the contemporary relevance of traditional expressions of Christian belief and, like Smart, sees the Eden myth as being about an inevitable 'evolution from a state of subconsciousness to a state of self-consciousness' (1996: 207). What the myth tells us, contends Smith, is that humans 'found their identity, their individuality, through recognising their separateness, their opposites. "The eyes of them both were opened and they realised that they were naked" (Genesis 3:7) describes their awakening to otherness, to difference' (1996: 197).

The question of whether this 'awakening to otherness' was an inevitable part of the evolutionary process and in some sense positive (in so far as it took us a step closer to salvation/liberation) or whether it was an entirely retrograde step from which we must return could be debated from within both a Christian and a Buddhist perspective.[4] But if the myth of the Fall is interpreted along these lines, then powerful resonances begin to emerge with the Buddhist understanding of our predicament, as stemming from the conceit 'I am', and particularly with the Mahāyāna contention that dualistic thinking is the problem. Large parts of Mahāyāna Buddhism identify our discriminative consciousness which conceptually divides the world into self and not self, me and you, this and that, good and bad, as a deluded way of apprehending reality which causes us to suffer. The Eden myth seems to echo something of this analysis but to the extent that it does, what in the myth is referred to as 'Knowledge' seems akin, ironically, to what Buddhists refer to as 'ignorance' or 'mis-knowing' (*avidyā*): it is eating from 'the tree of the Knowledge of good and evil' which causes Adam and Eve to become *self*-conscious; to experience themselves as separate from God and from each other and hence to perceive themselves as naked, to cover themselves, to hide, and, ultimately, to suffer and die. Thus the 'Knowledge' gained in the Garden of Eden seems to have similar connotations to the 'deluded consciousness that reifies and grasps to a substantial sense of self and world' referred to by Makransky as 'mis-knowing'.

This possible parallel is not lost on Buddhists. Buddhadāsa, for example, sees the underlying meaning of God's forbidding Adam and Eve to eat of the tree of the Knowledge of good and evil as being that '[a]ny suffering that arises in man is a result of his getting attached to what is considered good and evil', since this attachment 'generates desire and craving and illusion which rate as suffering itself' and 'may also account for the all-round growth of greed, anger and delusion which causes man to suffer'.[5] Having eaten the forbidden fruit, Adam and Eve underwent a spiritual death, says

Buddhadāsa, as they 'began to think in dualistic terms ... to the point that their minds were flooded by indescribable sufferings. ... Death, in the original-sin sense, occurs whenever we partake of the fruit of dualism' (1989: 149–50), and we begin to partake of this fruit, as individuals, at an early age (1989: 155). While participating in a retreat at Suan Mokkh (the Thai Monastery founded by Buddhadāsa), I attended a Dharma talk by an English monk who, ela-borating on this theme, asserted that what we need to realise is that *we are in the Garden of Eden now*; we just don't see it. As a Pure Land Buddhist would put it, we are in the Pure Land now.

The contention that our task is to realise that we are, metaphorically speaking, in the Garden of Eden now, chimes in with those strands of both traditions which emphasise that the spiritual task is not so much a quest for salvation/liberation, as a realisation and acceptance that we are already saved/liberated (strands strongly emphasised by a number of my interviewees). In Mahāyāna Buddhism we find the notion that there is no difference between *saṃsāra* and *nirvāṇa* and the idea that our minds are originally pure insofar as our truest nature is Buddha Nature. Through greed, hatred, and delusion we have come to perceive the world dualistically and have become separated from our true nature. Liberation, therefore, is the realisation of emptiness in which one discovers what one has always been. From a Christian perspective, the Genesis myth can be read as telling us that our original nature – 'original' in the sense of truest or most fundamental, rather than first – is pure. Habito argues that the term 'original sin' is, in this sense, 'a gross misnomer' since 'our original condition is a state of grace. Being the image of God is what's "original" in our created being – not sin' (2006: 17).

King sees both traditions as helping people realise and develop that which is innate in them (393). As a Quaker, she does not think in terms of human sinfulness but in terms of the Light Within, emphasising that God (rather than Adam) is inside us (2003a: 11). The task is to live in ever greater accor-dance with the Spirit or Christ Within, thinks King; from a Buddhist per-spective, it is 'to continue ... developing your own Buddhahood which is your birthright' (393). She notes that, in both traditions, it is expected that as one gets more and more in touch with Christ Within or one's Buddha Nature, one will increasingly exhibit selflessness, love of others, inner peace, fearlessness and so on (372): 'it's not a matter of liberation implying this whole separation and escape – that's not the right metaphor anymore ... *growth* is the right metaphor, development' (393). Habito also speaks of 'Christ nature' and 'Buddha-nature' as two different expressions which point to that which we, in some sense, already are and which we 'are continually called to cultivate and activate more fully in our lives'.[6] Similarly, Reis Habito says that from a Christian perspective she sees people as having a dimension that is timeless and 'already saved'; our task is the realisation of this dimension 'in our very limited kind of being'. She regards this as a process which is also recognised in Buddhism, though from a Buddhist perspective she 'might express it dif-ferently' (483). These reflections appear to be supported by Spae's assertion that Buddhism and Christianity 'converge in their soteriological intentions: they want to save ... man from himself so that he might become his "true self," which Christian mystics have identified with God, and Buddhist mystics with Nirvana' (1980: 39).

Habito thinks of our predicament in terms of our need for healing and finds it helpful to have two different but mutually reinforcing perspectives on our 'cosmic woundedness'. He sees this woundedness as manifest in our alienation from our fellow human beings, from the natural world, and also from our own selves. We are preoccupied with our 'selfish goals based on our idealised and false self-images', says Habito. He suggests that, when we recall the Buddhist characterisation in terms of *dukkha* – 'a state of dis-location, dis-ease, and of being out of touch with being itself – we can perceive a basic resonance with the Christian understanding of cosmic woundedness due to sin' (2006: 17–18).

Perhaps thinking about our predicament as one of broken relationship with God and others helps bring out the need to transform our relationships; the emphasis here will be on love, both for God and for other people (inspired by Jesus' demonstration that the power of love transcends suffering and death). Thinking about our predicament in terms of 'grasping to substantiality within duality' (Makransky 2005b: 210), on the other hand, might help bring out the need to see clearly the nature of reality so as to eradicate grasping and attachment; the emphasis here will be on wisdom, which dispels the ignorance that binds us to suffering and death. In this way Buddhism and Christianity can be seen as focussing, not so much on different problems, but rather on different *aspects* of the same problem.

Is grace the main principle that frees people?

However, even if there are ways of understanding Buddhist and Christian characterisations of the predicament from which we require salvation/liberation which resonate with – and even complement – one another, Makransky argues that Buddhists and Christians disagree over the main principle which brings about the salvific/liberative transformation. Christians think it is God's grace, says Makransky, whereas (Mahāyāna) Buddhists think it is non-conceptual, non-dual realisation of emptiness, and this realisation requires properly targeted practices; it is not simply bestowed on people by virtue of the nature of ultimate reality, i.e. salvation requires more than simply grace (2005a; 2005b).

As we noted in Chapter 4, the question of reliance on practice versus reliance on grace – or 'self-power' versus 'other-power' – is debated *within* both Buddhism and Christianity. Indeed Makransky acknowledges this and notes that in Buddhism, as in Christianity, 'there can be no freedom from bondage unless something transcendent intervenes. Only someone beyond such conditioning can point the way beyond it'. For Buddhists, that someone is the Buddha (2005c: 9). Makransky acknowledges too that the development of virtues through Buddhist disciplines does not occur 'by persons relying upon the inclinations of their egoic selves' (2005c: 11), and that in Pure Land Buddhist traditions, Amida's name is repeated 'with utter faith and receptivity, relying *totally* upon the Buddha's power of liberation' (2005c: 13, my emphasis). Indeed, Makransky explains that in his own Tibetan tradition, as in various Pure Land and Zen traditions, 'all power for practice is understood to derive from the power of the unconditioned itself' (2005c: 14). Perhaps, then, Makransky would agree with Corless when he asserts that 'there's really no such thing as total self-power in Buddhism'.[7]

The debate between Pure Land Buddhists and Zen or Tibetan Buddhists then, would seem to be one of how much can be achieved through reliance upon ultimate reality alone, and how much through practice, i.e. the debate concerns the right balance. When we turn to Christianity we find a parallel debate concerning the precise relationship and balance between what God does to bring about our salvation and what we must do. As Burch puts it: 'There is a difference of opinion as to whether divine grace is irresistible, that is, whether God throws us a rope or lassoes us' (1972: 33). This debate within both traditions appears to reveal that the supposed contrast between Buddhism and Christianity regarding the main liberative principle is a matter of emphasis rather than a serious disagreement: Christians, *in general*, rely more heavily upon the nature of reality than do Buddhists who, *in general*, rely more heavily upon specific practices.

However, it would seem that the contrast Makransky wishes to draw between Buddhism and Christianity is not simply a question of different ideas about how much we can rely on ultimate reality, and how much we must do ourselves. His point seems to be that, from a Mahāyāna perspective, it is non-conceptual, non-dual realisation of emptiness which liberates people, and this realisation can only be gained in full measure through properly targeted practices. '[T]he results of spiritual practice depend not only on the nature of ultimate reality but also upon the ways that specific practices render persons receptive to different aspects and qualities of that ultimate reality', insists Makransky (2005b: 210). Proper methods are needed for the development of the 'wisdom-emptiness' aspect of participation in the ultimate reality, which is 'the centre of soteriology, the very source of liberation' (2005a: 195); ultimately, 'fullest realization of ultimate reality (active *nirvāṇa*, *dharmakāya*) is fullest, non-dual insight into the *emptiness of all conceptualized appearances* and active compassion for all who have not realized the freedom of such insight' (2008: 61). Christians understand redemption to come 'mainly though the power of God's grace in communion' (2005a: 196), says Makransky, but while reliance on God's grace, expressed through the life of the Church, the practice of the sacraments, prayer, and so on can certainly increase love, devotional communion, and even wisdom to a limited extent, reliance on grace does not allow for the *full* development of wisdom which sees the non-dual, emptiness of all phenomena (2005a: 194–99).

As far as Makransky is concerned, then, the transformation from self-centredness to Reality-centredness depends inexorably on fully developed wisdom. Hence, we must look at whether he is right that there is a significant contrast between the traditions in this regard.

What is the most crucial aspect of the transformation?

There are various criteria offered within Buddhism for the judgement of truth and falsity in matters of religion. One fundamental set of criteria is the Noble Eightfold Path. Where the Noble Eightfold Path can be found, says the Buddha, there will be Enlightened ones; where the Noble Eightfold Path cannot be found, there will be no Enlightened ones (*Dīgha-Nikāya* 16). The eight elements of the Path (right view, right intention, right speech, right action, right livelihood, right effort, right mindfulness, right concentration) are traditionally understood as falling into three basic categories: wisdom (*prajñā*), morality (*sīla*) and concentration or meditation (*samādhi*). Buddhists who make a positive assessment of Christianity tend to do so because they believe the teachings of Jesus to be supportive of morality. But, when it comes to the criteria of wisdom and concentration/meditation, there is much more reservation. Buddhadāsa is very unusual in suggesting that Christianity may contain the requisite degree of concentration, though in a different guise from that in which it appears within Buddhism: '*What is generally known as faith,*' he says, '*does in fact imply a concentrated mind*' (1967: 40). He believed that the Sermon on the Mount, if practised, would be more than enough for the attainment of emancipation.[8]

For Makransky, it is the criteria of wisdom and concentration/meditation which prevent him from seeing Christianity as equal to Buddhism in terms of its ability to bring people to full liberation.[9] Indo-Tibetan and Zen traditions have striven to direct practitioners in cultivating in their own experience the wisdom of emptiness and non-duality since these traditions take the development of this wisdom to be the most crucial aspect of the salvific/liberative transformation. Christian traditions, argues Makransky, 'focus intensively on the love and communion aspects of participation in the ultimate reality', whereas Mahāyāna traditions include these aspects while also focussing more intensively than Christianity on the wisdom-emptiness aspect 'as the centre of soteriology, the very source of liberation' (2005a: 195). Wisdom practices foster direct insight into the lack of own-existence; and, as one realises the thought-madness of everything, the deepest patterns of self-grasping are eradicated. This wisdom, explains Makransky, in turn, informs Buddhist teachings of unconditional compassion and love: 'Deepest compassion', says Makransky, 'is non-dual awareness suffused with a tone of compassion that has transcended even the distinction of "self" and "other"' (Makransky 2005a: 196).

For Christians, salvation implies the repair of the human-divine relationship which is witnessed in a person's deep participation in God's unconditional love (*agape*) which pervades all creation. However, says Makransky, for the Christian, 'such love is a love within relatedness, mirroring the relations of

the Trinity, involving distinctions between poles of relatedness that are irreducible, not non-dual' (Makransky 2005a: 196). 'If, as most Christians are
taught,' says Makransky,

> someone relates to ultimate reality as a personal God most fully accessed
> by communing with Him through Christ in the Spirit, then the con-
> ceptualized poles of separation between oneself and God necessary for
> such communion are grasped as ultimate. The aim is not to transcend the
> conceptualization of such a dualism between self and God in Christ, but
> to adhere to that dualism as ultimate.
>
> (2008: 62)

Makransky and Heim, though taking different views of which tradition is
superior as a result, agree on this distinction. Whereas, for Makransky, it is
non-dual awareness which is the crucial aspect of the salvific/liberative transformation, according to Heim, the dimensions of perfected relationship and
communion with God are the most crucial aspects. Heim takes right relationship with God and others to be the highest goal and insists that essential
to this ultimate end is love within duality (Heim 2001a: 203–4); '[t]he salvation
Christians anticipate', insists Heim, 'is a personal communion of distinct
creatures with God their maker' (Heim 2001a: 203). Makransky and Heim
agree that in the final analysis, their soteriological goals are incompatible with
each other.

An ultimate dualism between self and God?

However, the characterisation of Christianity as resolutely affirming and
accepting attachment to an ultimate dualism between self and God is certainly not one which reflects the experience of most of my interviewees, none
of whom would – I think – recognise their aim, as Christians, as adherence to
the 'dualism between self and God … as ultimate'. It is tempting to conclude
that this is because their Buddhism, rather than their Christianity, is normative
with respect to this issue, and perhaps there is some truth in this. However, it
should also be recognised that the findings of our previous chapters suggest
that the characterisation of Christianity as resolutely affirming and accepting
attachment to an ultimate dualism between self and God may – on *Christian*
grounds – be considered misleading.[10]

Heim's position is based on ideas regarding the inner relations of the Trinity, but if the Godhead (God in God's self) is understood to be conceptually
transcendent, then it must be admitted that we are incapable of knowing
whether or not there are irreducible poles of relatedness within the Godhead
(which saved existence must necessarily reflect). In Chapter 4, we saw that, for
Haight, it is the economic Trinity (which concerns God's saving action
through Jesus) which is essential to Christianity and this can be preserved
without having to endorse 'the speculative language of how three persons

exist and are related within the life of the Godhead' (Haight 1992: 285). Moreover, the idea that all people have the divine within them as Spirit suggests that the poles of relationship between ourselves and God might not be absolute and irreducible, but rather that God is on a continuum with us – greater than, but not separate from us (see p. 70–72); God is the One in whom 'we live and move and have our being' (Acts 17:28). Remember also Rahner's warning that the difference between God and the world is 'radically misunderstood if it is interpreted in a dualistic way' (1978: 62). Further, if a Christology is accepted according to which Jesus, *qua* divine incarnation, is different from other human beings in degree rather than kind, then there may be soteriological inferences yet to be drawn from such statements as 'I and the Father are one' (John 10:30). If this statement faithfully expresses something of Jesus' experience, then perhaps this experience is available to all who overcome alienation from God. Might this experience not be akin to what Mahāyāna Buddhists would describe as an awareness of non-duality?[11]

Certainly, in the mystical tradition we find accounts of monistic or unitive experiences in which the poles of separation between self and God are not experienced as ultimate. Schmidt-Leukel points out that, although when it comes to the criteria of wisdom and concentration/meditation, 'most Buddhists detect a far-reaching deficit in Christianity', the exception to this is its mystical or contemplative tradition.[12] Makransky, however, argues that when Mahāyāna Buddhists talk about the realisation of emptiness as the end of the path to liberation, 'emptiness' (*śūnyatā*) should not be understood as 'an apophatic union with God attained by rare persons whose special vocation is mysticism'. Rather, what Buddhists mean by emptiness, says Makransky, is 'the insubstantial nature of all aspects of ordinary experience' (2005a: 195).

But perhaps Makransky is too quick to dismiss the possibility that the Buddhist's direct awareness of emptiness and the Christian's transformative experience of apophatic union with God are not relevantly equivalent. Certainly it is very difficult to make judgements of equivalence when comparing experiences within different traditions on the basis of what is said about them within those traditions, but can it not be equally difficult to be sure that two experiences are *not* in some sense equivalent? Furneaux, for example, is convinced that Buddhism and Christian mysticism come together on the issue of non-duality:

> I *know* that Buddhism and Christianity share certain things that other religions don't and it's those kinds of areas which inform the way I see things ... It's all around that whole issue of non-duality; that's where it all comes together: non-separation and non-duality and the way that Christianity and Buddhism try to work with that.
>
> (104)

She takes the overcoming of duality to be connected to what is referred to in Christianity as 'dying to self' (104).

Considering it the most crucial aspect of liberation, Buddhism has undoubtedly focussed more closely than Christianity on what Makransky calls the 'wisdom-emptiness' aspect of participation in ultimate reality (2005a: 195); whereas in Christianity, love (*agape*) has been emphasised as the most crucial aspect of salvation. Hence, Buddhism has developed more systematic methods for overcoming habitual tendencies to cling to conceptual constructs as if they captured reality. Insofar as this is the case, Buddhist methods might, potentially, be helpful to Christians. But this is not to say that the 'wisdom-emptiness' aspect of participation in ultimate reality is absent from Christianity; it may be present in a different guise.

'Wisdom', reflects Habito, from a Christian perspective,

> is the way of looking at things from the point of view of God's love. Looking at … everything around us – not as an object out there and I'm here separate from it – but from the standpoint of God's love where what I am is also something that's seen in God's love.
>
> (1996: 10)

He sees Zen practice that aims at the realisation of non-duality and emptiness as helping solve the problem of alienation from God: it helps us to 'see the miracle of ordinariness in daily life' (2006: 34); as Suzuki puts it, 'Zen … makes us live in the world as if walking in the Garden of Eden' (1949: 45). As we saw in Chapter 3, Reis Habito's experience of cracking the mu *kōan* (recognised as a genuine *kenshō* by Yamada Roshi, i.e. as an experience of non-dual awareness) was, from her Christian perspective, a profound experience 'of what might be called God's love' (446): 'the walls between yourself and God, or the walls between yourself and the Absolute – they become more transparent' (499). There is, she explains, the more literal level of truth at which one begins – 'where you are down here and God is out there … and you direct your devotion to something that is outside yourself' – and then there is another level, the level which Mahāyāna Buddhists call 'non-duality' (480). At this level, 'there is no outside and inside, so to speak; there is no self and other … you can't distinguish anymore' (480). 'These things are difficult to describe', she says; 'in the final result, it all depends on interpretation: on the words that we use for certain experiences' (481–82).

Perhaps Makransky should be more open to the possibility that what Mahāyāna Buddhists describe as the 'realisation of emptiness' might be described by Christians in different terms. In response to reflections such as Reis Habito's, however, Makransky might argue that there is a difference between claiming, as he does, that the duality of self and other is overcome in the salvific/liberative transformation, and claiming that at some stage in that transformation (or at least in some salvific/liberative experiences) it simply becomes *difficult to distinguish* between self and other. It could be that although some Christians can agree with Buddhists about what is experienced (i.e. they agree on the *phenomenology* of this aspect of the salvific/liberative transformation), they cannot agree that the transformation involves completely overcoming any distinction between ourselves and ultimate reality when this is interpreted as a *metaphysical* claim, since this claim, it might be argued, is inconsistent with the Christian understanding of the eschaton. In other words, Buddhism and the Christian mystical tradition converge to some extent in their accounts of the experience of practising the path, but they do not agree about what the final destination of that path will entail. Let us turn then to the eschatological question, before considering what the differing salvific/liberative emphases of Buddhism and Christianity might mean for how one should live in the here and now.

Where does the transformation end?

For the most part, Christian soteriological thinking does seem to assume that, in the eschaton, a person, even if radically transformed, in some way retains his or her individual personhood as distinct and separate from God and other persons; as Heim would put it, the 'middle' realities of ordinary life (persons, relations, community, communion) 'carry over into salvation' (2001a: 203–4). This does not seem to be the Buddhist understanding. Burch argues that '[w]hatever nirvana is, … it is at least clear what it is not. It is not continued existence as an individual. Whatever, if anything, is preserved in nirvana, individuality is lost' (1972: 72). Smart's portrayal of the Buddhist understanding is somewhat more nuanced, but he also sees a contrast between Buddhism and Christianity here. In Buddhism, says Smart, upon attaining liberation

> [y]ou see the immortal place, you gain the light, and yet the 'you' of you is lost. In losing individuality you gain release from rebirth. This is not like the full flowering of your gleaming personality which suffuses life with God in heaven.
>
> Empty impermanence and a flux of events, empty personhood through a combination of bundles of events, rebirth and non-individual liberation: these are very different ideas from those which have run through mainstream Christian thought.
>
> (1993:18)

Do these differing ideas imply that, however much shared experience there may be along the way, the end of the Christian path and the end of the Buddhist path are distinct?

Open-ended eschatologies pointing in the same direction

Let's first try to get a better grip on what Christians mean by 'heaven'. At its most basic, explains Hick, the notion of heaven is the notion 'that human personalities, made perfect, will enjoy an existence which is totally oriented to God' (1976: 202). However, this has tended to be expressed either in terms of the worship of God or in terms of 'a beatific vision of the divine Reality' and, as Hick points out, there's a tension between these two kinds of expression.

The first is derived from the book of Revelation which speaks of a new Jerusalem in which God is present with his people in Christ and worship takes the form of a community of people living together in the holy city and fully responsive to God. According to this understanding, the saints persist forever as separate and distinct individuals and the social and interpersonal character of human existence is perfected in this ideal society. But this notion, Hick points out, is fraught with difficulties, not least that it is hard 'to conceive of a worthwhile human existence in a situation in which there can be no needs, lacks, problems, perils, tasks, satisfactions or, therefore, purposes' (1976: 203).

The other expression of heaven, in terms of the beatific vision of the Godhead, Hick describes as '[t]he notion of a direct and transforming awareness of the divine Reality' (1976: 204–5). This idea begins with Jesus' statement 'Blessed are the pure in heart, for they shall see (*opsontai*) God' (Matthew 5:8). It is also evident in Paul's speaking of seeing face to face (1 Corinthians 13:12), and in the assertion that the saints in heaven will see (*opsontai*) the face of God (Revelation 22:4). It becomes an eschatological theology first in the hands of Irenaeus in the second century and is later developed by Aquinas. Aquinas takes the beatific vision to involve 'seeing all things in God and seeing them not successively but in total simultaneity of eternity' (Hick 1976: 205–6).

Hick gives various examples of Catholic writing in which the beatific vision is described in 'a profound and open-ended way', one of which is an analogy used by some Christian mystics:

> Throw a bar of iron into a blazing furnace and leave it there till it is molten metal in the midst of the fire, and the eye can no longer see the iron. As that iron knows the fire, so shall we know God. Our innermost being will thrill and throb in unison with God's life, and we shall be fully conscious of it.
>
> (1976: 206)

Does the iron bar retain its individuality here? If so, in what sense, given the heat of the fire burns within it and its boundaries cannot be determined? Is self-other duality overcome here or does one merely cease to be able to distinguish between oneself and God? Given that this description of the beatific vision gestures at an experience which is thought to occur beyond death and beyond all our current imaginings, it is not clear that we can ever be sure of the answers to such questions. As Knitter says, 'we really don't know what we're talking about'; 'Maybe the mystery of my life after my death will be so unexpectedly and wonderfully different', he suggests, 'that it will be beyond anything I can now describe as "my" or "me"' (2009: 75, 77). It is easy to sympathise with Hick's conclusion that while 'Christian thought about heaven, as the final state of the blessed, has been immensely varied', it has always tended 'at its best to be deliberately reticent and open-ended' (1976: 202).

Certainly, Buddhism and Christianity have tended to differ in emphasis here. As Hick acknowledges, Christianity's eschatological emphasis, 'has been firmly upon the value of the individual human soul, as an object of God's love, and upon the perfecting of finite personality and its eternal preservation in the divine presence' (1976: 426). This is in contrast to the emphasis of Buddhism, in which

> the individual personality is seen as merely a temporary bundling together of transitory elements. So far from the human ego being of permanent significance, the technique of salvation consists in a dismantling of this bundle by negating the craving for existence which holds it together.
>
> (Hick 1976: 427)

Hick argues, however, that the eschatologies of both traditions are 'pointers beyond the known which do not profess to delimit the boundaries or describe the contents of that towards which they point'. They 'offer convergent indications, each pointing beyond our present human experience and yet each pointing in the same direction'. Buddhists and Christians, he argues, look 'towards an ultimate human destiny which ... can only be conceived in the most general terms; and ... we observe these lookings to be oriented in the same direction' (1976: 427–28).

My interviewees clearly saw Buddhism and Christianity as effecting the same orientation. Following these two traditions is not a question of being lead in 'two different directions', insists Habito (161);

> Buddhists use the term '*nirvāṇa*' and Christians use the term 'heaven' but, if we get stuck on the conceptual imagery of these terms, then we will be limiting ourselves ... [I]t's something that keeps pointing beyond ... [I]t is ... a way of expressing ultimate destiny.
>
> (195)

Keenan says that he 'wouldn't mind attaining *nirvāṇa*' since *nirvāṇa* is the cessation of greed, hatred, and delusion which, as a Christian, he is aiming for anyway (304). Similarly, Reis Habito reflects that *nirvāṇa* is the 'complete extinction of ignorance, hate, and greed', and that heaven is the 'complete end to sin and complete happiness'; '[s]o how can we still qualify those states; if they are the same or if they are different?', she asks; '[t]hey're described differently but, to me, personally, they seem to point to the same reality' (484). She suggests that 'the smaller self becomes, the bigger God becomes in us', but asks,

> to be filled with God or to be filled with emptiness ... is this the same or is this different? ... [this] is the question that's so hard to answer.

> But ... both paths tell me that clinging to a very limited egoistic form of
> self ... – of 'I' – is wrong. So you have to enlarge that or let it go: however
> you want to express that.
>
> (480)

She reflects that 'salvation and liberation probably means to be in full communion with everything that is. The Buddhists ... have ... a Chinese expression –
'tong': just complete unity and interconnection, and I think that I probably
see that also as the Christian salvation' (467).

Even Corless, despite contending that Buddhism and Christianity 'may be
going in different directions' (14), when asked explicitly about the eschaton,
describes the beatific vision as a going up to love, as 'contact with the love
that moves the sun and the other stars' and says that this is true not only of
heaven but also of *nirvāṇa*, provided the wisdom aspect is also given emphasis
(74). He explains that over time he has come to believe that there's 'a progress
to a greater maturity, ... a progress to the light' (20). In connection with this,
he mentions an experience he once had in which he felt he was 'contacting a
realm ... of absolute love and wisdom and energy' (21). Corless is prepared to
affirm that Buddhism and Christianity have 'very similar' goals; it just seems
to him that 'the love of the Christian tradition is communion with God
and the love of the Buddhist tradition is sort of unconditional love with
everything; it's not directed towards a God' (75). At this point, however, he
reflects on the inadequacy of words: 'we're going to pass over into some other
condition with no conditions and we cannot explain it in words. ... [W]e ...
can't understand unless we're there' (75). Insofar as Corless sees the central
message of both traditions as unconditional love and wisdom, he does not
rule out the possibility that the destinations towards which these traditions
orientate people may turn out to be the same (63).

Reserving judgement and experiencing equality

Hick too thinks we are simply not justified in making any descriptive assertions about the ultimate state insofar as it is probably beyond our present
conceptual and imaginative capabilities:

> I believe that there is indeed a final state, a fulfilment of the project of human
> existence, beyond this life, perhaps beyond many lives. However, I do not
> profess to know what it is like. ... Following the Buddha's teaching about
> the 'undetermined questions', I also hold that we do not need to know
> now the answer to these eschatological questions in order to attain, or receive,
> the radically new state of existence which constitutes salvation/liberation.
>
> (1995: 72)

Provided dual belongers find that Buddhism and Christianity orientate them
in a single direction, is it necessary that they decide whether the Buddhist or

the Christian characterisation of the eschaton is most accurate in order to be able to move in its direction through their practice of both traditions? Even Makransky's and Heim's inclusivist views leave room for the possibility that Buddhist and Christian practice might be, to some extent, mutually supportive of progress towards the goal.[13] However, while Makransky's and Heim's inclusivism commits them to the assumption that there will come a point at which there is further progress to be made and only one tradition able to facilitate this progress, those who are committed to both traditions cannot share this assumption. Buddhist and Christian authenticity may afford the dual belonger a degree of agnosticism regarding the precise nature of the final goal, but it does not allow for the assumption that either one of these traditions is superior to the other with respect to the achievement of that goal. If I assume that Christianity will, in the end, be more efficacious than Buddhism, then, arguably, I am not an authentic Buddhist; likewise, if I assume Buddhism will, in the end, be more efficacious than Christianity, then, arguably, I am not an authentic Christian.

Hick argues that when we compare Buddhism and Christianity in terms of the effect of each on its adherents (by comparing the saints of each on the basis of the shared criterion of love or compassion), we find that there are no grounds to judge that either one is more efficacious than the other with respect to effecting the salvific transformation in this life (1993: 137). Makransky criticises Hick's criterion arguing that, '[t]o equate the world's religions in their results ... based on evidence of a broad similarly in the qualities of the world's saints is too rough a criterion'; it does not give us sufficient grounds on which to judge them to be equally efficacious (2008: 52). However, Hick is at pains to stress, 'not how easy it is, but on the contrary how difficult it is, to make responsible judgements in this area' (1993: 138); as he explains, all he intends to establish is

> the modest and largely negative conclusion that, so far as we can tell, no one of the great world religions stands out as more salvific than the others. Certainly the onus of proof lies upon anyone who wishes to claim that one particular tradition (presumably their own) stands out as uniquely superior.
> (Hick 1993: 139)

It may be unreasonable, as Makransky suggests, to assert that the world's religious traditions are equally efficacious, but is it not also unreasonable to assert that one tradition is more efficacious than all the others? It is far from clear that one could ever amass sufficient knowledge and experience to enable one to make this judgement. A number of my interviewees appeared to share this conclusion.

King, for example, employs a version of Hick's saintliness criterion: 'saintly behaviour – produced in all the major traditions ... [is] the only evidence that I have access to so that's what I go by and there are people who are so impressive in every tradition' (371). But King, nevertheless, feels that assessing the traditions on this basis is not enough to establish that they guide people to the same end or that they are soteriologically equal; all it allows her to say is that no one tradition stands out as superior to all the others. She explains that one of her most fundamental commitments is to be honest with herself about what she knows and what she does not know (404). Asked what she takes the eschaton to be, she is emphatic: 'I have no idea. No idea' (395); 'I can't really affirm definitely, definitively they're all headed to the same place; I can't affirm that until I'm there. I don't see how that's possible' (371–72). She reflects, however, that both Buddhism and Christianity 'inspire', and

> set a very high bar of what we aspire to ... so wherever one is, they call one on, to keep trying to take further steps; they both have different forms of methods and support – there are community supports ... , there are meditative structures and practices; there are moral norms ... and the example of illustrious people who have gone before. So there are encouragements and incitements and concretely helpful structures and practices which are both efficacious for me.
>
> (371)

Keenan says that he imagines that both Buddhism and Christianity are efficacious but has 'no way of knowing' about their long-term effectiveness: 'will they save you after death? I'm alive', says Keenan. He feels he cannot accept the word 'equally' regarding their relative efficacy, but qualifies this, saying, 'I would certainly accept the word "effective" simply because I've seen the effects' (253). Reis Habito, although also feeling unable to judge that they are equally efficacious with respect to salvation/liberation, says she thinks that the possibility of salvation/liberation is 'there in both religions' (465). Similarly, although Habito is also reluctant to say that Buddhism and Christianity are equally efficacious (167), he affirms that each has a message which is salvific and liberative: 'Now, how do those messages of salvation and liberation relate to one another? That's what I'm trying to continue to discern and reflect on and trying to live also in my own life' (167–68).

Since they did not feel that they could assert with certainty that Buddhism and Christianity are equally efficacious with respect to final salvation/liberation, a number of interviewees were reluctant to identify themselves as pluralists (see Chapter 1, note 38), apparently assuming that pluralism would require the certainty they lacked. Reis Habito says, for example, 'I have ... a little bit of difficulty with the term "pluralism" because I feel it's not up to me to say that Buddhism and Christianity are equally efficacious. How can I judge that?'.[14] Crucially, however, what distinguishes the position of most of my interviewees from Makransky's or Heim's inclusivist positions is that they do not *deny* the salvific/liberative equality of Buddhism and Christianity; they just do not feel they have sufficient evidence to positively *affirm* it.

Perhaps a distinction could helpfully be drawn here between what we might call 'hard pluralism' and 'soft pluralism': 'hard pluralism' would be the claim about the efficacy of the traditions, i.e. that Buddhism and Christianity are equally effective with respect to final salvation/liberation; 'soft pluralism' is the negative epistemic claim that it is not possible to know whether hard pluralism is true or false (hence, it is neither affirmed nor denied). With the possible exception of Corless, whose position is complicated by his at least partial rejection of bivalent logic, and perhaps also with the exception of Furneaux who, as we will see in the next chapter, appears to regard Buddhism as more efficacious than Christianity, my interviewees seemed to be soft pluralists with respect to these traditions. This position leaves open both the possibility that Buddhism and Christianity are equally efficacious and the possibility that one will turn out to be superior.

Perhaps Makransky or Heim will turn out to be right that to progress beyond a certain point on the path, one of these traditions will prove to be the more adequate vehicle. But notice, if any of my interviewees reach this conclusion, they will cease to be full and authentic adherents of *both* traditions, one being considered inferior to the other. But for as long as both are experienced to be equally efficacious, neither tradition is undermined since neither's claim to full salvific/liberative efficacy is denied. The Dalai Lama takes it to be possible for Christians to take Bodhisattva vows (1996b: 157–58), and 'to progress along a spiritual path and reconcile Christianity with Buddhism'. But, he says, 'once a certain degree of realization has been reached, a choice between the two paths will become necessary' (1996b: 155). Regardless of whether the Dalai Lama is right that a choice will at some stage be necessary (and note that he is speaking from his experience as a Buddhist, not from experience of practising both Buddhism *and* Christianity over time), his position indicates that, even if one assumes a choice *will* be necessary, it is nevertheless possible to accept that a person can be fully and beneficially committed to the practice of both traditions for as long as both are found to be helpful. Makransky would presumably agree that what is crucial from the Buddhist perspective is not that people recognise particular Buddhist practices as essential to the achievement of salvation/liberation, nor that they recognise those practices as superior to the practices of other traditions, but that they actually *engage* in those practices and experience them as salvific/ liberative in the here and now. After all, it is the practices which Makransky takes to be liberative, not the interpretation of the significance of those practices for which he argues.

Logical, psychological and spiritual coherence requires dual belongers to understand both traditions as orientating them in a single direction and, as we have seen, this is how most – if not all – of my interviewees do understand these traditions; and this understanding seems justified from a Buddhist and a Christian perspective. Moreover, dual belongers seem required by the demand for Buddhist and Christian authenticity, to see neither tradition as inferior to the other with respect to final salvation/liberation; and their soft pluralism means most of my interviewees also meet this requirement. Their position does involve a degree of uncertainty about what the end of the path they are treading will entail but, as we will now see, this uncertainty looks unproblematic from the perspective of both traditions inasmuch as it is arguably the case that neither Buddhists nor Christians should be concerning themselves with speculation about the end of the path.

Focusing on the present

Hick points out that in both traditions, 'the eschatological reality is not only a future state occurring beyond death but also ... a limitlessly better existence which can and should be entered upon now, in the midst of this present life' (1989a: 65) and, by describing salvation/liberation as a transformation which bears fruit in this life, he places emphasis firmly on our present participation in salvation/liberation. This emphasis chimes in with much contemporary Christian soteriological reflection. As Coward explains, many Christians today are looking for ways to adapt Christian belief to modern thought and this search has yielded an increasing emphasis on heaven and hell as possible ways of living in the here and now; on the need to focus on the demands of justice and the well-being of all *in this life*, and not merely be consoled with the thought of final justice; and an increasing acknowledgement of how little we know about life after death (2003: 56–58). On the basis of these emphases (clearly present in the reflections of my interviewees), it would seem that, from a contemporary Christian perspective, what is most important is a focus on what the salvific/liberative path requires of one in the here and now, rather than a focus on ideas about the completion of the path. Since this emphasis is traditionally strong in Buddhism too, this shared focus seems to reduce the significance of the gap between Buddhist and Christian eschatological thinking.

None of my interviewees tended to think in terms of religious ends, not primarily because of uncertainty about the nature of the eschaton, or which tradition would prove most efficacious in helping them reach it, but due to a conviction that the appropriate focus of the spiritual life, from both a Buddhist and a Christian perspective, is the here and now. They were more concerned with what was transformative in their present experience, than with eschatological speculation. Corless explained that, to the extent that he thought in terms of his having a *goal*, it was to develop kindness, clarity, and insight (42), and thinking in terms of ends he considered to be contrary to the spirit of both traditions: 'the real focus should ... be on ... how effective I am in helping others' (62–63). Keenan emphasises that salvation is not supposed to be something that happens after death: 'It's supposed to happen *now* and, certainly for Paul, resurrection's a *present* reality ... I *do* think about it in those terms and I think most mainline Christians do too' (275). Regarding the question of what the completion of an individual's salvation might be, Keenan says again, 'I don't know. It's not too important to me' (306); 'I would ... think it much more crucial that one practise the path than worry about the end point ... it'll take care of itself' (259). Similarly, Habito says: talk of *nirvāṇa* and of heaven points to our ultimate destiny, 'but that ultimate destiny is not just way way beyond ... it's already happening here and now, so if you ask me: "but what's ahead?" I don't know and I don't care' (195). He asserts that people 'look up to the sky, or to the next life, or to some idealized future, for the fulfilment of their desires, for the realization of happiness'. This attitude, says Habito, 'makes us forget and neglect the treasure that lies in the here and now' (2004: 69).

Asked what she takes the eschaton to be, Reis Habito says: '[t]o answer this question I just think about what Jesus says: the Kingdom of Heaven is right here'; she links this to the Mahāyāna claim that *nirvāṇa* is *saṃsāra* (483–84). What matters, thinks Reis Habito, is not what salvation means in future terms:

> what matters is: what does it mean right now? ... And I think for the Buddhists – for the Zen Masters that I have – it's the here and now that counts, not what you think about ultimate salvation, but [that] you do everything necessary in terms of mindfulness to be fully aware of now and what a transparent self might be.
>
> (468)

Like other interviewees, she feels that eschatology should not be a significant focus:

> I really think that what we can't know about we should not put all our energy into thinking about ... But what we can know about is just the here and now and so be fully aware of that, as much as possible.
>
> (497)

She explains that her Buddhist practice has helped her to interpret the Gospels in these terms: "the Kingdom of God is among you" ... Before, it wasn't as poignant as it is now. ... [T]he Buddhist's focus on mindfulness and the here and now gives me a new dimension to that – how it could be understood' (433). This emphasis is shared by King:

> I think about: this body is the body of Buddha; this land is the Buddha Land. It's not some place else. Heaven and *nirvāṇa* ... I think in terms of: it's right here. If I don't see it that's my shortcoming. So it's not an *end*. I can't think of it as an *end* at the end of the path. I don't think at all in terms of an end to the path. How could I think of that? That's immense. I have no concept. I don't even think in terms of 'end'. I think in terms of non-dualism, so ends and means are the same.
>
> (395)

Regarding the question of what Christians mean by 'heaven', Furneaux also places emphasis on 'here and now – as a stepping stone' (126), and this emphasis appears to be a point of convergence for her:

The Pure land on earth?
Dwelling in the Here and Now
Thy Kingdom is come.[15]

These reflections make the debate over whether Buddhism and Christianity share an end or not, or whether they are equally efficacious with respect to that end, seem of limited consequence; if both traditions emphasise that the end of the path should not be one's focus, then dual belongers seem justified in practising both religions for as long as both are found to orientate them in a single direction, i.e. for as long as they are found to be mutually supportive in the transformation from self-centredness to Reality-centredness, wherever and however that transformation might end. '[I]t is not up to me to figure out where it is going', says Corless; 'what happens to me is none of my business … I strive to be authentic at the moment and … presume it will … somehow, work out'.[16] From this perspective, the important question facing dual belongers is not 'where does it end?' nor 'which is best with respect to that end?' but, rather, 'can I live in the here and now according to the teachings of both; *are* these traditions mutually supportive?' Let's turn our attention, then, to this crucial question.

Is Christian conditioning compatible with Buddhist conditioning?

In the next chapter, we will look at questions relating to Buddhist and Christian formal religious practices. Our concern here is more general. Given their differing salvific/liberative emphases, is the Buddhist understanding of what the salvific/liberative transformation requires of a person in this life compatible with the Christian understanding of what the transformation requires of a person? Is it possible to meet the demands of both traditions? Do they condition thought and behaviour in mutually supportive ways? These questions are crucial, since if the answer is 'no' then attempting to be both Buddhist and Christian is likely to hinder rather than help facilitate the salvific/liberative transformation. In other words, even if both traditions foster the same transformation, if they foster it in mutually exclusive ways, then a choice between them may, nevertheless, be necessary for spiritual progress.

The *prima facie* worry is this. Christianity emphasises love (*agape*) as the most crucial aspect of the transformation and fosters loving engagement with the world as the key to heaven. In Matthew 25: 34–40 Jesus explains that those who will sit at the right hand of the Father in the Kingdom of Heaven are those who fed the hungry, clothed the naked, and visited the sick and imprisoned. Buddhism, by contrast, emphasises wisdom (which, in Mahāyāna terms, means direct non-conceptual, non-dual awareness of the emptiness of all phenomena) as the most crucial aspect of the salvific/liberative transformation and fosters the eradication of attachment to all phenomena. According to the Buddhist understanding, our dissatisfaction is caused by clinging to the perishable things of the world out of the illusion that they are permanent constituents of our own existence and can satisfy our deepest longings. It is this deluded orientation of our existential striving which Buddhism calls 'thirst' (*tanha*) and it is this 'thirst' which expresses itself in attachment and binds us to *saṃsāra*. The question which must be answered, then, is whether wholehearted commitment to growing in *love* is compatible with wholehearted commitment to growing in *non-attachment*? When we look at the kind of life each of these traditions advocates, are we looking at a contrast between engagement and escape; between passionate agapeic involvement in the world and cool non-attachment from the world? Are love and non-attachment mutually exclusive?

King describes a period of doubt and turmoil in which she grappled with just this issue. She felt that the message she was receiving from Buddhism was that life is characterised by the three marks, *duḥkha* (unsatisfactoriness), *anitya* (impermanence), and *anātman* (absence of self), that attachment is what binds us to *saṃsāra*, and that '[t]he proper response to the samsaric world is detachment', for there is 'no ultimacy, nothing of lasting value in this world'. In short: '[a]ttachment is a mistake, because whatever we attach ourselves to will inevitably change and slide through our fingers' (2003c: 162). King began to feel that, while all this is true, her experience of motherhood was convincing her that 'there is ultimacy in this world': 'In practice', writes King, 'it is an ultimate good, for me, to care for this child' (2003c: 163). In Quaker contexts, moreover, she was 'constantly hearing ... about love' – acts of selfless love were frequently extolled, love was a prominent theme in hymn singing and Bible study, and in the silence of Quaker Meetings what came up repeatedly and seemed most meaningful to King had frequently to do with love. 'I came to see learning to love more and more genuinely as the point of living a human life', writes King. 'And while I could see similar fruits of love in my Buddhist and Christian friends, I could see this kind of language and thinking only in Quakerism and Christianity, not in Buddhism' (2003c: 164). King did note the apparent value placed on a mother's love by the *Mettā Sutta*, in which we find the words: 'Just as a mother would protect her only child even at the risk of her own life, even so let one cultivate a boundless heart towards all beings' (*Suttanipata*, I.8). And she acknowledged that Buddhism certainly speaks of compassion and loving-kindness, but she nevertheless felt that, '[u]sually in Buddhist scripture, a cool detachment seemed to be part of the picture' and cool detachment, in King's experience as a wife and mother, 'was not part of the picture of love' (2003c: 164). Her quandary concerned 'the place of love in this world – ordinary, familial love'. 'It is true that nothing in this world lasts', reflects King. 'And yet we love. And it is the best thing about us that we love; love is the only setting in which we ordinary people are able to put ourselves aside and think of the other first' (2003c: 165).

So, is detachment or non-attachment necessarily at odds with loving involvement? In addressing this question, let's begin with a clarification of terms. There are two Pāli words which are sometimes translated as 'detachment':

viveka and *virāga*. Harris explains that the primary meaning of *viveka* is separation, aloofness, seclusion. This can take three forms: *kāya-viveka* (physical withdrawal), *citta-viveka* (mental withdrawal), and *upadhi-viveka* (withdrawal from the roots of suffering).[17] *Upadhi-viveka* links up with *virāga*, meaning the absence of lust, desire, and craving for existence. Harris suggests that 'non-attachment' is a far more appropriate translation than 'detachment' since,

> [p]hrases which overlap with attachment in this context and which can help to clarify its meaning are: possessiveness in relationships, defensiveness, jealousy, covetousness, acquisitiveness, and competitiveness. Through non-attachment, these are attenuated and overcome … , making way for their opposites to flourish.
>
> (1997: 3)

Non-attachment explains Harris, is 'a movement towards seeing the true nature of things more clearly. In contrast, *sarāga* (attachment) leads to biased and false perceptions, since objects are sensed through a net of predispositions towards attraction and aversion' (1997: 3). She points out that

> virāga does not imply apathy and indifference but a freedom from passion and attachment that is necessary if actions are not to become biased or partial. For what passes as compassion can cloak emotions of a very different kind, such as anger, attachment, or the wish to interfere. … Egoism seeks to use others for the material welfare and gain of self. Its 'love' is possessive and manipulative. Egoism has to be destroyed if *karuñā* is to develop.
>
> (Harris 1997: 8)

Compassion (*karuṇā*) and sympathy (*mudita*) are two forms in which loving (*mettā*, *maitri*) equanimity (*upekkha*, *upekṣa*) manifests itself. The Buddhist ideal of loving kindness is non-attached love because it is not self-centred and one who exhibits it does not seek his or her own pleasure. As Schmidt-Leukel says, the innermost form of attachment has the structure of clinging to oneself, of self-centredness;

> every form of genuine love, that is, of love which does not seek in the first instance one's own gratification, implies some degree of detachment. Ideal love – according to Buddhism – would be totally detached love, and that means a form of love which is indiscriminately directed towards everyone, high or low, friend or foe.
>
> (2003: 275)

In this light, the appearance of contradiction between the non-attachment emphasised by Buddhism and the love emphasised by Christianity begins to dissolve.

Complementarity and creative tension

Schmidt-Leukel argues that 'Buddhism and Christianity coincide in the ideal of detached love or loving detachment which is shown in an indiscriminate way to everyone'.[18] He explains that in the Christian understanding, '[r]eceiving and responding to the love of God goes along with a kind of detachment from the world of death' (2003: 274). Paul, for example, recommends that we possess the things of the world as though we had them not, 'for the form of this world is passing away' (1 Corinthians 7: 29–31) and, according to John, we are in the world but not of the world (John 17: 9–19). Schmidt-Leukel points out that, while 'in Christianity the correlate of divine, non-selfish love is a certain separation from the world, in Buddhism it is just the other way round, that is, selfless love is the correlate of detachment' (2003: 275). Buddhism tends to place greater emphasis on non-attachment than love, and Christianity, greater emphasis on love than non-attachment, but in both these traditions, non-attachment and love are understood as developing in a relationship of mutual dependence. If love is not accompanied by non-attachment, it is not unconditional but self-serving (one seeks one's own happiness and not simply the happiness of others). If non-attachment is not accompanied by love, it becomes indifferent to the suffering of others and fails to show compassion and empathy.

Schmidt-Leukel argues that it is the complementarity of detachment and involvement which accounts for the existential complementarity of these two traditions:

> It is here where both can enrich and spiritually stimulate one another. For within Christianity the dominance of involvement tends to supersede the element of detachment, and within Buddhism the dominance of detachment carries with it the danger of superseding loving involvement.
>
> (2003: 275–76)

Schmidt-Leukel acknowledges that there are, in each case, sub-traditions in which the complementary element is more strongly affirmed than elsewhere: Christian mysticism and monasticism have always emphasised the spiritual value of non-attachment,[19] and in Buddhism the Bodhisattva-ideal has upheld the supreme value of compassionate involvement. He points out that it is not surprising, therefore, that Buddhist–Christian dialogue has led to Christian revitalisation of contemplative practice and to Buddhist renewal of a sense of social responsibility (2003: 276).

Pieris also affirms the existential complementarity of these traditions. He describes *gnosis* (salvific knowledge) as the 'core experience' in Buddhism and *agape* (redemptive love) as the 'core experience' in Christianity, and sees these as 'complementary idioms that need each other to mediate the self-transcending experience called "salvation"' (1988a: 111); they 'are certainly not soteriological alternatives or optional paths to human liberation', but rather are 'two irreducibly distinct languages of the spirit'. Each of these languages, says Pieris, is 'incapable, unless aided and complemented by the other, of mediating and adequately expressing the human encounter with the ultimate. Any valid spirituality ... *must* and, as history shows, *does* retain both poles of religious experience' (1988a: 9–10).

If both traditions see love and non-attachment as virtues which, far from being mutually exclusive, can only be truly developed in conjunction with one another, then, far from impeding spiritual development, belonging to two traditions, one of which prioritises love the other of which prioritises wisdom, may even expedite that development. There was much in the reflections of my interviewees indicating that they experience and appreciate this existential complementarity. Furneaux writes, for example,

> [w]hile there is attachment, there is partiality, and thus what passes for love is attachment and not unconditioned. This is fully in accord with Christian and New Testament teaching. Agape is not conditioned. Where there is Fear there is no Love ... The whole of Buddhist training is the eradication of self servingness or attachment to ... ego.
>
> (125)

Habito acknowledges that, superficially, there can appear to be a contradiction between the Christian emphasis on love and the Buddhist emphasis on non-attachment, but he stresses that when one looks more deeply at the implications of Buddhist non-attachment, one sees that non-attachment is non-clinging, and 'underlying that non-clinging is the compassion for all beings, as a mother cares for her child and is willing to give her life to the child' (196). Similarly, the Christian emphasis is not on a clinging love but on a love which is devoted to the well-being of the loved one. In order to love in this way, says Habito, it is necessary to let go of one's clinging and possessiveness:

> there needs to be a letting go, and so that's where the Buddhist injunction not to be attached needs to be brought in, precisely in order to activate or make more concrete the implications of what love, in the Christian sense, is pointing to.
>
> (195)

In this context, says Habito, we see that 'there's no contradiction at all' (196), they are 'mutually reinforcing' (195).

Habito explains that he has found the interplay of the respective emphases of these two traditions very beneficial: 'my being Buddhist and my being Christian are now ... mutually enhanced by both sides of that polarity', he reflects; 'it's a unified vision informed by those two ... [M]y perception of things has become enhanced ... by these two traditions' (156–57). Similarly, King has gradually discovered, through the experience of motherhood, that both love and non-attachment are essential. She likens one's children eventually leaving home to a Zen joke:

> You gradually learn to forget yourself, to think only of them. You gradually, come to feel that they are the ultimate good, the ultimate truth. Then: Poof! They disappear! Oh yeah, what was that about *duhkha* and *anitya* again? ... A beloved grown child leaving home is the epitome of *duhkha*, the pain inherent even in the joyful ... How much I have benefited from the Buddhist insight into this situation.
>
> (King 2003c: 168–69)

King concludes that motherhood is an intense spiritual discipline:

> What better way to learn selflessness, love, and giving than to care for an infant? And what better way to learn letting go than to watch a grown child walk away? Yet the latter does not cancel or invalidate the former! Letting go well, in the right way, at the right time, to the right degree, is a part of love, even attached (devoted) love.
>
> (2003c: 169)

However, despite their complementarity, insofar as these two 'languages of the spirit' are irreducible and must be held together in tension, a certain amount of dialogue and mutual challenge between the agapeic and the gnostic idiom seems almost inevitable for a person struggling to maintain this tension through adherence to two traditions, one of which prioritises one pole and the other of which prioritises the other pole. The tension between the Quaker/Christian – and, importantly, *motherly* – emphasis on love and the Buddhist emphasis on non-attachment ceased to be experienced by King as a *troubling* dilemma after a dream she had one night, in which she was offered the opportunity to go through a door into "'bliss' (which clearly encompassed heaven, nirvana, *moksha* [liberation], and so forth)", but turned down the opportunity, adamant that she would rather return to her children, to be with them and to help them – and not only them, but all children:

> I saw in a flash that 'my' children were only 'my' children temporarily; at other times, other children were 'my' children, 'I' was a different 'me,' and indeed everyone was someone's child – 'my' child at one time or another. ... I wanted to go back, to live that life, knowing full well that in choosing that life over 'bliss,' I was choosing terrible pain and grief along with great joy.
>
> (2003c: 166–67)

Upon waking, King realised that this dream of hers had been a *Buddhist* dream insofar as she had chosen to return to this world of *saṃsāra* for the sake of sentient beings, but was at the same time a *mother's* dream insofar as she had wanted to return because she liked life and wanted to be with, and there for, her children and couldn't bear to abandon them. 'I felt I had finally solved my fifteen-year natural koan', writes King.

> The mother's love, her 'attachment' that keeps her bound to samsara, her gut-level inability to abandon her children who cannot make it on their own and truly need her help – these things are indistinguishable from the bodhisattva's willingness to turn away from nirvana and return to samsara for the sake of all sentient beings.
>
> (2003c: 167)

But the fact that King no longer finds the tension between the different emphases of her two traditions *troubling* does not mean that she no longer feels that there is any debate between the traditions on this score, nor that all her questions on this issue are answered.

The ongoing dialogical to-and-fro inherent in the attempt to find and maintain the right balance between loving engagement and wise non-attachment was particularly evident in King's reflections, and those of Reis Habito. One issue raised by both of them had to do with whether preferential love for one's children contains an element of attachment and, if so, whether this tells us that we shouldn't feel preferential love for our children or whether it tells us that not all preferential love is negative. 'I have preferential love', says King, 'and furthermore I feel that my children need my preferential love and … I think it is right for me, as a mother, to give them way more love and attention and care' (369). King feels that the Christian tradition is more affirmative of this familial preferential love than Buddhism (352), and this is an issue over which Christianity challenges Buddhism: ' … preferential love – is there a place for that? Is that *just* delusion?' (375). Elsewhere King is less rhetorical: 'Love of a child is indeed attachment, but that attachment is not delusion!' (2003c: 168). However, King appreciates the strength of the Buddhist insight too: 'preferential love can easily slide into clinging in a destructive way', and the Buddhist emphasis keeps one alive to this possibility (375). In this respect the traditions with their distinctive emphases are like two different languages, and 'one situation calls up one, another situation calls up the other' (352).

King explains that, over time, she has come to feel that what she needs to embrace is 'not clinging, as opposed to detachment' (376). Detachment, says King, doesn't work for lay people, especially those with children.

> So, is that rejecting something in Buddhism? Well, there's an awful lot of texts which make it sound like we're really meant to be very dispassionate and keep any kind of involvement at arm's length. To me that's monasticism. … [T]here's certain habits that monasticism is more liable to than a lay person's life … [D]etachment, which could be not clinging, … sometimes becomes a kind of aloofness and coolness. So, I don't really think

that's actively rejecting something in Buddhism, I think it's learning about nuances in a very tricky area.

(376)

King explains that deciphering the nuances in the Buddhist message about non-attachment was 'a matter of looking more deeply and coming to a point of clarification about it, but it was clarification which came about because of the challenge of Christianity' (377).

Reis Habito's reflections on the questions and tensions resulting from the respective emphases of Buddhism and Christianity are strikingly similar to King's. Reis Habito describes how, early in her encounter with Buddhism, she was troubled by the negative attitudes of the Buddhists she met towards child-bearing and marriage – attitudes born of the belief that family life leads to many attachments and keeps one from realising what is essential in life: 'I thought: how can that be?' (484). She explains that, over time, she has come to see the issue differently. She draws a distinction between what non-attachment means for monastics and what it means generally. She takes complete non-attachment to be a prescription for the monastics but thinks non-attachment is a prescription for everyone in the sense that 'if you're attached in your love to someone, there is some possessiveness' (484); 'for me', she concludes,

> emotional attachment is normal because you love someone and yet within this attachment there has to be non-attachment ... Also ... Jesus' words ... 'who clings to his father and mother ... cannot be my follower' – ... I see that very much in the Buddhist sense of being non-attached. It doesn't mean rejecting them ... but letting them be and seeing that they also have to let you be.
>
> (484–85)

Reis Habito reflects more critically that, at times, she feels that the Buddhist emphasis on non-attachment can obscure the beauty in personal relation-ships, focussing only on the negative effects of attachment when, in fact, 'there's also something positive in attachment' (497). She thinks that it might be possible for Buddhists to see some element of attachment in personal relationships in a different light, and suggests that attachment and non-attachment should not be thought of in too 'black and white' a manner (498).

Another, related focus of the internal dialogue between the respective emphases of these traditions has, for King and Reis Habito, been a sense that the Christian world-view accords value to individuals *qua* individuals whereas the Buddhist world-view seems to construe this emphasis as a form of ego-centrism. Again, it is King's experience as a mother which has drawn her attention to this contrast. King has found herself 'wanting to affirm the uniqueness, the individuality, the specialness [and] importance' of each of her children, and feels this instinct is supported by what she refers to as 'the individualism of Judeo-Christian culture' (369). Although King feels this individualism has gone too far in Western culture, she nevertheless appreciates this emphasis with respect to her children and feels that it is lacking in Buddhist cultures. She finds that Quaker practice, especially, stresses the value of the individual:

> I've seen children ... minister to the whole congregation, everyone listening to them with great attention and great seriousness. ... I just think that's fabulous – and ... what I'm valuing here is that Quakerism values my child as a *unique individual*. ... [I]n Buddhism, valuing a person as a unique individual is not ... on the radar screen at all, much less something they focus on.
>
> (419)

According to Buddhist teachings of *anātman* (no self), reflects King, 'ego's the whole problem', and she laughs to admit that she thinks that is right too. '[A]m I fostering ego in my children?', wonders King; 'I don't know' (419).

Reis Habito also tentatively suggests that the Christian notion of the individual before God and 'the great value that's put on individuality' in Christianity seems to contrast with the Buddhist notion that a person has this particular form only fleetingly and will soon have another form. She is keen to stress that she does not mean that Buddhism does not value human life as much as Christianity, but rather that Buddhism does not tend to emphasise the '*uniqueness* of *this* being right here and now' (498). She suggests that the sense of a person's uniqueness and of the value of *particular* human relationships is an aspect of the Christian world-view which Buddhists could perhaps be inspired by, but points out that Buddhists are cautious about such issues,

> precisely because when you say 'I'm unique and God loves me' that very easily ... translates into 'I'm special' and then this 'I', again, is becoming so strong ... Buddhists are very careful in not giving rise to a wrong notion of 'I' that's absolutised.
>
> (498)

The dual belonger's Buddhist and Christian perspectives come together to form a coherent picture to the extent that both traditions agree on the complementarity between their respective emphases on loving involvement and wise non-attachment. Yet at the same time, as King's and Reis Habito's reflections make clear, insofar as each tradition is allowed to maintain its own distinctive emphasis, it does not seem that these two perspectives converge in an entirely unified focus. In certain respects a kind of 'double-vision' persists. 'I cannot sit in complete comfort with either tradition', writes King,

> And yet I need both. For me, there is profound truth in both. I no longer see them as so nearly reconcilable, but more as two languages, each of

which speaks with great profundity truths of the spiritual life, yet neither of which (like any language) is really translatable into the other. In the end, all truth must be reconcilable. But I am well aware of my distance from that point.

(2003c: 170)

Similarly, Habito likens Buddhism and Christianity to two different sources of intravenous nourishment which 'somehow find a way of nourishing the same individual from their distinctive angles';[20] one achieves a degree of integration in which their compatibility is perceived, thinks Habito, and yet the dialogue between them persists (156–57).

To the Buddhist who sees insight into the nature of reality, leading to the relinquishing of all grasping and attachment, as the most crucial aspect of liberation, one can imagine the Christian responding: that is all well and good, but have you fed the hungry, clothed the naked, and visited the sick and imprisoned? As Paul says,

> If I have all the eloquence of men or of angels, ... understanding all the mysteries there are, and knowing everything, ... [i]f I give away all I possess, piece by piece, and if I even let them take my body to burn it, but am without love, it will do me no good whatever.
>
> (1 Corinthians 13: 1–3)

Conversely, to the Christian who sees loving engagement with one's neighbours (conceived of as anyone in need) as the most crucial aspect of salvation, one can imagine the Buddhist responding: that is all well and good, but unless you develop penetrating insight into the nature of reality, unless you cultivate the wisdom which sees that all is not-self and directly perceive the emptiness of phenomena, thus relinquishing all grasping and attachment, then even your most generous dealings with others will be tarnished by subtle manifestations of self-interest and you will continue to suffer and cause suffering to others. For Buddhist Christians then, Makransky's critique of Christianity's lack of focus on the development of wisdom becomes one side of an internal dialogue in which each perspective continually corrects the other, encouraging critical self-reflection and development on both sides. Even if this creative tension is at times a source of spiritual struggle for Buddhist Christians, there may be comfort in Pieris' insistence that '[i]t is the dialectical interplay of wisdom and love that ensures a progressive movement in the realm of the human spirit' (1988a: 9–10).

How long do we get to practise the path?

But a final question requires our attention. For even if we assume that the complementary emphases of Christianity and Buddhism assist participation in a single salvific/liberative transformation in the here and now, dual belongers must still contend with the discrepancy between the traditions regarding how long this transformation is thought to take.

In the Christian tradition a person's spiritual path tends to be thought of as being pursued over just a single lifetime. Protestant thinking tends to understand the soul not as surviving the death of the body but, rather, as dying with it and remaining dead until the end of time when body and soul are resurrected together and reunited. Traditional Catholic thinking, on the other hand, posits that, after death, a person's soul – incomplete without a body – enters either into the eternal suffering of hell; or into the eternal bliss of heaven, where it awaits unification with its body at the end of time; or into the intermediate state of purgatory where it undergoes further sanctification in order to make progression to heaven possible. From a Christian perspective, then, there are at most three *post-mortem* possibilities: heaven, hell, and purgatory (four, if limbo is included).[21] No notion of successive lives has ever been embraced by orthodox Christianity; in the Catechism of the Catholic Church, for example, we read: 'when "the single course of our life" is completed, we shall not return to other earthly lives. "It is appointed for man to die once" (Hebrews 9:27). There is no "reincarnation" after death'.[22]

Buddhists, by contrast, repudiate the idea of a permanent soul and believe in rebirth or reincarnation. According to traditional Buddhist thought, one lives countless lives. In Buddhist cosmology there are various realms into which one may be reborn, depending on one's stock of karmic merit. All rebirths are impermanent: one is born as a particular kind of being within a particular realm and one dies in that realm and then one is born again – perhaps as a human, or perhaps in hell, as an animal, a ghost, or a god, in accordance with the impersonal law of karma.[23] This is the cycle of death and rebirth – *saṃsāra* – to which we are all bound until such time as we gain the liberation and permanent bliss of *nirvāṇa*.

So do Buddhist Christians think spiritual progress takes place over the course of just one lifetime, or over the course of many? How do they deal with the apparent contradiction between Christian and Buddhist thinking regarding rebirth? They seem to have three options: (i) to reject the Buddhist teaching of rebirth as applying across lifetimes, i.e. to assume from one's Buddhist perspective that the process of rebirth refers only to the moment-to-moment death and rebirth of consciousness – a process which continues up to, but not beyond, death; (ii) to incorporate the notion that spiritual progress may continue over more than one lifetime into one's Christian perspective; or (iii) to reserve judgement on this issue, holding the teachings of Buddhism and Christianity in tension. Let's take a closer look at these alternatives.

(i) Rejecting a literal interpretation of saṃsāra

On this option, the dual belonger interprets the notion of *saṃsāra* as a mythological representation of this life, and interprets Buddhist cosmology in purely psychological terms, taking rebirth to refer only to the rebirth of consciousness in every moment of this life, and the various realms of the Buddhist cosmos as mythological representations of the various kinds of consciousness which may arise in this lifetime (rather than as the possible *post-mortem* destinies of unenlightened beings).

Habito is not sure about the question of repeated rebirths, but suggests that karma does not necessarily have to be understood as applying across numerous lifetimes (190). He points out that, just as there is much variety of interpretation in Christianity regarding bodily resurrection – from those who interpret it in terms of resuscitation after biological death, to those who interpret it as symbolising the newness of life found in death to self – so too there are various Buddhist interpretations of rebirth: 'in the Buddhist traditions there are different ways of taking this doctrine of reincarnation, from the more literal, as described in Tibetan tradition, to the more symbolic' (191). For his own part, Habito explains: 'I'm not sure about the literal implications but those doctrines do come from a long tradition that somehow work in those traditions. So, I'm listening to see what implications they would have ... [for] our contemporary society' (191).

There are a number of modern Buddhists who interpret the notions of *saṃsāra* and rebirth mythologically rather than literally – Nishitani, Cook, and Lai, for example.[24] Lai goes as far as to write of belief in rebirth that '[e]xcept for a minority of true believers and some in the forefront of a new age spirituality, it is true today, not as a literal reality, but as a metaphor, a fiction, a function of a religious imagination' (2001: 151). However, this statement is surely a gross exaggeration, ignoring as it does the vast majority of Buddhists in traditional Buddhist countries. As Schmidt-Leukel says, Lai's statement, at best, applies only to a *minority* of highly Westernised Buddhist intellectuals.[25] Let us be clear that the move made by a minority of Buddhists away from a literal interpretation of rebirth, is a move away from the traditional understanding. As Williams points out, to interpret the various realms of Buddhist cosmology merely as the various psychological states which one may experience here and now in this life is to depart from traditional Buddhism (2000: 78–79).

A non-literal interpretation of the doctrine of rebirth is, moreover, a highly *significant* departure from tradition since it arguably undermines the very premises upon which Buddhist faith rests: 'The idea of karma as creating spiritual tendencies could still be retained within the dynamics of one single life only', explains Schmidt-Leukel,

> [b]ut the aspect of a just cosmic order would vanish completely, together with any hope for those who were unable to attain the salvific goal within this single life. Nirvāṇa would presumably lose any metaphysical status as an unconditioned reality as well, and the idea of salvation would be reduced to the achievement of a relatively good but thoroughly conditioned state of personal development available, ultimately, only to a small elite.
>
> (2006b: 150–51)

If the bliss of *nirvāṇa* persists beyond death but one has just a single lifetime to achieve it (and otherwise one will simply die at the end of one's life), this is disastrous news for most people since unless one is able to devote serious time and effort to the achievement of *nirvāṇa*, one faces annihilation.[26] In contrast, as Hick – like Schmidt-Leukel – points out, the Buddha's teaching is an optimistic one, affirming as it does 'that each individual spiritual project will continue through life after life until *nirvana* is attained' (Hick 1989b: 177–79).

Admittedly, those Buddhists who deny that there is more than one life do not tend to believe in *nirvāṇa* as a *post-mortem* state, i.e. they deny that the bliss of *nirvāṇa* persists beyond death. But if one believes that death is the end even for those who have reached *nirvāṇa*, then this radically reduces the incentive to pursue the Buddhist goal, given one's slender chances of achieving it in just one lifetime. Would one not be better off foregoing the rigorous discipline of serious Buddhist practice and pursuing instead more attainable goals – with which serious religious practice might interfere, such as a fulfilling family life and professional life, good times with friends, romance, world-travel, good food and fine wines? Moreover, more earthly joys, such as these, seem to have much more worth if there is only one lifetime than they do if one assumes that one has been caught in a round of rebirth from beginningless time. To the extent that the drive to seek liberation is derived from one's awareness that one has been, and will otherwise continue to be, endlessly trapped in the cycle of death and rebirth if one does not achieve liberation, a belief in rebirth seems required as a foundational premise of Buddhism.[27]

Keenan is the only one of my interviewees who, despite believing in the notion of karma simply as cause and effect, emphatically does not believe in a series of rebirths. He is, however, the only one who does not see himself as a Buddhist and he is therefore entitled to a more relaxed attitude regarding what he accepts of Buddhist thought and what he rejects. Those of my interviewees who do see themselves as Buddhists seem right to be hesitant regarding the question of rebirth, for if Buddhists let go of the idea that we are literally caught up in the cycle of *saṃsāra*, then Buddhism either becomes bad news for the majority of people, or its goal is so diminished that there is no clear incentive to pursue it rather than other goals.

(ii) Incorporating the notion of rebirth into one's Christian perspective

Lai and Von Brück contend that, today, 'many Europeans have come to believe in reincarnation and the concept of *karma* is no longer a foreign word' (2001: 170), and studies suggest that approximately 30 per cent of people in the Western world believe in some form of reincarnation.[28] Could it be that rather than undermining the foundations of Buddhism by casting off belief in rebirth, a better option for dual belongers would be to incorporate that belief into their Christian world-view? Although all my interviewees believed in karma (even if simply under the description 'the law of cause and effect'), most were ambivalent about whether or not there is one lifetime or many.

Nevertheless, some did reflect that there have been certain experiences of theirs which seem better accounted for if rebirth is assumed than if one assumes there is just this one lifetime.

King, for example, has found that the notion of repeated rebirths has seemed to make sense of some of her experiences as a parent. For example, she and her husband had a sense of having been *chosen* by their children, 'a sense of that whole Buddhist story … , especially … from a Mahāyāna point of view: you're going from life to life … and, in some accounts, you do choose your parents; you're drawn to them and you … let yourself be pulled towards them' (399). King also says she has found the notion of rebirth helpful as an explanation of the distinctiveness, from birth, of each of her children:

> They do not come into the world as a blank slate, they come in with a formed *personality*; it's very clear, and they're extremely different from each other – from day one until now. So it seems like they're coming with their own agenda and their own baggage.[29]

King reflects that only the Buddhist world-view seems able to account for these strong experiences of hers and says that this is an issue about which she feels she needs to do some more thinking (400).

Reis Habito, although also being unsure about the question of rebirth and even leaning more towards a Christian understanding of a single lifetime, reflects, similarly, that there are some of her experiences which seem better accounted for on the Buddhist model of numerous rebirths, than on the Christian model. She gives the example of her non-dualistic concept of God and how different it was from her brother's understanding when they were children; this seems to Reis Habito to be evidence in support of her Dharma Master's claim that she had been his student in previous lifetimes: 'these things, they make me question: is there something to rebirth and are there really what the Dharma Master said he has gone through – many, many lives … ?' (467).

Only Corless, amongst my interviewees, went as far as to positively embrace belief in rebirth,[30] at least insofar as he took it to be 'more likely than not that after the dissolution of the body and mind that … the mind is still trying to do something and so it will become the condition for a new birth' (69). Corless, at least from his Buddhist perspective, took there to be numerous rebirths and numerous realms in which one's consciousness may be reborn after death. Indeed, he even thought that he might have visited one of these realms (Amitabha's Pure Land) during a near death experience he underwent during surgery, though he stresses that the realm in which he appeared to find himself had no explicitly religious content.[31] And, whereas a number of interviewees raised concerns with the idea that people's predicaments in this world can be put down to the fruition of their negative karma from previous lives (a notion they felt was fatalistic or uncomfortably close to blaming the victim),[32] Corless was much less perturbed by the idea, even finding that thinking in terms of the fruition of karma from previous lives offered him a useful perspective on his own cancer.[33]

Leaving aside any specific accompanying cosmology, the notion of rebirth was an example of something Corless felt he could accept in a unified way, from both his Buddhist and his Christian perspectives; he did not merely accept it from his Buddhist perspective and reject it from his Christian perspective, as with various other points of contention between Buddhism and Christianity. He draws attention to various New Testament passages which appear to provide grounds for Christian affirmation of something akin to the law of karma, and argues that the fruiting of action in heaven is well attested and is implicit in a number of the passages he quotes.[34] He admits that whether the karmic process extends beyond this present lifetime is more controversial, but argues that the notion of rebirth can – *on Christian grounds* – be incorporated into Christian doctrine (1978: 77).

> If the person is not that exulted then after death they have more to do and it seems reasonable that they would come back to another rebirth, possibly only as a human. I'm not sure whether Christian theology would be comfortable with the person coming back as an animal … .
>
> (69)

Corless points out that Origen upheld the pre-existence of souls and notes some relatively recent Christian writings in favour of rebirth.[35] He also points out that it was the notion of metempsychosis (successive clothings of an unchanging personal core in changeable bodies) which troubled the Church Fathers since this notion contradicts the Christian doctrines of the unity of the person and the resurrection of the body. But the notion of an unchanging self-entity, points out Corless, is also rejected by Buddhists in their rejection of an *ātman* which persists through repeated rebirths (1978: 78). He also points out from his Catholic perspective that there are theological problems with the notion of purgatory insofar as it appears to contradict the Christian contention that one cannot have a disembodied soul, and he suggests that these problems are overcome if purgatory is thought of in terms of repeated rebirths: 'I would propose … the investigation of the Buddhist notion of rebirth as a way of trying to solve the conundrum of purgatory' says Corless.[36]

Although King reserves judgement regarding the question of rebirth, she says she *hopes* there's more than one life in which to make progress (370); she does not believe in, and is not attracted to, the Christian idea of one lifetime followed by a judgement of eternal heaven or hell (391, 402). Certainly, the Protestant *post-mortem* options seem to present far too course-grained a dichotomy: eternal bliss or eternal suffering, based on the nature of one's short earthly life. Like King, Geddes MacGregor is repelled by the idea that a judgement of a few years of earthly existence could determine our eternal fate and argues that the notion that we have more than one chance to get it right is far more consistent with the Biblical revelation of a loving and compassionate God (1982: 11). The Catholic notion of purgatory at least makes some provision for the closing of what Hick calls the 'gap between the individual's imperfection at the end of this life and the perfect heavenly state in which he is to participate' (1976: 202). But, as Rahner says, these days the notion of purgatorial fire is implausible; reincarnation, he suggests, might represent a possible alternative (1982: 126–27). Might it not be preferable for Christians to stay with the spirit of the doctrine of purgatory but to understand the process of *post-mortem* purification as playing itself out through successive rebirths?

Such an interpretation may even help solve one of theology's most profound and persistent problems – that of how to reconcile the existence of an all-loving, all-powerful God with the existence of terrible evil and devastating natural disasters. MacGregor, for example, argues that '[b]y introducing the notion of reincarnation ... the absurdity in the problem of evil is immeasurably mitigated' (1978: 127). If salvation is understood as a gradual process, and if the idea that a single lifetime can result in eternal damnation is rejected,[37] then the notion of rebirth can be incorporated into an Irenaean Christian theodicy which envisages people as making gradual progress towards likeness to God.[38] Hick argues for just such an understanding, asserting that '[l]ife ... is a soul-making or person-making process. We exist in order to grow through our free interactions with a challenging environment towards a human perfection which lies far beyond our present state'. He takes it to be evident 'that such a completion is very seldom (if ever) achieved in the course of this present life' (1976: 408). According to this understanding, the world's being as it is is compatible with God's love and compassion insofar as its many challenges and hardships provide an environment conducive to our spiritual progress (Hick 1976: 210). Moreover, if we are all at different stages of advancement and require challenges suitable to the cultivation of the particular virtues we lack, the various inequalities between people at birth appear much more consistent with God's love than they do if there is only this life.

MacGregor suggests that, provided a naïve interpretation of the resurrection of the body is rejected,[39] Christians can think of people as embarked upon the purgatorial process of purification, each successive life a phase of that active process through which we strive for spiritual maturity.[40] Of course, there are still questions one would face if one were going to embrace rebirth from a Christian perspective: if, for example, one understands the nature of a person's rebirth as determined according to something like the law of karma, one would need to grapple with the difficult question of how to understand the relationship between karma and grace. Is God's grace manifest *within* or *through* the operation of the karmic principle, for example, or does grace *override* its operation?[41] But, on first inspection at least, there seems to be much to be gained for the consistency of Christian theology by incorporating the idea of rebirth, as Corless advocates. However, as we will now see when we investigate our third alternative, retaining the notion that there is one life only may have advantages not yet considered.

(iii) Reserving judgement about which teaching is true

On this option the contradiction between Christian and Buddhist teaching with regard to the number of lives we have is simply left unresolved by dual belongers – not in the sense of believing there are many lives from their Buddhist perspective and believing there is only one from their Christian perspective (and, therefore, affirming both P and not-P), but rather in the sense of leaving open the question of which teaching is correct. Apart from Keenan, who rejects the notion of rebirth, and Corless, who accepts it, my interviewees seemed to be, at bottom, agnostic with respect to the question of rebirth, emphasising that, since it is not a question which they have so far been able to settle decisively, they reserve judgement.[42]

This is true, for example, of King and Reis Habito. Despite the fact that some of their experiences have seemed to them to support the idea that there are many lives, these experiences remain insufficient to justify assured belief in rebirth: 'I do not try to force myself to believe something that I haven't affirmed in my own experience', says King, 'And I see no value and there's no appeal in believing things I don't know ... I can leave open the whole issue about a series of lives ... I would love to know that but I do not' (365). She emphasises, however, that not positively affirming either that there is one life or that there are many, is not the same as denying either of them: 'I don't firmly deny things of which I am not certain. ... I try to hold it open; I bracket the question' (363). Similarly, Reis Habito says that with regard to questions such as that of rebirth, she is 'somewhat agnostic':

> I don't worry about questions that I can't find an answer to ... So the option is: ... one life or ... many lifetimes and then, eventually (hope-fully), eternal life ... I know them as possibilities ... but as long as I don't clearly see the truth of it, I just reserve my judgement.
>
> (463–64)

Elsewhere she again says of rebirth: 'I can't say either I believe in it or ... I don't believe in it. ... I don't know ... because it's outside the realm of my own experience' (488).

This reservation of judgement does not mean that these dual belongers simply *ignore* the issue, however. The fact that for King, for example, the question of rebirth is 'bracketed' seems to mean precisely that it is an issue of ongoing investigation for her:

> I am challenged, intellectually, by ... the whole karma and rebirth thing, as well as challenged spiritually by it ... When I say 'I bracket the question' it doesn't mean I never think about it; I'm always thinking about

it ... I'm really trying to understand ... It's always in the back of my mind ... I don't dismiss; I take them very very seriously. ... I don't know this at the moment ... But I'm challenged by the tradition to ... really look into it; to really work with that possibility.

(375)

Reis Habito's reflections are similar. She explains that, especially since the death of a close friend of hers, she has become particularly interested in various understandings of death and afterlife and has read much on Christian ideas and at the same time asked Buddhist Masters for their views (472). Even though Reis Habito has found herself drawn more towards Christian notions of the afterlife in this regard, she has reserved judgement and continues to investigate both possibilities and to see what light is shed by each different understanding. She speaks too of keeping questions such as that of rebirth in her mind, 'without finding quick answers right away' (488). Reis Habito, like other interviewees, finds popular, mechanistic notions of karmic retribution difficult (as, for example, in the case of the suggestion that the Jews were in some way karmicly responsible for the Holocaust),[43] but says that this issue is also one with respect to which she feels she must 'do some more thinking and asking around, and letting the Buddhists explain how they feel ... ' (462). Habito explains that he too continues to listen to the traditions on the question of karma and rebirth (191).

Does this reservation of judgement matter when it comes to the question of whether these dual belongers are justified in considering themselves to be fully Buddhist and fully Christian? If one does not positively accept crucial elements of the Buddhist and Christian world-views, holding them in mind only as possibilities, it could be argued that this shows a lack of wholehearted commitment to these religions. Does this reticence confirm Cornille's judgement that multiple belonging 'always implies a certain holding back, an inability to fully accept some form of heteronomy' (2003: 49). As far as she is concerned, dual belongers grant themselves too much autonomy when it comes to deciding which elements of the traditions they are willing to embrace (2002b: 3).

Perhaps there is a certain holding back in the case of dual belongers who do not positively affirm either the traditional Buddhist position on rebirth or the traditional Christian position, and perhaps this does indicate a lack of complete commitment to these world-views, an unwillingness to fully accept the 'party line' of either of these traditions. King herself wonders whether her lack of positive acceptance of rebirth should make her hesitate to call herself *fully* Buddhist. She explains that the assumption of rebirth has not come naturally to her. However, she attributes this less to the fact that she is a dual belonger than that she is a *Western* Buddhist:

I often wonder if any of the American Buddhists are fully Buddhist ... I think we don't ... intuitively have these assumptions about ... living a series of lives ... It doesn't come naturally to me to assume that I've lived many lives. ... But for a lot of Buddhists ... that's a huge premise without which the rest of it doesn't make any sense. But they're raised with it ... .

(348)

Crucially, however, King's uncertainty regarding the question of rebirth is not even simply a case of what does and does not come naturally to her as a Westerner, but is, in the end, a question of what she feels it is possible, in the light of her present experience, to be certain of. She explains that, even if she belonged to just one of these traditions, she would anyway reserve judgement about whether there is one life or many:

> some of those unresolved areas [such as rebirth] ... would be unresolved *anyway*: *I do not know* how many lives we live ... If I were just one or the other I still wouldn't know. So, now I have a more complete way of not knowing. ... I prefer having different ways of *thinking about it* and not knowing, actually. In particular, ... I'm quite disinclined to believe ... that ... after death you face a judgement and you go one way or the other; I'm glad the only alternative in my mind isn't that or complete materialism.

(402)

Both King and Reis Habito feel that their withholding judgement over certain questions – such as that of rebirth, or of what the final destination of the path will involve – is perfectly consistent with the spirit of Buddhism and that it at least should be consistent with the spirit of Christianity too. Reis Habito claims that 'it's a really true Buddhist answer to say to many of these things that I don't know, and I think it should be a true Christian answer as well' (467). King, especially, feels that as a Quaker and a Buddhist, she has been 'given permission' by both traditions and the nature of their teachings 'to take with a grain of salt any kind of teaching, especially world-view/theoretical kinds of teachings' that she can't embrace; 'just to put them aside and be open about them and see what happens over time' (370). She sees herself as following the Buddha's advice (which she takes to be very much reaffirmed in Zen):

> that you know what you know and you rely on that; you don't rely on authority, you don't rely on tradition, you don't rely on popular opinion, or ... on some kind of a logical proof, or anything like that; you rely on what you know through your experience, directly, in a way that you are incapable of questioning ... and so that is very ... much my approach.

(370)

Given that King feels that she has the support of the traditions in reserving her judgement on questions to which she is unsure of the answer, contradictions such as that between the traditional Buddhist view and the traditional Christian view on the question of rebirth do not worry her too much. 'So, that's maybe a little bit of a slight-of-hand', admits King, 'but that *is* what the traditions teach, and so I guess ... that prevents any really final ... sort of world-view conflict' (370).

Habito admits that he has not yet investigated deeply the question of rebirth and thinks that perhaps he may never be able to. He explains that he does not feel that he has to be the one to resolve all such 'conceptual dissonances'. Perhaps, suggests Habito, they are irresolvable anyway (202). Reis Habito recalls the Buddha's simile of the arrow and his message concerning the importance of focusing on the task at hand (that of seeking liberation) rather than focussing on seeking answers to questions which are irrelevant to that task.[44] 'I think this is how I see these questions about eternal life and rebirth and so on', says Reis Habito (464). According to the Buddha, it is possible to practise the path to liberation without knowing the answers to such questions as whether the world is eternal, whether the soul is the same as the body, and whether a *Tathāgata* exists after death since, even though there are facts of these matters, it is not necessary to be in possession of those facts to achieve Enlightenment, and concerning oneself with them may even hinder one's practice of the path.[45] In the same way, perhaps dual belongers such as King, Habito, and Reis Habito are right not to be too concerned about the disagreement between the traditions over the question of rebirth.

Hick's reflections support this conclusion. Although he takes belief in *some sort* of afterlife to be necessary to the cosmic optimism which he takes to be an essential feature of religion, he says: 'if we ask today: Is belief, or disbelief, in reincarnation essential for salvation/liberation? the answer must surely be No' (1989a: 368). Echoing his conclusion regarding the question of the precise nature of the eschaton,[46] Hick concludes with respect to the question of rebirth that, like the Buddha's unanswered questions, it is not one which is 'soteriologically vital' (1989a: 369), and since there is not yet evidence or arguments which make the truth or falsity of the notion of rebirth a matter of public knowledge, 'we should regard the matter as one about which it would be unwise to be unyieldingly dogmatic' (1989a: 369). If each of these traditions is capable of accepting uncertainty among adherents regarding matters which are not considered soteriologically vital, provided that those teachings are taken seriously and are not rejected as false, then the uncertainty of dual belongers with respect to the question of rebirth – as well as to certain eschatological questions – need not disqualify them from counting as authentic adherents of these traditions. Indeed, to the extent that dual belongers who are undecided about such questions keep both the Buddhist teaching and the Christian teaching in mind and get on with the task at hand, perhaps a certain amount of agnosticism with respect to issues regarding which they do not yet have sufficient experience to make judgements can be regarded *positively* as indicative of an attitude which is in keeping with the spirit of these traditions, especially the spirit of Buddhism.

Preserving distinctions

Reservation of judgement on the question of whether there is one life or many is in some ways the best of the three options we have outlined, for on this option the distinctive insights of each tradition may be best preserved, and hence the benefit, in this regard, of dual belonging best maintained. We have seen how purging Buddhism of the notion of rebirth appears to have the unfortunate consequence of undermining the conceptual foundation of, and motivation for, Buddhist practice. But more than this, the assumption of rebirth also appears to foster the very goals of Buddhist practice since, arguably, it affords the Buddhist a perspective on life which cultivates non-attachment, equanimity, and patience: if one thinks of oneself and others as having lived many lives in the past and as likely to live many more in the future, this seems to encourage non-attachment to one's life and to one's worldly achievements and possessions, and even to one's family and friends. One can, moreover, afford to take a long view both in terms of people's religious practices (people will seek the truth when, eventually, they are ready for it) and in terms of conflicts and situations of injustice, since one understands that peoples' karma must play itself out over many lifetimes and not all will be resolved or achieved in this lifetime. Belief in rebirth, therefore, seems to undergird the whole Buddhist ethos and attitude to life and, consequently, to reject that belief is to risk radically altering that ethos and attitude.

Conversely, while there are clear benefits to abandoning the Christian assumption of one life only, this may be more of a sacrifice than it first appears: the assumption of one life (if it is assumed to be followed by some kind of afterlife) may help cultivate the goals of Christian living insofar as that assumption gives the Christian a perspective on life which cultivates a thirst for justice, a motivation to act, and a strong sense of responsibility towards people: if one thinks of oneself and others as having only this one earthly life, then what happens in this very life is the be all and end all – there are no second chances; no time for karma to play itself out over many aeons – this is it! This makes the demand for justice in this life great, and also means that one's familial relations assume a greater significance than they do in a world-view where one's children are only one's children for now and next time will be someone else's children and one's spouse, someone else's spouse. If there is only one life and the only mother my children will ever have is me and the only spouse I may ever have is the one I have now, then the demand to do justice to those bonds and do right by those entrusted to me is profound. To reject the traditional Christian assumption that there is only one life is, therefore, to risk radically altering the Christian ethos and attitude to life.

To be clear, I am not suggesting that there is a straightforward contradiction here between believing in one life only and emphasising the value of non-attachment, equanimity and patience; nor between believing in many lives and emphasising the value of this particular life. I am only suggesting that each of these beliefs might more readily cultivate one of these tendencies, tendencies which mirror the creative tension between loving involvement and wise non-attachment which both traditions advocate.

The Buddhist 'world' and the Christian 'world' overlap, contends King, but they are not the same: 'They are two life-worlds, two languages. On some points they can understand each other deeply; on other points they elude each other. This is exactly why they can learn from each other' (2005a: 100). When interviewed, King elaborated, giving as an example of a point on which they elude each other that of the Judeo-Christian concern for justice as against the Buddhist emphasis on acceptance of the fruition of karma and on letting go of one's anger. She had personal experience of the encounter between these two emphases while in Jerusalem with the Peace Council: Palestinians and Israelis, respectively, recounted the many wrongs and injustices done against them and spoke of the need for resistance and the demand for justice. The Buddhists were baffled by this since they felt this approach nourished suffering and a more appropriate response would be for each side to let go of their grievances.[47] King recalls that the Israelis and Palestinians had no idea what the Buddhists were talking about and vice versa; 'that's a place where they elude each other'. Nevertheless, King feels that neither perspective should be dismissed, since 'there is a certain truth in both' (413). She feels, moreover, that this is one of the areas in which there is a fascinating encounter between these two traditions which is currently playing itself out, not only inside people like herself, but also between communities (413). King has learned from Israelis that the Buddhist emphasis on letting go has been refreshing to many Jews in Israel for whom the burden to *remember* placed on them by their Jewish tradition has not offered them a way out of the cycle of violence in the ongoing Israeli–Palestinian conflict. Buddhists, on the other hand, through their contact with people of a Judeo-Christian mindset are encountering and being challenged by the notion of a demand for justice.

King points out that in order for this profound and creative encounter between these world-views to continue, it is necessary for the distinctiveness of each to be maintained, but she also wants them to learn from each other, and worries that these two wishes may pull in opposite directions.

> I want them to be themselves because how else are they going to learn from each other – and there's real richness on each side to learn from – and yet I feel they're both kind of incomplete so what happens when they have learned from each other? Is it better or worse? Maybe it's better – if they can really get the best of what the other has to say. ... [I]t's clear to me that that mess in the Middle-East would profit from a healthy injection of the Buddhist understanding of that whole thing ... But I think also, Cambodia, for example: they need more than they're being offered by their tradition.[48]

Although King wants Buddhism and Christianity to learn from one another here, she does not want to see the distinctions between the traditions fade, in case the particular insight of each is weakened. Hence, in this regard, at the same time as seeking to combine the insights of each in her own life, she is keen to see the distinctiveness of each tradition preserved and worries lest dual belonging become a force which erodes the distinctions.

> It's *essential* that Buddhism and Christianity preserve their integrity; their unique, being what they are. ... [S]o the kind of – I don't know whether to call it 'blending' or not – that I'm involved in and that the rest of us you're interviewing are involved in ... is based upon the separation of the two traditions. So once it starts getting blended by me and the others, people don't have the same resource anymore in the next generation.
>
> (407)

In other words, drawing on the insights of both traditions, as dual belongers do, is only possible if the traditions retain their separateness, yet dual belonging itself may – if it becomes sufficiently widespread – endanger that separateness.

King feels that the two world-views are incommensurable regarding the issue of letting go, on the one hand, and justice on the other: 'there's no way to translate one of those into the other. There's nothing to receive it, no approach to a parallel'.[49] Yet, as we have seen, she hopes that each side can learn from the other. King experiences this as a kind of paradox facing dual belongers. If both the Buddhist approach and the Christian approach contain truth, then it ought to be possible to integrate those truths:

> I would like ... to work out the integration, because my feeling is they both have a piece of the truth and, if that's the case, there should be a way to put it together ... on this *particular* point. ... Right now it's more – in my own mind – side by side ... I would like to work out, or I think it would be good if someone else worked out: that if they both have a piece of the truth, what are those pieces and how does it all work out in one single package?
>
> (415)

Whilst she desires this integration, however, King also feels – at a more general level – that there cannot be an integration of Buddhism and Christianity which preserves all the strengths of both traditions (407).

Could it be that the incommensurability King identifies regarding the encounter between letting go and justice is an incommensurability which relates to the fact that Buddhists assume that this present life is only one of innumerable lives, whereas in the Judeo-Christian tradition it is generally assumed that we have only one life? In other words, these approaches might be, to some extent, incommensurable because of the divergence between the metaphysical and cosmological assumptions which undergird them. Again, although each approach contains great value and truth, these truths cannot be easily integrated because the assumptions out of which they have emerged are straightforwardly contradictory: one of those assumptions must be false.[50] If this analysis is correct, then holding in tension these contradictory assumptions regarding the question of rebirth may be the best way of preserving both approaches – approaches which, though valuable in their own right, are especially valuable when each is kept 'in check' by the other: we should be non-attached, but non-attachment must not lead to apathy; we need to be concerned with justice, but we must not meet injustice with anger; we should be ready to act, but action must always take account of the conditions which lead people to act in unwholesome ways, and be motivated by compassion for both oppressed and oppressor. By working with both the possibility that there is one life and the possibility that there are many, the dual belonger may be best able to sustain the creative tension between these complementary insights.

Similarly, the balancing act in which King and Reis Habito are engaged between the Christian emphasis on the uniqueness of the individual and the Buddhist emphasis on no-self (see p. 143–4), may also relate to the question of whether this life is the only life (and the people we are now, the only people we will ever be) or whether it is just one of many (and the people we are now, merely transitory configurations of ever-fluctuating aggregates). The difference between the traditions regarding the question of the value of individuals *qua* individuals might, additionally, have to do with the question of which characterisation of the eschaton is the more correct: the Christian characterisation, in which individuality seems to be somehow preserved (and in this sense accorded ultimate, eternal value); or the Buddhist characterisation, in which individuality does not seem to be preserved (and in this sense is accorded no ultimate, eternal value). Perhaps, as with the question of rebirth, by remaining agnostic regarding the eschatological question, dual belongers are more likely to preserve the unique character of each tradition and are, thus, more likely to sustain the demanding but creative dialogical tension between the importance of each unique individual and the importance of not nurturing ego.

As Hick points out, even tradition-specific beliefs which turn out to be literally false, may still be mythologically true in the sense that 'the dispositional responses which they tend to evoke are appropriate to our existence in relation to the Real' (1989a: 370). I suggest that we think in this way about the Christian contention that there is one life and the Buddhist contention that there are many, and about their respective characterisations of the eschaton: in both these cases, their respective beliefs help undergird insights into the nature of the spiritual task; one fostering a concern for justice and motivation to act, a sense of the preciousness of individual persons, of the significance of this present life, and of responsibility for the lives of others; the other fostering acceptance and tolerance, non-attachment, a non-egotistical way of being, non-discriminating compassion, and the ability to let go of anger. These insights are *all* helpful in following the spiritual path, *especially* when held in tension with one another, and *all* have spiritual truth even though the assumptions which help undergird some of them will turn out to be literally false. If the dual belonger affirms only one of these assumptions in each case, and denies the other (as on options i and ii above regarding rebirth), then the pressure is on to find ways of maintaining both kinds of insight once one has removed one of the conceptual bases which encouraged one of these kinds of insight to flourish. Perhaps this will be possible, but it is a high risk strategy for those who are keen to preserve the distinctive insights of these two traditions, and since it is not clear that questions regarding rebirth and the precise nature of the eschaton are ones which anyone can answer for certain, perhaps the safer option – of holding in mind the teachings of both traditions as possibilities – is best. This way, the dual belonger is able to draw on the mutually corrective and complementary strengths of both approaches to life without risking the gradual decay of one or other of those approaches by undermining its conceptual foundations.

When discussing truth-claims such as those concerning whether or not there is rebirth, Hick rightly notes that every belief of this kind 'has arisen within a complex religious tradition ... to which it is integral, and each such belief contributes to one or more of the religio-cultural "lenses" through which the Real is humanly perceived' (1989a: 369). Given this, for dual belongers to opt too firmly for either the traditional Christian view that there is only one life, or for the traditional Buddhist view that there are innumerable lives, is to risk significantly altering one or other of the Buddhist or Christian lenses which they have found so beneficial. When she considers the alternatives to reserving judgement on the question of rebirth, King concludes similarly; that if one plumps for one or other side of the dichotomy, something will be lost:

> I'm agnostic on things that, as far as I can tell, really seem to *conflict* – one life or many lives? Well, I'm agnostic so that's fine, the differences are remaining intact but what happens if somebody goes one way or the other way? Then you've lost something. ... Pacifism looks really different if you believe in many lives and that gives the Tibetans and the others the patience, so that their form of pacifism can generate over several generations and then, as far as they're concerned, it all works out in the end. There's a certain truth in that, to me, and then there's also a certain truth in the other side which is ... : yeah, but what about this life right now? This is unique, this is precious: that's true too ... Well, they're both right, and if you really blend on that issue, *something's* going to be lost.
>
> (407)

For the time being, then, regarding the question of rebirth, King feels that the third option (in our schema) is preferable to the first or second:

> it's a *wonderful* thing to be in the position I'm in and have all that richness of these two different ways of talking and thinking, and being and to

be able to kind of swim around in both and see where there's something profound and, even if they seem to knock up against each other, that's OK – I can hold them both.

(407–8)

Following one's individual path

Our investigation suggests that, although Buddhism and Christianity characterise the transformation from self-centredness to Reality-centredness differently, there is considerable overlap between their characterisations. It also reveals that the tension created by their respective emphases on love and wisdom is recognised by both traditions as spiritually beneficial. Thus, it is possible to follow a single spiritual path which is both authentically Buddhist and authentically Christian, even if one is agnostic about the precise nature of the final destination of that path, about which – if either – of the traditions will turn out to be more efficacious in its final stages, and about how many lives one will have in which to complete it.

Habito recalls a Japanese saying which nicely encapsulates the possible objection to dual belonging which we have been addressing in this chapter: 'Those who chase after two rabbits will catch neither'. '[P]erhaps in declaring my aspiration to live as a Buddhist, and my aspiration to live as a Christian', says Habito, 'I am ... rendering myself unable to live up to either in a faithful and authentic way' (2007: 179). He does not, however, feel that this objection applies: 'what I have learned from Buddhism and what I have learned from the Christian tradition, somehow, tend to confirm one another', says Habito. 'They may challenge one another on occasions or from certain angles but, in that mutual challenge, there's also a mutual enrichment and a mutual transformation' (166); 'they're not two different paths pulling away and tearing me apart', he explains, but '[o]ne path, informed by those two traditions'.[51] Even Corless, who to some extent saw Buddhism and Christianity as orientating him towards distinct religious ends (and who, to that extent, perhaps, saw himself as 'chasing two rabbits'), reflects that, although 'there is some final end ... there's some kind of a process also' (73) and Buddhism and Christianity are mutually supportive in that process.[52]

Despite his monocentric pluralism, in *An Interpretation of Religion* Hick appears to deny the possibility of dual belonging (1989a: 373). One reason for this might be that he sees religious traditions as akin to different paths to the summit of a mountain. On the basis of this analogy, dual belonging seems impossible, virtually *by definition*, since one cannot reach the summit of a mountain by simultaneously walking up paths on different faces of that mountain. Although this analogy allows for the validity of Buddhist and Christian insights, on the model of religious belonging it suggests, the possibility of a dual belonger reaching the summit can only be accounted for if he or she is understood as forging a new Buddhist–Christian path, i.e. a new

'Buddhist–Christian' religion which is necessarily distinct from Buddhism and Christianity.[53] However, what the 'paths up a mountain' analogy fails to account for is the fact that it is not *religious traditions* which are saved/liberated, but *individual persons*. The analogy is, therefore, misleading: it fails to recognise that every person forges his or her own path up the mountain and no two paths are the same.[54] This affirmation of the uniqueness of every individual's salvific/liberative journey is supported by Smith's observations concerning the profoundly personal nature of faith:

> each man's faith is his own, is partly free, and results from an interaction within the personality between that confronting tradition along with all other mundane circumstances, external and inner, and the transcendent. A man's faith is what his tradition means to him. Yet it is, further, what the universe means to him, in the light of that tradition.
>
> (1962: 159)

There is no generic Christian faith or Buddhist faith, insists Smith, '[t]here is only my faith, and yours ... each of us is a person, not a type' (1962: 191). As Schmidt-Leukel says, then, the route one takes up the mountain is one's actual life, 'and religions should be instrumental in helping us to live it'.[55] He, therefore, suggests an alternative to the analogy between religions and paths:

> Religions may be compared to different maps or hill-walking guides, which give us some helpful clues to make our decisions, and some of the advice we get may be more helpful in some respect, while the advice coming from a different map may be helpful at some other junction.
>
> (2005e: 6)

Over time, Hick appears to have become more open to the possibility of dual belonging. In *The Rainbow of Faiths*, for example, he suggests that people might 'be able to share spiritual resources across traditional borders' (1995: 116); in personal correspondence in 2005, while still maintaining that being Buddhist and Christian would be difficult, he acknowledges that there is more than one Buddhism and more than one Christianity and among the possible combinations a compatible pair may exist;[56] and in 2009 he mentions 'important new possibilities' emerging from the ever closer contact between religions, among these the possibility 'even of "dual citizenship" in religion'.[57] Unlike the analogy of religious traditions as paths, Schmidt-Leukel's analogy of religious traditions as maps or hill-walking guides accommodates the possibility of an individual integrating ideas and practices from more than one tradition. The fact that maps can be drawn from different perspectives, with different considerations in mind, to different scales, and using different points of reference and different keys – such that one cannot be simply 'mapped' onto the other – recognises both the fact that the language of one tradition cannot be easily translated into the language of another, and the possibility that having two very different kinds of map could be useful to someone who has learnt to read both and who is undertaking a difficult journey.

Another analogy, employed by King, which construes Buddhism and Christianity in an instrumental way and which is also able to recognise the possibility of dual belonging is that of religions as tools. Cornille is critical of the tendency toward an 'instrumentalization of religious traditions' which she associates with multiple belonging, apparently seeing this as tantamount to a 'commodification' of religious traditions.[58] But if it is accepted that religions point beyond themselves and are not, therefore, ends in themselves,[59] then surely their value *should* be seen as primarily instrumental. King explains that she has been influenced by Buddhism here and especially by the 'Parable of the Raft' (*Alagaddupama Sutta*): 'Buddhism is a vehicle, a tool, for helping us to transport ourselves from our present condition to the condition of Enlightenment. It is not the end, it is a means' (2005a: 89). Quakerism, thinks King, is also an instrument; 'not an end in itself, not the embodiment of ultimate Truth, but a means, a method, a set of practices, the aim of which is to gain the individual (and, important in Quakerism, the group) access to the divine Spirit' (2005a: 90). Just as there is no inherent contradiction implied by a person employing various tools to carry out a demanding job, nor is there any inherent contradiction implied by the idea of a single person employing the insights and methods of more than one religious tradition in order to foster the salvific/liberative transformation. If the particular tools a person chose were to in some way work against each other, each undoing the work of the other, then using that combination of tools would be unadvisable. But, as we have seen, Buddhism and Christianity do not undo each other's work; rather, they are found to be mutually reinforcing and complementary.

6 Practice

In this chapter we will look at how Buddhist Christians combine the practices of these two traditions. Whereas, in the field of doctrine, dual belongers face numerous questions regarding the compatibility of Buddhism and Christianity, in the field of practice, as we shall see, the common ground is more immediately apparent. Many of the reflections of my interviewees suggest that in this area, especially, their integration of Buddhism and Christianity has been less a matter of consciously seeking to reconcile the traditions, than a matter of discovering deep convergences and allowing mutual influence over time.

Certainly, insofar as ethical behaviour is considered a dimension of 'practice', there is consensus in the reflections of my interviewees that this is one of the areas in which the compatibility and overlap between Buddhism and Christianity is most obvious. Of course, not all Western scholars would support this consensus, and in the late nineteenth century and first half of the twentieth century, few would have. Christian thinkers tended to interpret Buddhist ethics as individualistic (encouraging only the cultivation of one's own mind) and as indifferent to the sufferings of others, ignoring or dismissing anything which challenged this stereotype.[1] But, today, there is a growing consensus among scholars that Buddhist ethics is not deficient in comparison to Christian ethics and that there is broad overlap between them.[2] King reflects that, in a sense, all of life is practice and since, as far as she is concerned, the values of Quakerism and Buddhism are the same, in this sense, Quaker and Buddhist practice are one and the same,[3] – though she admits that those values are not easy to live up to (381). Even Corless, who took Buddhism and Christianity to be largely incompatible, or at least mutually irrelevant, felt that their ethical dimensions were an exception: 'at the ethical level there's not much conflict' (27). Hence, in this regard, he could consider both Buddhism and Christianity to be at once normative for him, and could assert that, even if it were not possible for him to *think* as both a Buddhist and a Christian at the same time, in the ethical realm it was nevertheless possible for him simultaneously to *act* as both (27).

But what about formal religious practice? There is clearly an overlap of purpose to the extent that both Buddhist and Christian practices are intended to foster selflessness, love and wisdom. But, given the differences between the theological and philosophical frameworks which give Buddhist and Christian practices their meaning, one might expect significant divergences. Indeed, a superficial comparison of Christianity and Buddhism could lead one to conclude that they are quite different in their fundamental formal practices: Christians pray whereas Buddhists meditate. While in prayer the individual addresses a personal 'Thou' (God, Jesus Christ or one of the Saints), praising or petitioning the one addressed; Buddhists do not address anyone but rather still their minds so as to investigate the nature of reality in the hope of realising the non-personal bliss of 'no self' or, in Mahāyāna terms, of discovering their own Buddha Nature through the experience of non-duality. Characterised as such, even if Christian and Buddhist practices both foster ethical behaviour and are understood as different ways of orientating people towards a single transcendent ultimate reality, those practices might, nevertheless, look mutually undermining. Deeper investigation, however, reveals that there is considerably more common ground between Christian and Buddhist practice than is captured by the cliché: 'Christians pray whereas Buddhists meditate'.

Prayer, meditation and everyday mindfulness: practice across traditions

To start with, contrary to popular Western misconception, there is much in Buddhism that one might legitimately identify as prayer. As Kenneth Tanaka explains, although Buddhists are stereotypically thought of as only meditating, the reality is that 'the vast majority of lay Buddhists in Asia primarily "pray" or express themselves devotionally, during which they give thanks but also petition for one thing or another of worldly nature'.[4] In the Mahāyāna countries of East Asia the objects of prayers are Bodhisattvas such as Avalokiteśvara, in the Theravāda countries of South-East Asia, Śākyamuni Buddha is the primary object of devotion (Tanaka 2003: 102), while the devas are the objects of petitionary prayer. Rita Gross identifies at least three different types of Buddhist 'prayers':

> The first ... involves prayer to many relatively existing beings. The second ... involves making aspirations or wishes, in which no one is addressed, but many hopes are expressed. The third, most elusive type ... comes from the liturgies of Tibetan 'deity yoga' ...
>
> (2003a: 91)

When we look at the practice of my interviewees we arguably find examples of – or at least akin to – all these types of Buddhist prayer, but especially the second and third types. Their reflections reveal, moreover, not only that all three types overlap in some way with their Christian prayer, but also that their understandings of Christian prayer have been influenced by these Buddhist understandings of prayer. Let's look at each of these types in turn.

In the first type of prayer, explains Gross, Buddhists petition various invisible super-human beings who, like human beings, are thought to exist as independent beings only at the relative level and not absolutely. Gross compares the kind of existence these beings are thought to have with that of saints or angels – who exist but do not have the total independence of existence Christians accord to God (2003a: 92–93). Such beings are believed by Buddhists to be able to respond to petitions and alter the course of events (Gross 2003a: 91–92). Although none of my interviewees included any prayer to Buddhist deities in their descriptions of their practice, Corless' Buddhist prayers to Bodhisattvas somewhat fitted this first category (whilst also shading into the third category, which we'll look at presently). He says of 'entities' such as Bodhisattvas that, while 'they're not walking around in the way that the humans are … they're quite real and they have a personality'. He says, for example, that he can relate to Tārā more easily than Chenrezi or Avalokiteśvara (37). From his Buddhist perspective, Corless expects these beings to help him make progress on the spiritual path (72). He explains that, although there are some differences, when he prays to Avalokiteśvara or Tārā, it is fairly similar to the way in which he might pray to Christian saints (37). Moreover, he accepts, even from his Christian perspective, a Mahāyāna Buddhist understanding of how beings of great attainment are able to assist people:

> it's as if they've attained to the *dharmakāya* and can then manifest instantaneously and simultaneously in all worlds, although not physically, to help all other beings and that's what happens when we pray to the saints … they are able to … manifest to us, individually.
>
> (69)

The second type of Buddhist prayer identified by Gross (2003a: 93) involves practitioners expressing wishes, particularly, for the fulfilment of goals towards which they are striving such as the well-being of all sentient beings, the fulfilment of the vision of a great teacher, or for their own spiritual progress in order that they might be of assistance to others. Gross takes 'dedication of merit' (a practice whereby the merit one has gained as a result of one's spiritual practice or virtuous actions is dedicated to all sentient beings) to be in this category of prayer (2003a: 94). With these prayers, explains Gross, 'there is no "you" to whom they are addressed, only an "I" making the aspiration and recipients of the wishes expressed in the aspiration or dedication' (2003a: 94). Buddhists consider such prayers valuable because of their effectiveness in helping the practitioners who express them to embody the ideals their aspirations express, and not because any god might act to fulfil their wishes (2003a: 95–96). Despite assuming a significant theological divide between Buddhists and Christians over the question of whether or not God is listening to such prayers, Gross sees overlap with Christian prayer here insofar as theists take it to be the person who prays who needs the prayer, rather than God. In Christianity, as in Buddhism, prayer plays an important role in the transformation and spiritual cultivation of the practitioner.

This second kind of Buddhist prayer was certainly a feature of the practice of my interviewees and a number identified *mettā bhāvanā* (meditation in which one cultivates loving kindness towards all beings by wishing for their happiness and well-being) or the dedication of merit, for example, as overlapping significantly with their Christian practice. Regardless of how each of them interpreted the theological divide between Buddhism and Christianity over the question of God (see Chapter 3), most interviewees anyway did not practise – or saw themselves as trying to avoid practising – petitionary prayer of a kind whereby one pleads with God to grant some specific wish. King, for example, says that she has recently taken a negative turn towards 'please, please' prayer, whether addressed to God or to anyone else: 'I'm not good with "please benevolent being, intervene here or help somehow"', says King (356). King is not sure whether or not to call it 'prayer' (356), but feels that practice in which one expresses the wish, for example, that all beings be happy and at peace constitutes a significant area of overlap between her practice in both traditions (355, 357):

> When there's someone who you're concerned about ... you hold them in the light, which is a kind of a prayer ... , but it's also mindfulness; it's also *mettā* practice – it's also sending loving kindness to that person. So that practice, to me, comes from the two different directions but ends up probably 90 per cent overlap.
>
> (355)

Even though there were other interviewees who did not share King's dim view of asking God, saints, and Bodhisattvas for help, it was nevertheless the case that most of their intercessory prayer for the wellbeing of others could be aptly described in King's Quaker terminology, as 'holding in the light' – holding the person in need in mindful, loving kindness (355). Despite not being a Quaker, Corless, for example, uses precisely this terminology: 'I try just to place the person or thing in the light because I don't know what is best' (34). Similarly, Furneaux explains that there is an element of what might be called intercessory prayer in her self-administered Eucharist; but, she says, 'I don't ask for anything or for anybody I simply offer up that person to whatever is useful for them and I don't presume to judge what might be useful for them' (102). Habito says that his petitionary prayer is not necessarily 'un-Buddhist', because in Buddhist practices 'there is also this sense of seeking the healing of other beings and so on, and so there is a sense of connectedness with other beings in situations of suffering, from a Buddhist angle' (147).

As in Christian prayer, moreover, there is, arguably, an expectation on the part of at least some Buddhists that the expression of compassionate wishes will have a positive effect on the world *beyond* their valuable effect on, and through, those who express them, despite the fact that they are not addressed to a god who is expected to act to fulfil them. Indeed, traditionally, Buddhists think of those to whom merit is dedicated as the primary beneficiaries of the dedication of merit. Other practices expressing wishes for the well-being of others are also assumed by many Buddhists to have a kind of magical or telepathic power to directly help bring about that which is wished for. King, for example, suggests that this is true of *mettā* practice, though she has never seen a Buddhist explanation of the mechanism through which such an effect is supposed to be brought about.[5] Despite not understanding how it works, this is King's own belief about her *mettā* practice. She does not take herself to be addressing anyone, yet understands this practice to be more than simply an expression of her wish: 'it's also partially, *somehow*, helping to bring that into being' (356). Furneaux also seems to believe that wishes for the wellbeing of others can directly affect their well-being,[6] even though, like King, she does not take herself to be addressing anyone ('I don't pray *to* anybody or anything', says Furneaux, 'I simply pray; or there's simply prayer'[7]). King's and Furneaux's understandings at least indicate that the question of whether prayer is effective beyond its positive effect on the practitioner and, if it is, what the mechanism is by which it is effective, are questions faced by Christians and Buddhists alike.

In the third type of Buddhist prayer identified by Gross (Tibetan 'deity yoga') utterances (including prayers for refuge, protection, and liberation) are addressed 'to a visualized being whose symbolic form represents ultimate reality and one's own true being' (Gross 2003a: 97). The being one visualises and addresses (and which is later visualised as dissolving into light and space, into a state of radiant emptiness) represents both ultimate reality and one's true self (as opposed to one's ego-self). Rather than being a supplication to something or someone outside oneself, Gross explains, the practice employs dualistic language to assist practitioners in their realisation of the ultimate non-duality between themselves and the reality they address (2003a: 97–98). References to practices akin to this third type of prayer can be identified in the reflections of most of those I interviewed (and not just in Corless' descriptions of his Tibetan visualisation practices). Reis Habito and Habito, for example, both of whom engage in some form of devotional practice addressed to a Bodhisattva, reflect that they understand themselves to be doing so at the relative level while, at the ultimate level, the one they address is not separate from themselves.

Reis Habito, for example, recites the *Great Compassion Dhāraṇī* (a long mantra dedicated to the praise of the Bodhisattva, Guanyin) and believes that, while at one level, she is praying to Guanyin (Kuan-Yin/Kannon/Avalokiteśvara), at another level, she is contacting the reality – represented by Guanyin – in herself (456). At the absolute level, explains Reis Habito, 'there is nothing like down here and up here and these people come to your help down here; it's just when you recite the mantra … you open up to reality and you open your heart up to compassion'.[8] Similarly,

Habito describes how devotion to Kuan-Yin is expressed in Zen practice communities, but explains that an important reminder is issued from the Zen perspective:

> we are told that Kuan-Yin is not 'out there' on the elevated platform, but that each and every one of us is Kuan-Yin. Our Zen practice is our way of realizing how to be Kuan-Yin, or of actualizing the reality of Kuan-Yin in our own lives.
>
> (2004: 100–101)

There is a chant which Habito recites with the community at Maria Kannon Zen Center (MKZC) which pays homage to the Bodhisattva Kannon: 'we don't chant it as if there were some being out there that we are chanting to', explains Habito, 'but it is simply reciting the name in order to activate that reality [of compassion] which is already in all of us' (160). Both Habito and Reis Habito understand their Christian prayer in a similar way. Habito suggests Mary as a parallel figure to Kannon within the Christian tradition, since she is the embodiment of compassion for Christians and is not only to be venerated, but is the model of all Christians; she represents the life which all Christians are called to lead.[9] 'In other words,' says Habito, 'the invitation ... as one reveres the figure of Mary, is likewise, to *be* Mary, to embody in one's life all that Mary signifies' (2004: 101). In Habito's own Christian Zen practice, these parallel figures come together in the figure of Maria Kannon: a Buddhist and Christian symbol of compassion.[10]

Similarly Reis Habito reflects that her understanding of Christian prayer is similar to this Buddhist understanding: 'so, that's one level that's also there in Christianity, of course: you pray to the Saints and they're out there and they come down to help you' (455). But then there is the absolute level of truth too, where there is no 'up here' and 'down there'. Reis Habito is not unaware that her Christian understanding of prayer has been influenced in this regard by Buddhism but nevertheless thinks it is an appropriate understanding of Christian prayer: 'it's also God opening myself up more to compassion, ... I don't think so much of God in terms of *out there*. I mean, if it's not in your heart, where is it?' (455). When asked for clarification regarding how she understands what is happening when she is praying to Jesus or the Saints, Reis Habito confirms that she understands Jesus Christ as, in a sense, 'an aspect of the reality that is called self'.[11] She explains, however, that she finds this a tricky area of discourse:

> because at some level it's true and at some level it's not and, when you start praying, you start from this level where there is I and Thou as a reality, and you come to a level where there is not a distinction and it is very hard to describe.
>
> (456)

Habito reflects that, even in modes of prayer such as petition (which he thinks clearly entails 'that sense of addressing something to a Thou that one understands as also listening to that prayer'), one is addressing a reality one also recognises as being 'more intimate to me than I am to myself'.[12] Hence, he also takes there to be an analogy between the type of Buddhist prayer in which one relates oneself to an external being in order to realise the reality of that being within oneself, and his devotion both to the Buddha and to Jesus Christ. With each of these figures, explains Habito, it is not 'just something out there that we're relating to but it is precisely a figure that stands for what we all are, deep within' (160). He suggests further that something like this understanding can apply not only to Christian prayer to saints but also to Christian prayer to God.

This experience, in Christian prayer, of God as both other and not other is not surprising when we consider, as Donald Mitchell (2003) and Taitetsu Unno (2003) urge us to, that even though in Christian prayer God is usually addressed as a transcendent 'Thou', ultimately, the subject and object of prayer are the same.[13] Mitchell notes with respect to prayers of petition, adoration, praise, and so on, that 'the prayers are the dynamics of a person's relationship with God, where God is both ultimate source and object of the prayers' (2003: 135). He draws attention to Saint Teresa of Avila's description of a prayer experience 'in which is revealed to the soul how all things are in God, and how within himself he contains them all'; he suggests that this kind of prayer experience is common in mature Christian spirituality (2003: 136).

At this point we begin to see the overlap, not only between Christian prayer and Buddhist prayer directed towards a being who represents both ultimate reality and one's own true being, but also between Christian prayer (particularly contemplative prayer) and Buddhist *meditation* practices in which one develops an awareness of one's non-separateness from ultimate reality. Indeed, when it comes to prayer experiences in both traditions in which the boundary between the one who utters and the one who hears the prayers seems to break down, the distinction between prayer (whether Christian or Buddhist) and forms of Buddhist meditation such as *shikantaza* (just sitting) or *Satipaṭṭhāna* (mindfulness) starts to blur.

As noted in previous chapters, not all forms of Christian prayer involve the experience of 'I–Thou' relationship. Rather, some involve non-conceptual, non-dual experiences (as in the contemplative prayer of some Christian mystics). We have also seen that there are non-personal conceptions of ultimate reality in Christian thought as well as the more prevalent personal conceptions, and that God is understood, by those who endorse God's conceptual transcendence, as neither object nor subject. We noted, moreover, MacInnes' observation that, while the Christian tradition has tended to place emphasis on the transcendence of ultimate reality, in the East the stronger tendency has been to place emphasis on the immanence of ultimate reality, and with King we speculated that the difference between Buddhist and Christian understandings of ultimate reality may derive, to some extent, from an ambiguity in the human experience of ultimate reality, an ambiguity which may have to do with our continuity with that reality. Against this background, it is clear that, when we compare prayer and meditation, far from looking at a contrast between utterly different and mutually irrelevant forms of religious practice, it is difficult even to discern a clear line between them: prayer simply revolves more around the experience of ultimate reality as greater than us (as the reality we worship, adore, beseech, and so on), whereas meditation revolves more around the experience of ultimate reality as not separate from us (as the reality in which we are to realise our participation experientially).

Reflecting on Buddhist and Christian practice, Ursula King also identifies a convergence between prayer and meditation. In prayer, observes King, 'the intentional direction ... is mostly one from inward to outward, from self to other, in that the prayer addresses another Person, the great "Other", so that the self finds a transcendent center for itself' (2003: 148). In Eastern meditation, on the other hand, we see 'a movement from outward to inward, and effort to reach the immanent center of the self in a deeper dimension within'. Hence, 'the direction of prayer and meditation differ; their center is found in a different place and experienced in a different way'. However, concludes King,

> ultimately this difference disappears in that the transcendent and immanent reality touch each other in the depth of being and are ultimately interrelated. One can therefore speak of an interweaving and a continuity between prayer and meditation – the deepest prayer experience of Christian mystics ultimately translates itself into a meditative depth experience of union with the divine ground.
>
> (2003: 148)

Perhaps we can say that prayer and meditation are two different ways of relating to ultimate reality but they are ways which are ultimately two sides of the same coin. My interviewees' reflections suggest that they very much experience this convergence in their own practice of each tradition and Reis Habito, for example, finds that she slips easily between prayer, in which there is a sense of God as 'Thou', and meditation, in which she focuses only on her breath until all distinctions drop away (453).

Some interviewees identified the everyday practice of maintaining mindful awareness as their main practice and reflected that this practice could be classed as both Buddhist meditation and Christian prayer. Furneaux, for example, takes *Satipaṭṭhāna* (Mindfulness) to be 'a unifying practice between the different Buddhist practices and between Buddhist and Christian practice'. For it is the basis of most Buddhist practices and is, says Furneaux, as far as we can tell, similar to early Church practice in the Patristic period.[14] She explains that although her practice does involve formal elements that would be more readily recognisable to others as prayer, she herself no longer draws a distinction between prayer and meditation. Her prayer does not involve 'I-Thou' experience, she explains, because in contemplative prayer there is no consciousness of an 'object' – of a 'Thou' (102–3). 'I' and 'Thou' 'are not collapsed into one' either, says Furneaux, 'but into the not-two', and she echoes King's reflections on the self undergoing transformation (see Chapter 3) when she explains that the one who prays is not the 'I' one normally thinks of as oneself (103). Similarly, says Furneaux,

> when you start mindfulness or *Satipaṭṭhāna* meditation … there is … clearly an observer, which is the 'you' doing the work. But as you go on and you keep seeing or experiencing the discomfort of that observer, it fades away and then there's no longer … any separation.
>
> (103)

It appears to be this similarity which has led Furneaux to the conclusion that, ultimately, there is little to distinguish contemplative prayer from *Satipaṭṭhāna*:

> Contemplative prayer *is* sitting. … The New Testament says (a) we do not know how to pray, and (b) be in continuous prayer. To be continuously mindful is to be continuously prayerful. Thich Nhat Hanh says mindfulness is the Holy Spirit – the energy of God. … the Holy Spirit teaches you mindfulness and that's the way I saw it when I was very young … When you come to see that there is just mindfulness and that what sits in meditation is not you or what you think of as you, then that distinction drops away as well. … [G]enerally the moving meditation is body prayer, the walking meditation is body prayer, the working meditation is a sacrament of everyday life.
>
> (102)

Similarly, Habito identifies his main practice as the attempt to maintain mindfulness in every moment, saying,

> at least, in terms of tuning in, that's really part of what I feel I've been accustomed to now; a way of maintaining mindfulness of the present moment and being grateful for each moment and so it's a way of returning to the breath, that I find that is my basic practice.
>
> (148)

He thinks of this as being both a Buddhist and a Christian practice:

> Buddhist meditation is … not just sitting … but also just coming to awareness of the here and now with each breath and so on … I've learned from the Zen practice to do that and … I've seen how that also makes sense as a Christian in terms of coming back to the Breath, now with a capital 'B'; the Breath which is the *rûach* of God … just returning to the presence of God in one's life. So I can articulate the same spiritual attitude from a Buddhist angle as well as from a Christian angle.
>
> (147)

King also identifies the everyday practice of mindfulness or prayerfulness as her main practice and likewise takes this practice to be both Buddhist and Christian: 'When I said "prayerful", I meant in a kind of a Christian sense, and mindful awareness ... – It's been both' (355).

Furneaux draws a traditional Buddhist distinction between 'peak' practice time, in the sense of formal practice time, and the continuous practice of mindfulness which, as far as she is concerned, is 'what the whole thing is about' (101). She explains that there was a time when she had to keep her 'peak' Buddhist practice separate from her 'peak' Christian practice, finding herself unable to say the Buddhist office or do any Buddhist chanting on the day each fortnight when she received the Eucharist, but she now attributes this to her own creation of distinctions which did not reflect reality. *Satipaṭṭhāna* is 'a practice of every moment', says Furneaux, 'so everything you do is practice' (101). She suggests that, although in the beginning one distinguishes between one's Buddhist and one's Christian practice, if one makes progress on this path, one eventually reaches a point in one's spiritual development where the 'dilemma' ceases to arise:

> it's not God or you, it's not God and you together, it's not all is one ... The question simply doesn't arise and, so, at that point you have fully integrated all the opposites of appearance and reality; conventional and absolute have come so close together there's not a jot of difference anymore ... So while we're saying ' ... this is Buddhist practice and this is Christian practice', ... hopefully, we'll be going, at some point, to the acceptance of 'eventually, it *simply doesn't matter*'. It no longer arises as a question for you, it's all so *absolutely* integrated.
>
> (115)

Today she feels no need to maintain a separation between her Buddhist and Christian practice, since she no longer distinguishes between them. 'I'm just practising', says Furneaux, 'or rather "there is just practice" ... being present is being present' (103).

Habito describes 'the wordless way of coming back to the breath' as his 'basic prayer' (150). He asserts that there are scriptural passages which point to this kind of experience of prayer and, like Furneaux (102), identifies this mode of contemplative prayer as consistent with what St Paul had in mind when he urged the Thessalonians to 'pray always' or 'pray without ceasing' (1 Thessalonians 5: 17): 'it's an invitation to live in a spirit of prayerfulness 24 hours a day, seven days of the week, 365 and a quarter days of the year and so on ... to have a constant attitude of being in prayer' (148). This interpretation of Paul's injunction to 'pray without ceasing' is a traditional one within the Christian contemplative tradition but, insofar as, for Habito, his practice of maintaining mindful awareness by coming back to the breath has been informed not only by the Christian tradition, but also by years of practice within the Zen tradition, he thinks of it as Buddhist practice too and is able to describe it in Buddhist as well as Christian terms (149–50). Vice versa, although Habito learned from Buddhists how to sit in silence, he cannot see his *shikantaza* as 'solely' Buddhist practice:

> I may have learned it from a Buddhist source but with my self-understanding as coming from the Christian tradition and with all of the, not just doctrinal and conceptual paraphernalia that comes with it, but also with my affective and emotional integrated being, there's a lot that is triggered by Christian images there. So in that sense I find that hard – to make that line of distinction: that it's *only* Buddhist, and so forth … I practise in a way that participates in both traditions so that's why it's not two practices but it's one practice that cuts across those two traditions.
>
> (150)

Habito distinguishes between the continuous practice of mindfulness or attitude of prayerfulness fostered by both traditions and *particular modes* of prayer (praise, thanksgiving, repentance, petition, and lamentation) which are specific to the Christian tradition. But he nevertheless understands these tradition-specific modes of prayer as underlain by that continuous prayer or mindfulness fostered by both traditions. And, as we have seen, even regarding petitionary prayer, there was a certain amount of overlap with Habito's more Buddhist forms of prayer.

King reflects that, although there are similarities between Buddhist and Quaker practice, there are also differences and, by and large, when in a specifically Buddhist place, she does Buddhist practice and, when in a specifically Quaker place, she does Quaker practice (at home, she says, it can be 'one or the other or both') (357). However, after further reflection, she admits that even in places which are specifically one or the other the distinctions are perhaps not that clear-cut. Although at Quaker Meetings she does Quaker meditation, she, like many other Quakers, uses Buddhist meditation techniques (focussing on the breath, for example) to assist her at the beginning of each Meeting in the process known as 'centring down', in which one quietens one's mind in preparation for the silence and openness of the Meeting (357). And, once one stops consciously centring down, explains King, the Quaker practice of sitting in stillness and silence is difficult to distinguish from the Zen practice of *shikantaza* (just sitting): 'it just so happens', says King, that 'both traditions have come to a practice that involves … quieting down and then trying to be open, still, connected, and just being there in the present' (357). Hence, although there are differences between Quaker sitting and Zen *shikantaza* (most notably, Quakers understand their maintenance of still, silent awareness as 'listening spiritually' for that 'still silent voice', listening for 'guidance or insights that come from the Spirit'; they also share spoken ministry – neither of which apply to Zen practice), King recognises that, even when she is practising Quaker meditation in a Friends Meeting House, her practice has still 'got an awful lot of Buddhist parts' (358). Similarly, Reis

Habito explains that even at Mass her practice includes meditation which could be deemed Buddhist:

> I love the readings but most of the time I don't like the sermons. So, when it's time for a sermon, I'm really doing meditation – I don't really listen, I just concentrate – and I find it's a good preparation for the Eucharist. So … even when I'm in church, maybe it's some kind of mixed practice again.
>
> (441)

A number of the reflections we have looked at so far suggest that the difficulty my interviewees have in identifying a clear dividing line between their Buddhist and their Christian practice results not only from their having *discovered* areas of overlap and resonance between Buddhist and Christian practice, but also from the *mutual influence* and *cross-fertilisation* naturally arising between the two traditions as both are practised. If, for example, Habito and Reis Habito had never encountered Buddhism, it seems likely that their understandings of what is happening in Christian prayer would not be quite what they are today; and if King and other Quakers had never come across Buddhist meditation techniques for calming the mind, it seems unlikely that they would currently be using precisely those techniques when 'centring down' for Quaker meditation. And there are plenty of other examples; one of these is Reis Habito's practice of Tibetan *Tonglen* meditation, which involves breathing in a person's pain and breathing out loving kindness to that person. Reis Habito finds *Tonglen* meditation can help to intensify prayer. When she practises it in a Christian context, she tends to think in terms of breathing out the loving kindness or compassion of God (at other times she thinks in terms of the compassion of the Virgin Mary or, in Buddhist contexts, of Guanyin) (449–50). She finds *Tonglen* meditation particularly profound and helpful as a Good Friday practice:

> you can breathe in Jesus' pain on the cross and really take it into yourself and then breathe out this loving compassion – and I think it's really transformative, and it's different from those prayers I knew from the Passion that are usually in that context.
>
> (450)

Is Reis Habito's Good Friday *Tonglen* meditation a Buddhist or a Christian practice?[15] And what of her *kōan* practice which, as we saw in Chapter 3, has included *kōans* couched in Christian terms[16] (given to her by Yamada Roshi because he perceived that, for her, the term 'God' was one which opened up her wisdom)? Although acknowledging that *kōan* practice comes specifically from the Zen Buddhist tradition, Reis Habito feels that, in her own life, it is a Buddhist *and* Christian practice (446).

Given her appreciation of deep convergences between Buddhist and Christian practices, and the cross-fertilisation between practices that has taken place in her spiritual life, Reis Habito explains that she would find it virtually impossible to take some particular aspect of her practice in isolation and classify it as purely Buddhist or purely Christian. Regarding her meditation in preparation for the Eucharist, for example, she suggests that, given its context, it could be deemed Christian practice, yet she is not convinced that she would ever have begun to pray in this way had she not encountered Buddhism.

> [W]hen I meditate and I pray, I never think, myself: is this now Christian or is this now Buddhist? To me, myself, it's not such a concern. But if I have to classify it, then there are certain difficulties coming up: how to describe it. ... [T]he meditation's more Buddhist because it starts from the breath and then it opens up to the awareness of all these people that are connected to my life, and the gratefulness, and all of that. So is that Buddhist, or is it Christian because it happens in church? See, I can't define it in the final result.
>
> (457)

The integration of her Buddhist and Christian practice is reflected in the combination of Buddhist and Christian imagery in Reis Habito's home, including the household altar: 'It's completely integrated ... Buddhist and Christian symbols; and our house, I think, is a complete mix' (455).

Furneaux, Habito, King, and Reis Habito were all reluctant to embrace the term 'dual practice' to describe their practice of two traditions, feeling as they did that the term implies a fundamental dichotomy in their practice which they do not experience. Habito, for example, feels that his main formal practice of sitting in mindful, prayerful silence, is best described by the term 'praxis across traditions', that this presents a more accurate picture of his practice than the term 'dual practice' (137; 1994b: 188 fnt. 1). He explains that his is 'a mode of practice that cuts through two distinct religious traditions, in a way that focuses on their mutually resonating elements, and ... not only reinforces ... [and] deepens, but also challenges each of the traditions involved' (1994b: 150). '[W]e are not dealing with two kinds of practices here', he says, '[i]t's the same practice, namely, of sitting in silence. But it crosses those two traditions' (137). Reis Habito would prefer to be identified as a 'Buddhist Christian' than as someone with a 'dual identity', or as a 'dual belonger'. The latter, she explains, seems to 'put a split into something that to me doesn't seem to have a split' (430).

But if one's Buddhist and one's Christian practice, and one's understandings of specific Buddhist and Christian practices, become so integrated that it is difficult to separate out anything as solely Buddhist practice or solely Christian practice, can one be sure that one's practice of Buddhism is authentically Buddhist and one's practice of Christianity authentically Christian? Is there not a danger here that one may have, inadvertently, incorporated one's Buddhist practice into a Christian schema or vice versa, or ended up with some third schema which comprises hybrid practices and draws on elements of Buddhist and Christian thought but which is itself neither Buddhist nor Christian?

Is Buddhist practice incorporated into a Christian schema?

Corless argues that 'Christians who do Zen most often do *Christian* Zen. *Zazen* is, for them, sitting in *contemplatio* (what English mystics call 'bare beholding') before God. A highly laudable but still a Christian practice' (1986a: 133). He particularly calls into question the Buddhist authenticity of the practice across traditions of Roman Catholics, like the Habitos, who practice within the Sanbô Kyôdan School of Zen (1996b: 1). Corless was not convinced that, in cases where Christian interpretations of the experiences to which Zen practice gives rise are maintained, it is really authentic *zazen* that is being practised:

> they appear to be practicing only sitting in lotus pose on a zafu and giving up words and concepts. They do not appear to be attempting to enter into the Buddhist universe in which there is no God, in which the Christian God is not relevant.
>
> (1996a: 10)

Winston King also questions whether the Zen meditation practised by Christians is genuinely Buddhist:

> I would say, in consonance with what William Johnston once wrote, that when a Christian sits on a pillow to meditate Zen fashion, he is sitting on a Christian pillow, and that the Zen Buddhist meditator in doing the 'same' meditation, even side by side with the Christian, is sitting on a Zen pillow, even though he would 'kill' the Buddha if he met him.[17]

Corless suggests that in order for dual belongers to be sure that they are practising genuine Buddhist meditation they should choose a form of meditation that contains some explicitly Buddhist content (1996a: 9–10).

Habito, however, denies the charge that when he practises *zazen* he is, in fact, sitting in *contemplatio*; or he denies, at least, that this is his 'default mode': 'I don't have a concept of God when I practice sitting in Zen, as such', says Habito. 'So, in that sense, I would not agree with Roger's description as applicable to what I practise when I practise Zen' (150). He explains that his practice in some moments does include a concept of God and could be interpreted as bare beholding before God but that his sitting is often a case of 'simply being there' (151). In Zen practice one lets go of concepts, says Habito, and one 'just sits there in a kind of wordless way before, well, Mystery with a capital "M", where the subject-object polarity is overcome, so there is no thing to behold there and no one beholding either. It's simply that' (151). To define sitting as *contemplatio* or bare beholding before God, suggests

Habito, limits the practice to a conceptual framework which is overcome. He acknowledges that Corless' description of his practice as bare-beholding before God, might apply to the Zen practice of Christians who do not move beyond their concept of God, but applied to his own practice, he finds it a one-sided description which fails to fully capture the reality (151).

Similarly, Reis Habito reflects that, although there are points in her Zen sitting to which Corless' description – *contemplatio* or 'bare beholding' before God – might apply, there are also points where his description would not quite capture what is going on in her practice: 'yes, there are stages where it's Christian Zen, and then there are stages where I wouldn't qualify it one way or the other' (452). And the situation is more complex still, as we discover when Reis Habito is asked whether she is *often* contemplating or bare beholding before God: 'It depends on the moment', she replies

> ... I mean, that is in there too, but then ... also sometimes ... there is ... *Tonglen*: when you feel that somebody is suffering, very naturally, ... as you sit in practice ... then I switch to *that* kind of meditation. Then I might come back and just concentrate and focus on the breath again. Then there might be an awareness of ... God's presence or something, and I would sit with that awareness of God's presence. But then you come to [a] stage where ... you don't even think in terms of God's presence. You know, in your heart, there is nothing that's *not* God's presence so it doesn't even have to be an object of your thought anymore.
>
> (453)

She concludes that Corless' description is true of certain stages of her sitting practice, but is not necessarily true of all of it, nor of the practice of all Christian Zen practitioners.

However, drawing heavily on the work of Robert Sharf (1995), Corless argues that, through the marginalisation of doctrine, Sanbô Kyôdan Zen leaves the Christian world-view of Christian practitioners *in situ*, yielding the possibility of a Christian having an intuitive experience, identified or authenticated by a teacher as *kenshō*, 'which is then interpreted as an intimation of the Christian God' (1996b: 6); and this, Corless argues, would clearly contradict the Buddhist understanding of the nature of reality.[18] Corless is disinclined to deem 'Buddhist' a practice which yields experiences interpreted in Christian terms (1996b: 6). Similar points (applied not to Sanbô Kyôdan Zen specifically but to the more general phenomenon of Christians practising Buddhist forms of meditation) are made by Rita Gross (2003b) and Grace Burford (2003), both of whom call into question the extent to which the meditation of Christians is Buddhist. Gross suggests that Christians who use Buddhist meditation 'are using a neutral, content-free technique associated with Buddhism to enhance their Christian practice' (2003b: 152). Burford points out that a practice can be Buddhist in the sense that Buddhists originated it, or in the sense that the experiences to which it gives rise are given a Buddhist interpretation. A technique which is Buddhist (in the first sense) may give rise to an experience which in itself defies dualistic categorisation, but interpretation happens within the realm of dualistic thinking, says Burford, and that experience may then be interpreted in Buddhist or Christian terms. 'So', concludes Burford, 'a Christian can engage in a Buddhist practice, gain from it something meaningful in Christian terms, and remain a Christian' (2003: 59). As a Buddhist, however, she

> might quibble with the claim that these practices remain Buddhist, even when Christians modify them to suit their purposes, when they impose on them conceptual frameworks and interpretations that fly in the face of basic Buddhist interpretations of the nature of reality.
>
> (Burford 2003: 59)

But, while these observations (and, in Corless' case, *criticisms*, since he is discussing the practice of people who explicitly claim that their meditation *can* be understood as authentically Buddhist) might well be applicable in some cases, are they applicable (as Corless takes them to be) in the case of the practice of dual belongers such as the Habitos? I would suggest that they are not straightforwardly applicable. For, while Habito and Reis Habito do deploy Christian concepts and are able to interpret their practice and experiences in terms of those concepts, these are not the only concepts they deploy. It is clearly not the case that they retain their Christian doctrinal framework and ignore Buddhist doctrine. Rather, they have over time immersed themselves in the Buddhist doctrinal framework *in addition* to their Christian framework and are able to interpret reality in general, and their own practice and the experiences it generates, within both of these frameworks respectively (and in cases of significant overlap between Buddhist and Christian interpretations, within both of these frameworks at the same time). Both Habito and Reis Habito profess veneration to the Triratna and accept key Buddhist interpretations of the nature of reality; they simply do not consider these to be fundamentally at odds with their Christian faith or with key aspects of the Christian interpretive framework (though it may not always be possible to work within both frameworks at once).[19]

In other words, it is not that Reis Habito, for example, operates only within the Christian conceptual framework and always attempts to express non-conceptual experiences in Christian terms, using Buddhist meditation techniques to simply enhance her Christianity; rather, she operates within both the Christian and the Buddhist conceptual frameworks and flits between them when attempting to give expression to her experiences. '[T]he *kōans* are all about letting go of concepts and expressing an experience right here and now, anyway you can', says Reis Habito (446). At times, she interprets her *kenshō* experiences, for example, in Christian language (as experiences of the love of God[20]) and, at other times, in more Buddhist language, as 'the opening of ... a very limited sense of "I"' (445), or as a 'glimpse into the interrelatedness of things' or as a 'stripping away [of] all the notions of self' (447). None of my interviewees understand themselves as merely using neutral, content-free techniques associated with Buddhism to enhance their Christianity. In other words, their practice is not only Buddhist in the sense that Buddhists originated the techniques they employ; it is also Buddhist in the sense that they embrace Buddhist interpretations of the experiences to which their practice gives rise (as well as Christian ones) because they accept Buddhist interpretations of reality (as well as Christian ones). This locates their approach with respect to the long-standing debate concerning Christian incorporation of Eastern meditation techniques.

When pioneers of Christian Zen such as Jesuit Hugo Enomiya-Lassalle began practising Zen meditation in Japan in the 1940s, this was met, initially, with considerable suspicion on the part of many Christians.[21] Attempting to justify his integration of Zen from a Christian perspective, Lassalle argued that Zen meditation should not be seen as a specifically Buddhist practice, but as a neutral practice technique which could, in principle, be received by any religious tradition.[22] As Werner Jeanrond explains, Lassalle

> did not share the Buddhist interpretation of the experiences gained during the Zen sessions. Rather, he attempted to interpret these spiritual experiences in a Christian way. ... [H]e considered Zen to be a natural method not linked with a particular religious confession and therefore explored its use within Christian faith ... to deepen ... contemplation on Christ.[23]

When he began practising Zen *kōans* from 1974 (after his *kenshō* was confirmed by Yamada Roshi), Lassalle again insisted that Zen practice had nothing to do with Buddhist philosophy (Jeanrond 2002: 113). This approach to the integration of Zen became widespread among Christians and in 1982 Winston King suggested that *most* Catholics who practice Zen meditation 'see it as a means or method for enhancing their own personal spiritual discipline with no doctrinal implications involved' (1982: 8).

There have, however, been dissenting voices. Pieris, for example, is critical of this approach, viewing it as exploitative of Buddhism insofar as it involves severing elements from their context without understanding, taking seriously, and appreciating that context. He speaks of 'the Christian guru who ... plucks Zen and Yoga from the religious stems that give them sap, and adorns Christian spirituality with sapless twigs!' (1988b: 85). Pieris calls this 'theological vandalism' and views it as a form of 'Christian triumphalism, which turns everything it touches to its own advantage, with no reverence for the wholeness of the religious experience of others' (1988b: 85). Pieris' call is for a more thoroughgoing immersion in the spirituality of the other. Similarly, Bettina Bäumer explains that she does 'not feel comfortable with most of the imitations of Eastern religious practices in the West', insofar as they 'lack the background on which those practices make sense' (1989: 40). She compares the common Christian approach to the integration of Eastern practices to 'somebody wanting to bathe in a river without getting wet!' (1989: 37). Informed by her own experience as a Christian immersed in Hindu spirituality, she reflects:

> What I came to realize was that 'adopting practices from other faiths' was not completely honest towards 'other faiths' – as if one had the right to extract certain beautiful experiences, practices or teachings from another tradition in order merely to incorporate them in one's own. No wonder that this attitude of 'appropriation' or 'utilization' practised by Christians has now led to the suspicion on the part of Hindus and Buddhists that this is a kind of spiritual theft. After all, Christians would also feel apprehensive if some Hindus started celebrating the mass without understanding the totality of meaning of which the mass is a part.
>
> (1989: 37)

Bäumer argues that the 'adoption of practices from other faiths' erroneously presupposes that practices can be isolated when, in fact, spiritual life is a totality:

> I could have easily said that what I learnt from Hinduism was a way of meditation – but in fact this meditation leads to a transformation of life itself, of one's experience of oneself, of others, of nature, of God. Meditation is not a particular yoga technique, or a zen way of 'sitting', taken out of their context. If one allows it to unfold with all its implications, one may be surprised at the transformation that is taking place.
>
> (1989: 38)

The reflections of my interviewees show them to be in greater accord with Pieris and Bäumer than with Lassalle. Interestingly, the conclusion Bäumer reaches, as early as 1989, is that a more authentic approach to the practice of another religion is dual belonging: 'One may sincerely and fully accept another spiritual tradition, without giving up one's own roots. This vocation may be rare, and it is not easy, but it can be pioneering also for others' (1989: 41). In other words, Bäumer recognises that dual belongers are precisely *not* Christians who attempt to extract practices from their Buddhist context and adapt them to their Christian requirements, but are individuals who accept the full import of those practices, immersing themselves in Buddhist spirituality – doctrine and all – and allowing that spirituality to become their own and to integrate as far as possible with their Christian spirituality.[24] This was clearly how my interviewees had come to regard their practice of Buddhist meditation. Habito admits that, in the beginning, he *did* understand himself as simply a Christian practising Zen meditation, but explains how this changed over time:

> as I continued to study Buddhism and continued to appreciate the richness of this tradition, I realised that I cannot prescind from the Buddhist

dimension or from the Buddhist fruits of Zen. ... I am now less inclined to just detach it from its Buddhist roots but precisely appreciate, with a renewed sense, the Buddhist background of Zen and I employ that also in my own verbal formulations of the Zen tradition; not prescinding from it but rather ... enabling it to come into full play.

(172–73)

Is Christian practice incorporated into a Buddhist schema?

However, when it comes to Christian Zen practitioners who interpret their experiences in Zen meditation in both Christian *and* Buddhist terms and understand those experiences as both Christian and Buddhist experiences as a result, Corless' criticism takes a different tack. At this point he starts to suspect that not only is their practice not authentically Buddhist but that neither is it authentically Christian. He argues that in such cases the experience of *kenshō* is taken by practitioners to solve the dilemma between Buddhism and Christianity and that, insofar as this is the case, what such practitioners prioritise is essentially a third position which is neither Buddhism nor Christianity but a quasi Vedantin Hindu transcendental monism which regards *satori/kenshō* as the essence of a presumed universal mysticism.[25] We will return to this argument in the next section; here, I wish to focus only on its relevance to Furneaux's practice. Furneaux arguably does at times come close to presenting the non-conceptual, non-dual experience of *kenshō* (or stream-entry, which she takes to be the equivalent in *Satipaṭṭhāna* practice) as actually solving – or at least as beginning to solve – the 'dilemma' (a term used by Corless and Furneaux) between Buddhism and Christianity, insofar as she takes this experience to be the beginning of a practitioner's progression 'beyond the opposites' of Buddhism and Christianity. I suggest, however, that in Furneaux's case, this approach relates not to the prioritisation of a third schema (quasi Vedantin Hindu transcendental monism), as Corless suggests, but to the prioritisation of a Mahāyāna Buddhist schema.

Furneaux speaks of 'the discriminative, divisive, associative and distinction-making faculties of dualistic mind that set up opposites, whether that is transcendent/immanent, self/other, grace/self-effort, subject/object, male/female or any other, and the layers of attributes we construct around them to identify with'. Particularly relevant to this group, says Furneaux,

is the distinction Buddhist/Christian. Sometimes it is necessary to refer to one or the other in a generic way, yet we need to be careful of not setting one against the other. The distinction is likely to be in our own mind; our task is to go beyond identified, beyond opposites, beyond trying to 'prove' something according to the distinctions in our own minds.

(2002a: 3)

Hence, the Morning Star Sangha[26] (MSS) is not simply a Buddhist–Christian dialogue group, but 'an opportunity to engage with the real and painful dilemma of *"separation"*,[27] since this dilemma can only be solved by engaging with it in diligent practice until one reaches *kenshō*/stream-entry (and subsequent deepens that experience) (111). Furneaux says of the practice of Christianity and Buddhism: 'for some of us – and increasingly because ... of the global world that we live in – it arises in this particular form and it can be, [for] those for whom it arises, the gateway to their liberation' (109); 'if you have come to the point where you can do nothing else, it may be "the ball of fire" which brings you to the not-two' (2006b: 15). '[W]hatever the "method"', contends Furneaux, 'to come at last to enter through the gateway of non-duality is the "one" or the "only" way' (123–24). She trusts that MSS participants are people for whom the Buddhist Christian '*kōan*' has become so painful that this *duḥkha* might be 'sufficient to energise the working on the *kōan* of "Beyond the opposites, beyond identities"' (2006b: 16). Committed participants 'are expected to continue to deepen their insight and practice with their own teacher or practice ... , since the first deep level of insight (stream entry, kensho, mu) is essential, for this endeavour'.[28]

Furneaux rejects ways of referring to a person's practice of Buddhism and Christianity which include the word 'dual' in the strongest terms of all my interviewees:

> '*dual*' in relation to the belonger is *really* problematic because ... it sets up these two *things* and the purpose of practice is to stop reifying them, making things out of anything (for which you have to have a subject and an object), and the practice is about seeing through that.
>
> (92)

One gets the sense in Furneaux's case that 'duality' terminology is found unacceptable not primarily because it fails to do justice to the degree of integration between her practice of each of these traditions (though clearly this is also the case), but because it seems to contradict her Mahāyāna understanding of the *purpose* of practising two traditions. Buddhist Christian practice across traditions seems to be interpreted by Furneaux as simply giving rise to the particular experience of duality which for certain people is a gateway into the experience of non-duality, and it is in the experience of non-duality that the Buddhist Christian *kōan* is solved.

However, if the *kōan* of Buddhist Christian dual belonging is treated as just one 'dharma gateway'[29] among many, and if the experience of *kenshō*/stream-entry (achieved through rigorous effort in Zen practice or *Satipaṭṭhāna*) is considered to be the first step through that gateway, then there is very little to distinguish MSS 'interpractice'[30] from straightforwardly Mahāyāna Buddhist practice, understood within a straightforwardly Mahāyāna Buddhist framework. Crucially, to the extent that Furneaux treats the tension of being both Buddhist and Christian as just one example of the experience of duality which is our fundamental delusion, and one which is to be overcome by MSS participants through practice leading to *kenshō*/stream-entry, she arguably incorporates her Christian practice into a Buddhist schema, since it is not clear that Christianity plays any important role here, beyond its role in being perceived to be in opposition to Buddhism (a role which could in theory be played by any other non-Buddhist system of thought and practice). In a discussion about MSS practice, recorded at the end of an MSS retreat, a Buddhist participant suggests that the retreat has been 'very strongly Buddhist oriented' with only 'snippets, bits and pieces of Christianity ... here and there'. He wonders, moreover, whether Christianity would have anything to *add* to what Buddhism readily supplies. Furneaux responds that it shouldn't be a question of whether something adds something to something else.[31] But while at the ultimate level (where all concepts fail to apply) this is, of course, true, it is *not* true at the conventional level and if this is not acknowledged, one may not be doing justice to the distinctiveness and particular strengths of each tradition. In this case, it is the distinctiveness and particular strengths of Christianity which seem threatened.

Moreover, can non-conceptual, non-dual experiences of reality really *solve* the 'dilemma' between Buddhism and Christianity, if that dilemma is one which occurs at the doctrinal and, therefore, conceptual level? Furneaux appears to think that comparing Buddhist and Christian ideas results from the confusion of the dualistic mind which asks 'is *this* the same as *that*?' (2001b: 3). '[M]y interest', she writes, 'is in practice, actually "engaging with it", "being it", rather than the confusions of dualistic mind'.[32] But has one really reconciled Buddhism and Christianity if this reconciliation in non-dual experience is not then worked out intellectually at the conventional level, i.e. at the level on which doctrines can be true or false, the same or different, compatible or incompatible?

Ironically, on this count, Corless' position is perhaps not so far away from the position he criticises since, at times, he too appears to present a non-conceptual – or, at least, non-binary – mode of experience as being, in a sense, the end of the dilemma between Buddhism and Christianity. Corless suggests that the incompatibility between Buddhism and Christianity 'is on the lower hierarchical level of *this* and *that. Either* God *or* the Buddha' (1986a: 121). But Christianity and Buddhism, he says, 'speak of a two-level consciousness – an everyday consciousness which does not tolerate paradox and which arranges things hierarchically, and an extraordinary or "super" consciousness which transcends paradox and hierarchies' (1986a: 118). He argues that 'only when Christian and/or Buddhist persons have contacted superconsciousness can there be any compatibility between the two religions'; the compatibility of Buddhism and Christianity is 'non-, or super-, conceptual' (1986a: 121).

However, it is less apparent in Corless' case than in Furneaux's that this emphasis on the role of 'non-, or super-, conceptual' compatibility with respect to the dilemma between Buddhism and Christianity relates to a prioritisation of Buddhism. Henry Smith *does* interpret this aspect of Corless' thinking as implicitly prioritising a Mahāyāna interpretative framework (1997: 168). I am not convinced, however, since it is not clear that Corless' theory deploys the notion of two truths, for example, in the way that it is deployed by Mahāyāna Buddhists. He does not seem to have in mind a way of experiencing reality which reveals the ultimate falsity of all conventional truth, whether Christian or Buddhist, since he is apparently unwilling to give up on the idea that Buddhist teachings are true even at the ultimate level, and likewise, that Christian teachings are true even at the ultimate level. Superconsciousness is the special kind of consciousness required in order to comprehend this. In other words, whereas Corless takes the doctrines of Christianity and Buddhism to be revealed as ultimately true in coinherent superconsciousness, Nāgārjuna takes all doctrines to be revealed as ultimately false, even those which are conventionally true. Although Corless' apparent contention that coinherent superconsciousness makes ultimate sense of Buddhist Christian dual belonging is clearly influenced by Buddhism and is intended to affirm the truth of both Buddhism and Christianity, there are significant discrepancies between his interpretative framework and that of both traditions, not least in his claim that there is more than one absolute (see pp. 45–48 above). We will focus on Corless' practice in the next section.

Furneaux's understanding seems to be closer to Nāgārjuna's and, in her case, there are further factors which suggest that Buddhism has priority for her. Although she says that she devotes 'the same attention in practice' to both traditions (91) and, similarly to other interviewees, feels that *Satipaṭṭhāna/shikantaza* is a Buddhist and a Christian practice, she at one point describes herself as 'a Christian hermit with a Buddhist practice' (107). She also seems to favour Buddhist language when it comes to explaining her practice and interpreting its experiential results, whereas Reis Habito and Habito seem to be equally happy with both kinds of language. For Furneaux, the conceptualisation of ultimate reality in I–Thou terms seems to be redundant with respect to her own experience. Reis Habito, for example, continues to experience ultimate reality in I–Thou terms during some forms of prayer and still finds this conceptualisation helpful and, as we have seen, even in attempting to express her non-dual *kenshō* experiences, she alternates between the use of Buddhist and Christian language (in Christian language, these are experiences of non-separation from the love of God). This suggests that Reis Habito thinks Christian I–Thou language is as conventionally legitimate as Buddhist language.

Returning to Furneaux, one gets the impression that she believes that, at a certain level of spiritual advancement, the Christian conception of ultimate reality and of how we are to relate to that reality, obscures rather than reveals the task, and that she employs Christian categories less frequently because she considers their conventional truth to be harder to grasp than that of Buddhist categories. It is not clear that she considers Christianity to have anything to add to what Buddhism makes abundantly clear. 'Buddhist practice and

Buddhist teachings', says Furneaux, 'say much more clearly or point much more clearly to things that are there in Christianity, for instance, the work of St John of the Cross is so clearly *Satipaṭṭhāna* but in much more difficult and convoluted words' (109). 'Obviously, when speaking to Christians,' says Furneaux, 'one tries the best one can to speak in Christian categories, and it is much easier to speak to Buddhists because it's simpler and more direct'.[33]

But to the extent that Furneaux takes Buddhist discourse to be a more accurate and helpful pointer to ultimate truth than Christian discourse, and to the extent that the language she herself uses most frequently to talk about her religious life is Buddhist, she is, I suggest, prioritising Buddhism. Her position can perhaps be seen as a form of Buddhist inclusivism which construes Christianity as helpful up to a point, but which takes Buddhist teachings and practice to be generally more effective in helping people attain the goal of the spiritual life, insofar as its doctrines and practices reveal the truth about the nature of reality more clearly and easily than do Christianity's.[34] As discussed in Chapter 5, belonging fully and authentically to a tradition would seem to require that one not take that tradition to be inferior to some other tradition; hence, full and authentic *dual* belonging requires the assumption that neither of these traditions is superior to the other overall. It is not clear from her reflections that Furneaux meets this requirement.[35] Consequently, it is unsurprising that she finds herself more readily accepted in Buddhist circles than in Christian ones. While Furneaux feels she is accepted in the Church by certain individuals, and says 'provided I speak in certain Christian kinds of ways, I can pass', she finds she is 'much more accepted by Buddhists' (98).

To be clear, I am not suggesting that there is anything inherently wrong with prioritising one of these traditions (and most people with Buddhist Christian multireligious identities do), but only that, in so doing, one cannot claim equal belonging to *both*.

Are Buddhist and Christian practices incorporated into a third schema?

I have suggested that, in Furneaux's case, the interpretation of *kenshō* as the gateway to resolving the 'dilemma' of Buddhist Christian practice seems to relate to the prioritisation of a Buddhist interpretative schema. But in other cases, might Corless be right that interpreting one's Zen experiences in Buddhist and Christian terms has to do with the prioritisation of a third position which is neither Buddhist nor Christian? Corless was particularly concerned, in this regard, about the authenticity of the practice across traditions of Sanbô Kyôdan Zen practitioners. Drawing on Sharf 1995, Corless argues that Sanbô Kyôdan Zen, especially, selects the experience known as *satori/kenshō* from the general body of Buddhist theory and practice and problematically regards it as the essence of the *Dharma* and 'even more problematically … as the essence of a presumed universal, or pan-religious, mysticism' (1996b: 1). The experience of *satori/kenshō*, he argues, is held up as solving the dilemma between the incompatible truths of Buddhism and Christianity when, in fact, this move only gives rise to a trilemma.[36] Corless is insistent: either there is God or there is interdependent arising and one can only have an experience that includes God and interdependent arising if that experience is of something (such as Nirguṇa Brahman) that 'transcends, and therefore diminishes, both' (1996b: 6).

But this criticism simply brings us back to Corless' sense of the incompatibility of Buddhism and Christianity and his rejection of the monocentric pluralist hypothesis (see Chapter 3). For dual belongers who, in contrast to Corless, endorse the monocentric pluralist hypothesis (either explicitly or implicitly), 'God' is just one way of thinking and talking about that conceptually transcendent 'Mystery with a capital "M"' (Habito: 150), Whom/Which is thought, and talked, about differently within a Buddhist conceptual framework. From the monocentric pluralist's perspective, this interpretation does not *diminish* the greatness of this 'Mystery', but rather underscores that greatness by emphasising Its/His/Her conceptual transcendence. This affirmation of the conceptual transcendence of ultimate reality opens up the possibility of interpreting the non-conceptual experiences to which one's Zen practice gives rise differently, though equally validly, within two different conceptual frameworks (and, insofar as one employs both a Buddhist and a Christian interpretative framework, one might consider one's Zen practice to be Buddhist and Christian). The Habitos (both of whom are Sanbô Kyôdan Zen practitioners) are not prioritising a third position by interpreting their Zen experiences thus, since, prior to conceptualisation, those experiences do not have content of the kind which could be captured by any position or view whatsoever, be it Christian, Buddhist, Vedantin Hindu, or anything else. It is only when those experiences are *interpreted* that any *positions* come into play and, for the Habitos, those positions are Christian and Buddhist. The difference between the Habitos and Corless is simply that the Habitos don't take those positions to be fundamentally incompatible.

It was Corless' sense of the incompatibility of Buddhism and Christianity that convinced him that specific practices could not be both Christian and Buddhist and that made him critical of approaches which appeared to him to blur the lines between Buddhist and Christian practice. He took the risk of dual belonging resulting in inauthentic practice to be very real and hence tried hard to prevent his practice of each from merging into his practice of the other. Unless one's formal Buddhist and Christian practices are clearly distinguishable from each other, thought Corless, how can one be sure that one is an authentic practitioner of either tradition?[37] And if one is not practising authentically within each tradition, he reasoned, one will undermine the dialogue between them. Although all those interviewees with a practice in both traditions, including Corless, would have preferred to avoid identity labels altogether, he was least uncomfortable with being identified as someone with a 'dual practice' and a 'dual identity' since he saw his own formal Buddhist practice and formal Christian practice as distinct activities relating to different 'absolutes', one undertaken by his Buddhist 'self', the other by his

Christian 'self'. Unlike, Reis Habito, for example, who found it hard to distinguish her Buddhist practice from her Christian practice and who felt that whatever practice she was engaged in she was always engaged in it as a Buddhist *and* a Christian, Corless went to considerable lengths to try to keep his practice of each separate from his practice of the other, in the belief that this was necessary in order to preserve the authenticity of both.

Corless' (1996a: 7) formal Christian practice was centred on the Mass and, before his health began to fail, his practice at home included Bible reading and chanting the divine office and the Psalms. While engaged in Christian prayer or contemplation, he would feel that he was a part of the communion of saints, 'praying in God'. Practising thus, 'only God and the consequences of there being a triune God comes to consciousness', explains Corless, 'and the Buddhist tradition is not an issue, it is not there' (1996a: 7). When he was engaged in Buddhist practice (consisting largely of liturgy and visualisation), however, the opposite was true. He opted for Buddhist meditation 'with form' because of his misgivings regarding formless meditation such as *Zazen*: 'I found that if I did silent sitting ... I would find the Jesus prayer would start to come up, or I would find myself doing Christian contemplation, and that I was not doing Buddhist meditation' (1996a: 7). Corless explains that he chose to take refuge in the Tibetan tradition and, particularly, within the Gelugpa tradition because it is 'one of the more intellectual and more image-full' types of Buddhism; he assumed that it would, therefore, be easier to ensure and maintain its uniquely Buddhist character (1996a: 7–8). 'I wanted to be as sure as I could that when I was doing Buddhist meditation, it was Buddhist and not Christian or a mixture' (9), he explains.

> If ... one is engaged in a Gelugpa visualization liturgy, struggling to relate to all kinds of oddly colored ladies and gentlemen improbably perched upon supportless lotuses, one cannot fool oneself that this has anything ... to do with God. Similarly, at Mass or Divine Office, there is no time to be thinking of the Triratna.
>
> (1986a: 133)

Corless initially structured his week such that he would practise Buddhist and Christian meditation on alternate days, starting on Sunday, and at separate shrines in his shrine room. His intention was that this alternate practice be,

> as far as possible, a dual practice of the Buddhist tradition in an authentically Buddhist way, and the Christian tradition in an authentically Christian way ... Only if I do that do I feel that I will be able to be a focus for the Buddhist-Christian tradition meeting in fullness.
>
> (1996a: 9–10)

On Saturday neither tradition was prioritised; rather this was a time of 'confusion, or co-inherence', when he would practice a self-designed 'Buddhist–Christian Coinherence Meditation' which he summarises as follows:

I ... realize myself to be in the presence of the triune God, and the Triple Jewel. I invoke them first separately, and then I invoke them both together, and then allow them to meet ... in my heart, or my consciousness ... and ... sit there, and then eventually allow it to dissolve ... [38]

His practice of both religions, and his Coinherence Meditation, had become less formal over time, and at the time of our interview he was no longer practising this rigid weekly regime, although he still avoided practising at either shrine directly after the other (30).

'A person cannot be authentically both a Buddhist and a Christian at the same time, since the systems are complete in themselves and, at several important points (such as the existence of God) contradictory', insists Corless. 'One can only be a "Buddhist–Christian" if one either ignores the differences between the systems or blends them in a transcendental unity' (1993: 13). Corless believed monocentric pluralism to be an example of the latter move. In contrast, he took his notion of the mutual coinherence of Buddhism and Christianity as two distinct absolutes to be a framework which allowed for the simultaneous acknowledgement of the truth of both traditions without ignoring or claiming to transcend the incompatibilities between them (thus threatening the integrity and self-sufficiency of each).[39] His belief in the possibility of a level of consciousness at which this coinherence might be directly experienced, provided Corless with some kind of integrated understanding of his dual practice, and this understanding was later bolstered by his affirmation of Gaia as the source of each tradition and the 'matrix' for their dialogue (10). This integrative framework was made explicit in his Coinherence Meditation, practised at a third 'Earth-centred shrine', or 'Shrine of the Heart', i.e. a shrine, as Corless explains, containing items relating to one's spiritual auto-biography. These items, he says, should speak to 'your Deep Self', which is 'a microcosm of Gaia, the planet Earth considered as a living and conscious being, the womb from which both Buddhism and Christianity ... have sprung and the common matrix that they now coinhabit' (1994a: 139–40). Corless' Earth-centred shrine contained both Christian and Buddhist elements. It 'speaks to my own heart, to the hearts of the Christian Gospels and the Buddhist Dharma, and to Mother Gaia, from whose heart all other hearts have come', explains Corless (1990b: 124, fnt. 31).

By 1994, the meditation practised at his Earth-centred shrine, began with an invocation of the Earth, personified as 'Mother Gaia' in which she is repeatedly praised (1994a: 140–41) and this is followed by an acknowledgement of dependence upon Mother Gaia through the recitation of prayer-like verses (1994a: 144). The main purpose of the meditation, explains Corless, is 'the acknowledgement of Buddhism and Christianity as two Absolute Systems coinhering on the same planet (in humanity as a whole) and in your own consciousness' (1994a: 139). When practising the formal version of the meditation, using the mantras 'MARANA-THA' and 'OṂ-ĀH-HŪṂ', he took himself to be practising as a Christian and then as a

Buddhist, and then the other way around, until the point at which he would allow the mantras to 'dissolve' into a single syllable, 'MAH' – 'a sound contained in, and therefore symbolizing the coinherence of, the mantras MARANA-THA and OM-ĀH-HŪM' (1994a: 142): 'I'm then the host of the two traditions and at that point I am kind of neither Buddhist nor Christian', says Corless; the host, he explains, 'is like the hotel manager' (34). Over the course of his last decade, Corless had ceased to practise the meditation in the formal way it is described in print, sometimes practising a simpler version (31–32); at other times, simply sitting before the Earth-centred shrine in silence. He explained that sitting before this shrine had come to be his 'default mode', particularly if he was feeling confused or didn't feel like a form of Buddhist or Christian practice. Often, he would light incense 'and just sit there in a sort of confusion and see what happens', and would usually feel better for having done so, feeling that he had 'contacted some level of consciousness or level of reality which is healing and nurturing' (32).

Corless preferred to describe his Coinherence Meditation as *supporting* his Buddhist and his Christian practice, rather than as *integrating* them (35). But centring on Gaia as the 'matrix' and 'context' for the dialogue between Buddhism and Christianity, nevertheless, seems to provide the sense of coherence which is lacking in Corless' theory of 'Many Selves, Many Realities' (Corless 2002). Indeed, this latter theory seems to recede into metaphor as the concrete reality of Gaia is affirmed as Mother of all. In this sense, the notion of Mother Gaia had seemingly begun to play a unifying role for Corless, the psychological function of which was similar to that played by the affirmation of one ultimate reality in monocentric pluralist thought; only, rather than being an ultimate transcendent reality, Gaia is a conventional, underlying reality, whom Buddhists and Christians alike depend on, praise, and mirror in themselves.[40] Dual belongers, according to Corless, in acting as 'hosts' to two traditions, are microcosms of Gaia. Speaking of the Buddhist–Christian dialogue going on within himself, he writes: 'I do not propose in any way to blend Buddhism and Christianity ... All I am doing, like the planet earth itself, is sitting in the midst of the confusion which I have discovered' (1989: 3). It is understandable that sitting in front of the Earth-centred shrine had become his default practice since, arguably, this was the only context in which Corless could gather all of himself together as *one* self in *one* reality, even if so doing was the source of confusion. In need of some common centre which would integrate his otherwise 'incompatible' and 'mutually irrelevant' religious 'lives', the possibility of coinherent superconsciousness and the reality of Mother Gaia became that centre; and his ordination as a multi-faith minister in 2005 in the Universal Church of the Master arguably became a further integrative factor.[41]

I suggest, however, that Corless' concern for authenticity and fear of syncretism, when combined with his natural need for coherence (the absence of which had been a source of considerable psychological strain[42]), had resulted in an integrative framework for his practice of both traditions (made explicit in his default practice at his Earth-centred shrine, and given quasi-institutional expression in his ordination as a multi-faith minister) which was arguably neither Buddhist nor Christian (though clearly influenced by, and containing elements of, both). Indeed, the emphasis on, and personification of, the Earth as 'Mother Gaia' shares more with Native American, Pagan, or New Age thought and practice than with either Buddhist or Christian thought and practice,[43] and the eclectic nature of Corless' Coinherence Meditation seems to display something of the New Age tendency – sometimes characterised as 'pick-and-mix' spirituality – to select elements from different traditions and create new hybrid practices. The meditation (as described in Corless 1994a), and the shrine at which it is practised, is composed of elements (mantras, prayers, visualisations, *yantras*, symbols, poetry, and so on) drawn from various traditions (not only Buddhism and Christianity, but also, for example, Islam, Occultism, and Native American traditions),[44] not all of which Corless is fully immersed in but which represent influences upon him. Thus, while this meditation, and his ordination in a multi-faith church, bring together many of Corless' 'selves', the overall result is a practice and an ordination which would likely be unrecognisable within most of the contexts from which those individual 'selves' are gathered.

By comparing the integrative dimension of Corless' practice to pick-and-mix spirituality, I by no means wish to suggest that his practice lacked depth, thoughtfulness, or integrity. On the contrary, the irony is that it was his uncompromising concern for Buddhist authenticity and integrity, and Christian authenticity and integrity – construed by Corless as entailing Christian exclusivity and exclusivism, and Buddhist exclusivity and exclusivism – which prevented him from endorsing a more organic integration of his Buddhist and his Christian practice which would have exhibited greater continuity with the traditions and therefore been more authentically Buddhist and Christian. His theory of many absolutes did not provide him with a framework which could enable him to make sense of the deep convergences he admitted to experiencing between his Buddhist and his Christian practice.[45] Moreover, his belief that it is not possible to be Buddhist and Christian at the same time meant that he felt unable to condone cross-fertilisation and natural integration between his Buddhist and his Christian practice since he assumed this would entail inauthenticity. But since, for his own sanity, he needed *some* kind of integrated understanding of his practice of two religions which he perceived to be, in important respects, incompatible, he carefully constructed an integrative framework which he believed was capable of protecting the integrity and authenticity of both traditions. The trouble is that his default practice is not, therefore, an integration of Buddhist and Christian practice which grows naturally out of each tradition and the dialogue between them, but is rather a novel, artificial invention which bears little resemblance to the practice of either tradition. Thus, of all my interviewees, Corless seems to come closest to seriously jeopardising his Buddhist and Christian authenticity, despite the fact that he seems to have striven hardest to protect that authenticity.

Corless seemed determined not to give up on the idea that the truth of each tradition is absolute (in *this* respect, his religiosity was very *dissimilar* to New Age religiosity).[46] When questioned directly regarding whether or not he saw the Buddhist and the Christian traditions as absolutes *in themselves*, he denied this (and instead claimed they *related to* different absolutes).[47] I suggest, however, that this reveals an ambiguity in his thinking, or at least in his use of the term 'absolute', since elsewhere he says, for example, 'a Christian who really takes the Christian message seriously sees the Christian message as absolute' (14) and, from his Buddhist perspective, he describes Buddhist teaching as 'absolute' in the sense of being the 'ultimately correct teaching about reality' (52). Again, he reiterates: 'I'm accepting the truths of Christianity and Buddhism as absolute' (24). Moreover, he describes the main purpose of Coinherence Meditation as 'the acknowledgement of Buddhism and Christianity as two *Absolute Systems*' (1994a: 139, my emphasis), and explains that 'the coinherent practitioner seeks only *to be of service to the Christian and Buddhist traditions*, and whatever aims they wish to set forward' (1994b: 181, my emphasis).

But does Buddhism conceive of itself as an 'Absolute System'? And is the aim of the Christian really to serve the Christian *tradition*, or is the Christian's aim rather to serve *God*? 'To be a participant in a religious movement', says Smith, 'is to recognize that that movement points to something or Someone beyond itself' (1962: 129). One cannot help feeling that Corless places too much emphasis on the absoluteness of the traditions themselves; an emphasis which is at odds both with the Mahāyāna conception of Buddhism as a 'finger pointing at the moon' and with the Christian contention that only God is absolute and that God utterly transcends human comprehension. Surely the ideal is not to be committed to one's religious tradition *as such*, but to be committed to the ultimate reality towards Which/Whom one's religious tradition orientates one.[48] However, whereas for monocentric dual belongers the idea that Buddhism and Christianity point beyond themselves provides an implicit integrative framework which allows them to relativise both Buddhism and Christianity with respect to Mystery with a capital 'M' (to use Habito's term), the problem for Corless was his belief that Buddhism and Christianity are either distinct absolutes in themselves, or are 'teachings about or pathways towards different realities' (53). The former position entails that these traditions *cannot* be relativised; the latter, that they can be relativised, but only in relation to *distinct* realities, such that this relativisation does not provide a framework in which the traditions can be related to one another.

Is integration a threat to the traditions?

While I have suggested that in order to be an authentic adherent of a religious tradition one cannot assume that tradition to be *inferior* to some other tradition; Corless goes a step further, reasoning that in order to be an authentic adherent of a tradition, one must assume that tradition to be *superior* to all

others. Corless' fear of integration and unwillingness to relativise the traditions with respect to a single ultimate reality related to his conviction that
when he practised as a Buddhist he must be exclusively Buddhist, and must
assume Christianity to be inferior, and when he practised as a Christian he
must be exclusively Christian, and must assume Buddhism to be inferior. 'To
be fully Christian', he insists, 'one has to believe that somehow the Christian
message is superior to other messages of other religions' (15); '[i]t's only possible to have a dialogue between two positions which are very entrenched' (22).
Corless thinks that exclusivity and exclusivism are required if one is to be fully
Buddhist or fully Christian, 'and not something else, like a person who is
attracted to Christianity but attracted to other things also' (15). His idea of
someone who tries to be both seems close to Winston King's image of a
person 'who is semi-ex-faith A (his inherited one) and interested/attracted to
faith B, but not yet willing to be committed to it'.[49] In other words, Corless
shares Cornille's worry that attempting to be both Buddhist and Christian
entails a less than complete commitment to both (see p. 153). Ultimately,
integration is undesirable, thinks Corless, because being both undermines the
traditions both directly (through the lack of complete commitment to each,
made necessary by the contradictions between them), and indirectly (by
undermining the mutually beneficial dialogue between them due to one's lack
of complete commitment to each).

But does it not undermine both traditions more to consider each to be inferior
to the other half of the time? And would it not show a greater commitment to
both to allow them to integrate sufficiently that one can bring all that one is
to the practice of both, such that one is Christian all (or at least most) of the
time, and Buddhist all (or at least most) of the time; rather than denying one
of them simply because the thought or practice of the other is holding sway
on that particular day? In other words, is integration not something that the
dual belonger is obliged, *precisely by* his or her commitment to both traditions,
to strive for, rather than against? I suggest it is.

Corless argues that 'Dual Practice, or Practice Across Traditions, represents
itself as the authentic practice of two traditions ... with a single practitioner
functioning as if s/he were two independent, or autonomous, practitioners'
(1996b: 1). But this cannot be what practice across traditions involves or
requires, not least because, if one has practised for many years within the
Buddhist and the Christian tradition, whether one likes it or not, it is, psychologically speaking, very difficult *not* to be Buddhist and Christian at the
same time. 'I am constructed by now of Buddhist and Christian parts, which
have over time developed their own interconnections', recognises King. 'I do
not respond to events "as a Christian" or "as a Buddhist," but simply as a
person conditioned by both' (1990: 125). In a similar vein, Reis Habito
reflects that she cannot leave God or Jesus on the doorstep of the *zendo* anymore
than she can leave her transformative experiences in Zen practice on the
doorstep of the church (441, 448). '[T]he fact is that I took refuge with a
Buddhist Master and I have a Buddhist Dharma name', says Reis Habito;

'[s]o ... that's a reality that's there ... and I don't want to deny that reality' (454). However, she also sees herself as having been karmicly formed within the Christian tradition and recognises that this means that Christianity provides the 'predispositions into which the Buddhism is integrated'.[50] (Note that even in describing her Christian formation, the influence of Buddhist thought is present, providing a case in point.) '[W]hat I bring to ... Buddhism is my Christian background and what I bring to Christianity is this very heavy influence and Buddhist understanding of things', she explains. 'So I wouldn't say that there are moments where I think purely as a Buddhist or purely as a Christian because I am I, and this is a mix of these two things in myself' (438). Reis Habito was particularly cognisant of the inevitability of integration: 'I can't stop the blending, it's not possible', she says (451).

Despite his attempts to 'quarantine' his Buddhist practice from his Christian practice and vice versa, evidence of mutual influence and cross-fertilisation can be easily found, even in Corless' case. It is clear, for example, in his use of the symbolic structure of Tibetan Maṇḍala visualization as a template for engaging with and finding new meaning in the Mass,[51] and in his understanding of how prayer to saints works – an understanding he himself describes as 'borrowed' from the Buddhist tradition (69). The other way around, he notes, for example, that his involvement with Christianity has encouraged him to focus on the personalities of the Buddhas and Bodhisattvas, and to emphasise the personal dimension of love and wisdom in a Buddhist context (80). Hard as one might try, it is virtually impossible, unless one is suffering from some sort of pathology, to partition off a significant part of who one is so as to isolate it from the influence of other significant parts of who one is. Corless is, to a limited extent, prepared to acknowledge this, conceding that if his Buddhist 'self' and his Christian 'self' were entirely cut off from one another it would mean that he were 'suffering from multiple-personality disorder since the Christian would not recognise the Buddhist as a part of the same person, it would be a different personality'. In his own case, he says, 'the two are aware of each other and in a sense defer to each other as two friends might' (17); '[t]hey don't understand each other but that doesn't mean that they have to part company' (19). But this acknowledgement does not go far enough, since there is plenty of evidence to suggest that these internal 'friends' not only *understand* one another in important respects, but also *agree* on various issues relating to doctrine and practice, and *assist one another* in practice by sharing ideas and practical tools with each other. (Corless himself describes the Gospel and the *Dharma* as 'complementary to each other' and suggests that 'each can somehow illuminate the other so as to establish the other on a surer foundation'.)[52]

Practising as though one were two separate beings might be necessary, provisionally, in order to allow one to experience, as far as possible, the other on its own terms; indeed, a number of those I interviewed spoke of initially having to put their Christian notions to one side in order to immerse themselves thoroughly in Buddhism.[53] But it cannot be a long-term solution to the 'dilemma' of dual belonging. Indeed, Corless at times comes close to acknowledging this. There is a clear tension in his thinking insofar as he describes Buddhism and Christianity as incompatible or irrelevant to each other, and eschews the notion of integration between them, yet at the same time calls for their 'mutual transformation'[54] and 'mutual enrichment'[55] through dialogue (as do many who are involved in Buddhist–Christian dialogue. What, after all, is the point of dialogue if the process leaves both participants unaltered and no closer to mutual understanding, to the discovery of common ground, or to a cross-fertilisation of ideas than they were to begin with?). If Buddhism and Christianity are to transform or enrich each other, then there must be an exchange of ideas or practices between them, i.e. there must be mutual influence and cross-fertilisation (and we see evidence of this mutual influence and cross-fertilisation when we look at Corless' reflections on his religious life). But he cannot have it both ways: does he want his Buddhism and his Christianity to be mutually isolated and impermeable, or does he want them to interact and to integrate what they can of each other's insights and practices so that each is enriched and transformed?

Corless had, over time, become much more willing to acknowledge the interaction and mutual influence between his Buddhism and his Christianity than he had once been. 'I can't function as a Christian with blinkers', he admits; 'I don't think they can ever be entirely separate ... The very fact that I'm practising both means that they're ... somehow influencing each other' (32–33). The trouble is that his concessions to the inevitability of mutual transformation sit comfortably neither with his hypothesis that Buddhism and Christianity are incompatible or mutually irrelevant and that any meeting (other than in superconsciousness) is beyond them (1986a: 121), *nor* with his notion that dialogue requires a Buddhist who is only Buddhist and a Christian who is only Christian. With these assumptions in place it is difficult for Corless to make sense of the organic cross-fertilisation and integration he experienced between his Buddhist and Christian practice, or to welcome it as a good thing, though he speaks positively of the potential benefits of mutual transformation and enrichment.

Corless' reflections are shot through with this unresolved tension and, at times, he seems to be aware of it. At one point in our interview, for example, he acknowledges that through their mutual influence on one another in his own life, the traditions are changing. He then says:

> it's a problem because I don't want to be the architect of the change: I don't have the authority to change the whole direction of Christianity or Buddhism, but I don't want to be stuck in the tradition, not recognising that they are both dynamically changing. So, I'm somewhat in the middle of all of that and it isn't that consistent.
>
> (25)

And when discussing Henry Smith's identification of a tension in his position,[56] Corless acknowledges the possible provisionality of that position:

[Smith] says, how can Buddhism and Christianity be in me total absolutes when they're interacting; surely something must be happening between the two? And, yes, there is something happening; I don't know quite what it is but I don't feel that I can direct what happens next (15) ... I'm accepting the truths of Christianity and Buddhism as absolute for the moment because that's the traditional understanding and yet, if there's to be an evolution of consciousness, something else will happen. So at the same time that I take seriously the truths of Christianity and Buddhism, I am prepared for them to change.

(24)

Corless is at pains to emphasise that his approach is experimental and he seems aware that it may not be the right approach long term:

I don't know where I'm going ... it's a continuing quest which is open to changing of direction, to back-tracking and revising what I've said ... I am experimenting with this dual-loyalty and the coinherence to see if it makes any sense – if it goes anywhere – and it may be wrong.

(85)

But even if Corless' approach is problematic and even if there are positive advantages to allowing integration, is he nevertheless right to worry that unless dual belongers draw a clear line between their Buddhist and their Christian practice, the integrity and distinctiveness of each tradition may be threatened? Although my other interviewees were more accepting of integration, Corless was not alone in expressing this kind of worry, and something like his desire not to be an 'architect of the change' was expressed by various interviewees, keen that they not change the traditions through their adherence to both.[57] As we saw earlier, King, for example, although grateful to be able to draw on both traditions and accepting of the inevitability of their interaction and cross-fertilisation in her own life, explains that she is 'not drawn to syncretism' (359) and does not want to contribute to the decay of the distinctions between Buddhist and Christian practice such that future generations may be unable to benefit from the distinctions as she does. 'I'm very wary of that and that's why when I go to a Buddhist place I want to do a Buddhist thing, [and when I go to a] Quaker place I want to do a Quaker thing', she says, continuing:

I really hope we don't lose that ... I really feel the practices have, in one case, two and a half millennia of processing and testing and validation and understanding the nuances and everything else, and hundreds of years in the other case: that's precious beyond measure. I *dread* seeing any of that lost. ... I respect them just as they are.

(408)

Having said this, however, King immediately back-tracks, saying: 'Now I'm going to ... completely negate everything I'm saying: there are places in the practice where I think they have to learn from each other'. Like Corless, King recognises her own ambivalence: 'I want them to stay the same and I want them to learn from each other. ... I hate being contradictory *that* much! Anyway, that's where it is' (408). As an example of this ambivalence, she says the following of the Buddhist elevation of monks and nuns over the laity, and of teacher over disciple:

> To a certain extent that's excellent and how it must be. ... I mean, as far as spiritual guidance [goes], you need it. But if I compare that with Quakerism, ... there's a spiritual truth and power – ... pretty awesome in its own way – in ... Quaker practice; it comes from an egalitarianism [exhibited in Quaker Meetings and business practice] that's lacking in Buddhism. Now, just the reverse is true – how contradictory!
>
> (408–9)

King is not sure whether this is a point where she would want to see the traditions learn from each other or not:

> the different spiritual practices – maybe they shouldn't learn from each other ... *I don't know.* I have not enough wisdom to know how these great things should play out but there's *great power* in both of those practices, both of those approaches.
>
> (410)

As a practitioner in both traditions, however, King is grateful that she has both approaches to draw on for her own benefit. She emphasises, moreover, that, when it comes to practice, she has not *intentionally* or *consciously* taken any steps to try to integrate her Christian and her Buddhist practice:

> I don't want to invent a new religion here and I don't want to ... consciously take one from column A and one from column B. ... [T]hese practices developed within a context and they have meaning and make sense in that context. They do overlap with each other so that context isn't everything ... but ... I don't want to create something new. ... I just want to ... appreciate and try to make use of things that very profound people have discovered.
>
> (359)

So how might we distinguish between legitimate and illegitimate forms of integration?

The legitimacy of organic integration

Giving the autobiographical example of a Jesuit working in a Theravāda Buddhist country, Pieris speaks of such a person's need to be 'rooted in two soils' but warns that an 'unguided zeal for personal integration' might expose one to two temptations: 'One would be to mix up the two idioms to form a kind of hybrid spirituality, a sort of cocktail in which we taste both components though not in the purity of their individual flavors', the other, to create 'a tertium quid (a third reality) in which neither one nor the other retains its identity even in a mixed form' (1996: 184). However, while Pieris' concern may be well placed with respect to some kinds of integration, it does not, I suggest, apply to all. My interviewees appeared to be very well rooted in both soils, and while most of them have welcomed the natural integration of Buddhist and Christian practice in their own lives, they have not sought to merge these traditions into one, but find the main benefit of dual belonging to lie in the distinctiveness of each.[58] Given this, the internal integration which has emerged *naturally* between their practice of these traditions – as opposed to being artificially forced in some way, thereby distorting one or both traditions – has simply been a case of their becoming *aware* of overlap and allowing each tradition to *enhance* the practice of the other. Such integration is unlikely to threaten either tradition since its results are continuous with the spirit and purpose of both.

This kind of organic integration, strongly evident in the life of Reis Habito, for example, is the result of having been deeply nourished by Buddhist and Christian spirituality rather than of 'picking and mixing' Buddhist and Christian elements to create an artificial hybrid. If a plant has roots in two different kinds of soil, the nutrients from both soils will mingle within it. Reis Habito's rootedness in both traditions has led to the natural growth of an integrated way of practising which draws on the strengths of both traditions in their distinctness. I saw no evidence that allowing this integration to occur had damaged the integrity of either; rather, each appears to have retained its identity even in this 'mixed form'.

Dual belongers have no interest in 'collapsing everything in to an amorphous mass' (Furneaux: 104). Habito, for example, while allowing the traditions to integrate, explains that he is concerned to protect the integrity of the traditions and, in this regard, emphasises the necessity of *thoroughly* practising a tradition rather than simply taking elements from it without an appreciation of their context (209, 212). The problem with picking and mixing elements and building something new, thinks Habito, is that one ends up with a 'truncated version' of what one is trying to assimilate. To put this point in terms of Pieris' earlier analogy, if one is well grounded only in Christianity, one ends up adorning Christian spirituality with 'sapless twigs'; and if, on the other hand, one is well grounded in neither tradition, one ends up with only a mixed bundle of 'sapless twigs' cut from the Buddhist and Christian trees.[59] Habito seems to take the latter to be the approach of New Age religiosity, in which 'people just take this or that from this or that other tradition and they build their own little supermarket kind of spirituality' (212). Similarly, Furneaux emphasises that although people may, for a time, 'window shop for what is on offer', they should eventually come to a point where they are prepared to settle into their practice, and she points out that each tradition contains checks and balances which may be missed if one picks and chooses only the bits and pieces one likes (2006b: 15).

Recalling the Dalai Lama's warning against attempts to 'put a yak's head on a sheep's body',[60] Habito suggests that, although there are artificial kinds of integration which he would class as such attempts, there are also more organic kinds of integration which fall outside the scope of this warning (177, 209). Organic integration occurs, suggests Habito, when practices from other traditions are integrated into one's religious life in 'a way that is not simply eclectic and arbitrary, but respects the integrity of the traditions involved and also does not compromise any aspect of one's own original tradition' (1994a: 153). He speaks of '[p]reserving the differences but integrating them in one's own life' and explains that part of what this means is that 'you acknowledge where certain practices and certain expressions come from' (209). In other words, allowing one's Buddhist practice to integrate naturally with one's Christian practice does not mean that one ceases to draw distinctions between them. Even though Reis Habito, for example, is unable to draw a neat line between her Buddhist and her Christian practice, she still operates within two distinct conceptual frameworks, and there is still liturgical oscillation in her religious life and an awareness and appreciation of the differences between certain practices. She explains, for example, that Buddhist meditation has helped her 'gain a much deeper understanding of the Eucharist' (particularly regarding the meaning of the real presence), such that she would now describe her understanding of the Eucharist, not as a Buddhist or a Christian under-standing, but as 'a complete blend' (494–95). However, this does not mean that she has ceased to draw any kind of distinction between her participation in the Eucharist and other types of practice. In this sense, the traditions remain separate:

> participating in the Eucharist is not exactly the same thing as reciting the Heart Sūtra, for example. Some people might disagree with that, they say 'you participate in the Eucharist and you're fully there and then you recite the Heart Sūtra and you're fully there, and the fully there is what counts'. But I would say they are still liturgical or ritual elements that are different and I don't like to blend *those* differences.
>
> (451)

A number of interviewees objected to attempts to amalgamate Buddhist and Christian practice in a way which did not emerge naturally out of the practice of both (attempts to put a yak's head on a sheep's body, we might say). Habito explains that he is not, for example, striving to see Buddha statues appearing in churches or crucifixes in Buddhist temples: 'that would be kind of a grasping something extraneous into an organic whole that may not be able to fit exactly'.[61] Images are combined at Maria Kannon Zen Centre (MKZC). (There is, for example, a statue of Kannon and a statue of Mary next to one another.) But he argues this differs from the juxtaposition of images in church or temple, not only insofar as there are people who come to MKZC from different religious backgrounds (and different images might therefore be evocative for different people), but also insofar as the combination of images, in this context, relates to the fact that MKZC has grown out of the vision of people such as himself who are both Buddhist and Christian; it is an organic development – rather than an artificial amalgam – because it emerges from the integrated spirituality of dual belongers:

> we put … images there little by little … just because they, somehow, come to embody something in our practice, … I'm trying to be careful not to put too many in a way that would be a hodgepodge of things, in a way that people would say: 'oh, that's syncretistic' … .
>
> (179)

Although here Habito hesitates, suggesting that perhaps some re-examination of the term 'syncretism' ought to be undertaken since 'the history of religious traditions is one of assimilation of practices and images from other traditions … [which], somehow, … become part of the organic whole'. At MKZC, explains Habito, 'we're trying to continue growing and deepening our practice and trying to find expressions that would be significant and … evocative of what we're seeking to experience together'.[62] He is not suggesting that communities such as MKZC should replace temples and churches;[63] MKZC is simply an external expression of the internal integration which for some people is already taking place as a result of their practice within both traditions. He explains that a key concern, as more and more practitioners join MKZC, 'is the maintenance of the integrity of the Zen tradition as well as of the Christian, while being open to organic growth with the interaction of these traditions' (1992a: 228–29).

Pieris warns against an 'unguided zeal for personal integration'. But what our investigation of Corless' practice suggested is that an unguided zeal *to preserve the distinctions* between the traditions can be equally detrimental to their integrity insofar as it can result in a form of practice and understanding of one's practice which, though containing Buddhist and Christian elements, is not recognisably either Buddhist or Christian. Corless was, of all my inter- viewees, the most wary of the danger of ending up with a religious practice which was neither Buddhist nor Christian,[64] yet by adopting an interpretative frame- work and practice of his own invention in order to try to preserve the integrity of the traditions (rather than letting an interpretative framework and integrated practice across traditions develop *out of* his practice of both), he in fact seemed to come closest to building the foundations of a *tertium quid* – his own third hybrid religious system. '[A] single entity can't be both', says Corless (14), but what our investigation suggests is that a single entity *can* be both and, moreover, that *allowing oneself to be both* helps one avoid putting 'a yak's head on a sheep's body', i.e. combining elements which are not organically related. Habito stresses that, although one should preserve the differences between Buddhism and Christianity, one should not *cling* to those differences,

> because, as one takes ... [the traditions] for what they are, in their differences, then one might be able to come to a point where one says: well, there's something beyond these differences that one can accept and, therefore, integrate into one's being and, therefore, be enriched in the process.
>
> (209)

Habito speaks of the 'enrichment of our own spiritual life and understanding as we open ourselves to practices from other paths to the Mystery' (1994a: 153), thus indicating an implicit assumption that organic integration happens within a monocentric pluralist framework (even if Habito himself would not use this terminology).

Difficulties and benefits

Of course practising thoroughly across traditions is not without practical difficulties, and it is revealing that none of those I interviewed would *advise* dual belonging. Whether it is an unguided zeal for personal integration towards which one leans, or an unguided zeal to preserve the distinctions between Buddhism and Christianity, the fact is that, for now at least, there are very few people who are sufficiently well grounded in their own dual belonging to be able to act as competent guides to others in helping them strike the right balance between integration and the preservation of distinctions. 'I didn't find anybody who was equally comfortable in both traditions whom I could take as a director', says Corless, for example (8).

Perhaps, for the time being, the best that most practitioners across traditions can hope for is that they be well guided in their practice of each of these traditions individually, so that their rootedness in each is thoroughgoing. Reis Habito, Furneaux, and King, all emphasise the importance of teachers in this respect. Yet here too there are difficulties since while one might well have a teacher to guide one's lay Buddhist practice, it is unlikely that one will have a teacher to guide one's lay Christian practice. Moreover, while those I interviewed were highly educated in matters of religion, most people's opportunities to study their traditions will be few. There may also be a risk of asymmetry here: reflecting on her experience of guiding Morning Star Sangha (MSS) participants, Furneaux explains that she has found a greater level of ignorance with respect to Christianity than with respect to Buddhism, because in the Buddhist case, 'they've had to be taught' (111).

Time constraints present dual belongers with another practical challenge. King has found that the need for thoroughness of practice within each tradition has tended, in her case, to mean that at different periods in her life she has devoted more time to the practice of one tradition than to the practice of the other. Which has commanded more of her attention at any given time has depended on her geographical circumstances[65] and on which tradition specific events in her life have attracted her to. King explains, for example, that grief led her into Buddhist practice more than into Quaker practice: 'It's a place of Buddhist practice – working with that – and ... I'm thinking in a Buddhist framework ... in trying to process my parents' death', whereas she reflects that she has been drawn more to Quaker practice by the challenges of raising a family (400–401). However, King nevertheless sees herself as '100 per cent Buddhist and 100 per cent Quaker' and thinks that the time she has devoted to each will work out roughly equally over the course of her life (348).

An aspect of dual belonging which might be experienced as a drawback is the fact that it may be difficult and even ill-advised to raise one's children within both the traditions to which one belongs oneself. While awareness of, respect for, and openness to, both traditions is likely to be transmitted from dual belongers to their children, dual belonging itself may not be a religious way of life which is easily passed on. It is more of a vocation. Moreover, the children of my interviewees had typically been given a more comprehensive introduction to Christianity than to Buddhism, partly because of the greater access to Christianity in the West and partly due to doubts about the confusion which may result from trying to raise children in two traditions. King, for example, found it virtually impossible to raise her daughters in the Buddhist tradition without the support of a community in her area (405), and also expressed worries about the confusion which attempting to bring them up in both traditions may have caused. 'I kind of think you have to pick one', says King (406). She, anyway, has doubts about how well Buddhism caters for children. She feels that for some women, herself included, there is a strong link between religious identity and motherhood (in her case, she initially became a Quaker primarily because of what it could offer her children).[66] She notes that the Buddhist teachings have been developed in a monastic context and has observed, in South-East Asia, that teaching to the laity is poor and even poorer when it comes to children. She does feel, however, that provision for Buddhist laity (including children) is developing and hopes that it will evolve still further in American Buddhism (418).

Despite the challenges of practice across traditions, all my interviewees felt that the benefits more than compensated. Having more than one route into practice means that, depending on one's spiritual disposition and needs at a particular time, or in a particular phase of one's life, one may use one route more than the other. 'I–Thou' prayer, for example, might feel appropriate at one time, whereas *shikantaza* might feel more appropriate at another time, even if one understands these practices to be ultimately convergent. If incorporating *shikantaza* and *kōan* study into one's Christian practice helps one experience

God's love, and if using Christian *kōans* helps one achieve *kenshō*, then integration has, in this instance, enhanced rather than jeopardised one's Christianity and one's Buddhism. As Henry Smith says, 'why cannot someone experience enrichment in both directions by practicing both? Interreligious experiences leave us no doubt that this happens' (1997: 170). Moreover, Habito reflects that, as well as finding Buddhist and Christian practice mutually enriching, he also finds them to some extent mutually *correcting*: Zen Buddhist practice does 'a better job in leading people to a direct non-dual experience and negation of concepts' than has Christianity with its tendency to neglect its more mystical strands (207), whereas the Christian emphasis on 'love of neighbour and transformative action on behalf of the world' can, by drawing attention to the fact that Zen practice also invites one to active compassionate engagement towards reforming the world, 'challenge Zen Buddhists from their safe haven of ... thinking that, if you've gotten your transformative experience sitting facing a wall, then ... all's right with the world' (214).

One does not have to be a thoroughgoing dual belonger to benefit from incorporating spiritual practices from other traditions. As we have seen, Bäumer, Pieris, and Habito are critical of those who employ practices from other traditions without being fully immersed in the contexts which give those practices their meaning, but even a 'truncated version of something' (to use Habito's expression) can enhance one's practice significantly.[67] While Bäumer is right that dual belonging is the ideal when it comes to practising across traditions in a way which preserves the integrity of both traditions (1989: 38–41), provided Christians approach Buddhism in a spirit of openness, humility, and reverence, it does not seem that there is anything wrong with their benefiting from the incorporation of particular practices without full immersion in the context in which those practices originate. Ursula King argues, for example, that the neglect of meditation in churches is a problem:

> There is far too much emphasis on the spoken word and external action, and yet many people can no longer easily relate to the art of praying. In contemporary culture we are externally overstimulated by words, images, and constant noise, which seem to drown the quiet search of our inner being.
>
> (2003: 149)

She suggests that many people today are seeking a new wholeness and that is why so many people are turning to meditation: 'they need a time and place for quietness and spiritual nourishment'. Annewieke Vroom's reflections support this:

> Sitting in church I feel suffocated with form. The images, the songs, the sermon, the communion – the fullness of it all is overwhelming. Where is the emptiness? Even in the two minutes silence we need to pray. I long to sit on a pillow and meditate. I feel estranged from my own place of worship.
>
> (2005: 3)

Vroom explains that although her loyalty to Christianity is not exclusive, she still feels a greater commitment to the Christian tradition than to the Buddhist, and wants to assist in developing the Christian tradition in order to help it survive in Europe. Yet she feels that if it had not been for her contact with Buddhism, she might well have lost contact with Christianity altogether (2005: 3–4).

These reflections suggest that the influence of Buddhist practice upon the Christian tradition, far from being a threat to it, might rather be sustaining and renewing. Sallie King says she dreads seeing anything lost from the traditions should there come to be cross-fertilisation of ideas and sharing of practices between them on a grand scale, but perhaps she should place more trust in the process of 'testing and validation' which she values so highly in each tradition (408). To be a living tradition is to be a changing tradition. Buddhism and Christianity have never been static, but have, over thousands of years, assimilated much from outside their original boundaries which was found to be true and helpful. As King herself notes elsewhere, Christianity is often presented as a synthesis of Hellenistic and Semitic world-views, and Chinese Buddhism as a synthesis of Indian Buddhism and indigenous Chinese world-views. 'How do such syntheses occur if a worldview is so self-referential, and ... resistant to blending with alien factors?', asks King (1990: 125). To participate in a tradition is, inevitably, to participate in processes of change and development; why should dual belongers fear *their* participation in these processes? King values the traditions as she knows them today, but without these processes of change, they would not be the traditions as she knows and loves them. Yet King seems to realise this, and despite her anxieties regarding the practice of each being influenced by the practice of the other, in a more decisive moment, she declares:

> Definitely Quakerism should learn from Buddhism. ... [T]hey should be ... more systematic about teaching meditation. There are *methods* and they *work* and people are so unguided in Quakerism and that's a waste ... they could get that so easily from Buddhism, and there's some of that going on. ... Then, yes, I guess something like ... Quaker business practice – for the Buddhist side. It's too authoritarian when there's one person who rules all aspects, beyond the spiritual: it doesn't need to be that way. So maybe ... one head for spiritual practice, a different head for business matters or something – distribute the power a little bit.
>
> (410)

As more people practise across traditions and as more external expressions of internal integration emerge (such as MKZN and MSS), it seems likely that this will gradually have some effect on the Buddhist and Christian traditions at large. Over time, perhaps the traditions will increasingly recognise their deep convergences and respective strengths, and influence one another's thought and practice, such that in some respects they may end up resembling one another more than now. (Indeed, regarding King's suggestions above, she herself observes that very many Quakers are already learning and benefitting from Buddhist meditation methods, and Carl Bielefeldt's reflections on contemporary Zen Buddhism in the USA suggest that there is already a movement towards more egalitarian styles of leadership as a result of Protestant Christian influence (2008: 7).) However, it also seems likely that, whatever ill there may be in participating in processes which result in Buddhism and Christianity becoming more similar, this ill will be outweighed by the positive benefits of this mutual understanding and mutual sharing. Moreover, the Buddhist and the Christian philosophical, theological, mythological, cosmological, historical, and geographical structures are sufficiently different from one another, that it seems very unlikely that the sharing of practices – and ideas about practice – will lead to the eradication of their differences.

7 Conclusion

The emergence of a coherent world-view and spiritual path

Our investigation has revealed that, through a process of increasing familiarity with, and deepening understanding of, Buddhist and Christian thought and practice, dual belongers are able to arrive at a coherent self-understanding informed by both traditions. As their understanding of how Buddhist and Christian insights relate to each other grows and they make new connections between them, their Christian and Buddhist thought and practice gradually integrate.[1] This process of integration involves flitting back and forth between one's Buddhist and one's Christian perspectives, attempting to make sense of Christian insights from a Buddhist perspective and Buddhist insights from a Christian perspective, and living within the growing area of convergence and complementarity between those two perspectives. '[A]s you progress on the spiritual path', says Reis Habito, 'knotty problems tend to become less and less knotty and ... you come to a deeper understanding where you find ... common ground' (486).

Discovering the respects in which the Buddhist and Christian perspectives converge is not just a case of coming to better understand *Buddhist* doctrines and how they function within their context,[2] but also a case of coming to better understand *Christian* doctrines which may have previously been taken for granted. One is prompted by one's new perspective to interrogate one's original perspective and, in so doing, to deepen it and appreciate its truth more profoundly. As Rosemary Radford Ruether reflects, '[g]etting to know and understand others also means knowing and clarifying better what is essential for one's own faith' and, conversely, '[t]he more one is clear about what is normative for one as a Christian, the more one can also open to the truth in other religious perspectives' (2005: 29). Fabrice Blée (1999: 1–2) insightfully describes the process in which genuine dual belonging emerges as a 'twofold conversion' in the sense that one comes to share the Buddhist vision and to appreciate its truth, and at the same time one returns to the heart of Christianity.

While these traditions need to be acknowledged as distinct from one another, says Habito, through their mutual assimilation in one's own life, one can reach a point whereby 'one comes to see them, no longer as contradictory nor as just adventitious mixing, but ... as an integral perspective' (155); 'there are ways of understanding these expressions and these doctrinal positions in a way that [they] are not mutually exclusive' (197). Habito has found that, increasingly, his Buddhist and his Christian world-views have come to inform a single, integrated world-view:

> I'm trying to articulate a world-view that would be integral but which derives from the Buddhist tradition as well as the Christian tradition without being unfaithful to either. So that's my continuing attempt. ... [T]here's no way of integrating the Christian world-view and the Buddhist world-view, as such, but my own world-view is informed by both perspectives and so my hope is that it's an integrated world-view and not a disjointed one.
>
> (144)

He explains that, although the Buddhist and the Christian conceptual frameworks differ, and the theological task he faces as a dual belonger is ongoing, there is an area in his life where those frameworks have found their intersection and he is 'trying to live within that intersection' (141).

In the course of our investigation, we have been exploring this area of intersection and attempting to discover its boundaries. I have tried to show that there are orthodox strands of thought within both traditions which make it possible to conclude, from a Buddhist and a Christian perspective, that there are deep convergences between these traditions and mutual benefits in their cross-fertilisation, and that the tensions between them are spiritually beneficial. Crucially, the Buddhist Christian can, consistently with both traditions, affirm that there is one ultimate reality; that Jesus Christ and Gautama Buddha mediate that reality, each in his own unique way; and that what the salvific/liberative path requires in the here and now is the replacement of egotistical, selfish ways of being with loving, wise and compassionate ways of being, regardless of what the precise nature of the end of that path may be, and regardless of how many lives one may have in which to pursue it. These agreements all contribute to the area of intersection which gives Buddhist Christian dual belonging its coherence.

Most fundamental to this intersection is the affirmation of one ultimate reality, found in both traditions, since this shared affirmation becomes the hook upon which both the dual belonger's distinct religious commitments can be hung. Cornille and Dupuis worry that thoroughgoing commitment to, and engagement with, two traditions may not be possible.[3] But what our findings suggest is that authentic dual belonging (i.e. faithfulness to both traditions) does not require the division of absolute commitment and engagement between two objects, as Cornille and Dupuis suggest, insofar as the singularity of wholehearted and unambiguous religious commitment depends, not on commitment to the thought and practice of a single tradition, but on commitment to one ultimate reality. Even regarding the ordinary diversity that exists within the life of any individual, Fowler asks,

> [a]re we each, in effect, 'many selves,' adapting and reshaping our identities as we move from one role, relationship or context to another? ... Or can we authentically claim faith in an infinite source and center of value and power, in relation to which we are established in identities flexible and integrative enough to unify the selves we are in the various roles and relations we have?
>
> (1981: 19)

Dual belongers are committed to two traditions, but those who understand both commitments as orientating them towards one ultimate reality *are* able to claim a faith and identity of the kind Fowler extols. Their primary, absolute, and undivided commitment is to this one ultimate reality; they simply orientate themselves towards It/Him/Her *through* more than one tradition.

Cornille asserts that religious belonging involves

> abandonment to a transcendent reality mediated through the concrete symbols and rituals of a particular religion. Surrender is thus not to the ultimate as such, but through – and in the end – *to* the teachings and practices embedded in a concrete religious tradition.
>
> (2003: 44)

But this latter claim is inconsistent with the traditional recognition on the part of Buddhists and Christians of the limitations of all concepts and symbols with respect to that reality which transcends them. As Smith says, authentic faith, 'is concerned with something, or Someone, behind or beyond Christianity, or Buddhism'.[4] Hence, King is able to say that she has 'one faith' in that which is 'before Buddhism and Christianity' (365). 'I *most* identify with that', she explains (364). Buddhism and Christianity 'just offer ... tools. They offer languages for me to try to speak' (390).

Except for Corless, all my interviewees inclined towards a monocentric understanding of the ultimate orientations of Buddhism and Christianity (i.e. they inclined towards the assumption there is one ultimate reality with which both traditions are concerned), even if only in the most general terms (as when Habito, for example, speaks of Buddhist and Christian ways of relating to 'Mystery with a capital "M"'). They also understood themselves to be following a single spiritual path. Corless had the least unified conception of his spiritual path insofar as he took Buddhism and Christianity to be – or to be relating to – different absolutes, but even he reflected that he experienced his Buddhism and his Christianity as mutually supportive, reinforcing, and complementary.[5] Moreover, from the most to the least unified conception, none of my interviewees demonstrated the 'arrested spiritual development and growth' Cornille speaks of in connection with dual belonging.[6] Indeed, rather than inhibiting their spiritual progress, dual belonging seemed to have increased their understanding of each tradition, of themselves, and of the nature of the spiritual task, and to have deepened, enhanced and enlivened their practice of each tradition.[7]

The continuation of oscillation

As we have seen, the experience of convergence and formation of new inter-connections between one's Buddhism and one's Christianity can make it increasingly difficult to separate out these two ways of thinking and being in one's own integrated world-view and practice (in this sense the Buddhist perspective becomes integral to the Christian perspective and vice versa), but this does not mean that one merges Buddhism and Christianity into a single conceptual or ritual system such that one is no longer able to speak authentically in the 'language' of each of these traditions separately or to identify the source from which certain elements of one's thinking and practice derive.[8] We have seen that authentic integration is a matter of allowing the distinctive insights and practices of each tradition to contribute to one's overall outlook and practice, and not a matter of conflating Buddhism and Christianity or of mixing them together in a manner which obliterates the distinctions between them. Indeed, their differences and tensions are cherished by authentic dual belongers as mutually complementary and corrective. '[T]hey do offer different insights', acknowledges Habito, 'one cannot just conflate them … [T]hey are two different systems of understanding reality … coming from two different cultural and historical backgrounds' (205). Yet, he says, these different systems 'somehow resonate' in one's own spiritual practice and world-view, such that one is 'enriched by both' (205). As Abhishiktānanda – who clearly exhibited a serious two-fold commitment (to Christianity and Hinduism) – puts it,

> [t]here is no question here of that facile syncretism which seeks to reduce all religions to their lowest common denominator, or what is often called their 'essence,' in the form of a few universal truths, and then, on the basis of some hasty and superficial comparisons maintains that their fundamental elements and essential beliefs are really the same.[9]

Habito is at pains to emphasise, moreover, that he is not interested in creating 'a hodgepodge of Christian elements and Buddhist elements', describing this as 'an irresponsible way of approaching spirituality' (153–54). All my inter-viewees made similar points, emphasising the distinctiveness of each of these traditions and likening them to different languages or separate pieces of soft-ware, each of which retains its distinct integrity even when one appreciates its overlap with the other and allows cross-fertilisation between them.

The distinctions between the traditions mean that faithfulness to each of them still requires some oscillation between Buddhist and Christian ways of thinking and being, notwithstanding the overlap between them. Thus, at times, one or other tradition may be dominant in the dual belonger's thought and practice. Oscillation takes place, for example, between the symbols and some of the formal practices of each, despite overlap and cross-fertilisation between them; thus liturgical distinctions are preserved. Another kind of oscillation was exhibited by some interviewees in relation to particular circumstances, such that one or other dominated when its particular insights or emphases were found to be the most relevant (as, for example, in the case of King's finding that Buddhism had more to say to her regarding the death of her parents, whereas Christianity had more to say to her regarding family life). To this extent, Phan seems to be right that 'the question of the primacy of one religious tradition over another is not a matter that is settled once and for all; it continually fluctuates, depending on circumstances' (2004: 73).

While we identified fundamental respects in which Buddhism and Christianity, as King says, 'understand each other deeply', we also identified respects in which they appear, to some extent, to 'elude each other' (King 2005a: 100). This seemed to be the case, for example, regarding the Christian emphasis on the value of the individual *qua* individual, and on the primary importance of justice, as against the Buddhist emphasis on realising the truth of not-self, and on the primary importance of letting go of grievances. Here the distinct emphases of the traditions seemed to contain pieces of truth, even though those pieces didn't appear to perfectly fit together. In these instances, remaining faithful to their respective insights seemed to be a matter of holding the Buddhist and the Christian perspectives side-by-side and oscillating between them, insofar as neither perspective seemed able to fully integrate the strength of the other without eclipsing its own particular emphasis. A number of my interviewees seemed to feel that this was where they benefitted most from having a Buddhist and a Christian perspective, precisely because each had strengths the other was unable to fully accommodate. 'One, in effect, supplements the other', explains King; 'there are strengths that each has that the other lacks and so that's good: to be able to draw on all those strengths' (362).

The divergence between the different strengths of Buddhism and Christianity seemed to relate to their distinct salvific/liberative emphases – Christianity on loving involvement, Buddhism on wise non-attachment – and to mirror the tension between them. Integrations of Buddhist and Christian perspectives which are legitimate from the point of view of each perspective, respectively, do not eradicate this tension but see living within it as spiritually beneficial insofar as each pole corrects the other. This beneficial tension seemed best maintained by treating certain pivotal points of disagreement between the Buddhist and Christian world-views as 'bracketed questions',[10] rather than siding firmly with one tradition or the other. This was my suggestion regarding the question of the precise nature of the eschaton (whether or not individuality is ultimately maintained), for example, and the question of rebirth. Agnosticism on these points is likely to help dual belongers preserve the distinctive character and salvific/liberative insight of each of these traditions (as well as helping them avoid unwarranted dogmatism concerning matters beyond the range of their current experience). By treating the eschatological question and the question of rebirth – neither of which are 'soteriologically vital'[11] – as bracketed questions, dual belongers can flit between both perspectives and attempt to live by the mutually complementary and corrective insights best supported by each of them respectively.

Cornille assumes that dual belonging entails an unavoidable encounter with 'incompatible claims to absolute truth' (2003: 45). However, as I have tried to show, no religious person who affirms the conceptual transcendence of ultimate reality should be claiming the *absolute* truth of religious doctrines which concern the nature of that reality. As Harris says, 'Ultimate Truth' is beyond all linguistic formulations. She suggests, therefore, that '[i]n seeking to move closer towards it, we need insights that complement each other, which even seem to contradict each other, so that we do not cling to one formula in the belief that all truth lies therein' (1999b: 2). In other words, the internal dialogical to-and-fro between mutually challenging conventional perspectives is not something to be avoided; rather it can be of benefit by rendering one less susceptible to the danger of becoming attached to one particular conventional perspective, and reminding one of the inadequacy of all concepts. King's reflections confirm this:

> I do feel it's very useful to have two in order to not slip into idolatry ... into thinking the words one was using ... were really adequate ... [I]t's a good reminder: there are two sets of words, they do not translate into each other, they both do reasonable jobs in their own ways, they have a lot going for them; but neither of them are fully accurate or really *name* reality or any of those things. So it *relativises* each tradition and that's good.
>
> (362)

This appreciation of the relativity of both traditions with respect to that which is beyond them means King is not profoundly troubled by the respects in which her Buddhism and her Christianity pull apart:

> My basic commitment is to the place before there's a Buddhism and before there's a Christianity; that's my deep commitment and I *know* that neither Buddhism nor Christianity nor anything else is ever going to perfectly express that ultimate reality. So that's alright: if neither of them is going to perfectly express it, it doesn't really matter if they're not perfectly reconcilable.
>
> (397)

Focus and bifurcation

As dual belongers practise both traditions over time, their increasingly integrated world-view does not gradually *replace* their Buddhist and their Christian perspectives, since that world-view precisely depends upon those perspectives in their distinctness. The resonances, agreements, convergences, and cross-fertilisations between these distinct perspectives all contribute to the coherence of the dual belonger's thought and practice across traditions; while their dis-agreements, failures to fully understand one another, and inability to fully embrace one another fuel the creative internal tension and internal dialogue between them, in which each continues to listen to the other and tries to see things from the other's perspective. When you 'delve deeply' into Buddhism and Christianity and 'put them vis-à-vis one another', says Habito, 'there can be "aha!" experiences' (206) as one is afforded 'a single vision of ... reality that ... the two perspectives in combination serve to enhance' (158). Yet, as Dupuis points out, '[t]o the comparison of the two eyes combining in one vision could easily be opposed that of a prism, whose different facets it is not possible to embrace at one glance' (2002: 74). Both Habito's analogy and Dupuis' capture a truth about what an optimum balance between integration and the preservation of distinctions consists in, inasmuch as faithfulness to both traditions results in *both* integration *and* oscillation.

A helpful model for envisaging authentic dual belonging might be to think of oneself as having two lenses through which to view the world: a Buddhist lens and a Christian lens. Initially, these two lenses are separate and one flits back and forth between the views they respectively afford. But as, over time, one is able to focus more successfully through each lens and to make increasing sense of what one is seeing through each, these lenses begin to converge, affording a single vision of reality as seen through the area of overlap between them. However, in addition to this emerging area of focus, there remains also some bifurcation to the extent that the overlap between the lenses remains complete. Insofar as one's Buddhist and Christian perspectives do not *fully* coincide, some 'double vision' persists (in which each lens reveals something different), requiring one to continue flitting to-and-fro between each perspective in turn, rather than viewing the world entirely in terms of the synoptic vision afforded by the area of convergence. The vision of reality shared by the traditions can go no further than the internal dialogue between them will allow, otherwise coherence is bought at the cost of eradicating important distinctions between them.

To fully merge the Buddhist and the Christian 'lenses' is to distort one or both of them. This may be the result of ignoring, or failing to recognise, differences between the Buddhist and the Christian perspective; or of collapsing the tensions between them by prioritising the salvific/liberative emphasis of one of them; or by choosing one perspective over the other in areas of disagreement, thus threatening the integrity of the other. If one pushes the integration of one's Buddhist and one's Christian perspectives too far, exceeding the capacity of one or both of them to assimilate the insights of the other, eradicating any need for oscillation between them, then one or both of these perspectives will be distorted. Moreover, while natural cross-fertilisation between these perspectives is to be welcomed, to fail to recognise each 'lens' as a distinct conceptual and ritual system, is to fuse them into a single lens and, hence, to destroy the integrity of both. Mindful of the danger of distortion, Habito acknowledges that his analogy of two perspectives combining in a single vision has its limits insofar as some 'bifurcation' remains: 'conceptually speaking', he reflects, 'there will never be a complete gelling or a complete integration' (143). He would no doubt share Harris' sentiments when she says that Buddhism and Christianity 'converge in remarkable and life-affirming ways. However the differences between them remain' (2002b: 17); 'I prefer the tension of living with difference and paradox', says Harris, 'to creating a unity that may do an injustice to the riches within each religion' (1999b: 2).

Furneaux describes her Buddhist and Christian practice as '*absolutely* integrated' (115). This sense of absolute integration appears to derive from the experience of having *transcended* the distinctions between these traditions. Perhaps Furneaux is right that the conceptual 'dilemma' between Buddhism and Christianity can be a gateway to non-conceptual, non-dual experience;[12] but if one is to faithfully and authentically represent both these traditions when one expresses one's insights at the *conceptual* level, one must retain the differences and dialogical tension between their respective emphases. Furneaux, however, appears to prioritise her Buddhist perspective, interpreting her Christianity so thoroughly in its terms that she arguably risks eclipsing Christianity's unique contribution to her overall world-view and undermining the beneficial tension which exists between the Buddhist and the Christian perspectives when each is allowed to be entirely itself. I am not suggesting there is anything regrettable about Buddhism being one's primary identity (and remember that each of these traditions individually affirms the beneficial tension between wise non-attachment and loving involvement). I am simply claiming that Buddhism appears to have overall priority in Furneaux's religious life and questioning whether, if this interpretation is correct, she can be thought of as participating *fully* in the Christian tradition and as authentically representing that tradition. Furneaux might well object that I have *not* correctly interpreted her reflections and, of course, this is possible.[13] Then let my question apply to any dual belonger who *does* instantiate the approach I have associated with Furneaux.

Although too great a degree of integration between one's Buddhism and one's Christianity can endanger full and authentic dual belonging, our investigation has revealed that this danger can also arise from a refusal to welcome whatever agreement, convergence, and cross-fertilisation emerges naturally from the internal dialogue between one's Buddhism and one's Christianity. The *extreme* oscillation between perspectives which remains if one tries to prevent this organic integration creates a dilemma which is, potentially, psychologically problematic, if left unresolved. By insisting that this extreme oscillation be retained, therefore, one risks, in the end, unwittingly subsuming both perspectives within a third perspective so as to achieve the psychological coherence one otherwise lacks.

This seems to be what had happened in Corless' case. Corless tried hard to isolate his Buddhism and his Christianity from one another in order to prevent his Buddhist and Christian 'lenses' converging. This meant that the to-and-fro between Buddhist thought and practice and Christian thought and practice was much more marked in Corless' case than in others'. The dichotomy in his own thought and practice that this produced appears to have been made psychologically tolerable by his incorporation of his Buddhist and Christian commitments into an integrative framework external to them both, which was premised on the possibility of coinherent superconsciousness and which construed his identity as a microcosm of Mother Gaia (understood as both the source of Buddhism and Christianity and the matrix for their dialogue). The marked degree of oscillation in his thought and practice continued but was no longer experienced as an intense dilemma, since Corless now had a meta-framework in which to make some sense of this oscillation. However, this framework was, in a sense, like a third lens placed over his Buddhist and Christian lenses: it allowed him to acknowledge his Buddhism and his Christianity at once, but was itself neither Buddhist nor Christian. Corless had striven hard to avoid this outcome, and had rejected the interpretation of Buddhism and Christianity as concerned with one transcendent ultimate reality precisely because he believed that this interpretation prioritised a framework which was neither Buddhist nor Christian.[14] But monocentric pluralism is *not* the result of viewing Buddhism and Christianity from a third perspective outside them both. Rather, it is simply an aspect of the overlap between the Buddhist and Christian perspectives, emerging as it does from their agreement that there is not more than one ultimate reality and that ultimate reality is conceptually transcendent.

Corless was reluctant to embrace overlap between his Buddhist and his Christian perspectives because he had applied to his dual belonging the wide-spread but erroneous assumption that dialogue requires a Buddhist who is exclusively Buddhist and a Christian who is exclusively Christian.[15] This idea fails to do justice to the reality of dialogue, ignoring as it does the fact that, if dialogue is fruitful, then the perspective of each of the participants is broadened as it assimilates what it can of the other's perspective.[16] Faithfulness to the traditions requires dual belongers to retain bifurcation between their Buddhist and Christian perspectives *only* to the extent that each perspective cannot entirely assimilate the other. Only to this extent is Corless right that the dialogue seems to require a Buddhist who is solely Buddhist and a Christian who is solely Christian. But, as we have seen, there are numerous respects in which the participants in the internal dialogue are able to agree with each other and to take on board each other's insights, and this convergence and cross-fertilisation is what leads to the emergence of a logically, psychologically, and spiritually coherent world-view and a practice across traditions which is genuinely Buddhist *and* Christian. Preserving the distinctions between these traditions is crucial, but not at the cost of the shared vision of which they are capable. Where, in dialogue, one's commitment to one's tradition allows one to assimilate one's interlocutor's insights, one is obliged by one's commitment to truth to do so. Thus, the extreme form of perspective-switching which seemed to characterise Corless' dual belonging should ideally be no more than a *provisional* response to finding oneself equally convinced of the truth of both traditions. The next step must be the ongoing attempt to integrate their truths by trying, from each perspective, to assimilate the insights of the other.

Our investigation reveals, then, that too great a zeal for the integration of one's Buddhism and one's Christianity, and too great a zeal to preserve distinctions between them, can be equally distorting. The full and authentic dual belonger is held by the traditions in a tension between a movement towards integration which draws the views through each of these 'lenses' into a single area of focus through the area of overlap between them, and an opposing movement which pulls these lenses apart, requiring the Buddhist Christian to flit back and forth between the view afforded by one and the view afforded by the other. Pushing the agreement and cross-fertilisation between one's two perspectives further than those perspectives will support – either by subordinating one to the other or by failing to recognise them as distinct – is detrimental to full and authentic participation in both traditions. Likewise, striving to hold one's Buddhist and one's Christian perspectives apart, such that one fails to appreciate agreement between them and obstructs their mutual enrichment, is also detrimental to authentic participation in both. Authentic Buddhist and Christian belonging requires that *the traditions themselves* dictate the balance: where they can agree, the Buddhist Christian should allow them to agree; where they cannot agree, the Buddhist Christian should allow them to disagree.

Risks associated with syncretism are risks faced by all

Is the Buddhist Christian's integrated world-view and practice across traditions syncretistic? As Cornille observes, despite attempts to rid the term of pejorative meanings, 'syncretism' still denotes 'the (illegitimate) mixing of irreconcilable truths' (2003: 46). But we have seen that, when an optimum balance is struck between integration and the preservation of distinctions, Buddhist Christian dual belonging involves only the *legitimate* integration of *reconcilable* truths. Authentic integrations emerge out of a growing understanding of how these distinct traditions reinforce, complement and enrich one another. Such integrations preserve the distinct insights of both traditions, show continuity with major strands of both, and include only those aspects of the traditions which can be shown, from both perspectives, to be consistent and mutually reinforcing; aspects which are inconsistent are left in tension. Although integrating the insights of different traditions can be thought of as a kind of interreligious mixing, as Habito stresses, it is not an *adventitious* mixing (155); rather, it emerges as mutually compatible strands of thought and practice which are already present within each tradition are drawn out and developed. Hence, integration is not a matter of attempting to fuse to each tradition something extrinsic to it, but is a matter of letting each perspective grow organically to include the truth of the other. This presents us with two choices: either we can, in acknowledgement of its pejorative connotations, use the term 'syncretism' only in connection with Buddhist Christian integrations which are *not* continuous with one or both of the traditions they claim to faithfully represent, or we can deem all multireligious identities syncretistic, and strive harder to rid this term of its pejorative connotations, simply evaluating particular integrations on the basis of how faithful they are to the traditions involved.[17]

Perhaps dual belonging will resolve itself in 'a new and highly individual integration reminiscent of New Age religiosity', suggests Cornille (2003: 46). Certainly, every individual dual belonger's way of integrating Buddhism and Christianity will be unique in its details, but provided an integration is demonstrably authentically Buddhist and authentically Christian, this uniqueness need not be a cause for concern. After all, no religious person, whether multireligious or not, can absorb and reflect the whole of a given tradition; as King says, '[l]ook at how varied Christianity is! look at how varied Buddhism is!'.[18] Even an individual who knows only one tradition, absorbs and reflects that tradition in his or her own unique way. Amin Maalouf, discussing identity in general, suggests that a person's identity is 'made up of many components combined together in a mixture that is unique to every individual' and what those components are depends upon 'a person's whole journey through time as a free agent; the beliefs he acquires in the course of that journey; his own individual tastes, sensibilities and affinities; in short his life itself' (2000: 3–4). Religious identity (*qua* aspect of one's overall identity) seems to be similarly constituted. One confronts only those elements of a tradition with which one's particular life-circumstances bring one into contact, and one assimilates or rejects elements on the basis of one's particular history so far, one's particular character, and one's degree of intelligence. Hence, one could say that there are as many branches of a tradition as there are practitioners in that tradition.

On the basis of such considerations, Jeffrey Carlson argues that *all* religion is, ultimately, syncretism:

> To have a religious identity is, inevitably, to be a 'syncretic self,' the product of a process of selective appropriation, internalizing elements drawn from vastly varied pools of possibility. We are this amalgam, this ever-changing assemblage of diverse elements ... (2000: 118–19). Each of our 'inventories' shows the influence of *many* places and times. We are all, and each, intrinsically plural. Together we share that formal complexity, that syncretic identity.
>
> (2000: 124)

Schmidt-Leukel also recognises this, asserting that *all* individual religiosity is 'patchwork-religion' inasmuch as every individual's religiosity is 'nourished by those extracts or "patches" of a religious tradition which have become significant to his/her very personal spirituality in the course of one's life and were digested in the very same personal manner' (2009: 58).

'In the realm of exclusive religious identities, of beliefs and techniques and interpretations of experience,' writes Burford, 'you are either in a different group, or you are in my group. Either you focus your meditation on Christ, or you don't; you assume the grace of God, or you don't' (2003: 60). But what if your life circumstances have brought you into sustained contact with both groups; what if your history is such that your religiosity includes Christian and Buddhist 'patches'?[19] The identities of my interviewees, for example, do not fit neatly into Burford's categories, but rather draw our attention to the more complex picture which is often the reality. 'To claim "I am a Christian" after one has read or otherwise encountered and been influenced by Buddhist thought and practice', says King, 'is to understate the case ... [A] person, however committed to the Christian path, who has nevertheless been exposed in any significant degree to Buddhism, is constructed out of Buddhist as well as Christian elements'. King insists, therefore, that 'religious identity should not be understood in black and white, either/or terms' (1990: 121–22).

And this applies not only to the religious identities of individuals but, relatedly, to the religious traditions themselves. Recognising this, Carlson suggests we 'rethink our notions of "insider" vs. "outsider"' (2000: 124). The boundaries of religious traditions have always been fuzzy insofar as the people within those traditions continually assimilate elements which – until assimilated by sufficient numbers – might generally be considered to lie 'outside' those traditions. Hence, as Carlson says, each tradition is 'itself an amalgam, the product of a process of selective reconstruction by those who came before' (2003: 79), or as Peter van der Veer puts it, 'every religion is syncretistic, since it constantly draws upon heterogeneous elements to the extent that it is often impossible for historians to unravel what comes from where' (1994: 208). Buddhism and Christianity are no exception. Moreover, it is *fortunate* for the traditions that they are not impermeable static entities, since growth and positive transformation would be impossible if they were.

Cornille compares authentic religious belonging to complete surrender to another person in marriage. Dual belonging is, by implication, likened to adultery or at least an avoidance of thoroughgoing commitment (2003: 48). But, rather than deciding *a priori* that the boundaries of truth and goodness must be determined by what one perceives as the boundaries of one's home tradition, perhaps pinning one's colours to the masts of *truth* and *goodness* wherever one finds them should be considered a mark of thoroughgoing commitment (rather than lack of it) and of spiritual courage and maturity (rather than juvenile promiscuity).[20] Of course, one's criteria for establishing what counts as truth and goodness outside one's home tradition, will initially depend in large measure on what counts as truth and goodness within one's home tradition as one understands it. But, as one's participation in the thought-world and practices of another tradition deepens, one's criteria expand to include, as far as possible, those of the other tradition. The structure Smart suggests for the assessment of another religion's truth-claims offers a way of thinking about how this process of expansion might legitimately (from the perspective of one's home tradition) occur:

> If faith F presents C as a criterion of truth, then faith T may turn out to do well or badly by that criterion. If well, then that is a ground for respecting criterion D put forward by T, and so something like an inter-system consensus about criteria cannot be ruled out.[21]

For those whose immersion in faith T is so thorough that it becomes as much a 'home' to them as faith F (the tradition in which they were raised), this process eventually becomes two-directional, the growing area of consensus between T and F giving coherence to their increasingly integrated world-view.

Multireligious identities are sometimes associated with a superficial 'pick and mix'[22] approach to religion, in which religion is seen as a 'smorgasbord of ... beliefs and practices' (Phan 2006: 181). Phan characterises this approach as a

> postmodern form of syncretism in which a person looks upon various religions as a supermarket from which ... one selects at one's discretion and pleasure whatever myth and doctrine, ethical practice and ritual, and meditation and healing technique best suits the temperament and needs of one's body and mind, without regard to their truth values and mutual compatibilities ... [demonstrating] the unbridled consumerism, excessive individualism, and the loss of the collective memory that are characteristic of modernity and its twin, globalization.
>
> (2004: 62)

No doubt this describes the religiosity of some people with multireligious identities, but it does not describe dual belongers, who are deeply grounded in both traditions. Even though Corless' practice seemed to show some similarity to New Age eclecticism, there was nothing in his reflections, nor those of any of my other interviewees, to suggest the presence of a superficial consumer mentality. Indeed, most of them explicitly criticised 'supermarket' spirituality or New Age religiosity, and the superficiality they perceived in it.[23] They exhibited such concern for the integrity of the traditions, moreover, and for thoroughness of practice within each, that there was arguably a danger of their dismissing unnecessarily the potentially beneficial sharing of ideas and practices between people deeply grounded in only one of these traditions.[24]

One element of the 'supermarket spirituality' critique seems to be an objection to the exercise of personal choice, clearly evident if one commits oneself to beliefs and practices beyond those prescribed by one's home tradition. Cornille argues that 'multiple religious belonging bypasses the very purpose and dynamics of religious belonging', which should be 'about the complete surrender of one's own will and judgment to a truth and power that lies beyond or beneath one's own rational and personal judgment' (2003: 48). But, while she may be right about the surrender of one's *will*, can Cornille really mean that in religious belonging one must surrender one's *judgement*?[25] Perhaps, it is only after having judged that a particular truth and power is worthy of submission that Cornille thinks personal judgement should be put aside. But, since all knowledge of truth and power is filtered always and inexorably through the limited and fallible understanding of human beings, surely a certain amount of discernment is always called for.

It is, moreover, erroneous to assume that those who are *only* Buddhist or *only* Christian do not also exercise personal choice. Defending her selective approach to religion, King rightly points out that the fact of diversity both within religious traditions and among them makes choice inevitable, even if one does not choose consciously (1994b: 190–91). She acknowledges her own fallibility and, therefore, the danger that exercising personal choice will lead her into error, but contends that there is no alternative available to her or anyone else (1994b: 192). If one accepts this, then the question of 'supermarket spirituality' becomes a question concerning the basis on which one makes one's choices, and whether one sticks with one's choices once they become demanding.

Schmidt-Leukel challenges the assumption that patchwork-religiosity is undesirable because it displays an essentially non-religious consumerist attitude, whereby escape is sought from a religious claim once it becomes a genuine existential challenge rather than a mere consolation, edification or spiritual thrill.[26] Is this not 'a danger that everybody has to face regardless of whether his or her religiosity is nourished by several or by just one religious tradition?', asks Schmidt-Leukel (2009: 59). He concedes that there is a danger that people will choose their religious 'patches' on the basis of primarily consumerist motives, but argues that freedom of choice is in and of itself a religious necessity (2009: 60).

Perhaps those with multireligious identities must strive harder than others to avoid the risk of superficiality to the extent that, if one is practising two traditions, one may be able to devote less time to each (it is on the basis of such constraints that King feels that belonging to more than two traditions would not be possible for her).[27] It is probably also true that dual belongers must work harder than single belongers to establish coherence amongst their beliefs by working out what is compatible with what. As Phan points out, without the 'hard and patient intellectual work' we witness among pioneers, 'multiple religious belonging runs the risk of shallowness and trendiness' (Phan 2004: 74). But those I interviewed count among such pioneers. All were highly reflective individuals with backgrounds in academic theology and religious studies. They had given much consideration to the question of the compatibility of their Buddhist and Christian perspectives, and made considerable inroads into achieving coherence. Certainly, as multireligious identities become increasingly common amongst ordinary believers, academic theology, as Schmidt-Leukel points out, 'can and will have to provide far more assistance' (2009: 65). It will hopefully also be the case that the more common dual belonging becomes, the more practical spiritual guidance will be available for those following in the footsteps of the pioneers.[28]

But although the challenge of avoiding superficiality might in some ways be greater for dual belongers than for single belongers, why should the fact that they derive spiritual nourishment from more than one source necessarily make them less willing to acknowledge and to strive to meet this challenge than those who belong to only one tradition? I suggest that, in this regard, dual belongers are actually *less* susceptible than others to the risk of superficiality since they are less able to take their commitments for granted, the presence of two complete and distinct perspectives being a potential source of genuine existential angst unless one submits to the challenge of investigating both in order to try to understand how they might fit together.[29] Single belongers, on the other hand, may live their whole lives without ever feeling challenged to investigate their religious beliefs.

We must, as ever, be wary of demanding more from those who practise across traditions than we do from those who practise within just one. No doubt there are people with multireligious identities whose immersion in the traditions from which they derive nourishment is shallow, who harbour many ill-considered and incompatible beliefs, who pick only the bits of a tradition they like and reject the rest, and who drop commitments which become demanding; but is this not also true of many who know only one tradition? Furneaux notes that those who practise across traditions are often charged with creating 'a mish-mash of things taken from one religion which you like and tacked on to the other, conversely ditching what doesn't suit you' (2006b: 15). She acknowledges that there are people who do take this approach, even with respect to a single religion, but it is clear that she does not take this approach to be her own.

Despite being critical of the superficiality he perceives in some approaches, Phan recognises the possibility of deeper and more fruitful approaches, and sets out four conditions for the kind of dual belonging he takes to be 'both spiritually fruitful and compatible with Christian identity'.[30] First, suggests Phan, dual belonging should not emerge primarily out of uncertainty over one's Christian identity, or out of spiritual crisis, discontent with one's church, or ignorance of the Christian tradition; and nor should it be based on a 'spiritual dilettantism', but on a firm rootedness in the Christian tradition. Second, deep and lasting dual belonging, thinks Phan, must involve ongoing and serious engagement with the doctrines and practices of the other religion and cognisance of the danger of 'facile syntheses of ideas and practices'. Third, *practical* participation in the other tradition is essential and, where necessary, practice should be guided by a Master and should ideally include a period of time with a monastic community. Fourth, the dynamic and evolving process of Christian identity formation will be more complex and demanding for the dual belonger than for one who is solely Christian and, consequently, there should be a willingness to live with irresolvable tension (Phan 2006: 181–82). Of course, Phan might not necessarily agree with my interviewees about precisely where this tension lies but, arguably, all my interviewees except Keenan (who does not practise within both traditions) meet the criteria he outlines and by no means are they the 'religious butterflies' Phan speaks of in connection with the superficial approaches he criticises (Phan 2006: 184).

Indeed, my interviewees demonstrate that it is possible to be thoroughly immersed in both Christianity *and* Buddhism, to achieve a considerable degree of overall coherence, to take the demands of both seriously without reservation, and to respect – even to cherish – the tensions between them. The very fact that they have sustained their commitment to both traditions over many years, despite experiencing tension (as well as overlap) between them, should provide sufficient evidence that these are not people who jettison their religious commitments when they become challenging: 'you need the things in the tradition that challenge', says King, 'not only challenge morally and experientially, but ... that challenge intellectually' (375). She admits, for example, that she is challenged by aspects of the Buddhist world-view such as karma and rebirth, but she does not drop these aspects because she is challenged by them; rather she takes them 'very seriously' (375). She feels, moreover, that the areas where the traditions challenge *each other* are areas of growth for her.

Questions remained in certain areas for all those I interviewed (as they do for reflective single belongers), but their reflections suggest that it is not necessary to have all questions answered in order to follow a salvific/liberative path informed by both traditions, and Buddhism and Christianity do not need to be experienced as consistent in every regard in order for one to draw valuable inspiration from both. King explains that the Quaker emphasis on love and the Buddhist emphasis on non-attachment, especially, have been for her a natural *kōan*, the Spirit leading her forward:

> this questioning mind fixed in not-knowing at the confluence of love and emptiness, has been, in Quaker language, the movement of the Spirit, the presence of the sacred. I am grateful that both traditions encourage me to regard this questioning mind with respect and seriousness.
>
> (2003c: 169–70)

A priori suspicion of dual belonging is often rooted in the assumption of the exclusive truth of just one of the traditions. In other words, for some the problem with dual belonging is not so much the exercise of personal choice but more the outcome of that choice.[31] Schmidt-Leukel points out that when the assumption of exclusive truth is in place, choosing to expose oneself to the influence of another tradition inevitably appears as 'the mixing of light and darkness, of truth and lie, of the divine and the demonic' (2009: 48). But if a more positive view of other religious traditions is embraced, then this view requires reappraisal:

If one can assume, for good theological reasons, that the good, true and holy is not confined to one's own religious tradition but can also be found within others, then the idea of a spiritual formation by various traditions can no longer be seen as a priori devious or dangerous.

(Schmidt-Leukel 2009: 48)

Endorsing efficacy without assuming superiority

My interviewees tended towards 'soft pluralism' in the sense that, while they did not feel able to affirm Buddhism and Christianity as equally efficacious with respect to (final) salvation/liberation, nor were they able to affirm either tradition as more efficacious than the other. (The exceptions are Corless, whose self-contradictory position embodied a form of mutual inclusivism or even mutual exclusivism, and possibly Furneaux, whose position is arguably a form of Buddhist inclusivism insofar as, though seeing both traditions as effecting the same salvation/liberation, she appears to see Buddhist thought and practice as doing so more competently than Christian thought and practice.) This pluralism is crucial to full and authentic dual belonging, for if Buddhism is affirmed as superior, it is hard to see how one can claim authentic Christian belonging and, if Christianity is affirmed as superior, it is hard to see how one can claim authentic Buddhist belonging.

I suggest, however, that many of those who rule out *a priori* the possibility of full and authentic dual belonging do so on the basis of the widespread assumption that one does not fully and authentically belong to a religious tradition unless one takes that religious tradition to be superior to all others.[32] Were this assumption correct, it would indeed make full and authentic dual belonging logically impossible, whatever the theology and self-understanding of the practitioner, since one's not being a Buddhist (among other things) would be logically entailed by one's being fully and authentically a Christian, and vice versa. It was this assumption on Corless' part (15, 22) which accounted for the intensity of his dilemma when he found himself equally convinced of the truth of both Buddhism and Christianity. However, I hope my arguments in Parts I and II go some way to refuting this assumption by showing that monocentric pluralism does not undermine the traditions but rather mirrors key aspects of their self-understandings.[33]

In Chapter 1 we noted that there is an objective dimension as well as a subjective dimension to religious identity. Hence, if one's understanding of oneself as Buddhist and Christian is to be justified, then one's Buddhism should be recognisable to at least *some* Buddhists, and one's Christianity to at least *some* Christians. I have tried to show that it is possible for a Buddhist Christian's thought and practice to be continuous with major strands of both these traditions and, to the extent that this is the case, we can assume that their thought and practice will be recognisable to at least some Buddhists and Christians. Moreover, if one practises in a Buddhist community and a Christian community, then one can be seen to have anyway received at least a superficial degree of acceptance on the part of those communities. However, one could argue that fulfilment of the objective dimension of identity requires that one's thought and practice be potentially recognisable not merely to some practitioners of the religion to which one claims to adhere but, more specifically, to the relevant religious *authority*. On this basis, it might be argued that, if the assumption of salvific/liberative superiority is made by the authorities in one or both of the traditions to which one claims adherence, then, in denying it, one fails to honour the objective dimension of identity in one or both cases and, therefore, cannot justifiably claim authentic belonging. Reis Habito contends that Buddhists generally regard a person's self-identification as a Buddhist as a sufficient condition for Buddhist identity and that the fact that she has taken refuge with a Buddhist Master anyway qualifies her as a Buddhist. She suggests that, traditionally, Christians would find it more difficult accepting her as a Christian (439).

This difficulty might not be too great were she a Quaker (indeed King joined the Society of Friends only after first receiving their explicit assurance that her Buddhism was no problem),[34] nor, perhaps, if she were an Episcopalian – '[t]hey're almost all pluralist in the Episcopal Church here', says Keenan, 'so they're not going to ... banish Mahāyāna theology' (245). (Although, the recent controversy over the election of Zen practitioner, Rev. Kevin Thew Forrester, as bishop of the Episcopal Diocese of Northern Michigan suggests Keenan's assessment of Episcopalian attitudes may be questionable.)[35] But, certainly, from the Vatican's perspective, acceptance of a Buddhist Christian as an authentic Christian seems unlikely, given its vocal criticism of pluralism.[36] For example, 'Dominus Iesus'[37] condemns the notion 'that the truth about God cannot be grasped and manifested in its globality and completeness by any historical religion', and states that 'the full and complete revelation of the salvific mystery of God is given in ... the ... historical event of Jesus'. This, it is argued, is what makes Christianity superior to all other religions and, consequently, what makes pluralism – however 'soft' – wrong.[38]

It has been argued in response to 'Dominus Iesus' that its claim that '[t]he truth about God is not abolished or reduced because it is spoken in human language' renders the current Vatican's theology unorthodox in the sense that it breaks with the traditional Catholic understanding of God as utterly transcendent of all human expression.[39] And Cobb goes as far as to characterise as sinful the belief that all that is needed for the salvation of the whole world is found in the past of one's own tradition, calling this 'an expression of ... defensiveness, which is faithless'.[40] However, there is still a question here which further research into dual belonging should consider: If the Habitos, for example, think of themselves as Catholics and if their approaches can be shown to be continuous with major strands of traditional Roman Catholic thought and practice (as I believe they can), how significant is the fact that the Vatican would denounce their religious world-views as unorthodox? This relates to more general questions concerning the role of religious authorities in determining religious identity and orthodoxy.[41] For now, let us just note that by denying the authenticity of Reis Habito's Catholic identity, one would risk imposing a more stringent criterion for belonging in her case than one would consider reasonable in the case of a single belonger. Were one to insist that honouring the objective dimension of Roman Catholic identity demands that one's theology be precisely aligned with the Vatican's in every regard, one might well find oneself hard put to find any authentic Roman Catholics among ordinary believers.

What would more clearly undermine the dual belonger's claim to Christian and Buddhist authenticity than his or her refusal to assume the superiority of either tradition, would be if he or she were to hold that Buddhist Christian dual belonging is superior to solely Christian or Buddhist belonging. As we noted in Chapter 1, faithfulness to Buddhism and Christianity requires that dual belongers affirm each of these traditions as efficacious in its own right, without need of supplementation by the other. But although those I interviewed had come to feel that both traditions were essential to their own spirituality, they did not take the salvific/liberative capacity of each tradition to depend on its being practised in conjunction with the other. All emphasised their love and respect for these traditions as they are and both traditions were very much affirmed as independently cultivating ways of thinking, being, and feeling which, for Buddhists and Christians respectively, have been spiritually transformative. No missionary zeal was exhibited regarding dual belonging. 'It's difficult to follow *one* practice seriously and deeply enough to actually come to liberation' exclaims Furneaux (109), for example, and Reis Habito is keen to stress that she has no agenda: 'I will not go out there and say "you know, it's not enough to be just Christian or it's not enough to be just Buddhist"' (430); 'I don't see myself as … saying "well, we can solve our problems by being Buddhist Christians". … [T]his is my personal path and karma … but I'm not … here to proclaim that I'm doing anything better … than someone who's only Christian or only Buddhist' (496).

Commitment and openness: dual belongers as microcosms of Buddhist–Christian dialogue

While the Christian and the Buddhist traditions are rightly acknowledged by dual belongers as having been salvific/liberative for generations of adherents, it may nevertheless be pointed out that the transformative power of each of them might be radically reduced should they fail to respond adequately to the challenge of religious diversity by discouraging adherents from appreciating what is good and true in other traditions, fostering, instead, exclusivism and fanaticism. Salvific/liberative efficacy is not necessarily guaranteed for all time, and the salvific/liberative capacity of each tradition is perhaps *tested* when it comes to its degree of openness towards the insights of other traditions. Habito, for example, surely does not undermine the traditions by claiming that, from each perspective, 'there should be an openness to explore and … to continually challenge one's own belief system to see whether there may be things that could be seen in a different light', nor by pointing out that 'one's own view of things becomes transformed and enlarged and expanded and deepened, as one submits it to the light of another tradition' (154).

To say that my interviewees, on the whole, affirmed the salvific/liberative efficacy of each of these traditions individually is not to say that they did not have criticisms of these traditions nor suggestions regarding how each could be assisted by the other to develop in its areas of weakness and to place greater emphasis on its neglected strands. '[B]oth offer deep wisdom and ... there have been many people who have had access to this wisdom in both traditions without having recourse to the other tradition', says Reis Habito;

> [b]ut now we live in an age where there is ... contact with the other tradition, and I think it helps to see what's highlighted in one tradition [and] to turn around and look at the other tradition and say: is it there, and would it be helpful, and is it something that has not been emphasised so much? – and this is more what I see happening between Buddhism and Christianity.
>
> (497)

Speaking from a Christian perspective, Cobb suggests that 'the challenge of Buddhism' be approached in 'an openended spirit to see what we can learn and appropriate for ourselves' (1978: 19). If Christianity is a living movement, says Cobb, then it requires Christians today to commit themselves to the task of learning from other traditions:

> In faithfulness to Christ I must be open to others. When I recognize in those others something of worth and importance that I have not derived from my own tradition, I must be ready to learn even if that threatens my present beliefs.
>
> (1999: 45)

Mutual transformation is often stated as an aim or, at least, as a positive result of interreligious dialogue. For this transformation to come about, Buddhists and Christians must eventually grapple with the challenge of integrating into their self-understandings both the truth they have discovered in the other's tradition and the truth about their own tradition which they have discovered whilst looking at it from the other's perspective.[42] As Schmidt-Leukel emphasises, this challenge is not undergone in the abstract:

> [i]t appears precisely when Buddhists and Christians turn, seriously and dialogically, towards a comparative understanding of their visions of human existence: the human predicament and its prospect of liberation; the relation of human existence to ultimate reality; the role played by

their founding figures, Jesus Christ and Gautama Buddha, in mediating ultimate reality to human beings.

(2005b: 19–20)

Most participants in dialogue grapple with this challenge of integration primarily from the perspective of just one of these traditions. Keenan, for example, does so primarily from a Christian perspective since, although he has a multireligious identity, he understands himself as a Christian first and foremost. Using the Mahāyāna Buddhist perspective he has gained through decades of study, he attempts to integrate into Christianity what he can of the insights of Buddhism, and also to integrate what he has learned about Christianity whilst looking at it from his Buddhist perspective.[43] But dual belongers are those who have, in the dialogical process, come to identify roughly equally with both perspectives and they, therefore, become micro-cosms of the dialogue as a whole, grappling with the challenge of mutual transformation from *both* directions.

Working from both perspectives, the authentic dual belonger gradually establishes coinciding comparative understandings of key aspects of Buddhism and Christianity, not from some supposedly neutral ground outside the tra-ditions but from within each, as he or she flits to-and-fro between his or her two perspectives in the inner dialogical process of mutual integration. The gradual evolution of his or her integrated world-view mirrors the mutual transformation these traditions are undergoing through their encounter with one another on a grand scale, much of which takes place through what Schmidt-Leukel calls 'mutual inspiration with "catalyst effects"' (2005b: 18). As examples he cites the revitalisation of Christian contemplative practice due to the encounter with Buddhist meditation; renewed Christian interest in 'negative theology' due to the encounter with the Buddhist philosophy of emptiness; and Buddhist recognition of the social implications of the bodhi-sattva ideal due to the encounter with Christian social ethics and charity (2005b: 18). Certainly, my interviewees' examination of Christianity from a Buddhist perspective had encouraged them to draw out its apophatic, mys-tical, contemplative strands, as well as to emphasise in a Christian context the importance of effective meditation techniques and clearer thinking regarding the nature of self and mind. And looking at Buddhism from a Christian per-spective had encouraged them to draw out the social implications of the Buddhist emphasis on the importance of compassion.[44] Corless, for example, affirms that

Christians who practice ... Buddhism can be stimulated to look into the mystical tradition of Christianity which has been largely neglected ... and ... to look into the apophatic tradition ... Buddhists, on the other hand, can be stimulated by the social activism of Christians ... to look at their own tradition in a new way.

(1996a: 9)

As microcosms of the dialogue, dual belongers embody both the fruits of that dialogue (in their integrated comparative understandings and cross-fertilising Buddhist and Christian practice) and its remaining disagreements and questions (in their agnosticism regarding certain issues and their experience of tension and ongoing internal debate). Indeed, far from undermining the dialogue between the traditions, there is a sense in which authentic dual belongers epitomise the *ideal* dialogue between Buddhism and Christianity insofar as their spirituality involves both complete commitment on each side and complete openness on each side.[45] We might, therefore, expect that the mutual transformation of these traditions will move faster in the lives of reflective dual belongers than it will between the traditions at large, and that the reflections of pioneers may therefore point us in some of the directions future global theology will take as people increasingly come to see themselves as heirs to the whole religious history of humankind and embrace, within the context of dialogue, the challenge of working out how the insights of the various traditions of the world relate to one another.[46]

Authentic dual belonging as broadening and strengthening the traditions

As we saw, some of my interviewees raised concerns that their internal integration of Buddhism and Christianity might prove detrimental to the traditions in the long term insofar as assimilating insights from one into the other could cause the traditions to increasingly resemble one another, thus eroding the distinctions between them and weakening the distinctive strengths of each: 'they've got to remain distinct ... and I am a force of destruction, perhaps', worries King, for example (407). However, while it seems likely that, if authentic dual belonging were to become widespread, it would influence the traditions to become more similar, this would only be the case insofar as dual belonging contributes to the process of mutual assimilation the traditions are already undergoing through their encounter with one another.

Clearly, if Christianity is caused by its encounter with Buddhism in the hearts and minds of dual belongers to place a greater emphasis on wise non-attachment and Buddhism is caused by its encounter with Christianity to place a greater emphasis on loving involvement, then this process of mutual transformation will be one which causes the traditions to become more alike. However, it should be remembered that mutual assimilation is not usually straightforward. As Keenan stresses, the meaning of words is context dependent;[47] what is said in a Buddhist context will not necessarily mean the same thing when it is said in a Christian context. This makes assimilating a truth from one context into another a complex process. To make the point in Zen terms, if Buddhists and Christians are pointing at the moon from different directions, then there may be many instances in which we find, as Corless puts it, that 'the opposite of one profound truth is another profound truth'.[48]

The trick is to look beyond the pointing fingers, explains Habito,[49] i.e. to orientate oneself towards that greater reality which lies 'behind or beyond Christianity, or Buddhism' (Smith 1962: 13). However, since there is no neutral ground from which to observe the moon (ultimate reality) *and* both fingers (the traditions), coming to understand how what is said within each of these traditions relates to what is said within the other is a matter of flitting back and forth between the Buddhist and the Christian perspective, and seeing how the moon looks, and how each tradition looks, from each perspective. Mutual assimilation is often neither the result of direct copying from one tradition to the other, nor of direct translation, but rather the result of ideas in one tradition encouraging the discovery and organic development of functional equivalents within the other tradition through a complex and ongoing process of triangulation within the context of deep and searching dialogue. This makes the developments in Christianity genuinely Christian insofar as they grow organically from strands within that tradition, and likewise the Buddhist developments in Buddhism.

Thus the traditions become more similar as a result of mutual transformation but not in a straightforward sense, and not by either compromising its own distinctive approach. When it comes to practice there might be some more straightforward copying over – as in the case of Christian assimilation of Buddhist meditation techniques, for example – but precisely how these techniques are employed and the meaning they are given, will depend on their new context. Although they will share more of one another's insights, these traditions will express them in ways appropriate to their respective conceptual frameworks (just as dual belongers express their insights differently depending on whether they are speaking in a Buddhist or a Christian context) and hence these frameworks will continue to differ. Developments in each tradition which result from the encounter with the other may, of course, be more or less authentic (in the sense of developing more or less organically out of what has gone before); but given that dual belongers love the traditions and are deeply immersed in both, and in the dialogue between them, we can be optimistic that the developments they help foster within each will be organic evolutions of both traditions which will renew and refresh the neglected strands of both, rather than suppressing the strengths of either.

As long as dual belongers allow the traditions themselves to dictate the balance between integration and the preservation of distinctions, the movement towards global theology from within each tradition which they help foster, while leading to a greater resemblance between the traditions, will not be a movement towards a single theology which synthesizes the best of both. Rather it will lead to a celebration of differences and the richness of diversity: 'Global theology in a pluralistic age need not cut its ties to the particularity of such religious traditions', explains Cobb,

> [i]nstead it can work within each religion to make the theology of that tradition more global. In the name of what is most sacred, even what is

most particular, in each tradition, adherents can be called to more global religious thinking and practice.

(1999: 59)

Habito hopes the process of mutual learning and mutual assimilation which, in his case, contributes to a growing focus through the two eyes of his Buddhism and his Christianity, will continue to take shape. But he points out that, as it does, the duality of the 'eyes' remains: 'they're two but they're one when they see something together' (211). He hopes that, one day, as the result of his ongoing efforts to see his Buddhism and his Christianity in a more coherent picture, he will be able to fully articulate how he is able to join the Christian community in reciting the creed and how he is able to join the Buddhist community in affirming traditional Buddhist doctrines, but he does not suppose that these articulations will be identical (197–99; 2007: 177). In other words, it is the *intersection* or *coincidence* of a Buddhist global theology and a Christian global theology – in the sense of the *agreement between* them – which gives coherence to the Buddhist Christian's world-view, and not the *sameness* of these theologies. And, recall, it is the points where these theologies do not *fully* coincide – in the sense of not completely agreeing – which create valuable tensions for the participants in the global dialogue.

'The opportunities for adventure in Christian theology have never been greater', recognised Cobb as early as 1978, in his article, 'Can a Christian be a Buddhist, Too?'. 'The risk is real, for we cannot predict the outcome. ... But if we do not take this risk, we will forfeit all claim to universality and exist only as a relic of times past' (1978: 20). Dual belongers fully embrace this challenge and this risk and, at times, may feel uneasy in their role as facilitators of change. But as Fabrice Blée recognises, authentic dual belonging involves 'having two religious universes linked in dialogue inside oneself, each being welcome in its originality and deepened in its specificity' yet, at the same time, dual belonging opens up a way of being 'in which the other's universal truth becomes mine' (1999: 2). In so far as this is the case, authentic dual belongers are likely to help broaden each tradition through assimilation of the insights of the other, making each more comprehensive and hence more worthy of its claim to universality; yet, at the same time, they will help make each tradition more aware of its own conventional particularity, of the historical contingencies which have helped shape it, and of its own particular genius and, hence, of its specific contribution to global dialogue.[50] As each tradition becomes more universal, differences between them are not eradicated, since they maintain their distinct and differently functioning conceptual frameworks and, where they cannot agree, each retains its own particular view (though with a lighter, less dogmatic hold, acknowledging that there may be more truth in the other's perspective than can be discerned on the basis of experience so far). The mutual transformation which dual belonging helps facilitate, therefore, is not only no *threat* to each of these traditions, it actually *strengthens* each in its universality *and* uniqueness, making the survival of both of them more likely. Conversely, barricading the doors of church or temple, in the hope of keeping the influence of the other out, only weakens one's religion's claim to universality and fails to demonstrate its unique contribution to global dialogue.

If the dual belonger's Buddhism is gradually becoming more universal, and so too his or her Christianity, there is a logic to Cornille's speculation that '[p]erhaps the experience of double religious belonging can be understood ... as a temporary stage or transition, on the way to a final resolution in one religion or the other' (2003: 46) – i.e. perhaps we can expect that dual belongers will eventually settle for a more universal Christianity or a more universal Buddhism. I suspect, however, that Reis Habito speaks for most dual belongers when she reflects that she does not feel that there will ever be a point where, as a Christian, she has learned all the lessons that can be learned from Buddhism and can simply go on her way (500), and she would no doubt say the same from her Buddhist perspective regarding Christianity.[51] Rather she sees this mutual assimilation as an ongoing process. These rich traditions emerged in almost total isolation from one another's influence,[52] and now that they are encountering one another, they have much to discover in each other, for their mutual enrichment.

Moreover, and crucially, the reflections of my interviewees suggest that they remain committed to both traditions, not primarily out of a sense of the narrowness or weakness of each, but rather out of a sense of the great strength of each and out of a sense that they are benefitting not only from the presence of their respective strengths but particularly from the tension and the dialogue between them. In other words, it is the *internal dialogue itself*, as well as what each tradition offers, which makes Buddhist Christian dual belonging a rewarding, if challenging, spiritual path. Owing to their distinctive salvific/liberative emphases there will be a limit to what each of these traditions can assimilate of the other while remaining true to itself. But the reflections of my interviewees suggest that the respects in which Buddhism and Christianity refuse to fully coincide are precisely the respects in which most is gained from dual belonging, for it is this divergence which makes the presence of each perspective most valuable to the other; and it is the points at which they converge which make each of them aware of this, since both agree that right orientation towards ultimate reality requires both loving involvement and wise non-attachment and, therefore, that the tension between their respective emphases helps keep each of them 'in check'. Pieris describes the Buddhist's and the Christian's core experiences as *mirror images* of each other (1988a: 123) and explains that:

> there is a *Christian gnosis* that is necessarily agapeic; and there is also a *Buddhist agape* that remains gnostic. In other words, deep within each one of us there is a Buddhist and a Christian engaged in a profound encounter that each tradition – Buddhist and Christian – has registered in the doctrinal articulation of each religion's core experience.
>
> (1988a: 113)

Thus, for the dual belonger, the internal dialogue itself becomes a kind of spiritual training insofar as each perspective continually corrects the other, holding the dual belonger in the creative spiritual tension which both Buddhism and Christianity insist on.[53] For as long as these traditions retain their core insights, therefore, we may find that there will always be people who would rather accept the demanding vocation of dual belonging than settle for an eventual resolution in either a more universal Buddhism or a more universal Christianity.

Amaladoss suggests that people who feel at home in two symbolic worlds, moving with ease between them and living in a religious fellowship with both communities, 'are obviously called to be mediators' (1999: 5). Reis Habito's reflections, for example, suggest she has often found herself in precisely this role:

> it's like you talk from within but you can also talk from without and you can explain things in a double way ... [I]t makes ... [people] very much wonder where this openness can come from and where this acceptance of the other can come from ... So, in that sense, ... to have both traditions in me is a great blessing maybe also for others.
>
> (491)

Insofar as dual belongers encourage mutual openness and understanding between religious traditions, they have a role to play as global peace-makers and, insofar as they contribute to the sharing of salvific/liberative insights between traditions, they also help strengthen and broaden humanity's collective understanding of, and ability to grapple effectively with, the challenges we face. Reis Habito issues a helpful reminder, that '"what can we contribute to the world?" is a question that we always have to keep on our minds, over and beyond: "what does it mean to be a Buddhist Christian?"' (501). Yet these two questions are not unrelated: 'I'm more inclined to do a Zen retreat ... and sit twelve hours a day than I would be to ... go to Capitol Hill on a bus and protest ... the war or something', reflects Reis Habito, 'and yet, I think, in some way, those *two* things are necessary'; the question, therefore, is 'how to fully integrate them to the best of my ability?' (501). It is perhaps the integration of these two dimensions of how ultimate reality impinges upon us as human beings – so well symbolised, as Pieris says, by '[t]he Indian sage seated in serene contemplation under the Tree of Knowledge, and the Hebrew prophet hanging painfully on the Tree of Love in a gesture of protest'[54] – which will be the most precious reward of the encounter between these two traditions.

Notes

1 Introduction

1 See Yandell and Netland 2009: 175, 212.
2 Cornille takes Christian Buddhist and Jewish Buddhist multireligious identities to be the most common forms of multireligious identity in the West (2003: 43). In the case of Buddhist Jewish dual belonging there is already a new nomenclature ('Jubu'), and the prevalence of Buddhist Christian multireligious identities seems borne out by the significant internet presence of people identifying themselves as both Buddhist and Christian or discussing the compatibility of these traditions, some online groups having many hundreds of members. See, for example, 'A Christian Buddhist Gathering Page'. This site is run by John Malcomson, a self-identified 'Christian Buddhist', who explains: 'We discuss the similarities between Christianity and Buddhism as well as whether being a Christian/Buddhist or Buddhist/Christian is valid or possible'. See also Joseph Anderson's blog, *Lotus and Lily Field Notes* (Anderson 2007) and, for further relevant links, Victoria Scarlett's post: 'Links for Buddhist-Christian practitioners' (Scarlett 2007).
3 Knitter 2009: 216. Knitter is currently Paul Tillich Professor of Theology, World Religions and Culture at Union Theological Seminary, New York. He took refuge in 2008 with the Dzogchen Buddhist community in the USA. His recent monograph (2009) explores the interaction between Buddhism and Christianity that has shaped his beliefs over time. For another personal account of a dual commitment to Buddhism and Christianity, see Thompson 2010.
4 See Knitter, *Without Buddha I Could not be a Christian* (2009). See also Knitter's blog: *How a Buddhist Christian Sees it* (2010).
5 I am construing 'theology' so as to include Buddhist religious thinking (see p. 13).
6 See Phan 2004: 70; Dupuis 2002: 69; Amaladoss 2002: 297; Eck 1993: 160.
7 Of course, Judaism was also present but tended to be confined to those born into it and hence, for the great majority, did not constitute an available religious option.
8 See, for example, Winston 1998; Heelas and Woodhead 2005; Ahlstrand 2007.
9 This term is used by Joseph Spae as early as 1980 in his important work, *Buddhist-Christian Empathy* (1980: 63).
10 See, for example, Bernhardt and Schmidt-Leukel 2008; D'Arcy May 2007; Goosen 2007a, 2007b; Tilley *et al.* 2007; Kasimow *et al.* 2003; Knitter 2009; Phan 2003, 2004; Cornille 2002a; *Buddhist-Christian Studies* vol. 23 (2003); Scheuer and Gira 2000; Sharma and Dugan 1999; Thompson 2010.
11 According to Bielefeldt 2008: 2.
12 Here Bielefeldt is referring to the way in which Buddhism is portrayed in the media and its generally positive, but somewhat distorted and unrealistic image in the West (see Bielefeldt 2008).

13 See Cornille 2003: 44. See also Tilley *et al.* 2007: 161.

14 In the Christian case, baptism – together with personal faith – is traditionally understood as the criterion for Christian identity although, insofar as infant baptism means baptism is not always one's own choice, Christian practice and community membership are perhaps more accurate indicators of lived Christian identity. In the Buddhist case, the taking of the three refuges is, as Rupert Gethin explains, 'essentially what defines an individual as a Buddhist' (1998: 34). The Buddha is the teacher of the *Dharma* (the truth about the way things are as well as how to act in accordance with this truth) and the community of accomplished disciples established by him is known as the *Saṅgha*. The taking of refuge in these 'three jewels' is often realised in the recitation of a threefold formula: 'To the Buddha I go for refuge; to the *Dharma* I go for refuge; to the *Saṅgha* I go for refuge.'

15 See Smith 1997: 132. Panikkar goes as far as to claim that in order to understand another religion, one must believe in that religion (1978: 9–10). This overstates the case, however, and were it true it would have the unfortunate consequence that I would be unable to legitimately disagree with or condemn any religious perspective, since disagreement would necessarily imply that I had simply failed to understand that perspective.

16 Pieris 1988a: 120. Pieris takes the core of a religion to be 'the *liberative experience* that gave birth to it and continues to be available to successive generations of humankind by developing its own peculiar medium of communication' (see also 1988a: 110–11).

17 A member of the Jesuit order, he prostrated himself before an authoritative Buddhist monk and asked to be taught by him, whereupon he was placed for some time in a Buddhist monastery anonymously (Pieris 2005: 13–14). Elizabeth Harris describes how this period of immersion enabled Pieris to 'enter the worldview of Buddhism and to articulate the experience in Buddhist terms' (Harris 2002a: 90). See also Harris' reflections on her own experience of immersion in Buddhism in Harris 2010 (and especially pp. 9–34).

18 Panikkar's famous phrase for this internal dialogue is 'intrareligious dialogue'. He says that if real *interreligious* dialogue is to occur, it must be accompanied by *intrareligious* dialogue (1978: 40).

19 Harris 1994: 3; 2004: 342; 2010: 160–61.

20 Blée 1999: 1. John B. Cobb, Jr. speaks of 'those who seek multiple belonging' (2002: 25). But reflections such as Malcomson's and Blée's suggest that multiple belonging is not something which is *sought*: one does not set out to become a Buddhist Christian, it is more a situation in which one ends up, and one might not find it altogether comfortable.

21 Paul Knitter, who identifies himself as a Buddhist Christian 'double belonger' feels that his 'core religious identity' remains Christian. He also suspects that for most of those with 'hybrid' identities, one identity remains 'core' (2009: 215).

22 See Cornille 2008: 7–8; 2002b: 4.

23 See Cornille 2003: 46. While Cornille recognises the possibility of both traditions becoming normative, she assumes this would mean one tradition were normative in certain areas of belief and practice, the other in other areas. I am not endorsing this assumption here.

24 von Brück 2007: 199 (see also 204–5).

25 Where page references appear, as here, without a publication date, they refer to my own interview transcripts (see p. 15 for a full explanation of the referencing of this material).

26 For an introduction to Erikson's thought, see Coles 2000.

27 See Du Boulay 2005; Dupuis 2002.

28 Senécal 1993: 3. For a fuller account of the crisis of which Senécal speaks, see Senécal 1998.

29 Griffiths 2001: 13. Griffiths is speaking of Greek Orthodox Christianity and Gelugpa Tibetan Buddhism.
30 Since writing this in 1989 Hick's view has changed and, in personal correspondence, he explains that he would now modify this statement (see p. 162).
31 Dalai Lama 1996a: 105 (see also Kiely's preface: xii).
32 Panikkar helpfully proposes that the criterion for Christian identity lies ultimately in '*the sincere confession of a person, validated by a corresponding recognition of a community*'. Thus, 'I am a Christian if I sincerely confess to being one (subjective factor) and am accepted as such by a community (objective element)' (2002: 123). A similar criterion could be applied to Buddhist identity. In both cases, however, it should be noted that the subjective and objective elements of religious identity are not entirely separate since through one's self-identity one influences the identity of the community.
33 See Jackson and Makransky (eds) 2000.
34 I am grateful to an anonymous reviewer at Routledge for helpfully articulating this worry.
35 I have employed the punctuation which seems to best represent the speakers' intentions and italicised text only to reflect their own emphasis. The Furneaux transcript includes a section with her written responses to questions which were not covered during the interview.
36 See McCracken 1988: 17; Ritchie 2003: 27. For the beginnings of a more quantitative approach, see, for example, Paul Heelas' and Linda Woodhead's study (2005) based on empirical research in Kendal in the UK and Kajsa Ahlstrand's study of Enköping in Sweden (2007).
37 See McCracken (1988: 9) on the long interview.
38 Pluralism is one of three categories – alongside exclusivism and inclusivism – belonging to the taxonomy theologians often use to classify attitudes to other religions. Pluralists suppose that several (at least two) traditions may be equally true and salvifically/liberatively efficacious. The three-fold taxonomy was popularised by Race 1983 and, since then, a vast body of literature has emerged discussing it and, especially, pluralism. For an introduction to the typology and a critical discussion of some of the objections to it, see Schmidt-Leukel 2005g.
39 Habito, originally from the Philippines, was the only one of my interviewees who was not born and raised in Europe or the USA. However, he was nevertheless raised in a Christian (Roman Catholic) country and has been living in the USA for more than two decades.
40 See Cornille 2008: 9.
41 Ananda Abeysekara points out that what is considered to count as Buddhism (or Christianity) changes in accordance with fluctuations in what he calls 'contingent conjunctures' (2002: 3, 4, 236–38). He contends that persons, practices, discourses, and institutions conjoin in constantly fluctuating patterns, and that each new conjunction can foreground a new definition of a particular religious identity and its 'others'. In this way competing narratives and debates conjoin and converge to constantly throw to the centre or obscure from view particular understandings of what can and cannot count as Buddhism (or as Christianity). Insofar as these contingent conjunctures will differ significantly depending on one's geographical location, the fact that most of my interviewees live in the USA will influence their notions of what Christian or Buddhist identity consists in.
42 See Chapter 2.
43 Thus my approach differs from that taken by Tilley *et al.* in their discussion of multiple belonging (2007: 50–63, 160–91). They employ a set of 'rules' based on Roman Catholic teaching with which acceptable forms of multiple belonging are expected to comply.
44 It should also be not that English is not Reis Habito's or Habito's first language. Their first languages are German and Filipino, respectively.

45 On the unhelpfulness of various labels, see: Habito: 136–37; 2007; Furneaux: 92; Reis Habito: 430; Corless 1996a: 10.
46 Reis Habito, for example, suggests that she is a 'Buddhist Christian' rather than a 'Christian Buddhist' insofar as she was raised with Christianity and came to Buddhism later (431).
47 In Phan's usage, by contrast, the 'Buddhist' in 'Buddhist Christian' is taken as a qualifier which modifies the primary Christian identity (2004: 68, 72). Similarly, self-identified 'Buddhist Christian', Ross Thompson, explains that he intends Christianity to be the noun, and Buddhism the qualifying adjective (2010: 34).
48 See p. 12. I say 'primarily', here, because if a person is practising in two communities, this already implies at least a superficial level of acceptance on the part of those communities.

2 Interviewee profiles

1 For a more comprehensive biographical account, see Corless 1986a; 1996a; 2002.
2 See Corless 1986a.
3 The conditionality of his baptism and subsequent confirmation was due to doubt over whether his baptism in infancy (and therefore also his confirmation) had been valid.
4 An Oblate is a lay or clerical person formally associated to a particular monastery. Benedictine Oblates seek to live a life in harmony with the Rule of Saint Benedict, as far as their lay circumstances allow.
5 See Corless 1986a – the earliest paper in which Corless expounds the notion of co-inherence.
6 Owing to his deteriorating vision Corless was forced to suspend these plans.
7 'Kashin' means 'fruit/result of Shin'. Furneaux translates 'Shin' as 'heartmind/ Spirit/God' (letter from Furneaux to Drew, dated 23 January 2006).
8 Furneaux attributes her baptism into the Anglican Church, when she had until that point been attending a Methodist church, to her parents' lack of understanding of the process (2006a: 1).
9 John Garrie Roshi drew on several Buddhist traditions, including Zen, Theravāda, and Tibetan Buddhism. He described the mindfulness practice he taught as 'Sati' and, in 1974, founded the Sati Society.
10 Furneaux was unable to complete the PhD. She attributes this to the community she entered: doctoral research was not considered work of the community (2006a: 1; letter from Furneaux to Drew, September 2008).
11 From the statement which appears on the inside cover of MSS newsletters.
12 Furneaux: 110. At the time of writing the sustainability of MSS's activities is under review and its residential events and practice days are suspended. However, individuals are still going to Furneaux's hermitage to practice or receive spiritual counselling by arrangement (letter from MSS Trustee, Revd. Michael Gartland (20 April 2010) accompanying the Easter *Morning Star Sangha Newsletter*; 'Occasional Update' *Morning Star Sangha Newsletter* (October 2010)).
13 Furneaux: 91–92. The wooden symbol she wears over her habit is a copy of a ninth-century Chinese Nestorian cross.
14 For a more comprehensive biographical account, see Habito 2007; 2004; 2003a; 1992d.
15 These experiences are described in detail in Habito 2003a; 2007.
16 Habito 2003a: 136. Habito directs readers to Kapleau 1965 for a detailed description of the Zen style of the Sanbô Kyôdan lineage.
17 *Kōans* are questions or phrases given to Zen trainees to focus on in *zazen* (seated meditation). They are designed to lead the mind away from intellectual, discursive,

conceptual thinking and towards an awakening experience. On the 'mu' *Kōan*, see Koun Yamada 2004: 11–16; Habito 2007: 165–67.

18 Habito 2003a: 136. Here Habito gives a more thorough account of the experience. See also 2007: 166–67.

19 *Kenshō* – literally 'seeing the nature' in Japanese – is an initial awakening experience (a seeing of one's Buddha Nature. This experience can then be enlarged and clarified through further practice in daily life).

20 During the period of the Tokugawa shogunate in Japan, Christians were persecuted. Many 'hidden Christians' had in their homes figurines that appeared to represent the Bodhisattva Kannon (the Japanese form of Kuan-Yin/Avalokiteśvara). To these Christians, however, the figurines were also representations of Mary the Blessed Mother (see Reis Habito 1996). Ruben Habito explains how among some Christians in Japan today, 'Maria Kannon is being accorded renewed appreciation and given new signification as an expression of a mutually resonating theme in the Buddhist and Christian traditions: that of compassion, which cuts through these traditions though given expression in each of them in distinct ways' (1994a: 146).

21 Habito 2007: 178. Habito explains that he uses the word 'kindom' rather than 'kingdom' in order to refer to 'the circle of those bound together as kin' (as explained by Mujerista theologian Ana Maria Isasi Diaz) rather than to 'a vertical hierarchical rule'.

22 A more comprehensive biographical account can be found in Keenan's unpublished autobiography *lower case catholic – or What the Buddha Did for Me* (Keenan LCC).

23 Keenan LCC: 168. Illich himself subsequently suspended himself from the priesthood after he came into conflict with Rome over his radical opinions.

24 Keenan retired from St Mark's in 2009.

25 For a more comprehensive biographical account, see King 2003c.

26 AKA The Religious Society of Friends (a branch of Protestant Christianity). King's branch of Quakerism is associated with the Friends General Conference and maintains the original Quaker practices of unprogrammed Meeting for Worship and eschewal of paid ministry.

27 See King 2003a (*A Quaker Response to Christian Fundamentalism*) which King wrote for teenage Quakers. She explains in interview that what she lays out there as the Quaker view is 'pretty much' her own view (344).

28 King explains that frequent weekend retreats make attending retreats more possible for lay practitioners with short annual vacations. She also points out that Spirit Rock Meditation Center, CA, for example, rather than insisting that teaching be done only by enlightened Masters, relies on 'Community Dharma Leaders' who are able to reach communities around the US.

29 Emails from King to Drew, October 2010.

30 For a more comprehensive biographical account, see Reis Habito 2000; 2003a.

31 See, for example, Reis Habito 2003a.

32 For a full account of the occasion, see Reis Habito 2003a.

3 God

1 See Hick 1989a: 176.

2 Cupitt 1980: 57. Although Cupitt does seem to be prepared to speak of 'post-theistic consciousness' in relation to his view (1980: 135).

3 For Buddhist examples, see Jackson 2000: 220, 240–41; Loy 2002: 213–14.

4 See Hick 1989a: 206.

5 See Chapter 1, note 38.

6 Griffin (2005b), Kaplan (2002), and Harrison (2006) all expound versions of polycentric pluralism.

7 Corless: 46. He qualifies this by saying that it is true 'at the level of words and concepts', which introduces an ambiguity in his position, suggesting it may be less radical than it often appears to be.

8 Corless: 51–52.

9 In this regard Corless' theory is similar to Victoria Harrison's 'internalist pluralism', according to which each religious belief system is 'a self-contained world' and what is true in one world may not be true in another. See Harrison 2006.

10 See Corless 1986a – the earliest paper in which Corless presents these ideas.

11 See, for example, Whitehead 1927–28; Cobb and Griffin 1976. Process theology has been influential in Buddhist-Christian dialogue.

12 Griffin 2005b: 50. Cobb explains that religious language often blurs the distinctions between the three ultimates by relating to more than one of them at once (Cobb 1999: 185–86).

13 See, for example, *Summa Theologiae* I q.3, a.5; I, q.4, a.3, AD 2 and I, q. 6, a.2, AD 3 (see Shanley 2006).

14 See Aquinas, *De Ente et Essentia*, Chapter 6.

15 *Summa Theologiae* I, q.13, a.8, AD 2 (see Shanley 2006).

16 See Rolt 2004; Turner 1995.

17 *Summa Theologiae* I, q. 13, a. 1, AD 1 (see Shanley 2006).

18 *Summa contra Gentiles* I 14, in Pegis 1955: 96.

19 Alvin Plantinga, for example, speaks of God as 'a being with maximal greatness' (1974: 213), and Richard Swinburne describes God as 'a person without a body (i.e. a spirit), present everywhere, the creator and sustainer of the universe, a free agent, able to do everything (i.e. omnipotent), knowing all things, perfectly good, a source of moral obligation, immutable, eternal, a necessary being, holy, and worthy of worship' (1993: 2).

20 te Velde 2006: 177. For more on the pre-modern notion of God, see Burrell 1986.

21 See Griffin 2005b: 60 (fnt. 77).

22 Cobb, for example, suggests that major insights of the Bible were obscured in the process of Hellenisation, leading Christians too often to confuse biblical insights with their Hellenised expression (1999: 139).

23 See, for example, Johnson and Huffman 2002a: 23–24.

24 Hick (1989a), Knitter (1985, 1996), Race (1983), Schmidt-Leukel (2005f), and Smith (1981), for example, all expound versions of the approach I am calling 'monocentric pluralism'.

25 See, for example, Louch 1993: 109.

26 See Vardy 1990, Chapter 4.

27 John Chrysostom quoted in McGrath 1999: 118.

28 Aquinas, *De Potentia*, q.7, a.5 (quoted in Küng 1994: 126).

29 Bhikkhu Bodhi 1995: 24. For a Mahāyāna denial that Buddhism is atheism, see Abe 2000: 110.

30 Schmidt-Leukel 2003: 276. See also 2006b: 112; 2007a: 72–74, 85; De Silva 1982.

31 *Udāna* 8:3 and *Itivuttaka* 43. See Ireland 1997: 103,180.

32 *Milindapañha* 269–70; *Visuddhimagga* 507–9.

33 See Schmidt-Leukel 2007a: 73. See also 2006b: 113–14.

34 *Milindapañha* IV 8:61. See Rhys Davids 1894: 186.

35 See Baier 2005: 106.

36 *Mūlamadhyamakakārikā* 25:19.

37 Schmidt-Leukel 2006e: 121–22. See also Bhattacharya *et al.* 1978: 1; Baier 2005: 110.

38 Reis Habito: 466–67. See also Habito: 149.

39 Keenan: 257. See also Reis Habito: 467–69.

40 Schmidt-Leukel 2007a: 74. For further examples of Christians and Buddhists who have drawn comparisons between the Christian and the Buddhist ultimate, see Merton 1976: 93; Nhat Hanh 1995: 154; Suzuki 1957: 16.

41 Schmidt-Leukel 2006b: 120–21 (see *Milindapañha* IV 8:65–75).
42 Cupitt 1980: 164. See pp. 42–45, above.
43 *Mūlamadhyamakakārikā* 24:8.
44 Augustine: Sermon 67, section 5.
45 Eckhart: Sermon, *Qui audit me.*
46 Tillich 1951: 205 (see also 204, 206–10, 235–39).
47 See p. 50.
48 Reis Habito: 446. Her observation is supported by the remarks of Zen priest and teacher, Norman Fischer. He asserts that, although the word 'God' 'presents a serious problem for many', he himself finds it meaningful and uses if freely in his teaching, 'where it seems helpful' (2002: xix).
49 For a Christian example of this recognition, see Schmidt-Leukel 2007a: 87; for a Buddhist example, see Nhat Hanh 1999: 195.
50 Keenan sometimes speaks as if this is his view. See, for example, Keenan: 260; 1989b.
51 By affirming the possibility of non-conceptual experiences, we need not be affirming the possibility of *entirely* unconditioned experiences of ultimate reality (experiences are always conditioned by our being the kind of beings we are), but only the possibility that experiences are not always conditioned by *concepts*, even if attempts to *express* those experiences always are (see King 1988: 269).
52 Corless and Habito are both significantly influenced by Nichiren Buddhism, in which Śākyamuni Buddha (the historical Buddha) is understood as a manifestation of an eternal, transcendent, loving Buddha. This eternal Buddha is regarded as father of the world, and sentient beings as his children, whom he endeavours to save from suffering through every kind of skilful means.
53 See, for example, Keenan: 297–98; Habito: 184–85; King 2005a: 96.
54 Catherine of Genoa, for example, exclaims: 'My "I" is God, and I know no other "I" but this is my God' (see Robinson 1979: 10).
55 For a Buddhist appreciation of the Judeo-Christian emphasis on relationship and of the 'you' language found in the Psalms, see Fischer 2002.
56 See Schmidt-Leukel 2006c: 5. Schmidt-Leukel does note some exceptions (see 2006c: 5, fn. 24).
57 See, for example, Schmidt-Leukel 2006c: 6–8.
58 For a discussion of these arguments and examples of all three types, see Schmidt-Leukel 2006b: 123–41.
59 Reis Habito: 435. Reis Habito suggests that process theology 'goes a little bit in that direction ... [I]t's not such a linear way of thinking' (435). For an example of a discussion of a process theological approach to the question of creation, see Lande 2006 (see also Ingram 1988: 340). However, insofar as the approach of process theology is incompatible with understanding God or *nirvāṇa* as solely ultimate, embracing a process understanding of creation looks likely to cause dual belongers such as Reis Habito more problems than it would solve.
60 Habito: 186. Knitter makes some suggestions along similar lines. See Knitter 2009: Chapter 1.
61 See p. 45–46.
62 On these lines of thought, see Schmidt-Leukel 2006b: 177–78. Schmidt-Leukel points out that there may be other ways of bridging the gulf between Buddhism and Christianity over the question of creation, emphasising that his own suggestion only serves 'to indicate that much promising work lies before us in our efforts to discern the truth on both sides of the gulf' (2006b: 178). Other pointers towards possible levels of compatibility between Buddhism and Christianity on this issue are made by the contributors to Schmidt-Leukel 2006a.
63 See Dumoulin 1974: 178; Cobb 1982: 43.
64 See Keenan 2006a; 2006b.
65 See the *Cūlamālunkya Sutta* (*Majjhima Nikāya* 63).

66 Habito: 169.
67 Habito: 169, my emphasis.
68 See Corless 1986a: 133.
69 Corless: 21. This resonates with Hick's contention that all the religions converge in the belief that the Real is 'ultimately benign in relation to humankind' (2001: 86).
70 E.g., Corless: 21.
71 King 1994a: 161. See also Amaladoss 2002: 302, 311.
72 Corless: 54 (see also 55–56).

4 Jesus Christ and Gautama Buddha

1 See Kelly 1977; Young 1983.
2 Hick 1977a: 178 (see also 1995: 9).
3 See, for example, Cabezón 1999, 2005; Schmidt-Leukel 2001b: 28.
4 *Saṃyutta Nikāya* iii 120, *Itivuttaka* 92 quoted in Schmidt-Leukel 2005c: 155.
5 *Aṅguttara Nikāya* 3.54–56 (i 157–59) quoted in Schmidt-Leukel 2005c: 155. See also Buddhadāsa 1989: 127–28.
6 See Schmidt-Leukel 2005c: 157; 2006e: 105–6.
7 Founder (1173–1262) of the Japanese Jōdo-Shin Shū.
8 'The Church spoke up for the humanity as an equal partner with the divinity, but was "never able to give this idea any content"', writes Corless (referring to Hick's criticism of the doctrine of the Incarnation), 'because it failed to come up with the precision of the Buddhist Trikāya explanation' (1987: 341). See also Corless: 66.
9 Nhat Hanh 1995: 38–39. See also Kern 2001: 38, and the Buddhist contributions to Gross and Muck 2000.
10 See, for example, Swidler and Mojzes 1997; Knitter 1985, 1996.
11 Schmidt-Leukel 2005c: 169. See also 2006d: 118.
12 Haight 2005: 157. See also Ward 1991: 11; Schmidt-Leukel 2006d: 119. In 2004, after investigating Haight 1999, The Congregation for the Doctrine of the Faith reaffirmed its earlier verdict that the book contained serious doctrinal errors (see Congregation for the Doctrine of the Faith 2004). Haight, however, continues to insist that Spirit Christology is orthodox (see Haight 2005), and it could be argued that the Vatican's Notification itself contains assumptions the orthodoxy of which (in the sense of consistency with the historical tradition and with the spirit of the New Testament) could be called into question. See Schmidt-Leukel 2008b; 2008c.
13 Nhat Hanh public lecture quoted in Schmied 2001: 137.
14 King: 351, 363; 2005a: 99–100. 'Christian Buddhist', John Malcomson, says that, for him, '[t]he notions of being a Buddha or a Christ' have become 'synonymous' (2007a: 3).
15 Pieris notes that it is common for the Buddha to be interpreted by theologians as 'a "holy pagan" preparing the way for Christ, the only Savior' (1988a: 130–31).
16 Cabezón 1999: 28. Similar points made by the Buddhist contributors to Barker 2005.
17 Matthew 7: 21 (Reis Habito: 493). See also Harris 2004: 347.
18 See Hick 1989a: 45; 1993: 127; Schmidt-Leukel 2007b: 309.
19 Dhavamony draws attention to the *Śikṣāsamuccaya* in which the Bodhisattva, out of compassion for suffering beings, vows to save them all, saying: 'All that mass of pain and evil *karma* I take in my own body … I take upon myself the burden of sorrow … Assuredly I must bear the burdens of all beings … for I have resolved to save them all. I must set them all free' (Dhavamony 1978: 51). He contends that from this Mahāyāna perspective the Bodhisattva is 'a suffering saviour' (1978: 51).
20 See Pieris 1988a: 128; Keenan: 305. See also Bloom 2007 (with Foreword by Habito).

21 King: 345 (see also 344–46, 381). Likewise, Wolfhart Pannenberg explains that
   Biblical research reveals that 'Jesus differentiated himself as a mere man from the
   Father as the one God' and even rejected the respectful title 'good master' (Mark
   10:18), 'with a reference to God alone as good' (Pannenberg 1994: 372); and
   Schmidt-Leukel points out that the portrait of Jesus found in the synoptic gospels
   is one of a man who, 'like every devout Jew, strictly rejects even the remotest move
   of identifying himself with God' (2007b: 307).
22 King: 394. Furneaux also emphasises 'Christ Within' (105,118).
23 Reis Habito: 474. It should be noted that the Buddha accepted love and veneration
   from his followers, and in orientating herself towards the Buddha as teacher rather
   than as beloved, Reis Habito differs from many lay Asian Buddhists for whom
   there is a strong *bhakti* element in the way in which they relate to the Buddha.
24 E.g., Habito: 175; King: 380; Furneaux: 105, 118.
25 Buddhadāsa 1967: 48 (see also 114–15).
26 See Kiblinger 2008: 38–40.
27 Nhat Hanh 1999: 46. Suzuki famously makes a similar point: 'Whenever I see a
   crucified figure of Christ, I cannot help thinking of the gap that lies deep between
   Christianity and Buddhism', he writes (1957: 129). Suzuki sees the symbol of the
   peaceful contented Buddha entering *nirvāṇa* as by far the more adequate.
28 Kurata 1971: 230–31, translated in Thelle 1982: 43–44. See also Candasiri 2005: 28.
29 Cabezón 2005: 18. Harris suggests The Venerable Hatigammana Uttarananda's
   approach as another example of Buddhist appreciation of the distinctiveness of
   Jesus (see Harris 2003: 128–31; Pieris 1996: 127–37).
30 See Keenan 1989a.
31 Another possible example is Ayya Khema. See Schmidt-Leukel 2001b: 13; Schmied
   2001: 131–32.
32 See, for example, Bloom 2005: 31.
33 At times the Dalai Lama seems to indicate that he simply is not sure in which
   category to place Jesus: 'my attitude towards Jesus Christ is that he was either
   a fully enlightened being or a bodhisattva of a very high spiritual realization'
   (1996a: 83).
34 This assumption is based on texts such as the *Milindapañha*, in which Nāgasena
   explains to King Milinda that this world can only bear the virtue of a single
   Buddha (*Mph* II:48) and, moreover, that if more than one Buddha appeared, the
   Buddha would no longer be chief, best, most excellent, peerless, highest, without
   equal; 'whatever is mighty in the world is singular' (*Mph* II:50–51).

5 Salvation or liberation

1 See pp. 8–11, above.
2 Makransky 2005a: 195. Much of our discussion will focus on a comparison of
   Christianity and *Mahāyāna* Buddhism and, hence, on the issue of non-duality,
   since my interviewees practised predominantly within Mahāyāna schools. The
   conclusions I reach, however, will also be relevant to the combination of Christianity
   and Theravāda Buddhism (by which my interviewees were also influenced).
3 Makransky 2005a: 210.
4 Even from a Buddhist perspective it would be possible to argue that the sense of a
   separate self is part of the solution as much as it is part of the problem since
   Buddhists take a human rebirth to provide the best conditions for Enlightenment,
   yet only humans seem to have *self* consciousness.
5 Buddhadāsa 1967: 89. Although a Theravadin, Buddhadāsa is influenced by
   Mahāyāna thought and the identification of dualistic thinking as central to our
   difficulties.

6 Habito: 180 (see also 2004: 7, 69).
7 Corless: 73; 1992a. See also De Silva 1982: 62–63; Pieris 1988a: 132.
8 Buddhadāsa 1967: 29. Nhat Hanh also at times appears to present understanding and practising deeply the life and teachings of Jesus as soteriologically equivalent to understanding and practising deeply the life and teachings of the Buddha (see 1995: 56).
9 See Makransky 2008: 47–49.
10 See, especially, pp. 69–72 and 81.
11 A similar suggestion is made by Nishitani of the Kyoto school. See Ueda 2001: 48.
12 Schmidt-Leukel 2001b: 27–28. For example, Suzuki (1957: 16) and Ayya Khema (1996: 50, 57) draw parallels between Buddhist thought and the thought of Christian mystic, Meister Eckhart.
13 See, for example, Makransky 2008: 63.
14 Reis Habito: 465. A further reason stated by some interviewees for their reluctance to make judgements regarding relative efficacy and sameness or difference, was that thinking in terms of 'is this better or worse?' or 'is it the same or different?' is a manifestation of precisely the kind of dualistic thinking which they took to be illusory (see, especially, Furneaux: 91; 2001a: 3). I suggest, however, that to make judgements of any kind is to operate at the relative level and on this level comparisons are spiritually and morally indispensible, especially in matters of religious belonging, since without them one cannot decide which religious practices are worthy of one's commitment.
15 Furneaux 2001a: 3.
16 Corless: 74 (see also 1990b: 120–21).
17 See Harris 1997: 2.
18 Schmidt-Leukel 2003: 275. Although Schmidt-Leukel speaks of 'detachment' here, rather than Harris' preferred 'non-attachment', it is clear that his understanding of detachment is in line with Harris' understanding of non-attachment.
19 See also Harris 1997: 4.
20 Habito: 155. He is grateful to Susan Postal for this analogy. See Postal 1992.
21 Although never an official doctrine, according to traditional Catholic thought, the Limbo of Infants was taken to be a fourth post-mortem possibility for unbaptised children. Today, however, the Catholic Church emphasises instead the possibility and hope of heaven for the unbaptised.
22 Catechism of the Catholic Church (1994), section 1013.
23 Tibetan Buddhists include a sixth type of rebirth: the *asuras* – the jealous anti-gods who do battle against the gods. For an introduction to Buddhist cosmology see Williams 2000: 74–81.
24 Nishitani 1982: 73; Cook 1989: 154–76; and Lai 2001: 133–53.
25 Schmidt-Leukel 2006b: 150 (fnt. 25). Indeed, elsewhere, Lai himself makes statements which appear to contradict his assertion that rebirth is a minority belief. See, for example, Lai and Von Brück 2001: 17, 170.
26 Moreover, not having heard the teachings that will lead one to *nirvāṇa* could be the difference between *post-mortem* survival and lack of it, and this arguably makes traditional Buddhist insouciance with respect to proselytisation look quite misplaced. See Hick 1976: 456; Smart 1993: 19.
27 See Schmidt-Leukel 2006e: 14–16.
28 See Zander 1999: 598–602; Bischofberger 1996a: 18–21; 1996b: 76.
29 King: 400. Buddhagosa also thinks a person's distinctiveness should be taken as evidence of previous lives (*Visuddhimagga* 3:83–85), as does MacGregor (1982: 34). King has found that thinking in terms of children as coming into the world with many previous lives behind them and with their own karmic 'baggage' in tow, helps lessen the vast burden of responsibility parents in the West often feel for how their children turn out: '[i]t's as if how the child turns out is totally the parents'

responsibility ... *yet* ... I'm *convinced* that what the parents do for the child is the merest tip of the iceberg' (399–400).

30 It may also be the case that Furneaux positively affirms rebirth, but it is difficult to be sure of her position on the basis of the material I have.

31 See Corless 2005b.

32 E.g., Habito: 190; Reis Habito: 462, 434–35; Keenan: 235.

33 Corless: 17; 2005a: 3.

34 Corless 1986b: 143. See also Rudolf Frieling (1977: 76–91) who insists that the karmic principle is thoroughly Biblical.

35 See Weatherhead 1978; Howe 1974. Lynn De Silva also argues for a Christian notion of rebirth (1968: 161–63).

36 Corless: 69 (see also 1978: 78).

37 If rebirth is incorporated into Christian thought, hell – however understood – can be thought of as a temporary state which perhaps serves a corrective purpose.

38 For a discussion of Irenaean thought, see Hick 1966: part III.

39 To this we must also add: 'and provided, as a Protestant, one is prepared to reject the idea of the total death of a person (until that person is raised at the end of time) ... '.

40 See, for example, MacGregor 1982: 11, 21–25, 75, 69, 100. However, MacGregor's contention that this process is *endless* is highly problematic from a Christian and a Buddhist perspective (1982: 145–46).

41 See e.g. MacGregor 1982: 28, 132–33; De Silva 1968: 136–37.

42 See note 30 above.

43 Mechanistic understandings of karma, although common in Buddhist folk literature, are not the only ones available. Important Buddhist texts explain that not everything one experiences in life is created by one's karma; if it were, karma would be incompatible with human freedom. Karma gives us the spiritual disposition with which we're born, but not *necessarily* the circumstances into which we are born or the events which happen to us. (See Schmidt-Leukel 2006b: 147–55; 2006e: 44–46.)

44 *Cūḷamālunkya Sutta* (*Majjhima Nikāya*, II:63 – Ñāṇamoli and Bodhi 1995: 533–36).

45 See note 44 above.

46 See p. 130.

47 For a fuller account of this encounter, see King 2005b: 207–11.

48 King: 414. King suggests that over the centuries Buddhism has been too passive and, in the wake of the Khmer Rouge in Cambodia, the attitude of simply letting go and moving on is proving inadequate: 'Maybe something more needs to happen here than: "well, it'll all work out over several hundred years". ... If you don't process it somehow, people don't just forgive it and forget. ... [I]f you really want to *heal*, which is the Buddhist objective, ... maybe thinking in terms of justice is a way of doing that' (414). King notes that there is currently a debate about having some kind of war crimes tribunal in Cambodia, or something similar to South Africa's 'Truth Commission'.

49 King: 415. See also 2005b: 209.

50 Note that questions such as whether or not we are reborn are in a different category from questions such as whether or not ultimate reality is personal or non-personal (see Chapter 3). The latter concern a reality which is conceptually transcendent; hence, *everything* said about that reality as it is in itself is necessarily *literally* false. By contrast, the former concern matters which are, at least potentially, within our conceptual grasp. Assumptions regarding such matters can, therefore, be *literally* true or false.

51 Habito: 162 (see also Reis Habito: 460).

52 Corless: 27, 42. See also Thompson 2010: 16.

53 This seems to be Heim's contention regarding those who practice within more than one tradition. See Heim 1995: 178.
54 Schmidt-Leukel agrees (see 2005e: 5).
55 Schmidt-Leukel 2009: 54. For examples of perspectives within different religious traditions which concur with this emphasis on the uniqueness of every individual's spiritual journey, see 2009: 55–58.
56 Email from Hick to Drew dated 30 October 2005.
57 See Hick's endorsement on the dust cover of Schmidt-Leukel's *Transformation by Integration* (2009).
58 Cornille 2008: 17. Similarly, Phan contends that, among American youth, 'the "instrumentalist" view of religion ... is no doubt the child of the therapeutic individualism and mass-consumer capitalism prevalent in our culture' (2006: 171).
59 See p. 85.

6 Practice

1 See Kraft 1992b: 3.
2 One significant difference, however, is that Buddhist ethics includes animals to a far greater extent than Christian ethics. Whereas many Christians today would see this as a respect in which Christianity should learn from Buddhism, others feel the concern for animals obscures the unique dignity of human persons (see Dumoulin 1974: 119).
3 King: 358, 372. To say that their ethical values are fundamentally the same does not of course rule out differences in emphasis: Buddhism, for example, arguably places greater emphasis on non-violence than justice (see King 2005b), whereas in Christian tradition the opposite has tended to be the case.
4 Tanaka 2003: 102. See also Corless (33) on Buddhist prayer.
5 She points out, for example, that Ariyaratne, founder of the Sarvodaya Shramadana movement in Sri Lanka, has convened huge outdoor meditations for peace in Sri Lanka where thousands of people do *mettā* meditation; 'he calls it "sending these wishes into the psycho-sphere" ... it sort of seems like that's what Buddhists are doing when they say "may all beings be happy ... "': it is an expression of my wish but it's also, somehow, reinforcing the likelihood ... or the tendency of the whole universe ... or the total benevolence available in the universe, or something' (356). See King 2005b: 167.
6 Furneaux implicitly identifies intercessory prayer and the practice of transferring merit and appears to suggest that such practices have a direct effect on the people who are prayed for or to whom merit is dedicated (see 2003: 1–2).
7 Furneaux: 106.
8 Reis Habito: 455. Her first encounter with Guanyin took place more than twenty years ago in Taiwan, as she stood in front of a statue of Guanyin: 'Can't you see?', Master Hsin Tao said to her: 'That is you!' (see pp. 35–38 above).
9 See Second Vatican Council document: Apostolicum Actuositatem (AA4).
10 See Chapter 2, note 20.
11 Reis Habito: 456. She explains, however, that her prayer to Jesus is a little different from her prayer to Guanyin since, whereas in the Buddhist understanding there are numerous manifestations of Guanyin, in the Christian understanding there is only the historical Jesus and this provides her background understanding of her prayer to Jesus, at least in its initial stages (456).
12 Habito: 149. He is quoting Augustine (see *Confessions* 3.6.11).
13 Unno makes this point with respect to the Jesus Prayer but Mitchell points out that this understanding applies to other forms of Christian prayer too (Mitchell 2003: 136).
14 Furneaux 2006c: 1 (see also 2002b: 1).

15 A similar question could be asked of Keenan's participation in the Mass. Keenan does not identify himself as a Buddhist practitioner, but his Mahāyāna interpretation of the Eucharist is such that one might question whether the Mass is not, in a sense, a Buddhist practice for Keenan. See Keenan 2004.
16 Japanese Jesuit and Zen master, J. K. Kadowaki, has written, influentially, on Christian *kōans*. See Kadowaki 1977.
17 King 1982: 8–9. Johnson, like Lassalle (see p.), was an early pioneer of Christian Zen. King does not give a reference for Johnson's remark.
18 Corless points out that Sanbô Kyôdan Zen developed to be so accessible to non-Buddhists that there are now more Catholic priests involved in the Sanbô Kyôdan than there are Buddhist *bōzu* (1996b: 3). Keenan – who, like Corless, is influenced by Sharf – suggests that Sanbô Kyôdan Zen could perhaps be considered 'a very unique, hybrid tradition ... so open to other religions that they're in effect ... a kind of Buddhist-Christian sect' (253).
19 Habito says that there are some respects in which it is not possible to combine Buddhist and Christian language and symbolism. In some cases it would be like attempting to combine two kinds of software: 'that might get you jumbled up in all sorts of difficulties where you'll just freeze like the computer will freeze if you put two kinds of software together which may be compatible in certain aspects but, technically speaking, ... come from different systems' (141).
20 See Chapter 2 (pp. 35–38) and Chapter 3 (p. 61).
21 In the late 1960s and 1970s, after Vatican II and with the Catholic Church's revitalised interest in Christian mysticism, attitudes began to change, but prior to this, there was considerable Catholic opposition to the integration of Zen into Christianity (in 1961 Rome prohibited further publication of Lassalle's *Zen – Weg zur Erleuchtung* (Enomiya-Lassalle 1960) and banned him from teaching the 'Zen method' (see Lai and von Brück 2001: 164; Jeanrond 2002: 113)).
22 Lassalle was strongly influenced by D. T. Suzuki's understanding of Zen (see Suzuki 1949: 38–39).
23 Jeanrond 2002: 112–13. In his exposition of Lassalle's approach to Zen, Jeanrond draws heavily on Baatz 1998.
24 It should be noted that Lassalle's attitude to the practice of Zen changed to some extent over the course of his life as he became decreasingly concerned with Christian identity (Jeanrond 2002: 114). Jeanrond speaks of Lassalle's 'increasingly double religious belonging' (2002: 112). Surprisingly, given his criticism of Christian Zen practitioners who play down the doctrinal import of Zen, Corless apparently also sees Lassalle as an example of someone with 'dual loyalty' (1990b: 114–15).
25 Corless: 11, 33, 57; 1996a: 10–11; 1996b: 4–5.
26 See Chapter 2, pp. 23–25.
27 'Changes in Morning Star': 2.
28 'Changes in Morning Star': 3.
29 'Changes in Morning Star': 3.
30 The statement on the inside cover of all MSS Newsletters states that MSS 'is a group meeting together for interpractice and to explore intercommunion, on a basis of "Beyond Identities" "Beyond the Opposites"'.
31 'Talks from the Heart' (2005).
32 Furneaux: 122. Furneaux was critical of some of my interview questions for this reason: 'many of the questions rest on philosophical assumptions I do not share, in particular there is the category error of assuming subject and object' (122). I would suggest, however, that the category error is Furneaux's insofar as questions to do with the compatibility of Buddhist and Christian teachings are necessarily asked at the conceptual level and at this level the dualism of subject and object must be assumed (even if it is agreed that this way of experiencing the world is an illusion which can be transcended); otherwise, it is virtually impossible to speak at all and

any dialogue between Buddhism and Christianity at the level of ideas is impossible (and I agree with Winston King that 'doctrinal questions must sooner or later be squarely faced if there is to be any genuine, fully existential encounter between any two religious traditions' (1982: 8)).

33 Furneaux: 96. Furneaux also says: 'it is much easier to talk with Buddhists because the *sīla* (the morality), the precepts and the ontological understanding is much, much clearer in Buddhism than in Christianity and the practice of transforming "internal formations" is clearer' (96).

34 Furneaux's position differs from Makransky's inclusivism (see Chapter 5), however, insofar as she does at least appear to see Christianity as capable of leading people to full salvation/liberation (even if it is less effective at so doing than Buddhism). Given that this is the case, it is debatable whether the term 'inclusivism' should be applied in Furneaux's case.

35 Of course, with only limited material to go on, my interpretation of Furneaux as inadvertently prioritising Buddhism might be erroneous.

36 Corless 1996b: 4–5 (see also 11, 33, 57; 1996a: 10–11).

37 See, for example, pp. 45–48.

38 Corless 1996a: 8. This meditation changed and developed over time. For detailed descriptions of the practice, see 1986a: 131–34; 1994a.

39 See Chapter 3, pp. 45–48.

40 It is perhaps the fact that Gaia is not a transcendent reality which, as far as Corless is concerned, prevents Mother Gaia from falling foul of the criticisms he levels against those who make sense of their dual belonging within a monocentric pluralist framework: the ultimate reality of monocentric pluralism, thinks Corless, '*transcends, and therefore diminishes*, both [Buddhism and Christianity]' (1996b: 6, my emphasis).

41 See Chapter 2, 'Roger J. Corless'. Corless explains that UCM is a Church that supports the individual spiritual path of each member, 'so you could call it multi-faith, in that sense, or inter-faith' (12). (UCM's symbol (see www.u-c-m.org/new/, accessed 28 October 2010) was designed by Corless and incorporates the symbols of many different religions, including Buddhism and Christianity.)

42 Corless 1996a: 5. See Chapter 2 'Roger J. Corless'.

43 Perhaps this emphasis has some precedence in Buddhism to the extent that the Buddha legend tells us that the Enlightened Buddha, when challenged by Mara, calls upon the earth as a witness to his Enlightenment; the Earth Goddess is subsequently thought of as the key witness to the Buddha's Enlightenment and Buddha statues portraying the Buddha in earth-touching mudrā are common.

44 See Corless 1994a.

45 His experience of convergence is evident, for example, in his claim that, when it comes to 'transforming consciousness through prayer and meditation', often Buddhism and Christianity 'help each other or are almost the same thing' (44) and, like my other interviewees, he identifies his main practice as maintaining mindful awareness throughout the day and finds it difficult to say whether this practice is Christian or Buddhist (31).

46 As Cornille explains, 'New Age is characterized by a rejection of the absolute truth claims of all institutionalized forms of religion' (2002b: 3).

47 Corless: 52–53.

48 See p. 85.

49 This approach, says King, does not engage in dialogue religious traditions as such, and 'may end up, both religiously and psychologically, nowhere in particular, with the engine of existential significance and action still in neutral' (King, W. 1982: 9).

50 Reis Habito: 454. Of course, the fact that the early religious formation of my interviewees occurred within the Christian tradition (Christianity is, in this sense, their religious 'mother tongue' – see von Brück 2007: 199–205), means it is easier

for them to identify the influence of their Buddhism on their Christianity than vice versa; they know what their Christianity was like prior to the influence of Buddhism, whereas they have no analogous experience of Buddhism. '[I]t would be hard for me to say what I would be like, had I been raised completely as a Buddhist', says Reis Habito, 'how my Buddhist understanding would be different' (490), and King acknowledges that although she is aware that her 'formation was Christian' and that this must be hugely significant, she is not always conscious of the effect it has on her understanding (380).

51 See Corless 1981.
52 Corless 1990a: 89–90.
53 E.g., Furneaux: 104; Habito: 154. Pieris and Harris also speak of having to temporarily let go of their Christian preconceptions in order to immerse themselves in Buddhism. Pieris describes this as 'a total letting go' (2005: 14) and Harris, as 'a form of death' (2004: 336); yet, both concur with my interviews that the eventual results of this temporary renunciation, or 'passing over' (see Chapter 1, pp. 2–7), were positive.
54 E.g., Corless: 83.
55 Corless: 84. Here he explains that he would now speak in terms of 'mutual enrichment' rather than in terms of 'mutual fulfilment' (see Corless 1986a).
56 Corless, Smith argues, pins the success of his coinherent model 'on the internal stability of the various religions as relatively static explanatory systems' and 'thereby settles for a separate and static coherence for each religion', relating the traditions to one another but not organically, allowing only for fine-tuning within each system but not for an interreligious coherence. Corless, 'appears to recommend, contrary to the broad movement of Buddhist-Christian dialogue, that Buddhism and Christianity *not* mutually transform each other. But surely the theoretical reconceptualization of our inherited traditions conforms both to the precedent of history', says Smith, 'and to the challenge of interreligious dialogue' (Smith 1997: 167). Corless was aware of Smith's critique and had, in response, become more acknowledging of the inevitability of mutual influence and change, even if he was yet to draw out the full implications of this acknowledgement.
57 The only clear exception to this was Keenan, who appears to *embrace* an understanding of himself as an architect of change, describing his theological project as an attempt to 'graft Mahāyāna philosophy onto the root of Christian faith' (LCC: 263). As far as Keenan is concerned, Greek-influenced talk of 'essences' no longer resonates for people. He therefore wants to see the Christian tradition change and believes that integrating Buddhist insights will effect that change (226). Perhaps less than full dual belongers (Keenan sees himself as a Christian, albeit a Mahāyāna Christian) are more attracted to change than full dual belongers. There might be a number of reasons for this. First, those who see themselves as belonging primarily to one religious tradition may be keen to import as much as they can of what is true and good from the other tradition, whereas dual belongers may feel less need to do this, insofar as they belong to both religious worlds and move freely between them. Second, single belonging Christians, for example, may not be so concerned about making sure what they end up with is authentically Christian since there is no *prima facie* danger of their Christianity shading into their Buddhism (inasmuch as they do not see themselves as Buddhists). Third, to the extent that authenticity and integrity concern them at all, single belongers may only be concerned with the authenticity and integrity of the tradition they consider their own and this makes the process of integration less complex and less risky than it is for those who are trying to preserve the integrity and authenticity of both traditions.
58 E. Burke Rochford found the same to be true of his interviewees. See Rochford 2003: 219.
59 See pp. 177–82 above.

60 Habito: 177. See Chapter 1, note 31.
61 Habito: 177. King is also averse to mixing symbolism in specifically Buddhist or Christian places: 'That's where you get into: this tradition has its integrity and really needs to maintain that. ... [I]t'll get confusing: everything will end up mush if you go too far that way', says King (382).
62 Habito: 179. Elaborating with respect to the juxtaposition of the statues of Kannon and Mary at MKZC, Habito explains that both are images which can be seen from a Buddhist or a Christian perspective as embodiments of the feminine principle of compassion (178).
63 Similarly, on the online forum of the Seattle-based Buddhist-Christian study and practice group, *Lotus and Lily* (2010), it is explained that many members 'continue to maintain a spiritual practice and/or involvement in another religious community (e.g., a Buddhist sangha or Christian church). But ... are glad for the unique and important mutual support and communal spiritual practice that Lotus and Lily provides them'.
64 See Corless 1990b: 121.
65 King: 348. King was not alone in reflecting that her location had to some extent dictated which of the traditions was given more attention at a given time. See e.g., Corless: 26, 31 and Keenan: 221.
66 King: 418–19; 2003c. I am sure there is much truth in King's suggestion, and the effect of parenthood upon religious identity would certainly be an interesting focus for further research.
67 The Christian contributors to Gross and Muck (eds) 2003, for example, would not necessarily see themselves as fully immersed in Buddhism, but have nevertheless benefitted considerably from their incorporation of Buddhist practices. See also O'Hanlon 1981.

7 Conclusion

1 As Reis Habito puts it, for example, '[a]ll these are new things that you then have to figure out and somehow fit into what you have known so far and how much can you integrate it and how much does it confuse you and so on and so that's an ongoing process and, so, I would say: from getting more familiar with the things you are able to integrate them more' (462).
2 Keenan is emphatic that understanding doctrines (and consequently their compatibility or lack thereof with other doctrines) is a matter of understanding how they function within their context (e.g. 246–47, 249, 265–68, 279, 331).
3 See Chapter 1, p. 9–11.
4 Smith 1962: 13. See also Mazzocchi 1999: 5. Two-fold belonging, says Mazzocchi, is only a serious problem from the perspective of one for whom religion rather than truth is absolute.
5 Corless: 27; 1990a: 89–90.
6 See Chapter 1, p. 9–11.
7 It might also be argued that in the cases of Habito and Furneaux, who have both completed formal Buddhist training, objective confirmation of their spiritual attainment is available – from the Buddhist angle at least – in the form of their having permission to teach within their respective lineages.
8 Habito: 141; Reis Habito: 495; King 1990: 125.
9 Abhishiktānanda 1975: 25.
10 King: 365, 374–75. 'I know them as possibilities' is Reis Habito's equivalent (464).
11 See p. 155.
12 Such experience no doubt contributes to the sense of sharing between these traditions. In this sense, Corless captures a reality when he speaks of a 'dialogue of silence' between Buddhist and Christian monastics (1985).

13 See pp. 18–19.
14 E.g., Corless: 21
15 For another example of this reasoning, see Thurston 1994: 178.
16 King (1990) and Smith (1997) make this point persuasively. See also Harris 2004: 346. Here Harris argues that 'encounter with "the other" is not simply a case of learning a different "language" alongside one's own and appreciating the world-view that language represents. If it is a true encounter, it will involve the bringing of the "other" within'.
17 Schmidt-Leukel recommends that instances of syncretism be assessed on their particular merits, or lack thereof, and not assessed negatively simply because they are instances of syncretism (2009: 67–89).
18 King: 384. See also Reis Habito: 454; Smith 1997: 172.
19 By endorsing Schmidt-Leukel's 'patchwork religiosity' metaphor in this context, I only intend to gesture at the way in which a person's religious identity can be shaped by more than one tradition; I do not have in mind the construction of a bricolage of elements extracted from different contexts without immersion in those contexts (an approach from which we distinguished authentic dual belonging in Chapter 6).
20 This interpretation would seem to be supported by Fowler's contention that there are six progressive stages of faith and that a feature of the two highest stages is an openness to, and integration of, the truths of more than one religious tradition (see Fowler 1981).
21 Smart 1995: 68. See also Amaladoss 2002: 303.
22 See Sutcliffe 2000: 19, 28.
23 E.g., Reis Habito: 451–52; Habito: 212; King: 375; Furneaux 2006b: 15.
24 Habito, for example, appears critical of the use of Zen practice simply to enhance Christian faith: 'if one is attracted to Zen practice, then be thorough with it and go the full length' (208–9). This concern for thoroughness, born of a respect for the integrity of both traditions, is crucial to authentic dual belonging, but it is not clear that it is necessary or realistic to require this thoroughgoing immersion from people for whom one religious identity is primary, when such people may never-theless be capable of deriving benefit from Zen practice.
25 See Chapter 5, note 14.
26 This criticism of the logic of 'the subjective choice of faith' is made, for example, by Polish theologian, Józef Niewiadomski (1996: 89).
27 King does not feel she could not practise more than two religions with care: 'I could not give myself to them with any seriousness … [nor] bore into them in any depth' (1994a: 158).
28 Furneaux and Habito have acted in this capacity formally to some extent (and Corless would also have, had he lived long enough to carry out pastoral duties as a UCM minister), and it is likely that all my interviewees will do so in more informal ways. Reis Habito says, for example, 'I hope that in the future I could be as helpful to those people as, for example, Father Lassalle or Yamada Roshi were to me' (496).
29 As Reis Habito reflects, 'to start out as a Christian and … find another perspective that questions everything that you had vaguely believed up to this point: I think it's a great blessing' (461).
30 Phan 2006: 181. See also Phan 2003.
31 See Schmidt-Leukel 2009: 61.
32 This relates to Rosemary Radford Ruether's observation that Christians often assume that religious identity and openness to pluralism are in opposition to each other, that strong Christian identity means knowing that non-Christian religions are defective, and that being open to truth in other religions weakens one's Chris-tian identity and 'waters down' one's appreciation of the truth of one's own faith (2005: 29).

33 Therefore, as Radford Ruether argues, Christian identity can be constructed in such a way that it 'both clarifies norms of what is authentic Christianity and affirms other religious paths, not in opposition to each other or as a vague compromise between the two, but in mutual affirmation' (2005: 29).

34 King: 353; 1994b: 193.

35 Thew Forrester, Episcopal priest and Zen practitioner with a lay Buddhist ordination, came under intense scrutiny after being elected as bishop of the Episcopal Diocese of Northern Michigan in February 2009, his election becoming the subject of an explosion of conservative Christian opinion in the blogosphere. Confirmation of his election required the consent of a majority of Episcopal Church bishops and standing committees but, very unusually, this consent was not granted and on July 27, 2009 the Episcopal Church of the United States declared Thew Forrester's election 'null and void'. One of the central questions on which the controversy had focused was whether his practice of Zen Buddhist meditation compromised his commitment to Christianity.

36 The Vatican recently censored Phan's theology of multiple religious belonging (see Phan 2004 and Committee on Doctrine … 2007). The committee focused on three areas of concern: Jesus Christ as the unique and universal Saviour of all humankind; the salvific significance of non-Christian religions; and the Church as the unique and universal instrument of salvation.

37 See Congregation for the Doctrine of the Faith 2000.

38 See Congregation for the Doctrine of the Faith 2000. Gideon Goosen comments that '[i]f, on a spectrum of approval of other faiths, *Dominus Iesus* represents the negative end of the spectrum, then Corless is the positive end' (2007a: 240). But Goosen fails to grasp the ambivalence of Corless' position. In line with his intention to treat Christianity and Buddhism as absolutes, Corless *explicitly endorses Dominus Iesus* and its claim that Christianity is the absolute truth (Corless: 15).

39 See Schmidt-Leukel 2008b: 274.

40 1999: 48. As early as 1978 Cobb published an article asking, 'Can a Christian be a Buddhist Too?' (Cobb 1978). Although this is not to say that he would recommend – or even recognise – the possibility of *full* dual belonging, since he apparently thinks it would entail having two primary religious identities and is unconvinced that this is possible (2002: 23). I would suggest, on the contrary, that the authentic dual belonger does not have *two* religious identities but one *complex* religious identity which is both Buddhist and Christian. The coherence of this identity depends, however, on the assumption that there is one ultimate reality, and Cobb, as a process theologian, does not share this assumption (see Chapter 3, pp. 48–53).

41 The 2009 conference of the European Network of Buddhist-Christian Studies focused on questions of authority in Buddhism and Christianity. See *Buddhist-Christian Studies* 30 (2010). See also Phan 2006.

42 See Schmidt-Leukel 2005b: 18; Eck 1993: 188–89.

43 Keenan himself speaks of looking at Christianity through a Mahāyāna 'lens' (326; LCC: 269).

44 For examples of all the above, see Corless: 82–83; 1996a: 9; Habito: 203, 214–15; Reis Habito: 498; King: 411; 1990: 125; Keenan: 249–50, 327.

45 By complete commitment and complete openness, I mean that they are completely committed to Christian truths and completely open to Buddhist truths, and vice versa.

46 See Smith 1981; Cobb 1999: 60.

47 See note 2 above.

48 Corless 1986: 133. Whereas Corless believes that in order to comprehend this we need to move to a higher level of consciousness (47), I am arguing that it can be comprehended at the conventional level through deep and searching dialogue.

49 Habito: 141–42. See also Furneaux: 116.
50 This prediction is in line with Masao Abe's vision of Buddhism and Christianity realising their universal nature without eradication of distinctions between them. See Abe 1989: 270, 275.
51 However, as Reis Habito acknowledges (490), she is less *aware* of what her Buddhism is assimilating from her Christianity. See Chapter 6, note 50.
52 See Schmidt-Leukel 2005b: 2.
53 In this sense, I agree with Judson Trapnell, who speaks of 'the dialogical relationship that itself constitutes a kind of ascesis' (1998: 233).
54 Pieris 1988a: 86 (see also 134–35).

Bibliography

'A Christian Buddhist Gathering Page'. http://webspace.webring.com/people/bu/um_12337/christianbuddhist.html (accessed 28 October 2010).

Abe, M. 2000. 'On John Paul II's View of Buddhism', in Sherwin and Kasimow (eds) 2000: 108–12.

——1989 *Zen and Western Thought*. Honolulu: University of Hawaii Press.

——1982 'Man and Nature in Christianity and Buddhism', in Franck, F. (ed.), *The Buddha Eye*. New York: Crossroad (1982): 148–56.

Abeysekara, A. 2002. *Colors of the Robe: Religion, Identity, and Difference*. Columbia: South Carolina Press.

Abhishiktānanda 1975. *The Further Shore: Two Essays by Abhishiktānanda*. Delhi: I. S.P.C.K.

Ahlstrand, K. 2007. 'Boundaries of Religious Identity: Baptised Buddhists in Enköping', in D'Arcy May (ed.) 2007: 155–64.

Anderson, J. 2007. *Lotus and Lily Field Notes*. www.lotuslily.net/ (last post 1 June 2007. Accessed 28 October 2010).

Amaladoss, M. 2002. 'Double Religious Belonging and Liminality: An Anthropological Reflection', *East Asian Pastoral Review*, 39 (2002): 297–312.

——1999 'Double Belongingness in Religion: An Anthropo-Theological Reflection' (paper given at the Voies de l'Orient second European Pastoral 'Assises'. Brussels, 11–14 November 1999. Used with the permission of Voies de l'Orient. A longer version was published as Amaladoss 2002 and, in French, as 'La double appartenance religieuse', in Scheuer and Gira (eds) 2000: 44–53).

Arai, T. and Ariarajah, W. (eds) 1989. *Spirituality in interfaith dialogue*. Geneva: WCC Publications.

Baatz, U. 1999. 'Double Belonging?' (paper given at the Voies de l'Orient second European Pastoral 'Assises'. Brussels, 11–14 November 1999. Used with the permission of Voies de l'Orient. A French version was published as 'Ce qui reste', in Scheuer and Gira (eds) 2000: 147–50).

——1998 *Hugo M. Enomiya-Lassalle: Ein Leben zwischen den Welten*. Zurich and Düsseldorf: Benziger Verlag.

Badham, P. (ed.) 1990. *A John Hick Reader*. Houndmills, Basingstoke and London: Macmillan.

Baier, K. 2005. 'Ultimate Reality in Buddhism and Christianity: A Christian Perspective', in Schmidt-Leukel (ed.) 2005a: 87–116.

Barker, G. (ed.) 2005. *Jesus in the World's Faiths: Leading Thinkers from Five Religions Reflect on His Meaning*. New York: Orbis.

Barnes, M. 2007. 'Expanding Catholicity – the Dialogue with Buddhism', *New Blackfriars*, Vol. 88, No. 1016 (July 2007): 399–409.

Bäumer, B. 1989. 'A Journey with the Unknown', in Arai and Ariarajah (eds) 1989: 36–41.

Bernhardt, R. and Schmidt-Leukel, P. (eds) 2008. *Multiple religiöse Identität. Aus verschiedenen religiösen Traditionen schöpfen*. Zürich: TYZ.

Bhattacharya, K. *et al.* (transl.) 1978. *The Dialectical Method of Nāgārjuna (Vigrahavyāvartanī)*. Delhi: Motilal Banarsidass.

Bielefeldt, C. 2008 (date of last access). 'Divisions and Direction of Buddhism in America Today'. www.american-buddha.com/carl.bielefeldt.stanford.htm?signup (accessed 28 October 2010).

Bischofberger, N. 1996a. *Werden wir wiederkommen? Der Reinkarnationsgedanke im Westen und die Sicht der christlichen Eschatologie*. Mainz: Kok Pharos.

——1996b. 'Der Reinkarnationsgedanke in der Europäischen Antike und Neuzeit', in Schmidt-Leukel, P. (ed.), *Die Idee der Reinkarnation in Ost und West*. Munich: Eugen Diederichs: 76–94.

Blée, F. 1999. 'Which Christian-Buddhist Way? For an articulation of the *twofold* religious *belonging*?' (paper given at the Voies de l'Orient second European Pastoral 'Assises'. Brussels, 11–14 November 1999. Used with the permission of Voies de l'Orient. A French version was published as 'Quelle voie chrétienne-bouddhiste?', in Scheuer and Gira (eds) 2000: 151–60).

Bloechl, J. 1999. 'Identity, Event, Context: Phenomenology and Religious Experience' (paper given at the Voies de l'Orient second European Pastoral 'Assises'. Brussels, 11–14 November 1999. Used with the permission of Voies de l'Orient. A French version was published as 'Identité, événement, contexte', in Scheuer and Gira (eds) 2000: 95–108).

Bloom, A. (ed.) 2007. *The Essential Shinran: A Buddhist Path of True Entrusting*. Bloomington, IN: World Wisdom Press.

——2005. 'Jesus in the Pure Land', in Barker (ed.) 2005: 31–37.

——1994. 'A Buddhist Perspective on Dual Worship', *Buddhist-Christian Studies*, 14 (1994): 163–67.

Bodhi, Bhikkhu 1995. 'Replies to Questions from "Source"', *Dialogue* (N.S.) 22, 1995: 20–28.

Borg, M.J. 1999. 'Jesus and Buddhism: A Christian View', in Gross, Muck (eds) 2000: 77–82.

Brück, M. von 2007. 'A Theology of Multiple Religious Identity', in D'Arcy May (ed.) 2007: 181–206.

——2001. 'What do I Expect Buddhists to Discover in Jesus? "Christ and the Buddha Embracing Each Other … "', in Schmidt-Leukel (ed.) 2001a: 158–75.

Buddhadāsa 1989. *Me and Mine: Selected Essays of Bhikkhu Buddhadāsa*, ed. Swearer, D.K. Albany: State University of New York Press (1989).

——1972. *Toward the Truth*, Donald Swearer (ed.). Philadelphia: Westminster Press.

——1967. *Christianity and Buddhism, Sinclaire Thompson Memorial Lecture*. Bangkok: Karn Pim Pranakorn Partnership.

Buddhist-Christian Dialogue in Action. Boston, 1992. http://innerexplorations.com/catew/1.htm (accessed 28 October 2010).

Buddhist-Christian Dialogue in Action. Chicago, 1996. http://innerexplorations.com/catew/2.htm (accessed 28 October 2010).

Buddhist-Christian Dialogue in Action. Tacoma, WA 2000. http://innerexplorations. com/catew/14.htm (accessed 28 October 2010).

Buddhist-Christian Studies 30 (2010).

Burch, G.B. 1972. *Alternative Goals in Religion*. Montreal: McGill Queen's University Press.

Burford, G. 2003. 'A Buddhist Reflects (Practices Reflection) on Some Christians' Reflections on Buddhist Practices', in Gross and Muck (eds) 2003: 55–60.

——1999. 'If the Buddha Is So Great, Why Are These People Christian?', in Gross, Muck (eds) 2000: 131–37.

Burrell, D. 1986. *Knowing the Unknowable God: Ibn-Sina, Maimonides, Aquinas*. Notre Dame: University of Notre Dame Press.

Cabezón, J. 2005. 'Buddhist Views of Jesus', in Barker (ed.) 2005: 15–24.

——1999. 'A God, but Not a Savior', in Gross and Muck (eds) 2000: 17–31.

Candasiri, Ajahn 2005. 'Jesus: A Theravadan Perspective', in Barker (ed.) 2005: 25–30.

Carette, J. and King, R. 2005. *Selling Spirituality: The Silent Takeover of Religion*. London and New York: Routledge.

Carlson, J. 2003. '[Double Religious Belonging: A Process Approach]: Responses', *Buddhist-Christian Studies*, Vol. 23 (2003): 77–83.

——2000. 'Pretending to Be Buddhist and Christian: Thich Nhat Hanh and the Two Truths of Religious Identity', *Buddhist-Christian Studies*, 20 (2000): 115–25.

Carter, R.E. 2006. 'Living Zen, Loving God. (Book Review)', *Philosophy East and West*, 56: 2 (April 2006).

Catechism of the Catholic Church (1994). London. Geoffrey Chapman.

'Changes in Morning Star' (undated letter sent by Morning Star Sangha trustees to members and others in c. January 2006).

Chappell, D.W. (ed.) 2003. *Socially Engaged Spirituality: Essays in Honor of Sulak Sivaraksa on His 70th Birthday*. Bangkok: Sathirakoses-Nagapradipa Foundation.

Cobb, J.B. 2002. 'Multiple Religious Belonging and Reconciliation', in Cornille (ed.) 2002a: 20–28.

——1999. *Transforming Christianity and the World: A Way beyond Absolutism and Relativism*, Knitter, P. (ed.). Maryknoll, New York: Orbis.

——1993. '[Mahayana Theology: A Dialogue with Critics]: Response', *Buddhist-Christian Studies*, 13 (1993): 44–47.

——1988. 'Being Itself and the Existence of God', in Jacobson, J.R. and Mitchell, R.L. (eds), *The Existence of God*. Lewiston, NY: Edwin Mellen (1988): 5–19.

——1982. *Beyond Dialogue: Toward a Mutual Transformation of Christianity and Buddhism*. Eugene, Oregon: Wipf and Stock (1998 edition). First published by Fortress Press in 1982.

——1980. 'Can a Buddhist be a Christian, Too?', *Japanese Religions* 11: 35–55.

——1978. 'Can a Christian be a Buddhist, Too?', *Japanese Religions* 10: 1–20.

Cobb, J.B. and Griffin, D.R. 1976. *Process Theology: An Introductory Exposition*. Philadelphia: Westminster.

Coles, R. (ed.) 2000. *The Erik Erikson Reader*. New York: W. W. Norton & Company.

Committee on Doctrine, United States Conference of Catholic Bishops 2007 'Clarifications Required by the Book *Being Religious Interreligiously: Asian Perspectives on Interfaith Dialogue* by Reverend Peter C. Phan'. www.usccb.org/dpp/StatementonBeingReligiousInterreligiously.pdf (accessed 20 September 2008).

Compendium of the Catechism of the Catholic Church 2006. Dublin: Veritas Publications.

Congregation for the Doctrine of the Faith 2004. *Notification on the book 'Jesus Symbol of God' by Father Roger Haight S.J.*. www.vatican.va/roman_curia/

congregations/cfaith/documents/rc_con_cfaith_doc_20041213_notification-fr-haight_en. html (accessed 20 September 2008).

——2000. *Declaration 'Dominus Iesus' on the Unicity and Salvific Universality of Jesus Christ and the Church*. www.vatican.va/roman_curia/congregations/cfaith/documents/rc_con_cfaith_doc_20000806_dominus-iesus_en.html (accessed 20 September 2008).

Cooey, P.M. 1999. 'Response to Alan Sponberg's "The Buddhist Conception of an Ecological Self"', in King and Ingram (eds) 1999: 128–32.

Cook, F. 1989. '*Memento Mori*: The Buddhist Thinks about Death', in Davis (ed.) 1989: 154–76.

Cooper, J.W. 2006. *Panentheism – the Other God of the Philosophers: From Plato to the Present*. Michigan: Baker Academic.

Corless, R.J. *Where do we Go from Here? The Many Religions and the Next Step* (unpublished novella).

——2005a. 'Cancer as a Dharma Teacher', *Gay Buddhist Fellowship* Newsletter (April/May 2005): 1–4.

——2005b. 'A Round Trip to the Bardo', *Gay Buddhist Fellowship* Newsletter (October/November 2005): 1–5.

——2002. 'Many Selves, Many Realities: The Implications of Heteronymy and the Plurality of Worlds Theory for Multiple Religious Belonging', *Pacific Coast Theological Society Journal*, October 6, 2002. www.pcts.org/journal/corless2002a/index. html (accessed 28 October 2010).

——1996a. *Profiles in Buddhist-Christian Dialogue: Roger Corless*. http://inner-explorations.com/catew/9.htm (accessed 28 October 2010).

——1996b. 'Dual Practice With Form and Without Form: The Doctrinal Consequences' (unpublished draft paper delivered at the Fifth International Buddhist-Christian Conference, De Paul University, Chicago. July 27-August 3, 1996. Kindly provided by the author but should not be considered definitive).

——1996c. 'Idolatry and Inherent Existence: The Golden Calf and the Wooden Buddha', in Loy, D. (ed.), *Healing Deconstruction: Postmodern Thought in Buddhism and Christianity*. Atlanta, Georgia: Scholars Press (1996).

——1994a. 'A Form for Buddhist-Christian Coinherence Meditation', *Buddhist-Christian Studies*, Vol. 14 (1994): 139–44.

——1994b. 'A Reply to the Responses', *Buddhist-Christian Studies*, Vol. 14 (1994): 181–84.

——1993. 'The Coming of the Dialogian: A Transpersonal Approach To Interreligious Dialogue', *Dialogue & Alliance*, Vol. 7, No. 2 (Fall/Winter 1993): 3–17.

——1992a. 'Self-Power Practice with Other-Power Attitude: An Interpretation of Mind in Shin Buddhism', *The Pure Land*, N.S. Nos. 8–9 (December 1992): 166–206.

——1992b. 'Seimeizan: A Living Buddhist-Christian Dialogue', *Buddhist-Christian Studies*, 12 (1992): 233–40.

——1990a. 'Can Emptiness Will?', in Corless and Knitter (eds) 1990: 75–96.

——1990b. 'A Way of No Expectations: *Abgeschiedenheit* and the Development of an East-West Spirituality', *Vox Benedictina* 7:3 (July 1990): 317–34. Reprinted in *Vox Benedictina* 11, *On Pilgrimage: The Best of Ten Years of Vox Benedictina 1984–1993*, compiled by Elspeth Durie and Dewey Kramer, edited by Margot King (Toronto: Peregrina Publishers, 1994): 111–24.

——1990c. 'The Monastic Encounter', *Buddhist-Christian Studies*, 10 (1990): 209–12.

——1989. 'Newsletter of the Society for Buddhist-Christian Studies 4' (Fall 1989), cited in Magliola, R., *On Deconstructing Life-Worlds: Buddhism, Christianity, Culture*. Atlanta: Scholars (1997): 123.

——1988. 'Becoming a Dialogian: How to do Buddhist-Christian Dialogue without really Trying' (unpublished paper given at *The Colloquium on Buddhist Thought and Culture*. University of Montevallo, Alabama. April 29–30, 1988).

——1987. 'Can Buddhism Validate the Truth of God Incarnate?', *Modern Theology* 3, no. 4 (July 1987): 333–43.

——1986a. 'The Mutual Fulfillment of Buddhism and Christianity in Co-inherent Superconsciousness', in Ingram and Streng (eds) 1986: 115–36.

——1986b. 'Christian Karma? A Note on New Testament Passages Apparently Consonant with the Buddhist Notion of Karma', *Buddhist-Christian Studies*, Vol. 6 (1986): 141–44.

——1985. 'The Dialogue of Silence: A Comparison of Buddhist and Christian Monasticism with a Practical Suggestion', in Houston, W. (ed.), *The Cross and the Lotus: Christianity and Buddhism in Dialogue*. Delhi: Motilal Banarsidass (1985): 81–107.

——1982. 'Speaking the Unspeakable: Negation as the Way in Nicholas of Cusa and Nagarjuna', *Buddhist-Christian Studies*, 2 (1982): 107–17.

——1981. *I Am Food. The Mass in Planetary Perspective*. Eugene, Oregon: Wipf and Stock (2004) first published by Crossroad in 1981.

——1978. 'A Christian Perspective on Buddhist Liberation', in Geffré and Dhavamony (eds) 1978: 74–87.

Corless, R.J. and Knitter, P.F. 1990. *Buddhist Emptiness and Christian Trinity: Essays and Explorations*. New Jersey: Paulist Press.

Cornille, C. 2008. 'Many Masters? Multiple Religious Belonging in Practice and in Principle' (This paper was originally delivered at a consultation in Basel in 2007 and a German translation was subsequently published in Bernhardt and Schmidt-Leukel (eds) 2008: 15–32. The original English version used here was kindly provided by the editors).

——2003. 'Double Religious Belonging: Aspects and Questions', *Buddhist-Christian Studies* 23 (2003): 43–49.

——(ed.) 2002a. *Many Mansions? Multiple Religious Belonging and Christian Identity*. New York: Orbis.

——2002b. 'The Dynamics of Multiple Belonging'. Introduction to Cornille (ed.) 2002a: 1–6.

——1999. 'The Dynamics of Double Religious Belonging' (paper given at the Voies de l'Orient second European Pastoral 'Assises'. Brussels, 11–14 November 1999. Used with the permission of Voies de l'Orient. A French version was published as 'La dynamique de la double appartenance', in Scheuer and Gira (eds) 2000: 109–21).

Coward, H. 2003. *Sin and Salvation in the World Religions: A Short Introduction*. Oxford: Oneworld.

Craig, E. (ed.) 2000. *Concise Routledge Encyclopedia of Philosophy*. London: Routledge.

Crook, J. 2001. 'When the Morning Star Arose, There was I' (talk given by John Crook September 2001, transcribed by Julia Richmond).

Cupitt, D. 1980. *Taking Leave of God*. London: SCM Press.

Dalai Lama 1996a. *The Good Heart*, Geshe Thupten Jinpa (transl.). Boston: Wisdom (paperback edition, 1998).

——1996b. *Beyond Dogma: Dialogues & Discourses*, Anderson, A. (transl.). Berkley: North Atlantic Books (originally published in French in 1994 as: *Au-dela des Dogmes*).

——1990. 'Extracts from the Bodhgaya Interviews', in Griffiths (ed.) 1990: 162–70.

D'Arcy May, J. (ed.) 2007. *Converging Ways? Conversion and Belonging in Buddhism and Christianity*. Klosterverlag Sankt Ottilien: EOS.

Davis, S. (ed.) 1989. *Death and Afterlife*. Houndmills: Macmillan.

D'Costa, G. 2008. 'Orthodoxy and Religious Pluralism: A Response to Perry Schmidt-Leukel', *Modern Theology* 24, 2 (2008): 285–90.

——(ed.) 1990. *Christian Uniqueness Reconsidered: The Myth of a Pluralistic Theology of Religions*. New York: Orbis.

Dean, T. (ed.) 1995. *Religious Pluralism and Truth: Essays on Cross-Cultural Philosophy of Religion*. Albany: State University of New York Press.

De Silva, L. 1982. 'Buddhism and Christianity Relativised', *Dialogue* (New Series) 9 (1–3): 43–72.

——1979. *Emergent Theology in the Context of Buddhism*. Colombo: Ecumenical Institute for Study and Dialogue.

——1968. *Reincarnation in Buddhist and Christian Thought*. Colombo: Christian Literature Society.

Dhavamony, M. 1978. 'The Buddha as Saviour', in Geffré and Dhavamony (eds) 1978: 43–54.

Du Boulay, S. 2005. *The Cave of the Heart: The Life of Swami Abhishiktananda*. New York: Orbis.

Dumoulin, H. 1974. *Christianity Meets Buddhism*, Maraldo, J.C. (transl.). La Salle, Illinois: Open Court Publishing Company.

——1966. *Östliche Meditation und christliche Mystik*. Freiburg: Alber.

Dunne, J.S. 1972. *The Way of All the Earth: Experiments in Truth and Religion*. New York: Macmillan.

Dupuis, J. 2002. 'Christianity and Religions: Complementarity and Convergence', in Cornille (ed.) 2002a: 61–75.

——1997. *Toward a Christian Theology of Religious Pluralism*. New York. Orbis.

Eck, D.L. 1993. *Encountering God: A Spiritual Journey from Bozeman to Banaras*. Boston: Beacon Press.

Enomiya-Lassalle, H.M. 1960. *Zen – Weg zur Erleuchtung: Einführung und Anleitung*. Freiburg im Breisgau: Herder Taschenbuch (1992 edition).

Fernando, M. 1978. 'The Buddhist Challenge to Christianity', in Geffré and Dhavamony (eds) 1978: 88–96.

Fischer, N. 2002. *Opening to You: Zen-Inspired translations of the Psalms*. New York: Viking Compass.

Flew, A. (ed.) 1979. *A Dictionary of Philosophy*. London: Pan books.

Fonner, M.G. 1993. 'Toward a Theravadin Christology', *Buddhist-Christian Studies* 13 (1993): 3–14.

Fowler, J. 1981. *Stages of Faith: The Psychology of Human Development and the Quest for Meaning*. New York: HarperSanFrancisco, 1981 (paperback, 1995).

'Frederick J. Streng Book Award: An Interview with Harold Kasimow, John Keenan, and Linda Keenan' 2005. *Buddhist-Christian Studies*, 25 (2005): 205–7.

Fredericks, J.L. 2004. *Buddhists and Christians Through Comparative Theology to Solidarity*. New York: Orbis Books.

Frieling, R. 1977. *Christianity and Reincarnation*. Edinburgh: Floris (originally published in German by Verlag Urachhaus in 1974 as: *Christentum und Wiederverkörperung*).

Furneaux, R. 2008. 'A Bow in the Sky', *Morning Star Sangha Newsletter*, 20 (Epiphany 2008): 2–4.

——2006a. 'Practice c.v.' (a short autobiographical summary of Furneaux's religious practice. Sent to Drew in 2006).

——2006b. 'When the Iron Eagle Flies: Putting a yak's head on a donkey', *Morning Star Sangha Newsletter*, 18 (August 2006): 15–16.

——2006c. Untitled (update on changes in the Morning Star Sangha), *Morning Star Sangha Newsletter*, 18 (August 2006): 1–2.

——2003. 'Calling you home: It is nearer to you than you are yourself', *Morning Star Sangha Newsletter*, 7 (February 2003): 2–3.

——2002a. 'Setting up Opposites', *Morning Star Sangha Newsletter*, 4 (February 2002): 3.

——2002b. Untitled (on the purpose of the Morning Star Sangha), *Morning Star Sangha Newsletter*, 4 (February 2002): 1–2.

——2001a. Untitled (three line poem), in *Morning Star Sangha Newsheet*, 3 (November 2001): 3.

——2001b. 'Diary Dates Retreats and Practice Days … ', *Morning Star Sangha Newsheet*, 3 (November 2001): 3–4.

Garfield, J.L. (transl.) 1995. *The Fundamental Wisdom of the Middle Way: Nāgārjuna's Mūlamadhyamakakārikā*. New York – Oxford: Oxford University Press.

Geffré, C. and Dhavamony, M. (eds) 1978. *Buddhism and Christianity*, New York: The Seabury Press (1979) in *Concilium* (1978) 116–20.

Gethin, R. 1998. *The Foundations of Buddhism*. Oxford: Oxford University Press.

Gira, D. 1999. 'A Painful Profession of Faith' (paper given at the Voies de l'Orient second European Pastoral 'Assises'. Brussels, 11–14 November 1999. Used with the permission of Voies de l'Orient. A French version was published as 'Une profession de foi douloureuse', in Scheuer and Gira (eds) 2000: 78–94).

Goosen, G. 2007a. 'Towards a Theory of Dual Religious Belonging', in O'Grady, J. and Scherle, P. (eds), *Ecumenics from the Rim: Explorations in Honour of John D'Arcy May*. Berlin: Lit Verlag: 237–45.

——2007b. 'An Empirical Study of Dual Religious Belonging', *Journal of Empirical Theology* 20 (2007): 159–78.

——2005. 'Edith Stein: An example of Dual Religious Belonging?', *Australian E Journal of Theology* 5 (2005). http://dlibrary.acu.edu.au/research/theology/ejournal/aejt_5/goosen.htm (accessed 28 October 2010).

Gowans, C. 2003. *Philosophy of the Buddha*. London-New York: Routledge.

Griffin, D.R. (ed.) 2005a. *Deep Religious Pluralism*. Louisville, Kentucky: Westminster John Knox Press.

——2005b. 'Whitehead, Cobb, and Deep Religious Pluralism'. Part one of Griffin (ed.) 2005a: 3–66.

Griffiths, P. 2001. *Problems of Religious Diversity*. Oxford: Blackwell.

——1993. '[Mahayana Theology: A Dialogue with Critics]: Response', *Buddhist-Christian Studies*, 13 (1993): 48–51.

Griffiths, P. (ed.) 1990. *Christianity Through Non-Christian Eyes*. Maryknoll: Orbis Books.

Gross, R.M. 2003a. 'Meditation and Prayer: A Comparative Inquiry', in Gross and Muck (eds) 2003: 88–100.

——2003b. 'Conclusion', in Gross and Muck (eds) 2003: 150–57.

Gross, R.M. and Muck, T.C. (eds) 2003. *Christians Talk about Buddhist Meditation, Buddhists Talk about Christian Prayer*. New York and London: Continuum (essays originally published in *Buddhist-Christian Studies*, 21 [2001] and 22 [2002]).

——(eds) 2000. *Buddhists Talk about Jesus, Christians Talk about the Buddha*. New York and London: Continuum (essays originally published in *Buddhist-Christian Studies*, 19 [1999]).

Habito, R.L.F. 2007. 'Being Buddhist, Being Christian: Being Both, Being Neither', in D'Arcy May (ed.) 2007: 165–80.

——2006. *The Healing Breath of Zen*. Boston: Wisdom.

——2005. *Experiencing Buddhism: Ways of Wisdom and Compassion*. New York: Orbis.

——2004. *Living Zen, Loving God*. Boston: Wisdom Publications.

——2003a. 'Close Encounters of a Certain Kind', in Kasimow, Keenan, and Klepinger Keenan (eds) 2003: 129–42.

——2003b. 'Who is a Bodhisattva?', in Chappell (ed.) 2003: 87–93.

——2000. *Buddhist-Christian Dialogue in Action. Tacoma, WA 2000*. http://inner explorations.com/catew/14.htm (accessed 28 October 2010): 7–10.

——1996. *Buddhist-Christian Dialogue in Action. Chicago, 1996*. http://innerexplorations. com/catew/2.htm (accessed 28 October 2010): 10–11.

——1994a. 'Maria Kannon Zen: Explorations in Buddhist-Christian Practice', *Buddhist-Christian Studies*, 14 (1994): 145–56.

——1994b. 'Living Tension: A Five-Point Response', *Buddhist-Christian Studies*, 14 (1994): 185–88.

——1992a. 'Practice and Internal Dialogue: A Report on the Fourth Annual Conference of the Society for Buddhist-Christian Studies', *Buddhist-Christian Studies*, 12 (1992): 227–30.

——1992b. 'A Christian and Zen Self-Critique', *Buddhist-Christian Studies*, 12 (1992): 175–78.

——1992c. *Buddhist-Christian Dialogue in Action. Boston, 1992*. http://innerexplorations. com/catew/1.htm (accessed 28 October 2010): 2–4.

——1992d. *Profiles in Buddhist-Christian Dialogue: Ruben Habito*. http://innerexplorations. com/catew/13.htm (accessed 28 October 2010).

——1986. 'The Trikaya Doctrine in Buddhism', *Buddhist-Christian Studies*, 6 (1986): 52–62.

Haight, R. 2005. 'Pluralist Christology as Orthodox', in Knitter (ed.) 2005: 151–61.

——1999. *Jesus – Symbol of God*. Maryknoll: Orbis Books.

——1992. 'The Case for Spirit Christology', *Theological Studies* 53 (1992): 257–87.

Hand, T. 1992. *Profiles in Buddhist-Christian Dialogue: Thomas Hand, S.J.* http:// innerexplorations.com/catew/12.htm (accessed 28 October 2010).

Harris, E.J. 2010. *Buddhism for a Violent World*. London: Epworth Press.

——2004. 'The Other Within', in Crusz, R., Fernando, M., Tilakaratne, A. (eds), *Encounters With The Word: Essays to Honour Aloysius Pieris s.j.*.Colombo: The Ecumenical Institute for Study and Dialogue: 331–50.

——2003. 'Jesus and Buddhists', *The Way* 42, No. 2 (April 2003): 117–34.

——2002a. 'Double Belonging in Sri Lanka: Illusion or Liberating Path?', in Cornille (ed.) 2002a: 76–92.

——2002b. 'The Beginning of Something being Broken: The Cost of Crossing Spiritual Boundaries', in 'Spirituality Across Borders', *The Way Supplement* 2002/ 104: 6–17.

——1999a. 'My Unfinished Business with The Buddha', in Gross, Muck (eds) 2000: 89–94.

——1999b. 'Double Belonging' (paper given at the Voies de l'Orient second European Pastoral 'Assises'. Brussels, 11–14 November 1999. Used with the permission of Voies de l'Orient. A French version was published as 'Vivre la différence et le paradoxe', in Scheuer and Gira (eds) 2000: 161–64).

——1997. 'Detachment and Compassion in Early Buddhism', *Buddhist Publication Society* (*Bodhi Leaves* 141). www.enabling.org/ia/vipassana/Archive/H/Harris/detachmentHarris.html (accessed 28 October 2010).

——1994. 'A Journey into Buddhism', *Buddhist Publication Society* (*Bodhi Leaves* 134). www.enabling.org/ia/vipassana/Archive/H/Harris/journeyIntoBuddhismHarris.html (accessed 28 October 2010).

Harrison, V. 2006. 'Internal Realism and the Problem of Religious Diversity', *Philosophia* 34, No. 3 (Sep 2006): 287–301.

Hathaway, R.F. (transl.) 1969. *Hierarchy and the Definition of Order in the Letters of Pseudo-Dionysius: A Study in the Form and Meaning of the Pseudo-Dionysius Writings*. The Hague: Nijhoff.

Heelas, P. and Woodhead, L. 2005. *The Spiritual Revolution: why religion is giving way to spirituality*. Oxford: Blackwell.

Heim, S. Mark 2001a. *The Depth of the Riches: A Trinitarian Theology of Religious Ends*. Grand Rapids, Michigan/Cambridge: William B. Eerdmans Publishing Company.

——2001b. 'The Depth of the Riches: Trinity and Religious Ends', *Modern Theology* 17:1 (January 2001): 21–55.

——1995. *Salvations: Truth and Difference in Religion*. Maryknoll: Orbis Books.

Hick, J. 2001. *Dialogues in the Philosophy of Religion*. New York: Palgrave.

——1995. *A Christian Theology of Religions: The Rainbow of Faiths*. Louisville, Kentucky: Westminster John Knox Press (1995). First published by SCM Press in 1995 as: *The Rainbow of Faiths*.

——1993. *The Metaphor of God Incarnate*. London: SCM Press (2005 second edition).

——1990. 'An Irenaean Theodicy', chapter 6 of Badham (ed.) 1990: 88–105.

——1989a. *An Interpretation of Religion: Human Responses to the Transcendent*. New Haven, USA: Yale University Press (first published in 1989 by Macmillan).

——1989b. 'Response to Cook', in Davis, S. (ed.) 1989: 177–79.

——(ed.) 1977a. *The Myth of God Incarnate*. London: SCM Press (1993 edition).

——1977b. 'Trinity and Incarnation in the Light of Religious Pluralism', in Hick, J., Meltzer, E. (eds), *Three Faiths–One God. A Jewish, Christian, Muslim Encounter*. London: Macmillan, 1989: 197–214.

——1976. *Death and Eternal Life*. London: Collins.

——1966. *Evil and the God of Love*. London: Macmillan.

Hick, J. and Knitter, P. (eds) 1987. *The Myth of Christian Uniqueness*. New York: Orbis.

Hodgson P.C. 2005. 'The Spirit and Religious Pluralism', in Knitter (ed.) 2005: 135–50.

Honda, M. 1981. '"The Cloud of Unknowing" and the Logic of "Not-Two"', *Buddhist-Christian Studies*, Vol. 1 (1981): 93–96.

Howe, Q. 1974. *Reincarnation for the Christian*. Philadelphia: The Westminster Press.

Huffman, D.S. and Johnson, E.L. (eds) 2002. *God Under Fire: Modern Scholarship Reinvents God*. Michigan: Zondervan.

Ingram, P.O. 2004. '"That we may know each other": the pluralist hypothesis as a research program', *Buddhist-Christian Studies* 24 (2004): 135–57.

——2000–2001. '"Fruit Salad can be Delicious": The Practice of Buddhist-Christian Dialogue', *Cross Currents*, 50:4 (Winter 2000–2001): 541–49.

——1988. *The Modern Buddhist-Christian Dialogue: Two Universalistic Religions in Transformation*. Lewiston/Queenston/Lampeter: Edwin Mellen Press.

Ingram, P.O. and Streng, F.J. 1986. *Buddhist-Christian Dialogue: Mutual Renewal and Transformation*. Honolulu: University of Hawaii Press.

Ireland, J. (transl.) 1997. *The Udāna and Itivuttaka*. Kandy: Buddhist Publication Society.

Jackson, R. 2000. 'In Search of a Postmodern Middle', in Jackson, R. and Makransky, J. (eds), 2000: 215–46.

Jackson, R. and Makransky, J. (eds) 2000 *Buddhist Theology: Critical Reflections by Contemporary Buddhist Scholars*. London: Curzon Press (reprinted in 2003 by RoutledgeCurzon).

Jeanrond, W.G. 2002. 'Belonging or Identity? Christian Faith in a Multi-Religious World', in Cornille (ed.) 2002a: 106–20.

Johnson, E.L. and Huffman, D.S. 2002a. 'Should the God of Historic Christianity be Replaced?', chapter 1 of Huffman and Johnson (eds) 2002: 12–41.

Jonas, R. 1996. *Profiles in Buddhist-Christian Dialogue: Robert Jonas*. http://inner-explorations.com/catew/10.htm (accessed 28 October 2010).

Kadowaki, J.K. 1977. *Zen and the Bible*, Rieck, J. (transl.). Maryknoll, New York: Orbis books (2002). First published in Japanese by Shunjusha in 1977 as: *Koan to Seisho no Shindoku*).

Kaplan, S. 2002. *Different Paths, Different Summits: A Model for Religious Pluralism*. Lanham, MD: Rowman and Littlefield.

Kapleau, P. 1965. *The Three Pillars of Zen*. Boston: Beacon Press (1993 edition).

Kasimow, H., Keenan, J.P., Klepinger Keenan, L. (eds) 2003. *Beside Still Waters: Jews, Christians, and the Way of the Buddha*. Boston: Wisdom.

Katz, S.T. 1978. 'Language, Epistemology, and Mysticism', in Katz (ed.), *Mysticism and Philosophical Analysis*. New York: Oxford University Press: 22–74.

Keenan, J.P. LCC. *lower case catholic – or What the Buddha Did for Me* (unpublished autobiography).

Keenan, J.P. 2006a. 'The Genesis of all our Dependently Arisen Histories', in Keown, D. (ed.), *Buddhist Studies from India to America: Essays in honor of Charles S. Prebish*. London and New York: Routledge (2006): 260–69.

——2006b. 'Refuting Some Buddhist Arguments about Creation and Adopting Buddhist Philosophy about Salvation History', in Schmidt-Leukel, P. (ed.) 2006a: 69–80.

——2004. 'A Mahāyāna Theology of the Real Presence of Christ in the Eucharist', *Buddhist-Christian Studies* 24 (2004): 89–100.

——2003. 'The New Interfaith Context and Shifting Agenda for Religious Thinking', *Interreligious Insight* 1:2 (2003): 27–36.

——2002. 'A Mahayana Theology of Salvation History', *Buddhist-Christian Studies*, 22 (2002): 139–47.

——1999. 'Critique of 'Buddhism and Christianity: The Meeting Place'', *Buddhist-Christian Studies*, 19 (1999): 35–40.

——1998. 'Hybrid Theology (*A Response*)', *Eastern Buddhist*, 31:1 (1998): 139–49.

——1996. 'Emptiness as a Paradigm for Understanding World Religions', *Buddhist-Christian Studies*, 16 (1996): 57–64.

——1994. 'Dialogue and Language', *Buddhist-Christian Studies*, 14 (1994): 169–79.

——1993a. 'The Emptiness of Christ: A Mahāyāna Christology', *Anglican Theological Review* 75.1 (1993): 43–62.

——1993b. 'Mahāyāna Theology: A Dialogue with Critics', *Buddhist-Christian Studies*, Vol. 13 (1993): 15–44.

——1989a. *The Meaning of Christ: A Mahāyāna Theology*. New York: Orbis Books.

——1989b. 'Mahāyāna Theology: How to Reclaim an Ancient Christian Tradition', *Anglican Theological Review* 71.4 (1989): 377–94.

Kelly, J.N.D. 1977. *Early Christian Doctrines*. London: Adam and Charles Black (fifth revised edition).

Kern, I. 2001. 'Buddhist Perception of Jesus and Christianity in the Early Buddhist-Christian Controversies in China During the 17th Century', in Schmidt-Leukel (ed.) 2001a: 32–41.

Khema, Ayya 1996. 'Mysticism is no Mystery', in *Eckhart Review*, Spring 1996: 44–57.

Kiblinger, K.B. 2008. 'Buddhist Stances Towards Others: Types, Examples, Considerations', in Schmidt-Leukel (ed.) 2008a: 24–46.

Kim, B. 1999. 'Christ as the Truth, the Light, the Life, but a Way?', in Gross, Muck (eds) 2000: 52–58.

King, S.B. 2005a. 'A Pluralistic View of Religious Pluralism', in Knitter (ed.) 2005: 88–101.

——2005b. *Being Benevolence*. Honolulu: University of Hawai'i Press.

——2003a. *A Quaker Response to Christian Fundamentalism*. Religious Education Committee, Baltimore Yearly Meeting, Religious Society of Friends.

——2003b. *Friends and Other Religions*. Philadelphia: Quaker Press of Friends General Conference (written for the Christian and Interfaith Relations Committee).

——2003c. 'The Mommy and the Yogi', in Kasimow, Keenan, Keenan (eds) 2003: 157–70.

——1995. 'It's a Long Way to a Global Ethic: A Response to Leonard Swidler', *Buddhist-Christian Studies*, 15 (1995): 213–19.

——1994a. 'Religion as Practice: A Zen-Quaker Internal Dialogue', *Buddhist-Christian Studies*, Vol. 14 (1994): 157–62.

——1994b. 'On Pleasure, Choice, and Authority: Thoughts in Process', *Buddhist-Christian Studies*, Vol. 14 (1994): 189–96.

——1990. 'Toward a Buddhist Model of Interreligious Dialogue', *Buddhist-Christian Studies*, Vol. 10 (1990): 121–26.

——1988. 'Two Epistemological Models for the Interpretation of Mysticism', *Journal of the American Academy of Religion*, Vol. 56, No. 2 (Summer, 1988): 257–79.

King, S.B. and Ingram, O. 1999. *The Sound of Liberating Truth: Buddhist-Christian Dialogues in Honor of Frederick J. Streng*. Richmond: Curzon.

King, U. 2003. 'A Response to Reflections on Buddhist and Christian Religious Practices', in Gross and Muck (eds) 2003: 140–49.

King, W. 1982. 'Buddhist-Christian Dialogue Reconsidered', *Buddhist-Christian Studies*, Vol. 2 (1982): 5–11.

Knitter, P.F. 2010. *How a Buddhist Christian Sees it*. http://unionindialogue.org/paulknitter/ (accessed 28 October 2010).

——2009. *Without Buddha I Could not be a Christian*. Oxford: Oneworld Publications.

——(ed.) 2005. *The Myth of Religious Superiority: A Multifaith Exploration*. New York: Orbis Books.

——1997. 'Five Theses on the Uniqueness of Jesus', in Swidler and Mojzes (eds) 1997: 3–16.

——1996. *Jesus and the Other Names: Christian Mission and Global Responsibility*. Oxford: Oneworld. First published in the US by Orbis.

——1985. *No Other Name? A Critical Survey of Christian Attitudes Toward the World Religions*. New York: Orbis Books.

Kōun Yamada (transl.) 2004. *The Gateless Gate: The Classic Book of Zen Koans*. Boston: Wisdom Publications.

Kraft, K. (ed.) 1992a. *Inner Peace, World Peace: Essays on Buddhism and Nonviolence*. New York: SUNY Press.

——1992b. 'Introduction' to Kraft 1992a: 1–4.

Küng, H. 1994. *Great Christian Thinkers*, Bowden, J. (transl.). New York: Continuum.

Kurata, M. 1971. *Momozō Kurata senshū* [Selected Works of Kurata Momozō], Vol. 1. Tokyo: Shunjūsha.

Lai, W. 2001. 'A Renewal of Samsara (Rebirth) – New Heaven, New Earth, and New Hell in Buddhist China', in W. Schweidler (ed.), *Wiedergeburt und kulturelles Erbe: Reincarnation and Cultural Heritage*. Sankt Augustin: Academia Verlag: 133–53.

Lai, W. and von Brück, M. 2001. *Christianity and Buddhism: A Multi-Cultural History of Their Dialogue*, Jestice, P. (transl.). Maryknoll, New York: Orbis Books.

Lande, A. 2006. 'Creation and Process Theology: A Question to Buddhism', in Schmidt-Leukel (ed.) 2006a: 81–91.

Louch, A. 1993. 'Saying is Believing', in Runzo (ed.) 1993: 109–16.

Lotus and Lily 2010 (year of last access). http://groups.yahoo.com/group/lotusandlily/ (accessed 28 October 2010).

Loy, D.R. 2002. *A Buddhist History of the West: Studies in Lack*. Albany: SUNY.

Maalouf, A. 2000. *On Identity*, Bray, B. (transl.). London: The Harvill Press. Originally published in French by Editions Bernard Grasset in 1998 as: *Les Identités meurtrières*.

MacInnes, E. 1996. *Light Sitting in Light*. Great Britain: Fount Paperbacks.

MacGregor, G. 1982. *Reincarnation as a Christian Hope*. London and Basingstoke: Macmillan.

——1978. *Reincarnation in Christianity: A New Vision of the Role of Rebirth in Christian Thought*. Wheaton, IL: Quest Books.

Makransky, J. 2008. 'Buddhist Inclusivism: Reflections Toward a Contemporary Buddhist Theology of Religions', in Schmidt-Leukel (ed.) 2008a: 47–68.

——2005a. 'Buddha and Christ as Mediators of the Transcendent: A Buddhist Perspective', in Schmidt-Leukel (ed.) 2005a: 176–99.

——2005b. 'Response to Perry Schmidt-Leukel', in Schmidt-Leukel (ed.) 2005a: 207–11.

——2005c. 'Buddhist Analogues of Sin and Grace: A Dialogue with Augustine', *Studies in Interreligious Dialogue* 15: 1 (2005): 5–15.

——2003. 'Buddhist Perspectives on Truth in Other Religions: Past and Present', *Theological Studies* 64, no. 2 (2003): 334–61.

Malcomson, J. 2007a 'Not One, Not Two: Being a Christian Buddhist'. Part 1. www. geocities.com/jmalcomson/beingchristianbuddhist1.html?200717 (accessed 17 June 2007).

——2007b 'Not One, Not Two: Being a Christian Buddhist'. Part 1. www.geocities. com/jmalcomson/beingchristianbuddhist2.html?200717 (accessed 17 June 2007).

Matthews, R. 1993. '[Mahayana Theology: A Dialogue with Critics]: Response', *Buddhist-Christian Studies*, 13 (1993): 51–58.

Mazzocchi, L. 1999. 'Twofold Belonging' (paper given at the Voies de l'Orient second European Pastoral 'Assises'. Brussels, 11–14 November 1999. Used with the permission of Voies de l'Orient. A French version was published as 'Notre pratique commune du Zen et de l'Évangile', in Scheuer and Gira (eds) 2000: 171–80).

McCracken, G. 1988. *The Long Interview*. Newbury Park, CA: Sage.

McGrath, A.E. 1999. *Christian Spirituality: An Introduction*. Oxford: Blackwell.

Merton, T. 1976. *Thomas Merton on Zen*. London: Sheldon Press.

——1968. *The Asian Journal of Thomas Merton*. New York: New Directions (1975 edition). First published in 1968 by The Trustees of the Merton Legacy Trust.

Mitchell, D.W. 2003. 'A Christian Response to Buddhist Reflections on Prayer', in Gross and Muck (eds) 2003: 135–39.

——1996. *Profiles in Buddhist-Christian Dialogue: Donald W Mitchell.* http://inner-explorations.com/catew/11.htm (accessed 28 October 2010).

Morning Star Sangha Newsletters and Newsheets (September 2001 – October 2010).

Muck, T.C. 1999. 'Images of the Buddha', in Gross and Muck (eds) 2000: 95–106.

——1994. 'Joint Buddhist-Christian Practice: A Critique of Corless, Habito, and King', *Buddhist-Christian Studies*, 14 (1994): 173–76.

Ñāṇamoli and Bodhi (transl.) 1995. *The Middle Length Discourses of the Buddha: A Translation of the Majjhima Nikāya.* Boston: Wisdom Publications (2005 edition).

Nhat Hanh, Thich 2005. 'Jesus and Buddha as Brothers', in Barker (ed.) 2005: 38–45.

——1999. *Going Home: Jesus and Buddha as Brothers.* London: Rider (first published in 1999 by Riverhead Books).

——1995. *Living Buddha, Living Christ.* London: Rider (1996). First published in 1995 by Riverhead Books.

Niewiadomski, J. 1996. 'Begegnung von Religionen im weltzivilisatorischen Kontext', in Schwager, R. (ed.), *Christus allein? Der Streit um die pluralistische Religionstheo-logie.* Freiburg i.Br.: Herder 1996: 83–94.

Nishitani, K. 1982. *Religion and Nothingness*, Van Bragt, J. (transl.). Berkeley, CA: University of California.

Nyanaponika 1981. *Buddhism and the God-Idea: Selected Texts*, The Wheel Publication 47. Kandy: Buddhist Publication Society (3rd repr.).

O'Hanlon, D.J. 1981. 'Integration of Spiritual Practices: a Western Christian Looks East', *Journal of Transpersonal Psychology* 13, 2 (1981): 91–112.

Palihawadana, M. 1978. 'Is There a Theravada Buddhist Idea of Grace?', in Dawe, D. and Carman J. (eds), *Christian Faith in a Religiously Plural World.* New York: Orbis: 181–95.

Panikkar, R. 2002. 'On Christian Identity: Who is a Christian?', in Cornille (ed.) 2002a: 121–44.

——1978. *The Intrareligious Dialogue.* New York: Paulist Press.

Pannenberg, W. 1994. *Systematic Theology* 2, Bromiley, G.W. (transl.). Grand Rapids: Eerdmans.

Pegis, A.C. (transl.) 1955. St. Thomas Aquinas, *On the Truth of the Catholic Faith: Summa contra Gentiles, Book One: God.* New York: Image Books (1961 repr.).

Phan, P.C. 2006. 'Religious Identity and Belonging Amidst Diversity and Pluralism: Challenges and Opportunities for Church and Theology', in Heft, J.L. (ed.), *Passing on the Faith: Transforming Traditions for the Next Generation of Jews, Christians, and Muslims.* New York: Fordham University Press.

——2004. *Being Religious Interreligiously: Asian Perspectives on Interfaith Dialogue.* New York: Orbis.

——2003. 'Multiple Religious Belonging: Opportunities and Challenges for Theology and Church', *Theological Studies* 64 (Sep): 495–519.

Pieris, A. 2005. *Prophetic Humour in Buddhism and Christianity: Doing Inter-Religious Studies in the Reverential Mode.* Colombo: Ecumenical Institute for Study and Dialogue.

——1996. *Fire & Water: Basic Issues in Asian Buddhism and Christianity.* New York: Orbis Books.

——1988a. *Love Meets Wisdom: A Christian Experience of Buddhism.* New Delhi: Intercultural Publications.

——1988b. *An Asian Theology of Liberation*. Edinburgh: T & T Clark.

Plantinga, A. 1974. *The Nature of Necessity*. Oxford: Clarendon Press.

Postal, S. 1994. 'Zen Mind/Christian Mind: Practice Across Traditions', *Buddhist-Christian Studies*, 14 (1994): 209–11.

——1992. *Buddhist-Christian Dialogue in Action. Boston, 1992*. http://innerexplorations.com/catew/1.htm (accessed 28 October 2010): 8–14.

Race, A. 1983. *Christians and Religious Pluralism: Patterns in the Christian Theology of Religions*. London: SCM Press.

Radford Ruether, R. 2005. 'Religious Identity and Openness to a Pluralistic World: A Christian View', *Buddhist-Christian Studies* 25 (2005): 29–40.

Rahner, K. 1982. 'Das christliche Verständnis der Erlösung', in: Bsteh, A. (ed.), *Erlösung in Christentum und Buddhismus*. Mödling (1982): 112–27.

——1978. Foundations of Christian Faith: An Introduction to the Idea of Christianity, Dych, W.V. (transl.). London: Darton, Longman and Todd.

Reis Habito, M. 2003a. 'On Becoming a Buddhist Christian', in Kasimow, Keenan, and Klepinger Keenan (eds) 2003: 201–13.

——2003b. 'Bridging the World Religions: On being a Buddhist-Christian Woman', in Chappell (ed.) 2003: 81–86.

——2000. *Buddhist-Christian Dialogue in Action. Tacoma, WA 2000*. http://inner-explorations.com/catew/14.htm (accessed 28 October 2010): 19–21.

——1996. 'Maria-Kannon: The Mother of God in Buddhist Guise', *Marian Studies*, XLVII (1996): 50–64.

——1993. 'The Bodhisattva Guanyin and the Virgin Mary', *Buddhist-Christian Studies*, 13 (1993): 61–69.

Rhys Davids, T.W. (transl.) 1894. *The Questions of King Milinda*, Part II, SBE 36. New York: Dover (1963 reprint).

Ritchie, J. 2003. 'The Applications of Qualitative Methods to Social Research', chapter 2 of Ritchie and Lewis (eds) 2003a: 24–46.

Ritchie, J. and Lewis, J. (eds) 2003a. *Qualitative Research Practice: A Guide for Social Science Students and Researchers*. London: Sage (third reprint, 2005).

——2003b. 'Generalising from Qualitative Research', chapter 10 of Ritchie and Lewis (eds) 2003a: 263–86.

Robinson, J. 1979. *Truth is Two-Eyed*. London: SCM Press.

——1963. *Honest to God*. London: SCM Press.

Robinson, J. and Edwards, D. (eds), 1963. *The Honest to God Debate*. London: SCM Press.

Rochford, E. Burke 2003. 'Interfaith Encounter and Religious Identity: Sociological Observations and Reflections', in Kasimow, Keenan, and Klepinger Keenan (eds) 2003: 217–29.

Rolt, C.E. (transl.) 2004. *Dionysius the Areopagite on the Divine Names and The Mystical Theology*. Berwick, ME: Ibis.

Runzo, J. (ed.) 1993. *Is God Real?* London: Macmillan.

Santikaro, Bhikkhu 2001. 'Jesus and Christianity in the Life and Work of Buddhadâsa Bhikkhu', in Schmidt-Leukel (ed.) 2001a: 80–103.

Saunders 1957. 'Review (untitled): Mysticism: Christian and Buddhist by Daisetz Teitaro Suzuki', *Journal of the American Oriental Society*, Vol. 77, No. 3, (Jul. – Sep., 1957): 253–55.

Scarlett, V. 2007. 'Links for Buddhist-Christian practitioners'. www.lotuslily.net/?page_id=260 (posted 10 March 2007. Accessed 28 October 2010).

Scheuer, J. and Gira, D. (eds) 2000. *Vivre de Plusieurs Religions: Promesse ou Illusion?* Paris: Les Éditions de l'Atelier/Les Éditions Ouvrières.

Schleiermacher, F. 1799. *On Religion: Speeches to its Cultured Despisers*, Oman, J. (transl.). New York: Harper & Row (1958).

Schmidt-Leukel, P. 2009. *Transformation by Integration*. London: SCM Press.

——(ed.) 2008a. *Buddhist Attitudes to Other Religions*. St. Ottilien: EOS.

——2008b. 'On Claimed 'Orthodoxy', Quibbling with Words, and some Serious Implications: A Comment on the Tilley-D'Costa Debate About Religious Pluralism', *Modern Theology* 24, 2 (2008): 271–84.

——2008c. 'Orthodoxy and Religious Pluralism: A Rejoinder', *Modern Theology* 24, 2 (2008): 293–97.

——2007a. 'Light and Darkness' or 'Looking Through a Dim Mirror'? A Reply to Paul Williams from a Christian Perspective', in D'Arcy May (ed.) 2007: 67–88.

——2007b. 'Uniqueness: A Pluralistic Reading of John 14:6', in O'Grady, J. and Scherle, P. (eds), *Ecumenics from the Rim. Explorations in Honour of John D'Arcy May*. Berlin: LIT Verlag 2007: 303–10.

——(ed.) 2006a. *Buddhism, Christianity and the Question of Creation: Karmic or Divine?* Hants: Ashgate.

——2006b. 'The Unbridgeable Gulf? Towards a Buddhist-Christian Theology of Creation', in Schmidt-Leukel (ed.) 2006: 111–78.

——2006c. 'Introduction', in Schmidt-Leukel (ed.) 2006a: 1–42.

——2006d. 'Chalcedon Defended: A Pluralistic Re-Reading of the Two-Natures Doctrine', *The Expository Times,* Vol. 118 no. 3 (2006): 113–19.

——2006e. *Understanding Buddhism*. Edinburgh: Dunedin Academic Press.

——(ed.) 2005a. *Buddhism and Christianity in Dialogue*, The Gerald Weisfeld Lectures 2004. London: SCM Press.

——2005b. 'Intimate Strangers: An Introduction', in Schmidt-Leukel, P. (ed.) 2005a: 1–26.

——2005c. 'Buddha and Christ as Mediators of the Transcendent: A Christian Perspective', in Schmidt-Leukel (ed.) 2005a: 151–75.

——2005d. 'Response to John Makransky', in Schmidt-Leukel (ed.) 2005a: 200–206.

——2005e. 'The Impact of Inter-Faith Dialogue on Religious Identity' (unpublished paper given in Leicester 8 May 2005).

——(ed.) 2005f. *Gott ohne Grenzen. Eine christliche und pluralistische Theologie der Religionen*. Gütersloh: Gütersloher Verlagshaus.

——2005g. 'Exclusivism, Inclusivism, Pluralism: The Tripolar Typology – Clarified and Reaffirmed', in Knitter (ed.) 2005: 13–27.

——2003. 'Buddhism and Christianity: Antagonistic or Complementary', *Studies in World Christianity* vol. 9.2 (2003): 265–79.

——(ed.) (in cooperation with Götz, T.J. and Köberlin G) 2001a. *Buddhist Perceptions of Jesus. Papers of the Third Conference of the European Network of Buddhist-Christian Studies (St. Ottilien 1999)*. St. Ottilien: EOS-Verlag.

——2001b. 'Buddhist Perceptions of Jesus: Introductory Remarks', in Schmidt-Leukel (ed.) 2001a: 8–30.

Schmied, K. 2001. 'Jesus in Recent Buddhist Writings Published in the West', in Schmidt-Leukel (ed.) 2001a: 130–39.

Senécal, B. 1999. 'Drinking in Several Wells. Between Christ and Buddha. Is a Double Belonging Possible?' (paper given at the Voies de l'Orient second European Pastoral 'Assises'. Brussels, 11–14 November 1999. Used with the permission of Voies de l'Orient. A French version was published as 'Entre le Christ et le Bouddha', in Scheuer and Gira (eds) 2000: 65–77.

——1998. 'Jésus le Christ à la rencontre de Gautama le Bouddha'. Paris : Éditions du Cerf.

Shanley, B.J. (transl.) 2006. *The Hackett Aquinas: The Treatise on the Divine Nature.* Summa Theologiae I 1–13. Indianapolis: Hackett.

Sharf, R.H. 1995. 'Sanbōkyōdan: Zen and the Way of the New Religions', *Japanese Journal of Religious Studies* (1995) 22/3–4: 417–58.

Sharma, A. and Dugan, K.M. (eds) 1999. *A Dome of Many Colors: Studies in Religious Pluralism, Identity, and Unity.* Harrisonburg: Trinity Press International.

Sherwin, B.L. and Kasimow, H. (eds) 2000. *John Paul II and Interreligious Dialogue.* Maryknoll, NY: Orbis, 2nd print 2000.

Smart, N. 1995. 'Truth, Criteria and Dialogue between Religions', in Dean (ed.) 1995: 67–71.

——1993. *Buddhism and Christianity: Rivals and Allies.* London: Macmillan.

Smith, A.B. 2002. *A New Framework for Christian Belief.* Hampshire: John Hunt Publishing Ltd.

——1996. *The God Shift: Our Changing Perception of the Ultimate Mystery.* London: New Millennium.

Smith, H.N. 1997. 'Beyond Dual Religious Belonging: Roger Corless and Explorations in Buddhist-Christian Identity', *Buddhist-Christian Studies*, 17 (1997): 161–77.

Smith, W.C. 1997. *Modern Culture from a Comparative Perspective*, Burbidge, J.W. (ed.). Albany, NY: SUNY.

——1987. 'Idolatry in Comparative Perspective', in Hick and Knitter (eds) 1987: 53–68.

——1981. *Towards a World Theology: Faith and the Comparative History of Religion.* London and Basingstoke: Macmillan.

——1962. *The Meaning and End of Religion.* Minneapolis: Fortress Press (1991 edition).

Spae, J.J. 1980. *Buddhist-Christian Empathy.* Chicago: The Chicago Institute of Theology and Culture.

Streng, F.J. 1993. 'Mutual Transformation: An Answer to a Religious Question', *Buddhist-Christian Studies*, 13 (1993): 121–26.

Sutcliffe, S. 2000. ' "Wandering Stars": Seekers and Gurus in the Modern World', in Sutcliffe, S. and Bowman, M. (eds), *Beyond New Age. Exploring Alternative Spirituality.* Edinburgh: Edinburgh University Press (2000): 17–36.

Suzuki, D.T. 1949. *An Introduction to Zen Buddhism*, Humphreys, C. (ed.). London: Rider (1969 edition).

——1957. *Mysticism Christian and Buddhist.* London: George Allen and Unwin Ltd.

Swearer, D.K. 1999. 'Buddha Loves Me! This I Know, for the Dharma Tells Me So', in Gross and Muck (eds) 2000: 107–17.

Swidler, L. and Mojzes, P. (eds) 1997. *The Uniqueness of Jesus: A Dialogue with Paul F. Knitter.* New York: Orbis Books.

Swinburne, R. 1993. *The Coherence of Theism.* Oxford: Clarendon.

Tacey, D. 2004. *The Spirituality Revolution. The Emergence of Contemporary Spirituality.* London New York: Routledge.

'Talks from the Heart' (2005). A recorded discussion at a Morning Star Sangha retreat at the Maenllwyd Chan Meditation Centre, 27–29 July 2005. (Audio resource.)

Tanaka, K.T. 2003. 'Christian Prayer Seen from the Eye of a Buddhist', in Gross and Muck (eds) 2003: 101–8.

Thelle, N.R. 2001. 'What do I as a Christian Expect Buddhists to Discover in Jesus?', in Schmidt-Leukel (ed.) 2001a: 142–57.

——1982. 'Foe and Friend: The Changing Image of Christ in Japanese Buddhism', *Japanese Religions*, Vol.12:2 (1982): 19–46.

Thompson, R. 2010. *Buddhist Christianity: A Passionate Openness*. Winchester, UK and Washington, USA: O-Books.

Thurston, B. 1999. 'The Buddha Offered Me a Raft', in Gross and Muck (eds) 2000: 118–28.

——1994. 'A Christian Response to Joint Buddhist-Christian Practice', *Buddhist-Christian Studies*, vol. 14 (1994): 177–80.

Tilley, T.W. 2008. 'Orthodoxy and Religious Pluralism: A Comment', *Modern Theology* 24, 2 (2008): 291–92.

Tilley, T.W. *et al.* 2007. *Religious Diversity and the American Experience: A Theological Approach* (written with seven of his students: Albarran, Birch, Durbin II, Fannin, Robinson, Martin, and Minix). New York and London: Continuum.

Tillich, P. 1952. *The Courage to Be*. New Haven and London: Yale University Press (2000 edition).

——1951. *Systematic Theology*, vol. 1. Chicago: University of Chicago.

——1949. *The Shaking of the Foundations*. Harmondsworth: Penguin.

Trapnell, J. 1998. 'Indian Sources on the Possibility of a Pluralist View of Religions', *Journal of Ecumenical Studies*, 35:2 (1998): 210–34.

Turner, D. 1995. *The Darkness of God*. Cambridge: Cambridge University Press.

Ueda, S. 2001. 'Jesus in Contemporary Japanese Zen. With Special Regards to Keiji Nishitani', in Schmidt-Leukel (ed.) 2001a: 42–58.

Underhill, E. 1911. *Mysticism*. New York: New American Library (1955 edition).

Unno, T. 2003. 'Jesus Prayer and the Nembutsu', in Gross and Muck (eds) 2003: 109–17.

——1999. 'Contrasting Images of the Buddha', in Gross and Muck (eds) 2000: 138–42.

Van Bragt, J. 2002. 'Multiple Religious Belonging of the Japanese People', in Cornille (ed.) 2002a: 7–19.

van der Veer, P. 1994. 'Syncretism, multiculturalism and the discourse of tolerance', in Stewart, C. and Shaw, R. (eds), *Syncretism/Anti-Syncretism. The Politics of Religious Synthesis*. London/New York: Routledge: 196–211.

Vardy, P. 1990. *The Puzzle of God*. London: Fount (1999 revised edition).

Velde, R. te 2006. *Aquinas on God*. Aldershot: Ashgate.

Vroom, A. 2005. 'Struggle for loyalty: the impact of studying another religion' (unpublished paper given at the Sixth Study Conference of the European Network of Buddhist Christian Studies, St. Ottilien, Germany: 10–13 June 2005. Quoted with the author's permission).

Waldenfels, H. 1976. *Absolute Nothingness: Foundations for a Buddhist-Christian Dialogue*, Heisig, J.W. (transl.). New York: The Missionary Society of St. Paul the Apostle in the State of New York (1980 English translation. Originally published in German in 1976 by Verlag Herder Freiburg im Breisgau).

Walshe, M.O. 1982. 'Buddhism and Christianity: A Positive Approach', *Dialogue* (N.S.) 9: 3–39.

Ward, K. 1991. 'A Vision to Pursue: Beyond the Crisis in Christianity'. London: SCM Press.

——1990. 'Truth and the Diversity of Religions', *Religious Studies* 26: 1–18.

Weatherhead, L.D. 1978. *The Case for Reincarnation*. M C Peto. Seventh Impression (a lecture given to the City Temple Literary Society by Rev. Weatherhead in the 1950s).

Where Do We Go From Here? Buddhism, Christianity, And the Next Step: A Remembrance and Celebration of Roger J. Corless (1938–2007). (Unpublished booklet of memorial contributions collated by David Dupree for Corless' memorial service in San Francisco, CA, 10 March 2007.)

Whitehead, A.N. 1927–28. *Process and Reality, Corrected Edition.* Gifford Lectures 1927–28, Griffin, D.R. and Sherburne, D.W. (eds). New York: The Free Press (1978).

Williams, P. 2002. *The Unexpected Way: On Converting from Buddhism to Catholicism.* London and New York: T & T Clark.

——(with Tribe, A.) 2000. *Buddhist Thought: A Complete Introduction to the Indian Tradition.* London and New York: Routledge.

——1989. *Mahāyāna Buddhism: The Doctrinal Foundations.* London and New York: Routledge.

Winston, D. 1998. 'Campuses Are a Bellwether for Society's Religious Revival', *The Chronicle of Higher Education*, 16 January, 1998, A60.

Yandell, K. and Netland, H. 2009. *Buddhism: A Christian Exploration and Appraisal.* Illinois: InterVarsity Press.

Young, F. 1983. *From Nicaea to Chalcedon.* London: SCM Press.

Zander, H. 1999. *Geschichte der Seelenwanderung in Europa. Alternative Religiöse Traditionen von der Antike bis heute.* Darmstadt: Wissenschaftliche Buchgesellschaft.

Index